# SENTIMENTAL DEMOCRACY

MAN OF FEELING.

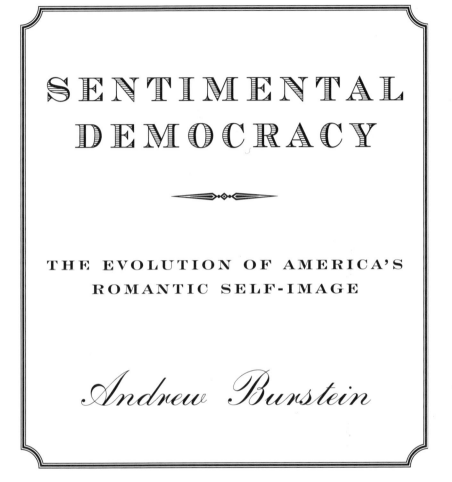

# SENTIMENTAL DEMOCRACY

### THE EVOLUTION OF AMERICA'S ROMANTIC SELF-IMAGE

*Andrew Burstein*

**HILL AND WANG**

*A division of Farrar, Straus and Giroux*

HILL AND WANG
A DIVISION OF FARRAR, STRAUS AND GIROUX
19 Union Square West, New York 10003

Distributed in Canada by Douglas & McIntyre Ltd.

Printed in the United States of America

*Designed by Gretchen Achilles*

FIRST EDITION, 1999

Frontispiece: Reproduced from the Frontispiece of the
1821 New York edition of Henry Mackenzie's *The Man of Feeling*

Library of Congress Cataloging-in-Publication Data

Burstein, Andrew.
 Sentimental democracy : the evolution of America's romantic self-
image / Andrew Burstein. — 1st ed.
  p.  cm.
 Includes bibliographical references and index.
 ISBN 0-8090-8535-6 (alk. paper)
 1. United States—Intellectual life—18th century.  2. United States—
Intellectual life—1783–1865.  3. Enlightenment—United States.  4. Political
culture—United States—History—18th century.  5. Politics and literature—
United States—History—18th century.  6. Political culture—United States—
History—19th century.  7. Politics and literature—United States—History—
19th century.  8. National characteristics, American.  9. Democracy—Social
aspects—United States—History.  10. Sentimentalism—United States—
History.  I. Title.
E163.B88  1999
306'.0973—dc21                                                    98-52046

TO JOSH
FOR ALL THE GOOD FEELINGS
IN FATHERHOOD

# CONTENTS

# PREFACE

———⟫◆⟪———

NO ONE MUCH BOTHERS about *The Man of Feeling* anymore. This 1770 novel by the Scottish Henry Mackenzie (1745–1831) was first printed in America in 1782 and then at least ten more times by 1828. It tells the story of Harley, a man of extraordinary generosity and sympathetic imagination who, in his travels, consistently thinks less of his own comfort than that of others. He is the embodiment of the eighteenth century's culture of sensibility, combining nature-given delicacy with self-conscious humanism, unable to turn from any person in need. Transfixed on noble ideals of liberty and happiness, Revolutionary Americans fashioned the dictates of sensibility into a romantic image of themselves.

As I was looking for ways to illustrate the Americanization of sensibility, I discovered a rare, undated pamphlet printed in New York, most probably in the year 1803, by a small publisher who specialized in sentimental literature.[1] It contains several vignettes highlighting themes of sensibility, including one from *The Man of Feeling*, and it opens with an excerpt from Thomas Jefferson's *Notes on the State of Virginia* (1787)—that sketch known as "The Speech of Logan." Here Jefferson recounts the story of a Mingo Indian chief whose wife and children were thoughtlessly murdered by white men on Ohio River land in 1774 and who took bloody revenge for these acts. According to Jefferson, the melancholy Chief Logan displayed his humanity in his fearlessness after the killings and in his solemn mourning ever after. Americans imbued with sensible values,* with compassion for those who have suffered, could not but empathize deeply with Logan's plaint. "There runs not one drop of my blood in the veins of any living creature," the Indian explained tearfully to an officer of the Virginia militia. "Who is there to mourn for Logan? Not one." This last statement appears as the epigraph on the title page of the 1803 pamphlet above a dour engraving of the taut-faced Indian.[2]

Jefferson succeeded in popularizing Logan's speech. The impressionable author of the Declaration of Independence meant his readers to feel the pain of Logan's loss and to marvel at the orator's sublimely simple words. The *Notes* had appeared while Jefferson was serving as American minister to the court of Louis XVI of France and was fresh from his own sentimental journey on the Continent. But owing to the enduring interest in Logan's symbolism, he felt obliged in the mid-1790s, after serving nearly four years in George Washington's cabinet, to satisfy those who doubted the authenticity of his description. Accordingly, Jefferson interviewed the aging General John Gibson, the man who had sat with Logan in the forest and translated his speech for Virginia's royal governor. *An Appendix to the Notes on Virginia Relative to Logan's Family* was published in the election year of 1800, when Jefferson was voted President.[3]

I find the association of Jefferson's sensibility with Mackenzie's quite extraordinary. In the 1803 pamphlet, "Old Edwards," taken from the later chapters of *The Man of Feeling*, immediately follows "The Speech of Logan." In this section of Mackenzie's novel, the character Harley comes upon an elderly man on the long path home from a military tour of duty for which he had selflessly volunteered in order

---

*The meaning of the adjective *sensible* intended here is the eighteenth-century meaning, "perceived by either mind or senses," according to Dr. Samuel Johnson's 1783 *Dictionary*, "having the quality of being affected by moral good or ill." The more common modern definition of the word, as "reasonable," developed only sometime in the nineteenth century. Noah Webster's *An American Dictionary of the English Language* (New York, 1828) began with a clinical definition ("Having the capacity to receive impressions from external objects"), followed by definitions consistent with Johnson's.

to spare his son from conscription and his son's children from being deprived of a father already crushed under the weight of an unforgiving justice system. Indeed, the son's sole crime had been one of a decent passion—the unpremeditated attack on an unfeeling gamekeeper who had wantonly shot his dog dead, a trusty pointer that had sprung the birds which put food on the modest family's table. Sentimental travelers Harley and Old Edwards arrive at their destination only to learn that things have gone from bad to worse. The industrious son and the son's wife have "died of broken hearts" under worsening financial pressures. Together Harley and "the unfortunate Edwards" are led by Edwards's three orphaned grandchildren to their parents' moss-covered grave site (see frontispiece). Here the Man of Feeling kisses away the flowing tears of the little girl, before resolving to bring the grieving Edwards and the orphans to his father's estate, where he establishes them on a small farm. "Even in this bad world," writes Mackenzie, "the lines of our duty, and our happiness, are so frequently woven together." The message—Jefferson's as well as Mackenzie's—is that in an enlightened society, positive passion and the sympathetic imagination can be applied to remedying ill and instituting social justice.

Two centuries later, American patriots customarily invoke the nation's legal-constitutional principles as the central component of their love of liberty. Yet the legacy of the culture of sensibility remains important, too. Americans have found it attractive to designate "Men of Feeling" as representatives of the national heart, safeguarding the national honor. "We the People" of the federal Constitution are still considered a People of Feeling who retain qualities of honorable sentiment and moral assertiveness. The altruistic model of behavior which animated early Americans and inspired them to declare their virtues to the world did not inhibit them from exercising an uncompromising power they deemed benevolent (which scholars today tend to judge more critically as violent acts of conquest). In the pair of episodes related above, good men—the Mingo chief and Old Edwards's deceased son—are deemed justified in their spontaneous if violent acts of righteousness. Nevertheless, America's founding generation sought to exhibit, and in the end did claim, a pronounced sensitivity to the wants of others, an infectious spirit of virtuous sympathy and generosity. If they had a penchant for violence, they did not acknowledge it, as they projected harmony among themselves and communion with others.

This is a book about the emotional sources of America's self-image and the sentimental foundations of the republic. It is a history of patriots during the critical years of nation building, 1750–1828, as Americans were becoming enamored with the *idea* of America, and as they confidently expressed a capacity to better the human condition with their transformative idea. Fashioning the still "new" land, they sought to turn their myths into power. And as they did, their creed developed into a culture I describe as "sentimental democracy." Emphasizing human compassion, they established a pattern of philanthropic mission, spiritual renewal, and global conversion still discernible at the end of the twentieth century.

All history is, in essence, emotional history. Terming this book an emotional history merely calls attention to its particular emphasis. Words convey perceptual experience; they represent how people qualify nature or life. With their words, historical subjects make emotionally significant efforts to demonstrate the nature of the self or of the external world, and to establish parameters of public participation. The actors in this nation-building drama profoundly concerned themselves with the creation and expansion of the United States of America and sought satisfaction in endeavoring to define and promote a deserving and desirable collective identity. But from the outset they faced dire struggles over how that national identity was to be shaped, classified, and sorted out. Consensus was rare, ideals too abstract to fix. Thus my narrative about their efforts focuses on how certain kinds of vernacular gained emotional resonance within their political and cultural context and amid shifting moods and tempers.[4]

An emotional history does not discount histories which engage with political ideology—in this case, the belief system which has sustained a modern democratic republic for more than two centuries. Rather, it is an adjunct to political history, presenting other features of the American state of mind at that time when the idea of America was being expressed most impressively in the documents and processes of nation building. It joins religious histories, too, especially those which emphasize civil millennialism—the idea of a combined spiritual and political triumph providentially assured to a righteous America. But it adds a new element: that positive passion, or generous sympathy (coercively applied), which was embodied in the democratizing language that Americans used to convey a sense of who they were and were becoming as a unified people.

This book springs from classic studies on the development of American intellectual energies. Bernard Bailyn's *The Ideological Origins of the American Revolution* (1967) reconceptualized the background of the nation's political birth, giving new force to words like *corruption, conspiracy,* and *slavery,* and to the idea of liberty. Ernest Lee Tuveson's *Redeemer Nation* (1968), Henry F. May's *The Enlightenment in America* (1976), and Sacvan Bercovitch's *The American Jeremiad* (1978) all showed how historians related the language of religious community to a broader public exhortation underscoring Revolutionary aims. Bercovitch observed: "Only *America* has united nationality and universality, civic and spiritual selfhood, secular and redemptive history, the country's past and paradise to be, in a single synthetic ideal." One's sense of Americans' longing for a community spirit is palpable in all these books.[5]

Jay Fliegelman's *Prodigals and Pilgrims* (1982) and Melvin Yazawa's *From Colonies to Commonwealth* (1985) explained the language of affection in the context of forging political union; in his resourceful examination of the moral imagination, Fliegelman in particular was attentive to the literature that Revolutionary Americans read. Subsequently, Gordon S. Wood's *The Radicalism of the American Revolution* (1992) went on to synthesize the way in which republican values surfaced and then spread. In the process, Wood humanized rising America's self-image, revealing the designs of proud individuals and the claims to legitimacy of a new national authority.[6]

Despite these historians' good work, the uncertain and varied descriptions of what was early conceived of as a definable national character still need to be explored and unraveled. May investigated the epistemology of the Enlightenment, the studies of nature and human motivations, in mediating between the intellectual and religious impulses of prominent men as they debated freedom and order, but he did not examine the emotional ties. Bercovitch and Tuveson persuasively argued that religious language underscored America's secular mission to reform the world, but they privileged Christian imagery over other expressions of social identity and personal intimacy, taking in only certain aspects of the vocabulary that came to constitute patriotic self-regard. Bailyn, Wood, and many others established the prominence of classical republicanism in shaping Revolutionary American protest, joining the civic humanism developed in antiquity with eighteenth-century English perceptions of political virtue and corruption. But as powerful as republicanism has been to the modern understanding of the American Revolution, its interpreters have not effectively incorporated the eighteenth-century concern with the workings of the human heart. So to these schools of thought *Sentimental Democracy* adds a related but largely overlooked temperament, the genteel language of the parlor and salon, the shared sympathy or "enlightened feeling" that conditioned public behavior and so informed political values—what G. J. Barker-Benfield has clarified for the British context and Anne C. Vila for the French in their persuasive books, *The Culture of Sensibility* (1992) and *Enlightenment and Pathology* (1998), respectively.[7]

On the related subject of nationalism, David Waldstreicher's *In the Midst of Perpetual Fetes* (1997) is an engaging work about celebratory practices in the service of nation building that will no doubt deepen appreciation for the organizing spirit of Revolutionary Americans. His Introduction provides a useful historiographic update on the literature of nationalism in preparation for an analysis of patriotic ritual. The national mind, so called, or "national psyche," or "national soul," has long been understood to be bound up in America's peculiar conditions—geographic protection from Europe, a much vaunted tendency (in comparative terms) to overcome social inequality, and other inventive myths. This perception of nationhood sanctifies a "moment" of consensus, the time when American independence was attained. Similar attributes are expressed in the notion of "American exceptionalism," that no other place, no other society matched America. Recognizing past historians' desire to find solutions to enduring tensions, Waldstreicher properly regards nationalism as a political strategy operating in the context of competing interests, rather than arising and developing of its own accord.[8]

And so this study as well proceeds with an underlying conception of nationhood, a distinct community of people of one or more nationalities (that is, who recognize the countries of their descent), who have come to identify with the established American creed elevating practical freedom and independence. Nationalism describes the connectedness of these people, their shared loyalty to national principles, and the persistence of a common cultural idiom. Contained within this definition of national consciousness is the moral standard whose traditional features include compassion, generosity, and benevolence. Whether or not these qualities are real and applied, at least they are consistently articulated elements of America's national goals and values.

Because neither the traditional political nor the religiopolitical histories have gone beyond their formulations to probe why Americans have thought themselves so decent, humane, and resilient, this book offers a new interpretation of the emotionally rich vocabulary ingrained in well-publicized documents, books and memoirs, newspaper and magazine articles, and pamphlets, poems, oratory, and private correspondence. Taken together, these lively texts reveal how zealous expressions of sympathy and affectionate ties joined with clear assertions of the reasoning intellect to promote national union—while concealing the unavoidably chaotic emotional life that most Americans experienced. A by-product of sentimental democracy has been the insistent demand for conformity from those already within or meant to come within the American orbit.

To be clear, in the pages of this book "democracy" means the American democratic spirit, and not merely that form of government which dates back to ancient Greece and gives power to the popular voice. Over time, democracy in America became a temperament, a moral quality, a vision of progress theoretically built on the encouragement of good works and public virtue, ideals said to have guided the American Revolution. In the minds of its confident promoters, democracy became rhetorically synonymous—if not in actual fact consistent—with egalitarian presumptions ("All men are created equal") and humanitarian progress. It promised happiness to its practitioners. It promised victory over authoritarian forms and transcendence over base desires. It can still call forth support for ostensibly benevolent "invasions"—Haiti in the 1990s is a recent example. It also explains why modern Americans think it is right that their country should take the lead in feeding the hungry or rescue earthquake victims elsewhere in the world. But my purpose is less to indulge in theoretical speculation than to narrate the story of America's romance with itself. In doing so, I do not prescribe, nor do I aim to subject to scientific analysis the minds of those whose words I cite, but simply to stir the pot of Americans' passions.

SENTIMENTAL DEMOCRACY OPENS with an expository chapter, "Sentiment and Sympathy." Mid-eighteenth-century Americans took the European idea of refined manners and delicate nerves—sensibility— and applied it to their own political culture. Revolutionaries identified sentiment and sympathy first with feminine traits and next with masculine self-control, and they made this moral calculus serve the republican ideal, ultimately using it to proclaim a national conscience. It was their conviction that high-minded Americans possessed greater natural bonds of affection and had developed an even-tempered philanthropy superior to that of any other people. Along with a virtuous passion properly applied to the establishment of a well-balanced government, sentiment and sympathy helped form an emotional covenant among Americans that promoted an optimistic view of the future of the nation and the world.

Each chapter thereafter charts transitions in the language used to express America's romantic self-image. Varying vignettes serve to set the mood for these discussions, noting the rhetorical conventions which animated the discourse of each period. During 1750–64, the sermonic convention underlay the colonial self-image, emphasizing respect, devotion, and a communal giving of thanks. During 1765–75, as resistance to the British Crown stiffened, the mood was expressed in memorials, beginning with daring drama in the streets and ending with the martyrdom of patriot Joseph Warren. In 1776, the revelatory metaphor of the dream served the cause of revolution. During 1777–88, the theme became captivity and release, physical escape from British containment and, through the Constitutional Convention, a codified escape from the past. During 1789–1800, as a new national authority grappled with internal contradictions, a fixation on death and dissolution became evident in gothic fantasy tales. With the election of 1800, one can detect the transformation of political culture in its satires on democracy; during 1801–15, appearances shifted, new voices were raised, distortions of the American dream were played out, and the rhetoric of national harmony was debated. Finally, during 1816–28, a grand nostalgia awakened, and the Revolutionary generation became enshrined through a new literature of enthusiastic national development.[9]

At the heart of these chapters lies an understanding of Americans' rhetorical pursuit of liberty and happiness. But their quest for an inviolable principle would not have been complete without a quasi-religious commitment to the land itself. And so, the final section of each chapter focuses on issues and conceptions of land and empire, measuring the specific relationship patriots claimed existed between the facts of America's physical surroundings and the unified nation's compassionate exploitation of that uncorrupted pastoral environment. Travelers wrote in praise of a fruitful earth which facilitated peaceful lives for a personable people; they urged settlement in a way that was meant to divert America from the path to diseased and overcrowded cities like those in Europe, where corruption and lust for power were bred. At the same time, this was land that supported the institution of slavery.

Nevertheless, early Americans sought to identify a common character, alternately describing themselves as curious, energetic, exuberant, free, good-natured, hopeful, inventive, invincible, passionate, persuasive, pragmatic, productive, righteous—an informed and sympathetic people. They also brought out qualities considered equally American that were generally less emotionally charged: integrative, introspective, calmly self-critical. They were meant to be a people fashioning an empire of generous humanity across a yielding land, maximizing social happiness and conveying a secure sense of liberty to their posterity. They would accomplish this feat of history, they thought, by holding to the heart-enriching principles of the American Revolution. Others around the globe, apprehending the moral conditions present in America and infused with hope, would reasonably desire to profit by example.

Arriving at the dynamic moment in the early nineteenth century when the culture of sensibility was overtaken by a more overtly ag-

gressive consciousness, the narrative returns to the concept of sentimental democracy and shows how sentiment and sympathy evolved over
the course of the early republic. Once it had cemented the union, the
old language of feeling, of sentiment under control, proved insufficient
to cope with an expansive capitalistic society bent more than ever on
shows of strength. The restraining values of the culture of sensibility
were supplanted by the language of manifest destiny, while chivalric
male protection of female delicacy and honor was reinforced. By the
age of Jackson, the ethereal and pure Man of Feeling became earthy
and fallible and could no longer stand for universal benevolence. The
eighteenth century's language of nerve structure and physiology relin-
quished its hold over the People of Feeling, and was succeeded by the
hardiness of raw American nerve. Sentiment and coercive power, long
seen in opposition, merged into the attractive combination that sentimental democrats have paraded at home and abroad ever since.

GENIAL MEMBERS OF the historical profession have contributed
substantively to my personal enjoyment in pursuing this project. Of
these people, Nancy Isenberg assuredly ranks first. From her perspective as a specialist in gender and American nationhood, she has offered
stimulating ideas and essential clarifications. She has been a patient and
perfectly poised critic. I am also most fortunate to have as friend and
adviser Peter Onuf, who knows how to take the materials of a complex
narrative and magically, it sometimes seems, reveal how to make it make
better sense. Joseph Ellis has challenged my ideas with good-natured
enthusiasm and supplied a ton of practical advice. Ken Burns has given
me a fascinating glimpse of his unique formula for conveying the historical imagination, reaching deep and reaching out. I have profited as
well from meaningful conversations with John Baskerville, Kathleen
Brown, Saul Cornell, Robert Dise, Jay Fliegelman, Linda Kerber, Jay
Lees, Jan Lewis, Edward Pearson, Camilla Rockwell, Herbert Sloan,
and David Waldstreicher.

I wish to thank Joanne Chaison, John Hench, Thomas Knoles, Ma-
rie Lamoureux, Dennis Laurie, and the committed staff of the American
Antiquarian Society for their expertise and support during my residence
as a Kate B. and Hall J. Peterson research fellow. Daniel P. Jordan,

Susan Stein, Douglas L. Wilson, Rebecca Bowman, Zanne Macdonald, and all the other outstanding members of the Monticello community have made me feel at home on Thomas Jefferson's still lively and productive mountaintop. Thanks as well to the good people at the George Washington Papers, especially Dorothy Twohig, Frank Grizzard, and Marlena DeLong, for their generosity and helpful suggestions. In Iowa, Judith Dohlman and Vickie Hanson helped me past technological and administrative hurdles of the modern age. Interlibrary Loan at the Donald O. Rod Library of the University of Northern Iowa was instrumental in acquiring essential materials. My agent, the wizardly Gerard McCauley, has worked tirelessly; at Hill and Wang, Elisabeth Sifton has buoyed me by her diligence, her wisdom, and her faith in the book. Finally, I want to acknowledge Robert and Lois Burstein for their spirited company during transitional days and my son Joshua, to whom this book is cheerfully dedicated, for occasionally turning off the television so I could think.

If national pride is ever justifiable or excusable it is when it springs, not from power or riches, grandeur or glory, but from conviction of national innocence, information, and benevolence.

—JOHN ADAMS, *inaugural address, 1797*

America stands alone as the world's indispensable nation.

—WILLIAM JEFFERSON CLINTON,
*second inaugural address, 1997*

# SENTIMENTAL DEMOCRACY

# CHAPTER ONE

————⊱◈⊰————

# SENTIMENT AND SYMPATHY:

# BEGINNINGS

INVENTING A NATION entails giving definition to the character of the people, identifying their compatible qualities and common understandings, cultivating a sense of moral community. In the United States, this process is still going on. It has provoked every emotion from the menacing rhetoric of nativists to the humbling acknowledgment of diversity. Almost every such attempt to define the nation's identity can be linked in some way to an embellishment of the language and events of the American Revolution—a romance with the pre-romantic age of the eighteenth century.

The most distinctive emotional force of those years was sentiment and sympathy. When citizens today claim that mastery of the continent was attained by the enterprising spirit of unselfish, fit pioneers, or when they avow the right of all to free speech and assembly, or whenever the U.S. government asserts that maintaining world peace can best be accomplished by a benevolent use of American power, the spokespersons for these ideals have relied on an inherited vocabulary of sentiment and sympathy. In his 1801 Inaugural Address, in words that Americans today still relate to, Jefferson termed his country "the world's best hope." Seeing the "rising nation" as a land that was "wide and fruitful," he urged its citizens to "unite with one heart and one mind," to restore after a decade of heated politics the sentimental values of "harmony and affection." For, without these, he insisted, "liberty and even life itself are but dreary things."[1]

From the time of the Revolution, if not before, Americans have tended to project a self-image of charitable concern and active self-restraint. Less persuasively, perhaps, their commitment to ordered liberty has dictated that righteous self-expression stop short of forfeiting reason through the degenerative effects of self-indulgence, greed, license, or political fanaticism—the unhealthy passions. During the Revolutionary crisis, loyalists decried rebel Americans' excesses in just such a vocabulary. The passion they witnessed in the activities of patriots during the 1770s appeared to them dangerous and unruly; they described the failure to check behavior in terms of "deformation," of a loss of reason and judgment. People recognized and feared their own base instincts; they knew they were vulnerable creatures subject to temptation. Freedom could not exist without morality—both sides in the American Revolution believed that—and both felt certain that the other lacked fortitude and enough moral strength to avoid being victimized by untrustworthy leaders.[2]

In part because mid-eighteenth-century Americans were thought (and acknowledged themselves) to be culturally and economically inferior to Europeans, the preeminent pens and leading voices of 1776 focused on what they believed was a widely held sense of moral superiority over the powerful mother country from whom they were to separate. Starting by describing their continent in idealized imagery as a promised land conducive to the growth of liberty, they highlighted the virtue of simplicity possessed by the people of the thirteen colonies, and they promoted a community spirit generated through popular resistance to an authority as unsentimental as it was unrepresentative.

Revolutionary America's eloquent polemicists could defend the inseparable causes of independence and American exceptionalism by the use of a potent, viscerally felt contrast: they claimed they were a patient, understanding, sensate people, and that the king and Parliament, who had sought to suppress their decent impulses, were necessarily dull, insensitive, and emotionally misaligned and misdirected. Jefferson's Declaration of Independence in particular played up the distinction between the feeling and the unfeeling, between a virtuous people and a tyrant who had "waged cruel war against human nature itself." Americans were resorting to war only after grievously suffering the "last stab to agonizing affection," while King George III had "plundered," "constrained," and "neglected" honorable subjects who had been simply seeking their rightful happiness. Because the colonists' British brethren were "deaf to the voice of justice and consanguinity," Americans had united to form a new consanguinity. Thus the nation of a just sensibility, with its "manly spirit" (here meaning one with sturdiness and conviction), had determined to "renounce forever these unfeeling brethren."[3]

As Jay Fliegelman has effectively argued, the Declaration of Independence was intended to be read aloud as well as in its printed form. Print culture in 1776 was secure in its authority, yet Jefferson aimed to preserve the special character of the spoken voice in his composition of a vigorous and passionate, politically persuasive document. When one member of Parliament denounced the Declaration as a "wretched" instrument "drawn up with the view to *captivate the people*," John Wilkes, a defender of American rights, rose to laud Jefferson's composition: "The polished periods [sentences], the harmonious happy expressions, with all the grace, ease and elegance of a beautiful diction, which we chiefly admire, *captivate* the people of America very little; but manly, nervous [vigorous] sense, they relish even in the most awkward and uncouth language. Whatever composition produces the effect you intend in the most forcible manner is, in my opinion, the best." Jefferson may not have seen his technique as Wilkes did, but he clearly aimed to mix style and sentiment in a way that affected listeners as well as readers. He was in effect announcing to the world a new oratorical ideal that combined masculine sentiment and a kind of theater. To "captivate," in the sense almost of ensnaring or bewitching (as the member of Parliament intended to convey), was not the effect of the Declaration; rather, Americans were responding to language that contained sensory power, that coursed through the nervous system and, in fact, made "sense."[4]

Self-serving distinctions between feeling and unfeeling persisted in American political rhetoric in the decades after the Revolution. A Fourth of July oration in Portland, Maine, in 1801, for example, reminded citizens of the meaning of independence: "We were no longer esteemed the rebellious subjects of Great Britain: but as a magnanimous people struggling for liberty—for our inherent birth-right . . . in opposition to men and measures instigated by the vilest motives; in opposition to men totally devoid of principles, of humanity, and of every spicies [sic] of fellow feeling." In Ohio, the *Scioto Gazette* that same year referred to a Great Britain likely to prevent farmers' flour from reaching the West Indies as an "unfeeling nation." Of the expected blockade, the newspaper editorialized: "The prospects of the enterprising citizens of the western country [are] blasted in the bud—their only avenue to foreign markets obstructed by an arbitrary and unfeeling nation, whose subjects are *starving* for the very article which they have prevented from proceeding."[5]

As the new republic grew, it continued to develop a sense of its special destiny grounded in its unique and unprecedented, emotionally rich and resilient, morally uplifting national creation story. Scholars who have written about sentiment have primarily related it to the sentimental literature of this period, especially to the female consciousness.[6] But sentiment and sympathy—and the culture of sensibility in general—were used to sustain the enterprise of nation building. It was as important for men as for women to cultivate this sensibility during and after the Revolution, and it went well beyond familiar characterizations to comprise an enduring counterpoint to plain masculine assertiveness and national aggressiveness.

The Enlightenment made an impression on the American founders not only in introducing a reverence for science, an appeal to intelligent judgment, and a tone of criticism but in asserting that harmony and sympathy existed in nature. "The prosperity of reason in the eighteenth century," Peter Gay has written, "was less the triumph of rationalism than of reasonableness."[7] The world of the literate was being emptied of religious mystery and filled with a philosophic understanding of humanity. In America, from the Stamp Act, which ignited Revolutionary protest, through the Jeffersonian-Hamiltonian party battles of the 1790s, anxious concern for the preservation of liberty and for the continued claim to happiness intensified Americans' fears of aggressive forces and aggressive behavior.[8] The language of sentiment and sympathy, used by a people who routinely called themselves peace-loving, constituted a defense against inner and outer turmoil.

THE CONCEPT OF *sensibilité* had arisen in the seventeenth-century French novel as a combination of *amour, amitié,* and the capacity to feel pain.[9] When medical research yielded more precise terminology, men with philosophic minds in eighteenth-century France and England combined their respect for science with social responsibility, as they came to identify the progress of civilization with decency, generosity, and optimism.[10] The meaning of sensibility expanded accordingly, linking the physiology of the nervous system with feminine delicacy and masculine self-control, with matters of private conscience and public virtue. To be endowed with sensibility in its most attractive (and at the same time most afflicted) form meant to have an enlarged capacity to perform benevolent deeds, to show affection readily, to shed tears and empathize strongly with human suffering. While women were easily acknowledged to possess such characteristics—tenderness and benevolence, fainting spells and languid spirits being extreme manifestations, positive and negative—men also possessed, to a certain and varying degree, a sensible nature.

Any understanding of sensibility begins, then, with its medical definition. British America's perspective on the psychoperceptual system in humans, of a mind that received impressions, dated from John Locke's *Essay Concerning Human Understanding* (1690).[11] Nerve fibers set off tremors; nervous tension within the body directly affected conscience and consciousness. Indeed, the words *conscience* and *consciousness* were for the most part interchangeable throughout the eighteenth century and coincided with hearts of compassion, with sympathetic emotions. While the heart combined circulatory power with vital equilibrium and expressions of love, a conscious person was one who commanded a moral sense.[12]

A revolution in understanding human physiology was underway. Dr. George Cheyne, who treated his friend the popular novelist Samuel Richardson, wrote the paradigmatic line in 1733: "Feeling is nothing but the Impulse, Motion or Action of Bodies, gently or violently impressing the Extremities or Sides of the Nerves, of the Skin, or other parts of the Body, which . . . convey Motion to the Sentient Principle in the Brain." Human feeling was understood to be simply the motion of nerve fibers; every response to a moral concern had a physiological referent. Popular writers thus spread, in the words of a modern critic, "the new science of man, directing thought about man from his visible eyes and expressive face to his unseen nerves and controlling brain, from what he looks like to what he feels to what he knows."[13]

Because the body was viewed as a mechanism that might be easily overwrought, sensible creatures, however respectable, disinterested, creative, or accomplished, might also "fatigue their Heads with intense Thought and Study," according to Bernard Mandeville, an early-eighteenth-century writer and physician specializing in nervous disorders.[14] James Madison's hypochondria, or possible "epileptoid hysteria," was explainable in these terms.[15] New Hampshire senator William Plumer wrote of his Kentucky colleague Buckner Thruston in 1807:

> He was educated to the profession of the law—& is a man of science—Is a good Greek & Italian scholar. Is a man of an amiable disposition—his manners are refined—His feelings exquisitely delicate—is subject to hypocendriacal complaints, &, of course, at different times appears very different & unequal. He assured me to day, that was he once attacked with rudeness in a news paper publication he would retire to private life. He is not like his late colleague Brackenridge [John Breckinridge], or his present fellow [Henry] Clay, *effective man.*[16]

By this time, traits considered feminine, or like the female constitution possessing and exhibiting an unusually high degree of sensibility, were thought to indicate an imbalance in males, making them less fit for the demands of public debate.

Fibers, connectors of the nervous system, figured prominently in sentimental literature. Thomas Jefferson, for one, frequently intensified statements where he wished to combine reason with an appropriate level of passion by referring to "every fibre of my frame" as an elemental component of his being; he wished to eradicate "every fibre" of aristocracy in America and in later years he explained that "every fibre" of his passion for public life had dried up.[17] "Vibrations" and "thrills" also accompanied human activity, words conveying the interpenetration of emotions and physiology. Around mid-century, the Swiss physiologist and poet Albrecht von Haller clarified the importance of sensibility as a primary life force with his experimental results distinguishing irritability (unfelt automatic responses) from sensibility (responses accompanied by feeling).[18]

Most profoundly, "sympathies" were what conducted feelings through nerves and organs. In his Lectures on the Mind, Dr. Benjamin Rush of Philadelphia stated that physiological sympathies were governed by the same laws as emotional sympathy. The pulsation of the heart was a sympathy, as was the "reciprocal" sympathy between the brain and the stomach. Rush called the senses "the inlets of ideas." He held that odors as well influenced morals: living near an active volcano aroused people to unusual passion, just as one's morning walk through a flower garden brought a natural composure. Arthur May, a candidate for the degree of doctor of medicine at the University of Pennsylvania, submitted a dissertation on sympathy to the trustees and medical faculty in 1799: "In warm weather appetite fails; because the impression of heat on the skin invites excitement from the stomach to the surface; and the system cannot bear both impressions of heat and aliment. Appetite is suspended in the same manner by joy, grief, expectation, etc." May found that impressions or sympathies "vibrate" throughout the body and "undulate" to the "remotest boundaries." "In a word," he claimed, "the whole system, mind and body, is one mass of general sympathy."[19]

In the eighteenth century, most Europeans and Americans were taught from birth how to curb their emotions, though they remained anxious about appearances. "Outward expression of the passions is a sort of universal language," wrote a contributor to *The Universal Asylum, and Columbian Magazine*, seeking insight into Americans' character. Passions were "commotions of the body as well as of the mind," which a sensitive, sophisticated observer could interpret. Countenance and constitution were the subjects of the "conjectural science" of physiognomy. One could search for fraud, deceit, or moral weakness. In a more positive light, the perfectly innocent, unsuspecting heroine in Susanna

Rowson's sentimental *Charlotte Temple* (1791) was described by her physiognomy: "The goodness of her heart is depicted in her ingenuous countenance." According to *The New-Hampshire Magazine*, the external manifestation of inner virtue was visible even to those with a less extraordinary perception: honor and love of truth wore the face of "vivacity" in a true gentleman. The young Bostonian author of *The Power of Sympathy* (1789), William Hill Brown, gushed in his prose: "But come thou spirit of celestial language, that canst communicate by one affectionate look—one tender glance—more divine information to the soul of sensibility, than can be contained in myriads of volumes!" Repeated references to Johann Caspar Lavater's *Essays on Physiognomy*, first published in America in 1794, attest to the popularity of this method of reading character. Lavater tauntingly illustrated his findings, which associated the shape of foreheads, eyes and eyelids, noses, lips, and chins with various temperaments. "Each part of an organized body is an image of the whole," the physiognomist claimed.[20]

The taxonomy of facial expressions and their corresponding revelations of character formed a literature that could be easily translated into political culture. The republican ideal of plain speaking, honest deportment, and apparent lack of concealment was contrasted with the seductiveness of heartless contrivance. Sociability highlighted sensibility. It was an important part of politics, at once art and strategy. It involved subtle self-promotion, at the same time avoiding a crass regard for notice or the appearance of glory seeking. But it was not easy to effect. As Jay Fliegelman has commented, "the triple injunctions to please yet persuade, to control oneself but stimulate passions in others, to reveal oneself and yet efface oneself, combined to create an exhausting challenge."[21]

At once sentient and rational, human beings needed to maintain a proper balance between these two facets of their behavioral system in order to achieve happiness. In *The Theory of Moral Sentiments* (1759), Adam Smith produced what was perhaps the most thorough work codifying the culture of sensibility into which eighteenth-century Americans and Britons alike came of age.[22] Smith described the sensations of sentiment and passion as "affection of the heart from which any action proceeds," and he characterized virtue and propriety, the experiences of grief and joy, taste and judgment, concord and discord, opinions and moral standards. "A man of sensibility," he wrote, "may sometimes feel great uneasiness lest he should have yielded too much even to what may be called an honourable passion." The man of virtuous sentiment, cultivating a sense of duty, overcame the impulse of self-love through reason, principle, and conscience—by reflecting on the precariousness of existence and discovering "the man within." He came to recognize that "we are but one of the multitude." Smith called such a feeling "moderated sensibility."[23]

The injunction to follow nature's dictates animated the mid-eighteenth-century Scottish philosophic school to which Smith belonged. Not inconsequentially, Edinburgh and Glasgow were centers of medical as well as moral discourse. The American Enlightenment plainly profited from the writings of these Scots (including Thomas Reid, Francis Hutcheson, David Hume, and Hume's cousin, Lord Kames), for the Revolutionary literati appreciated their pragmatic and intuitive qualities, and their argument that benevolence and public virtue demanded an engagement of the heart. Silent, pondering reason, they insisted, could not act as a moral restraint. America's language of sentiment drew upon the moral scheme of the Scottish Enlightenment, a system which may be said to have contributed structure to the culture of sensibility.[24]

The so-called father of sentimental ethics was the third Earl of Shaftesbury (1671–1713), a student of John Locke who conceived harmony and sympathy in cosmic terms and cherished the notion that an innate moral sense was present in all human beings. Shaftesbury believed that society was made strong and cohesive through the cultivation of intimate connections, the "natural, generous affections." While self-interest was said to govern the world, he wrote, *"Passion, Humour, Caprice, Zeal, Faction,* and a thousand other Springs, which are counter to *Self-Interest,* have as considerable a part in the Movements of this Machine."* Even as the metaphor of the cold, metal mechanism came into literary fashion—the balanced springs and wheels of a clock to represent the well-tuned human body—it required the "enlarg'd Affections" of the heart to perfect circulation. In his 1726 "Plan of Conduct," the twenty-year-old Benjamin Franklin found himself sensibly "excited" to this idea of moral virtue. Appreciating natural impulses and the value of emotional intimacy, he and his successors in America's enterprise to constitute a humane government responded to Shaftesbury's sentiment and to that nicely expressed in Alexander Pope's 1733 *Essay on Man*:

> In lazy Apathy let Stoics boast
> Their Virtue fixed; 'tis fixed as in a frost,
> Contracted all, retiring to the Breast;
> But strength in mind is Exercise, not Rest:
> The rising tempest puts in act the soul,
> Parts it may ravage, but preserves the whole.
> On life's vast ocean diversely we sail,
> Reason the card, but Passion is the gale.

Human abilities were best employed when the passions were recognized, not artificially stifled. The yearnings of the heart must give force to real progress in public affairs.[25]

Other works underscored these dictates. The Scottish Dr. Hugh Blair captured Americans' attention with his comprehensive *Lectures on Rhetoric and Belles Lettres* (1783), which immediately became a staple in libraries and remained so throughout the period of the early republic.[26] Blair described sensibility, in both physiological and moral terms, as integral to human development and the inseparable companion to reason and taste. Taste, he wrote, was "founded on a certain natural and instinctive sensibility to beauty, yet reason . . . assists taste in many of its operations, and serves to enlarge its power." Taste was a sense, like the moral sense, endowed by nature and "necessary for man's well-being." While individuals were unequally endowed with it, education and culture were by far the greatest determinant in the possession and active practice of this desirable faculty. Blair understood taste, then, as sensible behavior. Improvement of society depended on the enlightened exercise of taste and sensibility; just as a craftsman whose "nice exertions" of the sense of touch led to superior creations, the acuteness of "internal taste" led an individual or society to artful refinement and moral improvement.[27]

To those thinkers whose influence was most felt in America, sentiment was prime, and its authority was superimposed on reason. Taste and sensibility, or "delicacy of taste," expressed the conviction that human beings were perfectible. Reason applied to sensibility produced effective judgments. As Blair put it, "the ultimate conclusions to which our reasonings lead, refer at last to sense and perception." Reason appealed "in the last resort, to feeling. . . . It is from consulting our own imagination and heart, and from attending to the feelings of others, that any principles are formed which acquire authority in matters of taste." Taste in religion and forms of government suggested a multiplicity of standards: "popular humour, or party spirit" proved that human beings and the institutions they constructed, no matter how cultivated, were prone to dissolution and caprice owing to the inescapability of "native feelings." Blair nonetheless upheld Enlightenment optimism when he projected that "in the course of time . . . the genuine taste of human nature never fails to disclose itself and to gain the ascendant over any fantastic or corrupted modes of taste which may chance to have been introduced."[28]

The great French political thinker Charles-Louis de Secondat, Baron de Montesquieu, was interpreting a similar state of mind when he set out to examine the prospects of a free nation. Reason, he wrote in his 1748 *The Spirit of the Laws*, "never produces great effects on the spirits of men," and reason alone, without the passions, allowed a government to "undertake enterprises against its true interests." The mores, manners, and character of a nation, formed and confirmed by liberty, naturally produced a national life that was "always heated," "led by its passions." Montesquieu viewed this as a positive feature of free society: "This nation, made comfortable by peace and liberty, freed from destructive prejudices, would be inclined to become commercial," and to expand for the sake of commerce rather than to dominate other nations and peoples. The philosopher rhapsodized: "If there were in the world a nation which had a sociable humor, an openness of heart; a joy in life, a taste, an ease in communicating its thoughts . . . and which had with all that, courage, generosity, frankness, and a certain point of honor, one should avoid disturbing its manners by laws, in order not to disturb its virtues." And elsewhere: "we do nothing better than what we do freely and by following our natural genius." He was speaking of the positive political effects of sensibility.[29] As Hume stressed, the heart directed "the tender passions," accounting for "*generosity, humanity, compassion, gratitude, friendship, fidelity, zeal, disinterestedness, liberality,*" and other useful social qualities of benevolence and good character. But if passion could be enlisted to do good, it was also, again in Hume's words, "much better satisfy'd by its restraint, than by its liberty." As an ineradicable part of human nature, passion could be channeled into virtuous activity, satisfying self-interest and public interest at once.[30]

SENSIBILITY REACHED THE HEIGHT of its popularity in England with Samuel Richardson's epistolary novels of the 1740s and 1750s, the consciousness-probing works of Laurence Sterne in the 1760s, and Henry Mackenzie's emblematic *The Man of Feeling* in 1770. These and subsequent writings stressing sensibility communicated refinement to the middle class. They encompassed matters of individual self-cultivation, superior taste, criticism of aristocratic pride, and a spirit of prudence and self-restraint in human relations more generally. The elements available to these sentimental novels had developed over a century: the wronged but patient wife or husband whose patience yields the return of his or her loved one; the guide/philosopher/friend, generally a middle-class idealist, ready with good moral advice or meaningful sentiments; the reclaimed prodigal, led astray by a malevolent force, later able to return purified; the "conscious" or high-minded sentimental lovers, symbolizing the natural endurance of uncorrupted love; and especially, the often tested young female servant who finally "wins" virtuous marriage to the squire pursuing her.[31] As the subtitle of Richardson's first novel, *Pamela: or, Virtue Rewarded* (1740), suggests, moral strength had to be "rewarded" by society for it to possess more than spiritual significance. Private feelings became public revelations as the literature of the period extended beyond the imagination of the reader and into the political realm.

By the time the first professional American novelist, the Philadelphian Charles Brockden Brown, began seeking readers in the 1790s, this tradition was so widely accepted that moral fiction had worked its way into purposeful expressions of American identity—the good that issued from the susceptible national heart. While Brown was to make his mark as the author of disturbing gothic tales like *Wieland*, in which unbalanced reason and sensibility clashed, he avowed that it was Richardson's instructive texts which first inspired his talent. An unpublished sketch for an essentially autobiographical epistolary novel, "The Story of Julius" (1792), traced, in the author's words, "the mazes of the human heart" inflamed by noble passions. Love, friendship, social obligation, and self-sacrifice (key ingredients in the sentimental novel) figured crucially in this prose and influenced the impassioned Brown in a literary pursuit of happiness for his flawed, impressionable, and affecting characters. In a letter to a trusted friend, Brown communicated in breathtaking words: "Did you ever observe the extraordinary influence of imagination over the actions and sentiments of men?" In "The Story of Julius" he established that, as much as he aspired to be the American Richardson, he was already an American Man of Feeling.[32]

Sentimental fiction written by men did much to clarify American standards of behavior during the decade leading up to the Revolution. These works encouraged other men (gentlemen or, better, insensitive men with unwholesome appetites) to convert to sensible values, to become masters of their selves thereby. Their indulgence of emotion was for the purpose of aspiring to a certain sense of honor, to a superior level of moral sentiment. But part of the effect of Richardson's enormously successful *Pamela* and *Clarissa* in highlighting the heart as the source of writing was to improve men's treatment of women, who were understood to be prone to sensibility by their very nature, easily swayed by passionate suggestions in writing. Richardson's novels were psychological treatments of sexuality and power, of the female moral vision and male reformation. Virtue was put on trial. What female readers were understood to "need" in their encounters with this didactic fiction was a seriousness of tone and purity of content that would persuade them to remain modest.

In *A Sentimental Journey* (1768), Sterne announced unabashedly that he found all women to be ethereal creatures. They were a delight to him, and never to be trifled with or led on. "God bless them all!" he wrote. "[T]here is not a man upon earth who loves them so much as I do: after all the foibles I have seen, and all the satires I have read against them, still I love them; being firmly persuaded that a man who has not a sort of an affection for the whole sex, is incapable of ever loving a single one as he ought." Yet Sterne acknowledged, in the guise of everyman, that he desired all the women who so delighted him, and that he had to command his heart to make him behave virtuously toward them. Sterne's literary alter ego Yorick, when prodded by a French nobleman to admit that he has come to France not only "to spy the nakedness of the land" but also "*that* of our women," replies that he would wish to spy only "the *nakedness* of their hearts . . . [in order] to fashion my own."[33]

Sterne's playful and suggestive stories were popularized for women in a desexualized anthology entitled *The Beauties of Sterne, Including All His Pathetic Tales and Most Distinguished Observations on Life, Selected for the Heart of Sensibility*. Under the system of thought then prevailing, this sensible heart would restrict female sensuality and soften the masculine one. The male constitution had to be firm to promote the masculine traits of prudence and self-command, but masculinity as a code of conduct was coming to be understood in terms of an energizing humility, in discovering one's "better feelings." As Adam Smith succinctly put it, "our sensibility to the feelings of others, so far from being inconsistent with the manhood of self-command, is the very principle upon which that manhood is founded."[34]

Sensibility relied heavily on the shedding of tears. The Abbé Du Bos, an early eighteenth-century critic of poetry and painting believed to be the first to locate introspection in the nature of aesthetics, reflected on inner experience: "The tears of someone we don't know move us even before we know the subject which makes him weep. The cries of a man to whom we are attached only by humanity make us fly to his aid with an automatic movement which precedes all deliberation." Du Bos anticipated that the experience of reading would create for ever larger numbers of people the same illusion of presence as viewing a painting did—"becoming spectator to a moving spectacle," as one scholar describes it. While Du Bos claimed that this kind of secondhand experience enabled people to "enjoy . . . emotion" without displacing their reason, his contemporary, the novelist and playwright Pierre Carlet de Chamblain de Marivaux, stated in 1714 that it was the reader's "*plaisir de sa sensibilité*," the awareness of his or her own ability to be moved, to find compassion, through which the soul found fulfillment. Sterne ripened this art. "I am never so perfectly conscious of the existence of a soul within me," he wrote, "as when I am entangled in [melancholy adventures]." And Mackenzie echoed, "I imagine being somewhat conversant with the fine arts is one of the most powerful improvements of the mind. . . . The soul, as well as the body, has nerves, which are only affected in a certain indescribable manner, and gain by frequent exertion, a very superior degree of feeling."[35]

In his *Letters from an American Farmer* (1782), the French-born New Yorker Hector St. Jean de Crèvecoeur exemplified the American dream and at the same time the character of his welcoming countrymen by identifying his letter-writing persona as "the farmer of feelings." The farmer's love for his wife was so deep that in contemplating her he "cannot describe the various emotions of love, of gratitude, of conscious pride which thrill in my heart and often overflow in involuntary tears." His sensible receptors reacted to the beauties of nature as well: "The pleasure I received from the warblings of the birds in the spring, is superior to my poor description, as the continual succession of their tuneful notes is *for ever new to me*."[36] Like Crèvecoeur, Mackenzie's fictional Harley, the Man of Feeling, constantly describes tearful breakdowns and the good of nature which seems to prevail despite the existence of contrary impulses: "[He] checked for a while the yearnings of his heart; but nature at last prevailed and [he] mingled his tears in hers." In Mackenzie's later novel, *The Man of the World*, a seduced woman delivers her child and "mingled tears with kisses on its cheeks."[37] In "My Head and My Heart," Jefferson's 1786 letter to the artist Maria Cosway written in the form of a dialogue, the correspondent similarly marvels at the Heart's capacity to commit to others. Recollecting scenes he encountered with Mrs. Cosway and the involuntary nature of his response to them, Jefferson's sympathetic Heart exclaims: "The wheels of time moved on with a rapidity of which those of our carriage gave but a faint idea, and yet . . . what a mass of happiness had we travelled over!" The sensible Jefferson, ostensibly prone to rich, uncontrollable feelings, proceeded to describe the sublime landscape of America as that place where his friend might seek "an asylum from grief! With what sincere sympathy I would open every cell of my composition to receive the effusion" of her "woes," to "pour my tears into" her "wounds." Later in the letter he restates the cause of the man of sentiment: "And what more sublime delight than to mingle tears with one whom the hand of heaven hath smitten!"[38]

In his authoritative *Dictionary*, Johnson listed a series of combinations with the word *heart* which offer a glimpse of the imaginative possibilities which writers of the age of sensibility drew upon in their attempts to impress feelings upon readers. There was *heart-ach*, *heart-break*, and *heart-breaker* (at this time meaning nothing beyond "a cant name for women's curls" and not generally used in polite society). One was *heart-burned* when "the passions inflamed." *Heart-dear* meant "sincerely beloved," *heart-ease* a synonym for peace and quiet. *Heart-string* was, significantly, "the tendons or nerves supposed to brace and sustain the heart," *heart-struck* the effect occurring when something was "driven to the heart" and "infixed forever in the mind." An idea was *heart-swelling* when "rankling in the mind," and one was *heart-whole* when something external had not yet pierced one's affections—that is, "with the vitals yet unimpaired." Human vulnerability was the exclusive subject of *heart*-prefixed expressions.[39]

By mid-century, the French and English word *sentiment* was long in use and already employed in a neutral context; one could profess "sentiments" without expressing sentimentality. The adjective *sentimental*, however, was given vogue by Sterne. *A Sentimental Journey* was a favorite among men and women of letters in America. It told the story of the "Sentimental Traveller" Yorick, who rejoiced in simple pleasures in his human encounters, in "communicating our sensations out[side] of our own sphere." For Sterne *sentimental* meant precisely *sensibility*. Nothing was more real to him: after having insulted a Franciscan monk who was asking for alms, Yorick opens himself up to his natural emotions and finds pleasure in resolving to make amends with the beggar he has snubbed. Some period later, while he is "plucking up a nettle or two" at the monk's grave, Yorick's "affections" are so "struck" that he "burst out into a flood of tears—but I am as weak as a woman; and I beg the world not to smile, but pity me."[40]

Jefferson carried a pocket-sized edition of *A Sentimental Journey* on his 1787 excursion through the South of France, wrote letters in Sterne's style, and intentionally borrowed scenes from the novel to demonstrate his sympathetic communion with common people. In 1780 Abigail Adams wrote to James Lovell, "I have read Stern's Sermons and Yorick's Sentimental journey." She found in Sterne's works "a rich Stream of Benevolence flowing like milk and Honey, that in an insensible heart, he creates the sensation he describes—in a feeling one, he softens, he moulds it into all his own." But Sterne's moral fiction had reached the heart of America even earlier. A medical doctor named Eustace in Wilmington, North Carolina, exchanged sentiments with Sterne in correspondence of 1768, the last year of the author's life. Dr. Eustace claimed to be a "zealous defender" of Sterne's character Tristram Shandy, an ambiguous hero of the novel of the same name, published in nine volumes between 1759 and 1767. Eustace expressed his identification with the chaotic picture of life that Sterne adored taunting his readers to acknowledge, and concluded, "You know it is an observation as remarkable for its truth as its antiquity, that a similitude of sentiments is the general part of friendship." To the sympathetic colonist, who had sent the gift of a walking-stick along with his letter, Sterne replied, "There is so little true feeling in the HERD of the WORLD, that I wish I could have got an act of parliament, when the books first appear'd, 'that none but the wise men should look into them.'" Men of Feeling allowed themselves the pretense of being members of an exclusive fraternity, urging upon the world a better temperament through sentimental attachments and obligations.[41]

Sterne excited a consciousness that determined successors made even more dignified. Mackenzie's Man of Feeling, like Sterne's Yorick, exhibits an outstanding sympathy for his fellow creatures. It is part of his nature to do so. He rescues a starving prostitute and reunites her with her grieving father. He commiserates with "the unfortunate Edwards," tends to him in his suffering, and willingly, it seems, succumbs to a deadly disease rather than turn from this new friend in need.[42] The virtue of his humanity, while extreme,[43] symbolized the individual's use of the imagination to demonstrate social responsibility and actively contribute to civilization. To the obscure 1803 pamphlet associating Jefferson's "The Speech of Logan" with the excerpted "Old Edwards," the printer added John Potter's "The Shrubbery," another vignette in which a man showed that he could "feel the melancholy luxury of tears." The "exquisite sensibility" of a young woman named Julia has long "thrilled" the heart of Potter's character Melmoth, when he suddenly learns of her death. Then he "felt the intelligence in every nerve. It was as the cold point of a dagger at his heart. He did not utter a word . . . lost in the sensations which harrowed up his soul." In this tale, "spirits of love and sympathy" inspire "all the soft affections" and "all that is beautiful in feeling, and elevated in thought," that awake "trilling harmony from that sweet instrument the human soul."[44] The message was, as the entry under *sensibilité (moral)* in Denis Diderot's *Encyclopédie* declared: "Men of sensibility live more fully than others. . . . Reflection can produce a man of probity, but sensibility makes a man virtuous."[45]

The family of words linking sense and sensibility expressed a moral and political attitude which contained elements of rationalism along with enthusiasm and idealism. Humanity was expected in politics (the passage of humane laws, for example), because civility of manners and consistency in morals were expected everywhere else. The fraternity of Freemasons, which provided a forum for community-minded men who aimed to advance professionally through friendship, ritualized these values. The Freemason organization, termed "a lodge for the virtues" by brother George Washington in 1796, was described by a later member, Reverend John Clark of New York, as a "moral institution" that helped to rescue people from "moral degradation." "We are creatures of sense rather than intellection," he explained, and so the fraternity employed "sensible signs" to impress morality on its members.[46]

Cordiality and amiability, the softening of male manners, came to dominate eighteenth-century life. The early American champion of gender equality, Judith Sargent Murray, wrote in *The Gleaner* in the 1790s that women should raise themselves above dependence by learning "some particular branch of business," so as to gain the same freedom American men enjoyed. But, she added crucially, her intent was not to "unsex" women or make them less amiable, less affectionate. She insisted, in fact, that maternal instincts made women naturally superior to men in feelings and that society benefited as a result. Woman's virtue derived from "sentiment, at once sublime and pathetic," to be distinguished from the "frosty indifference, and the sour severity of some fathers." Using as her supreme example the tears of grief of a mother, Murray exclaimed: "It is she, who, with dishevelled locks, pale and distracted, embraces with transport, the body of a dead child, pressing its cold lips to her's, as if she would reanimate, by her tears and her caresses, the insensible clay. These great expressions of nature—these heart-rending emotions, which fill us at once with wonder, compassion and terror, always have belonged, and always will belong, only to Women." Woman was the model of soulful sensibility, the sex which alone could *naturally* transcend selfish desire and *naturally* act "above the standard of humanity"—in whose sensibility lay the means to save humanity.[47]

If women generally subordinated themselves and their private interests to the greater good of the world that men made, sensible men honored female self-suppression by accepting that their public virtue should parallel the gentle persuasions of domestic life and maternal sympathy and generosity. To this extent, Men of Feeling accepted that the traits associated with women's innate sensibility could and should serve them in republican political discourse. Delicate women, modest, graceful, and well dressed when subject to the public gaze, were meant to act with companionable efficiency to preserve harmony in the home; sensitive and uncorruptible men were meant to act virtuously and generously to public advantage.[48]

Men who styled themselves as enlightened critics hoped, as they systematized their social world, to project an air of meritorious self-control. Theirs was a disciplined sentimentality, whereas they regarded women's as an unconscious, unrestrained sentimentality needing a strong hand in support. Leading men empathized with "the American fair" as they simultaneously observed (looking for signs of weakness, of uncontrollable emotion) and shielded them. Their professed understanding of sensibility helped qualify them as protectors of the state's most vulnerable citizens. Sensibility, then, was a physiological phenomenon that found expression as voluntary self-monitoring behavior for any man who wished to evidence public spirit. If fearful republicans knew that untoward ambition could kill a republic, perhaps sensibility could at least contribute to stabilizing it.

# CHAPTER TWO

# SCHEMES OF FUTURE
# HAPPINESS: 1750–64

LANGUAGE TELLS the story of the evolution of America's romantic self-image. Documents like the Declaration of Independence advanced a community spirit at once sentimental and assertive, productive and powerful, and grounded in the self-constituted wisdom of a people whose outstanding commonness somehow made them uncommon. The sacramental terms of the republic, words and phrases like *liberty* and *pursuit of happiness*, became transcendent elements of culture and could not be understood outside of a belief in Americans' compulsive desire to sympathize. Whether or not individual self-consciousness actually merged with a national imperative, ennobling signifiers such as these sustained the national lore. Patriot spy Nathan Hale's "I only regret that I have but one life to lose for my country" instructed posterity that there *was* a country, that it was bigger than the self and greater than a British colony.

Nation building can adhere to novelistic conventions. To invent America, inspired writers of the founding generation drew up their setting, an inviting landscape with majestic properties. They then wrote in the land's inhabitants: they contrasted the "innocent" aboriginals with the new and burgeoning European population, doubling every twenty-five years, whose enterprising virtue was to be tested in later chapters by the mere existence of enslaved Africans who encumbered their consciences. The story was meant to be instructive: it pitted mildness and moral rectitude against aggressive power and moral laxity, and it matched humanity with seductive ambition. Language plotted this artful saga, and created America's political and cultural personality.

During the Revolutionary era, American citizens actively espoused a vocabulary rich in sentiment and productive passion that would distinguish them as a free and independent people with a special destiny. Their fabrication of a national identity, one that could be called American, inspired confidence even as it masked the reality of the nation's military and economic insignificance in the eighteenth-century world. Moreover, the pursuit of happiness was characteristic of these people well before Thomas Jefferson inserted this Lockean phrase into his Declaration. "Liberty," a concept inherited from the understood rights of free Englishmen, gradually took on an American tone. American "empire" became synonymous with the rich soil of a vast continent geographically isolated from the crowds, vice, fratricidal wars, and despair attributed to the nations of Europe.

The quest for a sentimental and assertive patriotic idiom began with a New England minister. Jonathan Mayhew (1720–66) was the son of Experience Mayhew, of Martha's Vineyard, a missionary to the Indians, and Remember (Bourne) Mayhew—parents with delightfully evocative Puritan names. Their son, born of Puritans, was bred a Yankee. In the historian Bernard Bailyn's words, the 1744 Harvard graduate was a "pre-eminent spokesman in the colonies for everything that was new, bold, and radically non-conformist."[1]

Reverend Mayhew rejected religious mysticism and believed instead that the reconciliation of human beings with God took place through the activity of the human spirit in virtuous self-development. His importance rests upon an unambiguous pamphlet he wrote which was published in 1750, *A Discourse Concerning Unlimited Submission*, which helped lay the groundwork for colonial American protest in the decades to come. In it, this rational Christian far exceeded the bounds meant to contain a Congregationalist minister. He avowed the legitimacy of civil disobedience, asserting that the authoritarian nature of the church was subversive of liberty, and that a people's love of liberty and practice of virtue ought to be coupled with resistance to oppressive rule of all kinds. Dogma which arrogantly claimed knowledge of unquestionable truth denied human growth. Mayhew's strategy was to fix the limits of submission by containing the force of the words which rulers used (or abused) to exact submission.[2]

Heretical and scandalous to conservative New Englanders, Mayhew's language defined the moral power underlying Whig political thought, the view pitting a virtuous citizenry against centralizers who intrigued to consolidate power and undermine popular liberties. When in his late years John Adams was attempting to recall for a younger generation the spark which kindled the Revolution, he praised Mayhew as a "transcendent genius," a man of wit and clever reasoning, an unstoppable force, who maintained his selfless concern for country "with zeal and ardor."[3]

The pastor's language positioned civil government against arbitrary rule, liberty against tyranny, the literal Bible against a twisted, deceptive priestcraft, common sense against nonsense. In the preface to his pamphlet Mayhew asserted: "Civil tyranny is usually small in its beginning," but became "at length, like a mighty torrent or the raging waves of the sea" that "deluges whole countries and empires." Sea metaphors consistently expressed Revolutionary Americans' anxiety about the conditions they faced; a tempestuous, untamable force of nature, the sea symbolized all that was dangerous in the lives of people on the move in the eighteenth century. The sea could be tranquil in repose and also the natural equivalent of excess human passion.[4]

While Mayhew was at first concerned with clerical bigotry and religious tyranny, he broadened his prescription when he further determined: "Tyranny brings *ignorance* and *brutality* along with it. It degrades men from their just rank into the class of brutes. It damps their spirits. It suppresses arts. It extinguishes every spark of noble ardor and generosity in the breasts of those who are enslaved by it. It makes naturally strong and great minds feeble and little, and triumphs over the ruins of virtue and humanity."[5] Mayhew used the terms of an emotional well-being which was understood to be at risk wherever liberty was threatened. Both the creative spirit and the natural disposition to be generous could be smothered by political or religious oppression.

Nothing so compactly characterizes the taste of mid-eighteenth-century Americans as this passage. The test of this people, they believed, lay in their desire to rise to a sublime level of thought and feeling, to be as advanced, as civilized, as distant from the savage state, as observant, science-marveling, and God-worshipping as humans could be. Each individual could seek moral progress and mental growth only by monitoring character. It was difficult enough to live up to one's promise in a world of temptation, but tyranny was insidious and productive only of lethargy in citizens. It "extinguished" one's spirit when it deprived the human mind of light ("spark") and heat ("ardor"). It debased character—private *and* social—by arresting the propensity to do good. Tyranny transformed noble into ignoble. And it followed that government tended either to encourage or to subvert the process of moral and intellectual perfectibility which so absorbed the literate public of Mayhew's age.

In the pastor's prescription, one submitted only to those rulers who acted for the good of society. And, significantly, it was the people themselves, sentient and humane, who ought to determine when a ruler had failed in his trust and should be dismissed. "A PEOPLE," he wrote, "really oppressed to a great degree by their sovereign cannot well be insensible [impervious to sensation] when they are so oppressed. . . . For a nation thus abused to arise unanimously and to resist their prince, even in dethroning him, is not criminal, but a reasonable way of vindicating their liberties and just rights." It was not for light and transient causes (to borrow the language of the Declaration of Independence of a quarter century later) that a people rose up; to Mayhew's essentially placid mind, "petulant, querulous men . . . men of factious, turbulent and carping dispositions" were comparatively rare in any society. Otherwise, "mankind in general have a disposition to be submissive and passive and tame under government as they ought to be," when "those who govern do it with any tolerable degree of moderation and justice." Theirs was meant to be, after all, the age of reason.[6]

Mayhew's sermon became a far-reaching pamphlet and would be reprinted momentously in 1775. It drew to a close with the piercing prose of a patriotic command: "Let us all learn to be *free* and to be *loyal*. Let us not profess ourselves to be vassals . . . but let us remember, at the same time, government is *sacred* and not to be *trifled* with." Contemplating other kingdoms in the mid-eighteenth-century world, Mayhew repeated what was at this time the Englishman's creed, that happiness was already safeguarded under the conscientious government of King George II: "We enjoy under his administration all the liberty that is proper and expedient. It becomes us, therefore, to be contented and dutiful subjects." Glowing as this report was, Mayhew's next warning was especially strong: "Let us prize our freedom but not *use our liberty for a cloak of maliciousness*. There are men who strike at *liberty* under the term *licentiousness* [that is, those who would undermine liberty by calling up a fear of moral decay attending an *excess* of liberty]. There are others who aim at *popularity* under the disguise of *patriotism*. Be aware of both. *Extremes* are dangerous."[7]

The prescient Boston minister had introduced a set of ideas capturing what was to become, soon after, the Revolutionary cast of mind. Patriot leaders of the next quarter century would consider themselves to be what Mayhew himself appeared: self-assertive moderates, as paradoxical as that might sound. Persons granted the public trust by the people at large were presumed to be of informed minds and enlightened temperament. British Americans would not be enslaved; they would not countenance despotic measures. And in return for justice, they acknowledged the authority of the sovereign.

But, as we have seen, the temper of the time was to recognize that the human character had flaws. The leaders who tempted and cajoled and *mis*led could, in difficult times, sway masses of vulnerable subjects. Mayhew urged his audience to keep a vigilant watch against corruption and betrayal. His final incisive thought was a typical eighteenth-century supplication: "to lead a *quiet and peaceable* life" in the sight of "the supreme RULER of the universe," the "KING eternal, immortal, invisible." It was, as well, a typical definition of happiness.[8]

Add to this directive an opinion from Mayhew's 1759 *Two Discourses . . .* , and an even fuller picture emerges. The colonies, he wrote in the later pamphlet,

> could become a mighty empire (I do not mean an independent one) in numbers little inferior perhaps to the greatest of Eu-

rope, and in felicity to none . . . mighty cities rising on every hill and by the side of every commodious port . . . happy fields and villages . . . through a vastly extended territory; there the pastures clothed with flocks, and here the valleys covered with corn . . . religion professed and practiced throughout this spacious kingdom in far greater purity and perfection than since the times of the apostles.[9]

Rhetorically, the American colonists, with their rich potential and good intentions, were already poised to rewrite human history. Mayhew had recast his Puritan forebears' idea of providential America.

## HAPPINESS AND LIBERTY

When he wrote of happiness in his 1750 pamphlet, Mayhew reflected the religious and social idiom of his generation. Religion stressed the harshness and persistence of grief attending earthly life, and moral philosophy stressed the elusive, tentative nature of happiness.[10] Typical was a 1758 poem in *The New American Magazine*, published in Woodbridge, New Jersey. "Life," the unidentified poet mourned, was "but a bubble."

> What a constant round of pain
> Mortals here on earth sustain!
> Real happiness requiring:
> Ne'er obtaining, still desiring.

Francis Bacon, in the previous century, had written: "The world's a bubble, and the life of man / Less than a span." John Dryden's 1697 poem "Alexander's Feast" contained similarly inspired lines: "War, he sung, is toil and trouble; / Honour but an empty bubble." Anything fragile and unsubstantial, worthless or deceptive, could be termed a "bubble."[11]

The same magazine two months later featured a column titled "Of false and true Happiness." It began with these words: "How vain, fugacious and empty, are all the little momentary pleasures of life! How blind and fond we are of being deceiv'd!" Absorbed with the same question, a later issue distantly wondered:

> O Happiness where's thy resort?
> Amidst the splendor of a court?
> Or dost thou more delight to dwell
> With the humble hermit in his cell
> In search of truth?

Ultimately, *The New American Magazine* settled on a happiness that equated with self-awareness and self-restraint, and found fulfillment in the mind's removal to a higher plane of thought. In the journey of life, one was best off by turning to "*Reason*, that bright refulgent beam of *Light*, that *Guide* to the *Soul*, that Lamp of the *Understanding*." The mind was naturally prone to vice and folly, bound to violate all laws, divine and human. Conscience helped one avoid corruption; soul searching led one to the "earthly *Paradise*" where flowed "rivers of *felicitous* thoughts." True happiness existed in calm contemplation of eternity, and in the comfortable merging of a decent imagination and closely scrutinized daily life.[12]

The metaphoric confluence of happiness with the light ("that bright refulgent beam of *Light* . . . that Lamp of the *Understanding*") which is reason prefigured the language of the generation ahead, when America would become "the land of light and liberty." Light was a dominant metaphor for truth, a truth meant to be clarifying, substantial and solid, the awakened reason of the mind. This is how Samuel Johnson's heralded English-language *Dictionary*, published from 1755, associated key words with fundamental values, supporting the lexicographer's definitions with standards of behavior. "Light" as awakened reason or essential truth had biblical origins, of course; because God was incomprehensible to the human mind, metaphorical language served to approach an understanding of divine purposes. John Locke characterized inspiration as "this internal light," just as Quakers repeatedly invoked "inner light" as the ultimate source of truth. "Liberty" was beginning to acquire the same kind of indivisibility; the "light of liberty," along with the sun's radiance, indicated a clear impression and future-directed happiness. "Slavery," then, existed in a rhetorical darkness.[13] It was this kind of slavery that British Americans associated with their traditional enemy the French, who by the mid-1750s were moving south from Canada and encroaching on the Pennsylvania frontier. Residents feared forced conversions to Catholicism, feared that captured children would be "enslaved . . . contrary to the Light of their Minds."[14]

Greatest emphasis continued to be put on the worthy, if often vain, search for earthly happiness in a vice-ridden world. The *Virginia Gazette* gave the general understanding: "There is no Topick more copiously treated by ancient Moralists, than the Folly of devoting the Heart to the Accumulation of Riches, since they can contribute very little to the Happiness of human Life." In the present as well, deference to learned moralists was the most effective answer to the temptation of riches: people who were "incited, by some violent Impulse of Passion" to equate wealth and happiness could be brought to reason by those others "whose Experiences and Sagacity has recommended them as Guides to Mankind."[15]

Often during the 1750s, the *Virginia Gazette* reminded readers of those human traits which gave rise to conditions favoring happiness: Prudence, Circumspection, Frugality, Fortitude, Temperance—resisting the "Superfluities of Life." Above all, people should not hope for too much; mere "empty Wishes and painful Comparisons" awaited those who dreamed of the power and eminence reserved for a fortunate few. Speaking for women, Esther Edwards Burr, the conscientious daughter of the famous theologian Jonathan Edwards and mother of the future Vice President Aaron Burr, wrote in her journal in 1756: "many poor young thoughtful cretures think nothing of [prudence] is needfull after marriage, but vainly immagine that happiness comes of consequence, but I would humbly ask such persons if they ever injoyed any great good without taking any pains for it." Happiness did not arise without persistent self-monitoring.[16]

Benjamin Franklin's restless nephew Benjamin Mecom, who later succumbed to a mental disorder, edited the short-lived *New England Magazine of Knowledge and Pleasure* in 1758. Its dual motto was "*Prodesse & Delectare*" (to do good and to delight) and, curiously, "*E Pluribus*

*Unum"* (out of many, one), which phrase, taken from the Roman poet Horace, Mecom's uncle would have a hand in contributing to the Great Seal of the United States eighteen years later. Mecom's magazine printed conventional verse, such as a lamentation over the "endless Toils" of an individual who had erred in life by choosing the wrong friends. In Mecom's pages happiness was a constant theme, unfixed and elusive because of the mass of uncertainty that prompted human discontent. People's only rescue came from turning to God, "Pow'r Supreme," and "the Worlds of Light that gild the sky." The imagination reaching to God invited the only known "rapture," in the hope for a better tomorrow: "So scanty is our present Allowance of Happiness that in many Situations, Life could scarcely be supported if Hope was no[t] allowed to relieve the present Hour by Pleasures borrowed from Futurity, of which the only proper use is to chase away Despair." Any thought of pursuing happiness had to be coolly weighed. The struggle for survival was moral as well as physical.[17]

The *Pennsylvania Gazette*, founded by Benjamin Franklin in 1728, printed pieces in the 1750s that examined two kinds of happiness: that joined to a consciousness of piety and that allied with the natural right to liberty. The "Road to Happiness" was deceptively short," one writer supposed, yet very few had ever traveled through it. They were those whose religion was firmest and whose understanding of liberty the most profound, for they could discern the difference between earthly "happiness" and earthly "pleasure."[18]

The distinction between "happiness" and "pleasure" occupied writers who questioned the consistency of the colonists' commitment to chaste living. They were mindful of the issues addressed by the eminent British political thinker Edmund Burke, who proposed in his philosophical treatise on the sublime and beautiful in 1757: "Pleasure of every kind quickly satisfies; and when it is over, we relapse into indifference."[19] To Americans deeply concerned with private and public morals, happiness (often interchangeable with "delight" and "felicity") was an uplifting sensation, generally sought; "pleasure" was a simpler and sometimes baser objective that might bring pain and moral decay along with it.

Pleasure was of the senses. According to an article adapted from a

British magazine and printed in the *Pennsylvania Gazette*, the Epicureans had understood a variety of pleasures, but the eighteenth century had to acknowledge that it could associate pleasure only with sensuality; though rational, even sublime—not simply sordid—pleasure was possible, modern readers could no longer relate to these ancient sensations. Happiness was a confounding prospect to the present generation, given the precariousness of life and the prejudice inherent in language: "Every individual Man disowns he is in Possession of [happiness], tho' every One hopes and expects he shortly shall be." The tangible ingredients of real happiness, after "Ease in a Man's person" and "Ease in his circumstance," were "Wisdom, Liberty, and Reputation." Liberty in particular was "so natural a Right, that one should scarcely call it a *Happiness*." Its absence, however, "casts a Gloom over the whole Mind" and "oppresses" the soul. It was such thinking that sustained Mayhew's thesis on vindicating rights.[20]

Another article used the same vocabulary to argue that happiness was only attainable through timely acts of goodness and the regular practice of humility and benevolence. Veering away from the standard themes of religiously inspired columns, the writer exhorted readers to direct the imagination to useful effects. One could not realize happiness without being rooted in the moment: "The Mind of Man is perpetually planning out Schemes of future Happiness, and contemplating distant Prospects of Pleasure . . . instead of endeavouring to enjoy the present with solid Satisfaction." But the "man of plain common Sense" who "jogs on contented in the Road of Life" could enjoy "the Pleasures that fall in his Way with Thankfulness, without flattering his Mind with the Hopes of future Enjoyments, which would certainly disappoint his Expectations." Happiness, at mid-century, remained an anxious pursuit.[21]

Americans' self-proclaimed love of liberty, on the other hand, was already legend, traced by mid-eighteenth-century writers and ministers to their seventeenth-century forebears, the first English settlers. Mayhew himself preached in 1754: "Our ancestors, tho' not perfect and infallible in all respects, were a religious, brave and virtuous set of men, whose love of liberty, civil and religious, brought them from their native land, into American deserts."[22] The historian Gordon Wood has observed that the language of English liberty used during the eighteenth century on both sides of the Atlantic was the mainstay of every cause that arose: "No people in the history of the world had ever made so much of it." The young Prince of Wales, who was shortly to be crowned King George III, stated unequivocally, "The pride, the glory of Britain, and the direct end of its constitution, is political liberty."[23] To British Americans, liberty was designated by a transcendent nature and was therefore sacred and inalienable. In political society, liberty was based on "natural rights" and granted within reasonable limits by legislatures acting with the consent of the people. Liberty preserved balance.[24]

As much as they had an understanding of their traditional liberties, colonial Americans sensed what the loss of these liberties could mean. The *New-York Evening Post* in 1747 had defined *slavery* as "a force put upon human nature, by which a man is obliged to act, or not to act, according to the arbitrary will and pleasure of another." The African slave trade was beginning to be condemned by white Americans, led by the introspective Quakers, who in the 1750s began to impose penalties on Friends who bought and sold slaves, and who by the 1770s had completed most manumissions among their sect. With the "discovery" of prejudice and the heightened consciousness this produced, white Americans tried to reason through matters of human differentiation, though for most people feelings of pity for the enslaved caste sufficed. Well-informed minds did not yet focus squarely on prospects for emancipation.[25]

It is important to understand why. Humane thinkers, shocked by the inhumanity of arbitrary power and comforted by the soft persuasion of sympathy, related Adam Smith's *Theory of Moral Sentiments* to the vicious system of enslaving dark-skinned people. But they did not have a modern liberal sense of the common potential for social equality and did not regard the African American as one who easily felt the absence of liberty. The colonial elite held their liberty dear because of the self-knowledge that refinement and a spirit of courtesy and consideration had nourished in them. At the same time, they believed that the African's historic memory did not contain a real appreciation for a quality of life comparable to that cultivated under long years of liberty. Thus, while reason and benevolence hardly seemed compatible with slavery, empathic feeling became mere condescending pity. More easily, Anglo-Americans who linked human happiness to the progress of science and philosophy reasoned that the *general good* would be served by eliminating this primitive form of economy. Newspapers, meanwhile, routinely advertised Negroes for sale.[26]

There was little momentum behind the movement to abolish the slave trade or slavery before the mid-1760s. In the North, where the black population, free and unfree, never amounted to more than 1 or 2 percent of the total population, some well-housed, well-clad slaves expressed their attachment to a benign paternalism; once freed, some followed their former masters or worked as hired hands. In the South, where blacks overall were at least one-third of the population, whites for the most part regarded them as a potential threat to civil order and as people of inferior intelligence. Here, rapid growth in the black population worried whites and caused them to stress racial differences and power relations more.[27]

It is impossible to dispute that American society prior to the Revolution was predicated on human inequality, and yet many of the larger planters commonly stressed their sensitivity and responsiveness to the slave communities. Masters recorded that they were intent on avoiding the breakup of slave families, and were unable to ignore feelings of sympathy and common humanity.[28] Such white "gentlemen," professing their enlightened sensibility, became a self-conscious, self-perpetuating ruling class intent on solidifying their control over the social hierarchy as well as the courts and local government. They exploited the labor of the white poor as well as their own black slaves and gave charity with self-satisfied condescension. In their vocabulary of power and morals, fundamental liberty was equated with their own responsible regime. With their prestige and good example, Southern "gentlemen" defined the public good, minimizing *public* concern with the demoralization and degradation their human chattel endured. In short, they accommodated themselves to slavery.

Domination over the slave population in fact strengthened these white Americans' professed love of liberty. Apologists for the institution of slavery compared what they knew or suspected of the slaves' lives in

Africa and concluded that this subordinated people were happier in bondage in America than enslaved or even free on their native continent. Some, infused with missionary purpose, went so far as to assert that slaves were happier enslaved in America than they would be *free* in America.[29] Typical of this self-congratulation is a statement made by Reverend Jonathan Boucher, who lived in both Virginia and Maryland between 1759 and 1775 and, as tutor to George Washington's stepson John Parke Custis, was a regular correspondent and often dinner companion of the future President. In his autobiography, written after his removal to England, Boucher took "comfort and satisfaction" that

> I have nothing very bad to charge myself with on the score of rigour or severity to my slaves. No compliment was ever paid me which went so near my heart as when a gentleman was one day coming to my house, and having overtaken a slave, asked him, as is common, to whom he belonged. The negro replied, "To Parson Boucher, thank God!" And few things affected me more than their condition on my leaving them. . . . Nothing is easier than to excite compassion by declamations against slavery. . . . The condition of the lower classes of mankind everywhere, when compared to that of those above them, may seem hard; yet on a fair investigation, it will probably be found that a people in general in a low sphere are not less happy than those in a higher sphere. I am equally well persuaded in my own mind that the negroes in general in Virginia and Maryland in my time were not upon the whole worse off nor less happy than the labouring poor in Great Britain.[30]

James Otis, a Boston activist, was one of the few who extended the definition of political liberty in 1764 by insisting that race enslavement was unconscionable. "The colonists are by the law of nature freeborn," he wrote, "as indeed all men are, white or black." He repeated the absurdity pointed out by the late Montesquieu, who had sought unifying principles in his masterpiece on government and society, *The Spirit of the Laws*: enslaving a man because he was black was no more valid than enslaving one because of "a flat nose, a long or short face." Slavery was "the most shocking violation of the law of nature" and tended "to diminish the idea of the inestimable value of liberty. . . . It is a clear truth that those who every day barter away other men's liberty will soon care little for their own." Otis reaffirmed the understanding of liberty that John Locke had put forward a century before—"The natural liberty of man is to be free from any superior power on earth": it meant that the liberty of independent states and the liberty of every individual were identical, and "This gift of God cannot be annihilated." Otis could write this way because the impulse to do good was implicit in British Americans' popular conception of themselves. But it scarcely mattered. African-American slavery as yet had only touched the surface of community consciousness—it had not yet exposed raw nerve. The land was scarred with a demeaning practice that human hearts could detest. But even the noblest intellects could not find, within their time-bound perspectives, a practical means to eradicate slavery.[31]

When liberty was not being expressed in terms of understood rights and the unwritten British constitution, it was associated with the virtue of public spirit and the quest for greater knowledge. Franklin's *Poor Richard's Almanack* for 1752 stressed that "PUBLICK SPIRIT" had filled the "Blank" of "neglected Nature," and "in wondrous Works" made "Myriads" happy. To this great innovator, public spirit was "Parent of Trade, Wealth, Liberty and Peace." *Poor Richard's* for 1757 rose to support liberty again, highlighting freedom of the press, in which enlightened reason stood to triumph over ignorance and "*lawless Pow'r.*" To "chain" the press was "Treason against sense," wrote Franklin. Liberty had a "thousand Tongues"; the American people's strength lay in their curiosity, and in their determination not to be silenced.[32]

It was a time for ardent feeling and polite sociability. Both were understood as forms of persuasion that characterized the moral order. In a 1764 pamphlet, *The Colonel Dismounted*, the Virginian Richard Bland expressed the colonists' language of rights when he taunted a detractor: "I do not suppose, Sir, that you look upon the present inhabitants of Virginia as a people conquered by the British arms. If indeed we are to be considered only as the savage ABORIGINES of this part of America, we cannot pretend to the rights of English subjects. . . . Under an English government all men are born free, are only subject to laws made with their own consent, and cannot be deprived of the benefit of these laws without a transgression of them."[33]

These words bring colonial self-respect to the surface. Bland meant to shame Britons, his rhetorical strategy insinuating that, in suffering indecent treatment by English society, no people appreciated their liberty more than the American colonists. If the English looked down on America as Anglo-Americans themselves looked down on "savage" Indians, unsuited for citizenship, there was an implied moral difference between the two; as in the later case of sympathy for Chief Logan, the colonists could at least imagine in their hearts a distant admiration for Indians, with whom they traded and to whom they ministered Christianity. In Bland's rhetorical and self-serving construction, Britons seemed so ungenerous in spirit that they could not even begin to appreciate the Indians' humanity and capacity for civilization.

Bland was giving voice to the ideology being nurtured ever more urgently in America: the colonists would never consent to being denied rights that other English subjects possessed. Self-regulated, they were capable of generous actions. A lesser status would degrade them and demean the value of their generosity; it would deny Mayhew's prediction that their religion would be "professed and practiced" in future times in "purity and perfection." The free American felt beyond the reach of Britain's executive power, beyond even the reach of Parliament. Legal protection was, as Bland put it, the "common consent of the people from time immemorial" and "the birthright of every Englishman." It followed him "wherever he goes." And that meant America.[34]

## LAND AND EMPIRE

When Reverend Mayhew wrote in 1750 that the British colonies of North America "could become a mighty empire," still dependent on the mother country but with "mighty cities rising on every hill" and "happy fields and villages" across an expansive pastoral landscape, he was no more visionary than Benjamin Franklin, whose "Observations Concerning the Increase of Mankind," written a year later, was the strongest statement to date regarding America's real prospects for growth. The piece was so well received that after its first publication in London in 1755, it was reprinted in British magazines and appended in 1760–61 to Boston and Philadelphia editions of Franklin's *Interest of Great Britain Considered*. In fact, the influential document was still being praised at the end of the century by Thomas Malthus amid his foreboding calculations concerning population growth, food supply, and social conditions.[35]

Franklin's "Observations" clarified differences in the use and development of land in America and England and addressed the consequences of these differences for their respective populations. America's relatively sparse settlement promised cheap land, early and fruitful marriages for generations to come, and a doubling of the population every twenty years, Franklin thought. Because the colonies would continue to need British manufactures, London had nothing to fear by allowing America to develop its own industries. Growth and expansion could only reflect well on the mother country.[36]

It was not merely Franklin's observations on growth and economic health that generated optimism among British Americans in the decade that would bring the contest with France for continental dominance to a head. Americans of different colonies marveled at the productive potential of the expanse they occupied. Most people outside the major towns grew their own food, wove their own cloth, made their own clothes and furniture. Rivers and roads linked outlying areas with larger population centers, and the variety of production—the apple orchards of New York's Hudson Valley or Pennsylvania's Lancaster County, the corn and wheat fields of Virginia's recently settled Shenandoah Valley—made the strenuous work of clearing wilderness worthwhile.[37] Even the newest colony, Georgia, established in the 1730s and 1740s, was advertised as an "Asylum to receive the Distressed" and a warm and temperate Eden, which offered unprecedented "Liberty of Conscience," "Comfort of Life," and easy prosperity. A 1748 travelogue predicted that it would soon be populated by "useful People," and a 1754 update noted that colonists were "crowding in every day, fill'd with expectations." In country that possessed "all the Advantages of Air & Soil," Georgians were "flourishing," their spirit of industry bringing "happiness & tranquillity."[38]

The promise of peace and abundance in agricultural America was conspicuous in the columns of *The New American Magazine*. An early issue ventured how it might be if a British subject of three hundred years past had been told to anticipate mid-eighteenth-century conditions. When informed "that the improvements were in great measure owing to the discovery and settlement of *America*, suppose him transplanted thither, how would his surprise increase, at seeing a country never heard of in his time, now peopled with millions of *Europeans*. . . . [H]e would cry out, *A new world has arisen, and will exceed the old!*"[39]

The editor of this literary magazine, who wrote under the pen name "Sylvanus Americanus" (American Woodsman), contributed a regular feature entitled "The Country Farmer." Bucolic verses rhapsodized love and beauty, and portrayed America as an open land offering all the advantages of an Eden, and no longer the dangers of a savage wilderness. As the land was softened into a pastoral setting comparable to the countryside of England and Scotland, the cultivators of that land became a "judicious" yeomanry, happily surrounded by family, friends, and dependents. The generous farmer, "boast of our nation," was, moreover, "remote from the troublesome scenes of fraud, malice, vanity, and ambition, cultivating domestick virtue, cherishing the principle of universal benevolence, and dispensing friendship to all." Even his looks were of "chearful innocence" and his words spoke "an elegant simplicity." With tongue in cheek, "Sylvanus Americanus" reported that this amiable, dignified common farmer used "no corruption but manure; he hatches not intrigues, but poultry; he brews not mischief but beer; he fears no blasts of envy, though he dreads the blasts of heaven."[40]

In fact, though, the middling sorts in America did not always view their distant neighbors with charity and tolerance. Intercolonial jealousies and rivalries were quite pronounced. When Dr. Alexander Hamilton of Maryland (no relation to the later statesman) journeyed north in 1744, he listened as Pennsylvanians boasted not only of their superior moral character compared to the "immorality, drunkenness, rudeness and immoderate swearing" of the Marylanders but of the "goodness of the soil as far more productive" than that of their southern neighbors. There was as much earthiness and bile as "chearful innocence" and "elegant simplicity."[41]

Still, the pastoral idyll grew. Commerce might be the lifeblood of early Boston, a writer for the *Boston Gazette* proclaimed in 1760, but "Agriculture is the most solid Foundation on which to build the Wealth, and give me Leave to add, the political Virtue of a Common Wealth: it is by this, by which Nations are cloathed and fed." Leading a life superior to "the constant Toil of the Merchant, who fatigues himself from *early to late* in loading his Vessel, pursuing a Bargain, or even handling his Pen in the Compting House," the farmer "rises with the Sun to go his Circuit; and if he takes Care not to eat the Bread of Idleness, he is as sure, as the common Indulgence of Heaven can make him, to eat the Bread of Health and Peace: and if he will but shut out imaginary Wants that would intrude into his Mind, he is as sure to close his every Day, and to see his final Sun set with as much Splendor as any other of Mankind."[42] Whether it was conveyed through sprightly wordplay (the American farmer "hatches not intrigues, but poultry") or metaphors of natural sustenance (he eats "the bread of Health"), agrarianism was early seen as the ground on which this liberty-loving people stood.

Where human beings proved limited, the beauty of nature supplied harmony and enchantment. The soul of the poet was drawn to "the calm, uncrouded rural scene," in another New Englander's verse. He or she willfully flew from fickle friends to "a gliding Stream" where "wand'ring o'er the flow'ry vale, / Imbibing Joy from every Gale," one could arrive at a "blissful State."[43] The land from New Jersey's coast inland was awful and sublime and still supportive of harmonious intercourse: "frightful crags, *Atlantic* heights, commanding prospects, spacious lawns," yet so inviting that Indian innocents ("thoughtless of wrong, they chase and roam the wood") could return to live in harmony with British Americans, once "false Frenchmen" were ousted from the continent.[44] And the western frontier along the Ohio River was, to a fighting militiaman, "the finest and most fertile Country of *America*, lying in the happiest Climate in the Universe."[45]

Though the journeying Dr. Hamilton described Philadelphia as an unpaved, dirty, monotonous town "obstructed with rubbish and lumber,"[46] the largest city in America boasted sylvan features as well. "Just as the morn had spread the skies / With rosy blushing light," a poet could stroll along the banks of the Schuylkill River, delighted with the "swelling surface, clear as glass," "lovely birds," and "golden sun-perch" at play. The charming river provided sustenance as well as sport. "Sure never streams beneath the sun / Such stores of pleasures knew." A contributor to *The New American Magazine* urged "Sylvanus Ameri-canus" to pay less attention to "former [European] writers" and more to "the taste and manners of the inhabitants of this new world," where "now, at last, deservedly," Great Britain was devoting some "attention and curiosity." In the writer's opinion, the mother country could de-cisively be shown that "the intellectual soil here, like the natural is extremely rich and fertile, capable of the finest productions, under due culture and encouragement."[47]

The French and Indian War that erupted on the frontier in 1754 was the final contest in a series of struggles, beginning in the late sev-enteenth century, between British and French interests in North Amer-ica, and it gave Americans the opportunity to establish their patriotic credentials. In his early twenties, Lieutenant Colonel George Wash-ington of Virginia fought bravely but unsuccessfully at Fort Duquesne in western Pennsylvania's backcountry. Massachusetts royal governor William Shirley, a successful strategist in the previous North American war against the French in 1745, led the colonial assembly in raising a force of two thousand to march north on Canada and another twelve hundred soldiers to combine with New York and New England troops in upstate New York.[48]

In 1755, as the war continued, Reverend Samuel Davies preached a sermon to volunteers in Virginia's Hanover County that was in many ways characteristic of the times. He deliberately portrayed the com-bined French and Indian enemies in such a way as to equate killing them with the cause of a righteous God. "The horrid Arts of *Indian* and *Popish* Torture" were carried out "leisurely," he suggested, evi-dence itself of their having abandoned human nature: "See yonder!" the preacher exclaimed. "The hairy Scalps, clotted with Gore! The mangled Limbs! Ript-up Women! The Heart and Bowels, still palpi-tating with Life, smoking on the Ground!" Invoking images of offended sensibility, Davies settled upon a secure British-American view of vir-tuous masculinity: courageous in meeting the challenge of the enemy's inhumanity, independent and uncoerced—exhibiting always the resolve of a free people. Theirs was not "a savage ferocious Violence: Not a fool-hardy Insensibility of Danger, or headstrong Rashness to rush into it: Not the Fury of enflamed Passions, broke loose from the Government of Reason: But calm, deliberate, rational Courage; a steady, judicious, thoughtful Fortitude, the Courage of a Man, and not a Tyger." Masters of their passions, these idealized American combatants were "brave Men, without the Compulsion of Authority, without the prospect of Gain, voluntarily associated in a Company, to march over horrendous Rocks and Mountains, into a hideous Wilderness, to succor their helpless Fellow-Subjects, and guard their Country." There was surely no better people for so challenging an environment.[49]

Understanding their land and liberty to be equally precious, colonial Americans insisted that their distance from mother England did not diminish their patriotism, nor could it undo the firmness of their collective character. In this vein, Jonathan Mayhew delivered a sermon, superior in eloquence if less colorful than Davies's, arguing that English liberty merited the ultimate sacrifice. Liberty was "a Cause wherein the Glory of God, the Honour of your King, and the Good of your Country, are so deeply concerned; I might perhaps add, a Cause, whereon the Liberties of *Europe* depend. For so great a Consequence is the Empire of *North America* . . . that it must turn the Scale of Power greatly in favour of the only Monarch, from whom those Liberties are in danger." To Mayhew as to Davies, every man's "Heart . . . Purse, and his Arms" were worth investing so that "our Liberties, our Religion, our Lives, our Bodies, our Souls" might be kept strong. Judging by the words of community leaders, it appeared that Americans' identification with the empire was deepening in war.[50] Responding to interest in his soon to be published "Observations Concerning the Increase of Mankind," Franklin opined in 1758 that it no longer seemed pressing to convince London to demonstrate its commitment to America's future, because "Britain seems so fully persuaded at this time of the Importance of her Colonies."[51]

Uneasiness did remain, however, over the extent of the mother country's practical influence in the struggle taking place in its dependent dominions. The war for empire was officially declared in Europe in 1756, but at this critical point the war was not going well for the British in America. The Pennsylvania naturalist John Bartram urged Franklin, when he arrived in London in 1757, to convey colonial anxieties: "Calamities of our provinces, Vast sums spent and nothing done to the advantage of king or countrey. How should I leap for Joy to see or hear that British Oficers would prove by their actions the zeal and duty to thair Prince and nation thay so much pretend in words."[52]

In Massachusetts, after Governor Shirley's recall, bad feelings festered between the colonial assembly and an imperious British commander, Lord Loudoun, who wanted to extract funds from the colonial government without promise of reimbursement. (Shirley had presupposed reimbursement from the royal treasury.) Facing a possible catastrophe, colonial Americans delivered their petitions in fretful words; they insisted on their patriotism while betraying confusion over Britain's withholding of economic support and refusal to acknowledge American initiatives in the war effort.[53]

Most historians concur with the British officers who directed the fighting that, when not pressed to defend their own homes, the independent-spirited colonists lacked the martial vigor of professional European troops. Colonel Washington did not agree, protesting that his Virginia regiment deserved recognition for its patriotic sacrifice. Writing to Royal Governor Robert Dinwiddie, he argued for the principle of equal treatment for British and British-American forces in obtaining royal commissions:

> We cant conceive, that being Americans shoud deprive us of the benefits of British Subjects; nor lessen our claim to preferment: and we are very certain, that no Body of regular Troops ever before Servd 3 Bloody Campaigns without attracting Royal Notice.
>
> As to those idle Arguments which are often times us'd— namely, You are Defending your own properties; I look upon to be whimsical & absurd; We are Defending the Kings Dominion . . . and there can be no Sufficient reason given why we, who spend our blood and Treasure in Defence of the Country are not entitled to equal prefermt.

Washington insisted that his men "labour under every disadvantage, and enjoy not one benefit which regulars do." Any advantage gained by the enemy along the frontier could not, he claimed, be attributed to the "Inactivity" of Virginians.[54]

In 1757 a champion of colonial America was found in Britain's controversial leading minister, William Pitt, who resolved to finance the war by reimbursing the colonists for their contributions and whose "great Soul," his American adherents claimed, "animates all our Measures." From Pittsburgh (as Fort Duquesne was renamed after its capture from the French in 1758), an optimistic appraisal received attention in the *Boston Gazette*, repeating the same aggressive tone of other printed exhortations: "The look'd for Day is arrived," one which would secure the western frontier and break the French "Chain of Communication betwixt *Canada* and *Louisiana*, a Chain that threatened this Continent with Slavery." As the tide of war turned in the colonists' favor, the extent of British America's achievement seemed mind-boggling, inasmuch as the land itself posed tremendous challenges— just to "maintain Armies in a Wilderness, Hundreds of Miles from the Settlements; to march them by untrodden Paths, over almost impassable Mountains, thro' thick Woods and dangerous Defiles [narrow passages or gorges]." Reconciling with the pliable Indians, who seemed merely to wish to live securely among whichever Europeans approached them in large numbers, the colonists could rest easier, "so that our Back Settlements, instead of being frightful Fields of Blood, will once more smile with Peace and Plenty."[55]

This ultimate success was attributed not only to the fighting farmers but to the yielding land itself. The *Boston Gazette* was proud to report on "the Happy Effects of Husbandry within these few Years past." New Englanders had "fed themselves and large Armies besides." The honorable Cincinnatus, Roman model of the soldier-farmer, had dropped his plow and marched off to conquer the enemies of his country, before returning to his laudable employment as a tiller of the earth. His American counterpart had held the economy together, while standing poised to reclaim the country from the French threat.[56]

Providential history, as American Protestants saw it, was a continuous battle between liberty and tyranny, and for the moment Roman

Catholicism was called the source of all that was cruel and arbitrary. The clergyman Mather Byles declared from the pulpit with millennial expectancy: "What a Scene of Wonder opens to our View!" Deliverance from the French prefigured future glory for America.[57] Soon Franklin was able to resubmit: "The Foundations of the future Grandeur and Stability of the British Empire lie in America," for England and America together were destined to "awe the World."[58] Liberty and the land went hand in hand in prose, expressed equally, at key moments, through ecstatic religion and secular optimism.

The war had demanded an unprecedented level of commitment from the American colonists. If at times it was given only grudgingly, the result was, nevertheless, the final removal of the French imperial presence from North America. This dramatic change on the continent made reliance on British military power less critical to the colonists' peace of mind. After the 1763 Treaty of Paris, their relationship to the land would be tied up with their perception of a debt—or lack of a debt—to the mother country, which, like them, had contributed men and money to the decisive war. But for the moment a balance seemed to have been struck.

No one seemed to shy away from acknowledging that Americans aggressively faced west. The language hailing God's empire in the New World was part of a crisis rhetoric entirely consistent with the civil and ecclesiastical liberty that Mayhew had described in his 1750 pamphlet. The promise of the continent was mediated only by Americans' willingness to acknowledge that it was as yet too vast and varied to know well.

A Marylander named Christopher Gist, for example, kept journals of his 1750–52 explorations on behalf of the Ohio Company, the first British-American topographical descriptions of the land beyond the Allegheny Mountains. Governor Dinwiddie of Virginia in the early fall of 1750 gave him a necessarily loose set of instructions:

> You are to go out as soon as possible to the Westward of the great Mountains, and carry with you such a Number of Men, as you think necessary, in Order to search out and discover the Lands upon the River Ohio, & other adjoining branches of the

Mississippi down as low as the great Falls thereof [Louisville, Kentucky]: You are particularly to observe the Ways & Passes thro all the Mountains you cross, & take an exact Account of the Soil, Quality, & Product of the Land, and the Wideness & Deepness of the Rivers. . . . When you find a large Quantity of good level Land, such as you think will suit the Company, You are to measure the Breadth of it. . . . You are to fix the Beginning & Bounds in such a Manner that they may be easily found again by your Description."[59]

Enterprising Americans looked for land that would yield crops, support permanent settlement, and be linked by land and water to the eastern markets. Nothing was going to stop them, not even the Proclamation Line established by London in 1763, which directed the colonists to refrain from settling west of the Appalachian Mountains (and which was put into effect solely to avoid a costly war with resistant Indian tribes). "Not even a second Chinese wall," ran an article in the *Virginia Gazette*, "unless guarded by a million soldiers, could prevent the settlement of Lands on the Ohio and its dependencies." In 1763, Virginia's governor notified the Board of Trade in London that colonial land speculators were likely to resent any constriction of their freedom to grab Indian lands and that these people would commence hostilities against "mischievous" tribes. A number of future leaders of the United States, such as George Washington and Thomas Jefferson, belonged to syndicates that aimed to circumvent official policies in order to acquire western territory. At least one scholar has linked land hunger (and London's conservative policy of conciliating the Indians) with the drift toward revolution.[60]

Benjamin Franklin had described Ohio in 1755 as a region "now well known both to the English and French, to be one of the finest in North America, for the extreme richness and fertility of the land; the healthy temperature of the air, and mildness of the climate; the plenty of hunting and fishing, and fowling; the facility of trade with the Indians; and the vast convenience of inland navigation." At the time Ohio appeared critical if British America was to prevail over its French rival. Fearing that "our debtors, and loose English people, our German servants, and slaves" might desert to the enemy, he proposed a more rapid rate of settlement and heightening of prestige among the western Indians. The year before, Franklin had observed that, with or without British encouragement, "many thousands of families are ready to swarm, wanting more land." The "old colonies," as he called them, were poised to take the lead in occupying the west.[61]

Ohio at mid-century featured rugged hills, dense forest, and open prairies, with white-tailed deer, black bears, wolves, turkeys, quail, and an abundance of fish in its rivers flowing both north and south. In a striking preview of things to come, a Delaware chief named Shingas observed to an English missionary, upon the expulsion of the French from the area: "We have great reason to believe you intend to drive us away, and settle the country; or else, why do you come to fight in the land that God has given us?" The British, of course, told Ohio's Indians that they only wanted to drive away the French, not to occupy the land themselves, and to foster a healthy trade. But by the early 1760s the Shawnee of Ohio were recognizing the threat in those who had become already "too great a People." In the ensuing decade, Virginia's colonial governor had to acknowledge that his power was "insufficient to restrain the Americans" from their relentless quest to identify and settle desirable areas within Indian territory.[62]

The value of the land that the various colonies claimed was open and exploitable could only be estimated. As Governor Dinwiddie had with Christopher Gist in 1750, George Washington wrote to a man he engaged to explore and survey land in west Florida for him, avoiding particular directions and recognizing that only a "general & perhaps just Idea of the nature of the Country" could be obtained. He hoped to learn "whether the Lands on the Mississippi—the Mobile—or elsewhere promises in Futuro, to become Most valuable." A letter written the following year, thanking the surveyor for his "obliging account," addressed the confusing reports Washington had received: "The contradictory Accounts given of the Lands upon the Mississippi, are really astonishing—some speak of the Country as a terrestrial Paradise, whilst others represent it as scarce fit for any thing but Slaves & Brutes." The unsettled parts of America possessed an allure tempered by the prospect of peril and unprofitability.[63]

For these reasons, colonial Americans of the mid-eighteenth century projected greatness in terms like those used by Mayhew and Franklin, alluded generally to nature's bounty in reflecting on the potential of their country, or simply inflated the frontier spirit as they organized to acquire more land. Land already under cultivation and close administration was their highest concern, where their presumptions about life and liberty were most at risk. For their own peace of mind, they sought a symbiosis of two forms of society, the already settled and the newly developing. The common denominator, ideally, was twofold: laws of property and rules of sensible conduct.

As Europeans transplanted to the Indians' world, the colonists were obliged to negotiate, intellectually and emotionally, between cultural ideals—between the autonomy of the Indian, unmediated by the legal complexities of government, and their own deliberative, bounded liberty. Presuming that the natives, overall, were "innocent" and they themselves advanced, they self-consciously plotted their future. If, as Richard Slotkin has written, the aboriginal American trusted his natural passions, "innocent of the consequences of his individualism and self-indulgence," then the Anglo-American colonist had to suppress nature by exercising reason. The "civilizers" believed that they would tame the physical wilderness of North America and improve humanity generally; armed with sentiment as well as reason, both of which the pliable Indian could be taught, they could even turn "tawny" Indians "white." Because in their minds conscience restrained uncivilized behavior, this kind of "sincere" conquest was a progressive act, an act of regeneration. Amid land hunger, the myth of American philanthropy defined an uneasy quest for continental dominance.[64]

Future-directed colonists, idealized as judicious, industrious, and peace-loving cultivators by "Sylvanus Americanus," professed that they were a people of decent passions, bringing their pastoral abundance under control. In their texts, they seemed to thrive on the belief that they had a surplus of energy in addition to the skills to manage a continental expanse, and that from the time their ancestors had first replicated the well-ordered English economy in New England, they had proven able to tame the wild without abandoning sentiment. In writing a new history, they were furthering the enterprise of improving humanity. This is why they so resented their inferior status as Englishmen, and why Richard Bland reacted to the unflattering comparison of Americans to "savage ABORIGINES." The French and Indian War had raised the issue of British indifference to American requirements. Colonists' marked refusal to submit passively to the natural environment— their rejection of the Proclamation Line of 1763—strengthened the steady belief that, as a people, they possessed not only English liberty but the emotional resilience that such liberty spawned.

# CHAPTER THREE

# A PEOPLE OF ENTHUSIASM AND SELF-CONTROL: 1765–75

*"THE REAL AMERICAN REVOLUTION"* consisted of *"radical change in the principles, opinions, sentiments, and affections of the people,"* wrote John Adams, an "alteration in the religious, moral, political, and social character of the people of the thirteen colonies, all distinct, unconnected, and independent of each other." It amazed Adams how "Thirteen clocks were made to strike together—a perfection of mechanism, which no artist had ever before effected." The Revolution, he explained confidently in the same letter in which he extolled the virtues of Jonathan Mayhew, would not have been possible without "a people possessed of intelligence, fortitude, and integrity." And he dated this transformation to the 1760s.[1]

Americans of that decade exhibited a curious blend of personality traits. Writers expressed equal amusement and concern with the variety of cultures in their midst. For one thing, Americans from different colonies typecast themselves in images of who they were that for the most part pleased them, and they found fault with the habits of others. People were both cheerful and volatile, possessing an intensity just below the surface, no better exemplified than in the witty commentary of the avuncular Benjamin Franklin, the sometimes humble, sometimes scheming, but always public-spirited moralist.

Industry, austerity, and pacifism were thought to characterize the basically egalitarian and morally demanding Philadelphia Quakers, with the women in their white caps and the men in equally plain attire. During his cross-colonial journey, Dr. Alexander Hamilton termed them "an obstinate, stiff-necked generation." Pious Congregationalist women of New England held themselves up as active reformers and guardians of public morals, leading their husbands and children to Christ and boosting the reputations of their local ministers. Another brand of New Englander, more inquisitive, was well symbolized by the young lawyer John Adams, who studied hard, felt deeply, quarreled with himself over his ambition, and always insisted on displaying his profound sense of honor and candor. The proud, hospitable Southern patriarch expressed strong kinship ties, liked to dance, play music, and engage in other social activities to prove his worth as a skilled, respectable person and affecting conversationalist, but Northerners considered Southerners boorish, promiscuous gamblers and smug slaveholders. Then there were the widely dispersed, politically less instrumental back-country subsistence farmers, who, in contrast to the nearer yeomen of "Sylvanus Americanus," were often regarded as "indolent" and quasi-savage by big property owners nearer the coast, who thought of themselves as the moral judges of their social inferiors.[2]

The historian Jack P. Greene has argued that these differences among the colonies are exaggerated. All of them, after all, experienced population growth, an acceleration of their economies, and integration into a larger Atlantic economy, and the standard of living throughout North America consistently rose. Equally true, geographical mobility influenced the people of both the North and the South to seek greater individual autonomy. Though political participation was limited to independent white adult males, America, says Greene, was "more inclusive and responsive to public opinion" than any other political system in the eighteenth-century world. Self-government was proving successful; local politics was in the hands of a "coherent, effective, acknowledged, and authoritative" elite. On the other hand, at the Albany Congress of 1754 Benjamin Franklin was disappointed when he failed to secure a defensive union of the colonies to coordinate relations with the powerful Iroquois and meet the French threat. That same year Governor James Glen of South Carolina advised his Virginia counterpart, Robert Dinwiddie, that the French understood that the colonies were a mere "Rope of Sand, loose and inconnected." Thomas Hutchinson of Massachusetts fatefully conveyed the same sentiment in 1765: "I know no two colonies which think alike."[3]

It was the 1765 Stamp Act that established a broadly based political identity for this disparate community, built around the new principles, opinions, sentiments, and affections to which Adams was attesting. Accustomed to government by their own provincial assemblies, Americans did not welcome the broadened exercise of power from beyond the seas. But from London's perspective, the cost of stationing a force of British regulars in North America during the conflict with France demanded just measures to raise revenues and reduce Britain's debt. When Chancellor of the Exchequer George Grenville urged Parliament to pass the Sugar Act in 1764, which placed a high duty on sugar imported into the colonies, the centralizing measure strengthened the customs service, which had recently been empowered in Boston to search vessels and punish smugglers of non-English goods—a customary practice that was technically illegal. It also served to remind Americans of the high taxes they had paid voluntarily over the course of the French and Indian War; but the measure did not arouse wide opposition, because it targeted only merchants.[4] In February 1765, however, stating that Americans owed "their proper share" if they were to be "entitled to the privilege of Englishmen," Grenville pushed through the Stamp Act, by which Parliament required all paper documents (including newspapers, pamphlets, private contracts, licenses, and even playing cards) to be embossed with a special stamp, paid for in hard currency. This new tax affected lawyers, printers, and many others besides merchants, and this time reaction across the colonies, from Massachusetts to the Carolinas, was emotional. Tax resisters consistently avowed Mayhew's antiauthoritarian logic, a "Spark of Patriotism" kindled and burned, the continent was "inflamed," and a people with common grievances, bound by "affection," aired their deep feelings. A new language of protest heralding liberty and virtue reverberated in published writings.[5]

That year, the Sons of Liberty (and its sympathetic counterpart, the Daughters of Liberty) banded together to declare their common suffering and prevent enforcement of this aggressive act of Parliament. In

New York and Boston, Albany and Providence, New London, Connecticut, and Annapolis, Maryland, merchants, tavernkeepers, printers, jewelers, and other "mechanics" (people who earned their living with their hands) led the resistance. Among them were Boston's Samuel Adams, a cunning, outspoken popular organizer who, despite his Harvard education, could not settle on a profession other than politics; Philadelphia's Charles Thomson, who had arrived from northern Ireland an orphan, had been placed in the home of a blacksmith, and would eventually become the indefatigable secretary of the First and Second Continental Congresses; and New London's Israel Putnam, a colorful, stalwart, massively built farmer-warrior who had been captured in combat during the French and Indian War and would fight again as an American major general at Bunker Hill in 1775. The Stamp Act resisters kept their identities secret and harassed the stamp distributors until resignations were tendered.[6]

It was a period of contentious reasoning and colliding ambitions. Fearing that lives of "elegant simplicity" could easily be transformed into dishonorable subjugation, colonial leaders North and South refused to be intimidated. Over the coming decade, America's proud Revolutionary propagandists would gain martyrs to the cause of liberty and a new and powerful vocabulary to distinguish the feeling and unfeeling.

## A CONTINENT INFLAMED

In autumn 1765, a writer for the *Boston Gazette* pronounced the community's lively rejection of the Stamp Act with a full-page alert: "Awake! Awake, my Countrymen, and, by a regular & legal Opposition, defeat the Designs of those who enslave us and our Posterity. Nothing is wanting but your own Resolution."[7] Enslavement meant, as it had earlier, capitulation before an arbitrary command; as Mayhew had put it, that which "damps spirits" and "extinguishes every spark of noble ardor and generosity." Tyranny destroyed the passion which actuated humane government; surrender of the will could only produce moral laxity among citizens. "Resolution" had new meaning, on the other hand; after the war against the French, it required clarification of the colonists' common purposes. Only unity would prevent their submission to the power of a centralizing government insensitive to their local interests. Public-spirited Bostonians reminded their compatriots that they were a tenacious people and that they needed their passion. Among the anxious preoccupations of these social critics was a fear that the transformation from liberty to slavery might occur surreptitiously, simply for a lack of public vigilance. Even an active, liberty-loving people could devolve into willing slaves of corrupt authority if they were not watchful; their progeny, born into such a state, would no longer know the impulse to live free. Contemporary examples were cited: the French, Danish, Swedish, Turkish, Russian, and Polish peoples had all surrendered their political initiatives.[8]

Another Boston newspaper mourned that when the Stamp Act was enforced Parliament would become "absolute Monarch" of the colonies. "Freedom thus gone," the column went on, "Slavery with all its horrid Train, immediately takes its Place.... The same Cause that brought Thousands from Europe, to settle these Haunts of Savages, will drive them back, or force them to seek Shelter deep in the Woods. Learning, which is about to fix her Abode here, will quickly retire, and rising Arts be depressed."[9] Nothing less than the disintegration of American civilization lay on the horizon. According to this nightmarish vision of happiness and liberty overturned, the colonies' otherwise predictable progress would be arrested. The imposition of slavery connoted something larger to the colonists than racial oppression; the loss of self-determination was a moral catastrophe that could easily plunge the entire continent into barbarism.[10]

A subsequent article proclaiming the political rights of the colonies reiterated the frightful formula: when an unfeeling minister like Grenville succeeded in his purpose, the result was an inevitable sinking from political happiness into a state of submission from which neither the first generation deprived of its liberties nor the sleepy generations to follow, indifferent to the lively sensations of freedom, would recover: "Even those who *counsel ignoble ease and peaceful sloth,* flatter themselves, that when we grow stronger, we shall shake off the yoke. Will the tyrannous minister suffer us to grow stronger? Does slavery give strength? . . . When an *American* and a slave are one, who is it that will voluntarily seek bondage in *America?*"[11] America's future greatness, its attractiveness to like-minded European emigrants, required that the existing population raise its voice and act to secure liberty at the first sign of oppression.

Joseph Warren, a twenty-four-year-old Harvard-educated physician, attended the same Congregational church as Samuel Adams and had begun a friendship with John Adams upon inoculating the lawyer against smallpox. Writing of the Stamp Act to a college classmate who had gone back to England, he expressed alarm and amazement that London could act so unreasonably, and on the basis of such ignorance of human nature and American manners. His letter spoke of enlightened self-knowledge as he adhered to the righteous idiom of the day. "Freedom and equality is the state of nature," he wrote, "but slavery is the most unnatural and violent state that can be conceived of." It was "absurd to attempt to impose so cruel a yoke," as Parliament had seen fit to do. Resentment ran deep: "The whole continent is inflamed to the highest degree." It was perfectly obvious to him that the common expression of outrage and indignation was enabling good minds across America to unite: "The colonies, until now, were ever at variance, and foolishly jealous of each other," Warren meaningfully observed. "They are now . . . united for their common defence against what they believe to be oppression; nor will they soon forget the weight which this close union gives them."[12]

The Stamp Act crisis, then, gave unprecedented attention to Americans' regard for their courageous collective character. The *Boston Gazette* proclaimed: "The Descendants of Britain, born in a land of light, and reared in the protective Bosom of Liberty—Shall you commence Cowards, at a Time when Reason calls so loud for your Magnanimity?" Magnanimity, a broad-minded quality uniting compassion and generosity, was coupled here with bravery and honor, measures of power. This key word *magnanimity* was invoked many times during the trying decade to come, a signifier for disinterested patriotism. Americans who possessed the will to take moral action knew that the penalty for a wait-

and-see attitude was slavery. As the same newspaper remarked, "I know you disdain the Thought of so opprobrious a Servility."[13]

Readers were assured that their world was based on justice, that truth was omnipotent and reason always victorious, that love of liberty was "natural to our Species and interwoven with the human Frame." The rhetorical power of this intensifying image joining human physiology to a politically lively emotion made citizens conscious of the inseparability of private inclinations and their political will. Because they were "inflamed" with a love of liberty, the natural combination of passion and reason accorded power to their sentimental consensus, and it also promoted happiness. If at moments of crisis the cries of "Liberty!" (hyperbolically claimed to be as inextinguishable as the sun itself) did not arouse the bright passion of this people, then reason would. Reason argued that London had pursued its own profit in the late war with France, had brought substantial benefit to itself and yielded "comparatively little Advantage to us." Given the real costs of military production, this logic went, the stamp revenues were entirely unwarranted.[14]

In towns across the colonies, mock funerals gave public display to the drama of popular disaffection and helped to define the patriotic personality.[15] In Wilmington, North Carolina, citizens produced an effigy of Liberty, which they placed in a coffin and carried in solemn procession to the churchyard, as a drum slowly beat in mourning and the town bell, muffled, rang out dolefully. Before burying the effigy, the mourners happily found that it was exhibiting signs of life; they placed it in a large chair, and rejoiced through the evening that "LIBERTY had still an Existence in the COLONIES." After a later demonstration, the Wilmington stamp officer, under pressure, agreed not to execute "any Office disagreeable to the People." That evening, after he wrote his resignation, "a large Bonfire was made, and no Person appeared in the Streets without having LIBERTY, in large Capital Letters, in his Hat."[16]

A correspondent from Newport, Rhode Island, reported on another, even more melodramatic mock funeral. The dawn was overcast that day, which recalled lines from Joseph Addison's *Cato*, in which clouds metaphorically represented the loss of liberty. "The glorious sun was darkened," wailed the Rhode Islander, "and Nature seem'd herself to anguish!—The Sons of Freedom sunk beneath this horrid Gloom, and every one was struck with the Melancholy, at the approaching Funeral of their departed, beloved Friend, LIBERTY!" This funereal wail persisted over two long, increasingly maudlin paragraphs, until:

> The Mourners were about taking their last FAREWELL. . . . Oh my ruined Country!—The mournful Aspiration was scarcely uttered, when a Son of LIBERTY, emerging from the horrid Gloom of Despair, addressed himself thus:—"O LIBERTY! the Darling of my Soul!—Glorious LIBERTY! Admir'd, ador'd by all true Britons! LIBERTY dead, it cannot be!" A Groan was then heard, as if coming from the Coffin; and upon closer Attention, it proved to be a Trance, for Old FREEDOM was not dead.—The Goddess Britannia had ordered a Guardian Angel to snatch Old FREEDOM from the Jaws of frozen Death, to the Orb of the reviving Sun, to remain invulnerable from the Attacks of lawless Tyranny and Oppression.

At that moment, the writer noted with a final flourish, "the Clouds dispersed, and once more clear'd the Face of Heaven." Expressions of faith in young King George III restored vigor and purpose to the erstwhile mourners, and a glamorized Chorus, as in Greek drama, pronounced the moral:

> Britannia's Sons despise Slavery,
> And dare to be nobly free.[17]

The theme of resuscitation in these funerals reminded citizens that resolution and persistence were lifesaving. If the Stamp Act was an attempt to murder Liberty by strangulation, then the people had to do more than merely gasp for breath. To fight meant both to demonstrate in public and to vocalize discontent in the press. On another level, the mock funerals transcended class boundaries, for they introduced a traditional category of natural emotion into the colonists' new political discourse. Rather than simply reveling in the sophisticated culture of sympathy which exquisite literature transmitted to the more refined elite, these public dramas appealed to an emotion all people understood—unabated grief.

Because they styled themselves a decent people long accustomed to a comfortable liberty, Americans made a point of their tendency to trust, until given cause for suspicion. The *Pennsylvania Gazette* related the train of events that led from the initial shock of the Stamp Act to the people's self-preserving reawakening. "A considerable Time we lay in silent Consternation," it posed, "and knew not what to do!—We seemed to be in a frightful Dream." Then came recognition, knowledge that in the Stamp Act could be discovered "the most deeply laid inveterate Design for the intire Extirpation of Liberty in America. . . . Slavery, with all its terrible Train, fenced us in on every Side.—We knew not what to say or write—even our Presses ceased to utter the Language of Liberty." Here was the surreptitious manner in which tyranny deprived the mind of light. "At last, by Degrees, we began to recollect our scattered Thoughts" until "the latent Spark of Patriotism . . . flew like Lightning from Breast to Breast—it flowed from every Tongue, and Pen, and Press, till it had diffused itself through every Part of the British Dominions in America; it united us all."[18] After the lightning of concerted action electrified the continent, the light of liberty again diffused peacefully, like the light of the sun. Shocked or numbed by unexpectedly waking to a new day without that sun, the resolute American "we" ultimately proved themselves able to retrieve or resuscitate liberty. British Americans would not submit.[19]

Grenville's side was expressed nearly as often in the patriot press, though as an unmerited position meant to prompt reaction and strengthen the colonists' resolve. The king's minister was quoted, for example, stating: "Great Britain protects America, so that America is bound to yield obedience. . . . Taxation is part of the sovereign power which the British legislature is granted."[20] Boston Sons of Liberty energetically lampooned Grenville, tying an effigy of him to the stake and holding him up to poetic ridicule:

> His guilty Countenance betrays
> His meanness in a thousand ways.[21]

In their rites of rebellion, Americans made it clear that they could mobilize support whenever their liberties were challenged. And by recounting events in the press, they showed the durability of their consensus while constructing for themselves a realm in which they possessed a righteous power.[22]

Throughout the crisis, colonists North and South expressed confidence in the eventual results of their outward efforts. Christopher Gadsden, a notably boisterous merchant of Charleston, South Carolina, later a member of the Continental Congress, wrote to an English friend: "Our affection to our *dear* Mother Country tis impossible to alienate and turn into absolute hatred all at once; we have therefore generally flattered ourselves that as the Stamp Act was . . . very precipitately and inconsiderately enter'd into[,] your Bowels [here meaning the source of compassion] would again Yearn over us as Brethren and Nature compel you to . . . repeal the dreadful Sentence."[23]

The repeal of the Stamp Act in March 1766 became known in the colonies two months later, producing a moment of euphoria. A commencement ode read by Thomas Hopkinson upon graduating from the College of Philadelphia in June described the return of liberty in the usual hallowed terms—"sacred Freedom, from her native Skies," "bright Liberty," "Freedom, sweet celestial guide," and "Heaven-descended sacred Liberty! How blest the Land where thou shalt deign to dwell."[24] Across the colonies there was wide recognition that an important precedent had been set. Resisters felt they had survived a test, that their passionate appeals for decency and justice had brought success and vindication. They imagined that they could at any time muster the warm spirit of self-denial and prove that they could live plainly and simply—if, for instance, there was a boycott of British goods. This augured well for an ardent, principled people, a sentimental, reasonable people. The image they had of themselves was an exceptional combination: a people of enthusiasm and self-control.

Again Jonathan Mayhew, pastor of Boston's West Church, weighed in. His "Thanksgiving-Discourse" of May 23, 1766, published that year as *The Snare Broken*, was gratefully dedicated to William Pitt for having twice saved the colonies from ruin: "once, by magnanimously conducting a just and glorious war" against a foreign foe, "and once, by preserving peace" within the extended nation, "exerting himself to prevent a fatal rupture between BRITAIN and her Colonies." The outspoken Pitt was understood to have helped sway Parliament and king to repeal a "dreadful act" widely judged "unconstitutional, oppressive, grievous," and potentially "fatal."[25]

Mayhew conjured well-known and sensational images of enslavement that others had already fixed upon, and he supplemented them with a catalogue of ills emotional and social, individual and cross-colonial. The "dismal mixed scene" on the American continent had prompted "murmuring, despondence, tumult and outrage," "private jealousies and animosities, evil surmisings, whisperings and backbitings," all symptoms of the diseased atmosphere produced by the "grievous" Stamp Act, a "galling yoke to be laid on our necks," which would have likely grown "heavier by length of time" and become unendurable. This vividly imagined prospect reached even to the sensibility of "our bought *Negro slaves*," he claimed in an interesting digression. At first Mayhew seemed puzzled that the blacks of New England had "shared in the common distress." Failing to attribute love of liberty to a people integral to society but excluded from its conversation about rights, he presumed their collective motive had been merely pragmatic: "if *the act* took place, their masters might soon be too poor to provide them suitable food and raiment; and [they] thought it would be more ignominious and wretched to be the *servants of servants*, than of freemen." The presumption was that slaves were well taken care of and not treated unjustly by their New England masters. But racial justice was clearly peripheral to the primary struggle as Mayhew saw it; the dominant culture in America feared for preservation of its own sacred liberty without apparently feeling more than a bland kind of compassion for blacks.[26]

In language no less dramatic, he went on to explain that "blood and slaughter" had been narrowly averted, as had "the ruin of the colonies and the downfall" of Great Britain. With the intercession of Pitt and the triumph of reason, Britain instead emerged "the envy and glory of Europe." The Stamp Act repeal restored order and contentment in

America, said the popular pastor. "Even our slaves rejoice," he repeated, unable to let go of this example, "as tho' they had received their manumission."[27]

Mayhew pursued the family metaphor next. During the crisis, Britain's children had come to feel "wrath" toward their fundamentally sincere parent; with the restoration of moral balance, they could now see that it was "human frailty" that had prompted the Stamp Act, a misunderstanding "about facts and circumstances." Sympathy rendered mutual understanding possible. "British kings are the political FATHERS of their people," he reminded his flock, "and the people their CHILDREN; the former are not *tyrants*, or even *masters*; the latter are not slaves, or even *servants*." Without reciprocal affections, without a spirit of generosity rooted in family feeling, there would not have been a champion of American liberty in Parliament. "What SON, either of AMERICA or of LIBERTY is there . . . who can help being touched and penetrated to the inmost recesses of the heart, by such magnanimous and generous expressions [as Pitt's] in behalf of the colonies?" The colonists could continue to warrant the king's confidence by displaying "spirited" moderation, "a prudent, temperate, wise behaviour" in consequence of the satisfying conclusion of the crisis.[28]

Mayhew's thesis was still that virtuous passion and calm reason combined were highly effective as a political instrument. The forty-six-year-old preacher would not survive the year, but until his death he continued to urge what he had no reason to regard as an incompatible prescription: "a close harmony with our mother-country" achieved without lowering the guard against any "grasping, encroaching" power that would infringe on the people's liberties. From childhood, he reflected, he had been educated "to the love of liberty, tho' not of licentiousness. . . . I would not, I cannot now, tho' past middle age, relinquish the fair object of my youthful affections, LIBERTY; whose charms, instead of decaying with time in my eyes, have daily captivated me more and more." It was an affecting public testament from an influential cleric raised not only on the holy scriptures but on the doctrines of the orator Demosthenes and the virtuoso Cicero, the poet Milton and the philosopher Locke. Jonathan Mayhew went to his grave believing that the "wise, brave, and virtuous" were "always friends to liberty."[29]

But Parliament soon struck again. When the Stamp Act was first proposed, Charles Townshend had assured the House of Commons that the Americans were "children planted by our care, nourished up by our indulgence," and thus ought to contribute to Britain's "burden." In early 1767, as the new Chancellor of the Exchequer (ironically appointed by Pitt), Townshend introduced a series of Revenue Acts that raised the stakes. Duties on American imports of glass, paint, lead, and tea, meant to pay the salaries of British officials in the colonies, met with well-coordinated protests and a wide boycott. Nonimportation quickly became the means of foiling parliamentary designs to create a more docile America, a willing act of self-sacrifice being considered the highest display of American character. Maintaining the boycott was, once again, broadly associated with the issue of liberty vs. enslavement, "whether, for the future, we shall have any Property at all, or not—whether we shall be Freemen or Slaves?" George Washington, for one, termed nonimportation a good "scheme" that promised "salutary effects" if widely enough practiced. He was incensed that "our lordly Masters in Great Britain will be satisfied with nothing less than the deprivation of American freedom," and he flirted with the notion that although a recourse to arms "should be the last resource," it was not out of the question when taken up "in defence of so valuable a blessing" as liberty.[30] Making matters far worse, in 1768 London transferred four thousand British regular troops from Nova Scotia and Ireland to Boston Commons. Without apparent purpose other than to silence the colonists' protest (the Indian frontiers were relatively quiet), these regulars clashed verbally with citizens. The end result came to be called the Boston Massacre.

## The Insolence of Unbridled Passion

Eighteenth-century Britons and American colonists alike perceived a standing army as a symbol of the loss of liberty. So sensitive were Bostonians to militarization of any kind that during the French and Indian War a lead article in the *Boston Gazette* had suggested that raising and training local militia might alter people's perceptions of the quality of liberty. "Necessity" was understood, but how could people be protected from "a *Military Power*, as may in Process of Time prove dangerous to our civil Privileges—those civil Rights, *to protect* which is the only Intention and the only Business of a Militia." The irony was not lost on Americans: soldiers in the midst of citizens, though meant to protect, had rarely in history stopped short of sacrificing the people's happiness to unscrupulous ambition.[31]

In 1769, another commentary evidenced the townspeople's predisposition to challenge the presence of coarse and unfriendly soldiers in their midst. According to "A Freeman," writing with sarcasm and derision, citizens should resist even the simplest of questions posed by unwanted British regulars on their streets. The interrogatory "Who goes there?" warranted no response in a time of peace. Or, better, why not turn things around, since the soldiers, or "Sentinels," were British subjects no different from the American "men, women and children, black, white and grey" among whom they lived. Everyone in Boston had an equal right to inquire of any other person, "Who goes there?" And the answer in every case should be "Friend," although, for that matter, every free individual "has a right to pass along in stubborn sullen silence, if he pleases." The *South-Carolina Gazette* wrote supportively that Parliament was driving the Bostonians to a state of exasperation by "*imprudent* and *arbitrary*" acts that could not but "*create confusion.*" Bostonians considered themselves good neighbors. Quartering troops during times of peace in the "very Bowels" of their town was, as their leading citizens reported to the royal governor, "truly alarming to a free People." The regulars were "Exercising a Discipline, with all the Severity which is used in a Garrison, and in a State of actual War." Samuel Adams told the Philadelphia physician and educator Benjamin Rush that independence was his wish as early as 1768, when the standing army, which he termed the "shoeblacks [shoeshine boys] of society," intruded upon the peace of Boston.[32]

Through to the fateful day of March 5, 1770, British regulars roamed the streets of Boston. The rude exchanges and taunts that passed between the red-coated troops and restless citizens finally yielded deadly results: "A particular Account of a most barbarous and HORRID MASSACRE!" ran the banner headline, a broadside within black borders, reprinted in the *Boston Gazette*. Across the top of the page were five black coffins, the initials of the dead inscribed on each, above skull and crossbones. Below this came the shocking intelligence: "Amidst the impending Wrecks and Ruins of Power that threaten a wide Destruction to American FREEDOM, the Revolutions of Time have produced a day ever memorable for the most cruel and inhuman Massacre, perpetrated by the Hands of Men, who may be justly stiled more savage than the savage Beasts." Vulgar power had roughly violated fragile freedom. It was important for Bostonians to assert that "Britannia," the feminized paragon of English liberty, would "blush with indignation" that one Briton had so unconscionably and in so grotesque a manner struck out at another. The murders of five young and promising colonists was a "stain" of the most disgraceful kind on the British character. But, the paper vowed, using the same hearty language summoned during the Stamp Act crisis, "the Spirit of LIBERTY will always prevail, whilst English Blood flows in the veins of free-born *Americans*." The love of liberty that colonial activists sought to communicate was not yet exclusively American, but thought of as a distinctly English trait.[33]

While speaking to the culture of enlightened sympathy, the language of the broadside was pure polemic. Now, with the presumption of prophecy, American patriots were communicating aggressively and unreservedly about the inevitability of their triumph over militant evil. A Rhode Islander traveling in England wrote to the Connecticut clergyman Ezra Stiles: "You will often hear the following Language— Damn those Fellows we shall never do any Thing with Them till we root out that cursed puritanick Spirit—How is this to be done?—Keep Soldiers amongst Them, not so much to awe Them as to debauch their Morals." No matter how unlikely that these words were actually uttered, proud New Englanders were infuriated by the attitude expressed. Their views were still informed by the earlier Puritan consciousness of sin and service to society, and they felt their morals to be substantial and above reproach.[34]

In this contest of monumental proportions, love of liberty had become as potent a moral system for New Englanders—and perhaps a majority of colonial Americans—as their professed religion. Their truth was absolute. The originators of English liberty across the Atlantic seemed to have forsworn allegiance to the sacred principle. "Vain," "base," and "diabolical" was the armed enemy of the true faith; they would "intimidate" Americans into a "*tame* Submission"; meanwhile, "humanity" and "compassion" belonged to those who protected right and taught civic responsibility and virtue. A flourish at the bottom of the *Boston Gazette* broadside lyrically pronounced: "FREEDOM'S SONS in quest of Truth pursue." That freedom was "spotless," its adherents "filial." The indispensable, "spotless" principle was equated with perfect peace. "Spotless" meant godly, deserving of providential victory—just as British Americans had portrayed themselves when they vilified the popish, unenlightened French enemy of the decade prior. As is so often true of the morale of an embattled people, it was critical to contrast the qualities of the "enemy" with one's own community of pure and just aims.

In a way, the details of the Boston Massacre reveal less than the passionate language it unleashed. The "tragical Affair" that occurred on King Street on Monday, March 5, began when soldiers of the 29th Regiment were seen, according to the *Boston Gazette*, "parading the Streets with their drawn Cutlasses and Bayonets, abusing and wounding Numbers of the Inhabitants." Four young men then encountered "a Soldier brandishing a Broad Sword of an uncommon Size," accompanied by "a Person of a mean Countenance, armed with a large Cudgel." Physiognomy mattered. When "admonished" to "take Care" of the sword, the soldier reportedly slashed the arm of the unoffending youth. A scuffle ensued, and more soldiers poured out of the barracks. When a Bostonian named Samuel Atwood approached and asked whether the soldiers intended to "murder People," he was struck with a club and abruptly told: "You'll see by and by." Defiant youths picked up staves, while others followed the soldiers to ascertain their purpose. "Thirty or forty Persons, mostly Lads," met the soldiers with a hail of snowballs, and then the enraged British captain, Thomas Preston, was heard to call out: "Damn you, fire, be the Consequence what it will!" Guns discharged and three lay immediately dead, two more destined to die of their wounds, "but what shewed a Degree of Cruelty, unknown to British troops, . . . was an Attempt to fire upon, or push with their Bayonets the Persons, who undertook to remove the slain and wounded! . . . Tuesday morning presented a most shocking Scene, the Blood of our Fellow Citizens, running like Water through King-street."[35]

On Thursday, the bodies of the "unhappy Victims" were carried to their graves. Shops were closed during the procession, as bells "toll[ed] a solemn Peal." The Bostonians' "Moderation & Loyalty," it was said, had prevented the massacre from growing into something much larger, "the Signal only wanting to bring in a few Hours to the Gates of this City many Thousands of our brave Brethren in the Country, deeply affected with our Distresses."[36]

Boston had made its case. But in England a very different interpretation of the events of March 5 was disseminated. According to the British account, the commander of the 29th Regiment had cautioned his troops not to quarrel with the residents. Yet during the two days leading up to the encounter, soldiers were routinely "knocked down" and otherwise "ill-treated." When a fire alarm was "intentionally" sounded, a "multitude" of Bostonians drifted onto King Street; goaded and jeered at, the regulars resisted involvement, following orders to remain in their barracks. But then the hundreds who had come out seeking a fight turned on the sentry who stood in front of the Customs House, "where the King's Money is lodged," and a small party of troops next emerged in order to "extricate" their threatened comrade: the "melancholy consequences" were impossible to avert amid the escalating insults and fistfights. Captain Preston had a responsibility to protect both his endangered men and the Customs House. He reported having withstood "cruel and horrid Threats against the Troops," while he waited for sufficient intelligence to prove the existence of a carefully planned conspiracy. When that moment came, Preston had his men advance cautiously, intending only to disperse the crowd by "parleying." He further insisted that he never gave the word to fire. But the mob supposedly yelled, "Come on, you Rascals, you bloody Backs, you Lobster Scoundrels; fire if you dare, G—d damn you, fire, and be damned; we know you dare not." One of the regulars then "received a severe Blow with a Stick" and, as he turned, fired his weapon. The captain himself was struck hard on the arm, as "a general Attack was made on the Men by a great Number of heavy Clubs, and Snow-Balls being thrown at them, by which all our Lives were in imminent Danger."[37]

Reports more sympathetic to the American cause were also published in London. The *London Gazetteer* printed in late April a commentary by "Junius Americanus" stating that "the streets of Boston are already flowing with blood, wantonly, cruelly, and cowardly poured forth from the unarmed multitude, by your military magistrates." Though Boston's patriotic press warned the British ministry that "your triumphs are written in blood, and are indelible," Americans assumed in this inflamed atmosphere that the British public would believe Captain Preston's explanation and have little sympathy for them.[38]

To correct British perceptions, Samuel Adams sent a letter to Benjamin Franklin, who was in London and would be serving officially, from that autumn, as agent of the Massachusetts legislature. In his letter Adams energetically decried the intolerance and unscrupulousness of those who opposed the American cause: "false Accounts," "notorious falsehoods," "the Malice of our Enemies" who had "wrought up a Narrative" to take advantage of the "lucky opportunity of Slandering the Town." These "Persons of wicked Intentions" were bent on injuring the various colonies "in the grossest Manner, with Impunity or even without Detection," "a few designing Men to deceive a Nation to it's Ruin," to "totally alienate [the] Affections" long shared by America and the mother country. The colonies, in contrast, had acted in the open, consistent, unconcealed, and "bound in faithfulness."[39]

Not long after, Franklin wrote a letter that was printed pseudonymously in *The London Chronicle*. It contained something of Adams's tone, but it also had Franklin's characteristic language of reasonableness: while citing "groundless calumny," Franklin insisted that Americans "love and honour the name of Englishman" and wished "a perpetual intercourse of good offices, commerce, and friendship." They had merely, and justly, complained that Parliament lacked the right to raise revenue from them without their consent. Britain, in overreacting, seemed contemptuous of America. "Instead of *preventing* complaints by removing the causes," Franklin went on, "it has been thought best that

Soldiers should be sent to *silence* them . . . treating the Province and People with every indignity and insult, proper to provoke their resentment, and produce some rash action that might justify making a massacre among them." After these representations, the Philadelphian, never fainthearted, plainly warned that it was folly to dismiss the American claims: "As nothing is likely to be well done that is done in anger; as customers are not naturally brought back to a shop by unkind usage; as the Americans are growing, and soon will be, a great people, and their friendship or enmity become daily of more and more consequence," only respect and "leniency" could "heal the wound effectually." As "customers," Americans were meant to be regarded as more than children whose blind obedience was assumed. And as a soon-to-be "great people" and potential "friends," they warranted greater respect. Franklin's message implied moral equality, which was not quite the same as demanding political equality. Physiologists and sentimental novelists were insisting in other contexts that sympathy had to be reciprocal; affection had to be naturally and demonstrably two-sided and could not be coerced.[40]

By the following winter, the *Boston Gazette* went so far as to report: "At present the sound of war grows louder and louder, and seems almost inevitable." Citizens knew that royal appointees were conveying detailed information back to England about American resistance; one such letter noted that "a state of disorders, confusion and misgovernment" prevented orderly administration. Protests and distractions made enforcement of parliamentary acts difficult if not impossible. While Franklin in London was urging leniency and respect, trusted British officials in America were complaining that activists' "Flagitious publications" were exciting "popular tumults." Grave dangers remained to what London viewed as proper constitutional authority, and few believed that soft treatment would resolve anything.[41]

The full lesson of the Boston Massacre was brought to captivated audiences in the years following. On each anniversary of the tragedy, pious orators spoke to citizens of the aggrieved town, promising heavenly favor to a people who understood right. A thirty-four-year-old schoolmaster, James Lovell, hoping to tap Americans' generous reservoir of sympathy, spoke in 1771 commemorating the "horrid bloody scene." He attested to the "true undaunted courage excited by a confidence in God" that had brought the original English settlers to America. It was in order to bestow upon their posterity "full *English liberty*" that they had risked all; and now, though their legacy was "much impaired," nevertheless "their brave spirit still exists in vigor." Ridiculing the "mercenary" standing army, fatally emplaced in a "free city," the Latin scholar asserted that a free people could only be one that had a constitutional check upon the power to oppress. There was no middle ground. "Watchful, hawk-eyed JEALOUSY," he cried, "ever guards the portal of the temple of the GODDESS LIBERTY . . . We are . . . SLAVES until we obtain such *redress*, through the justice of our King, as our happy *constitution leads us to expect*." The British Parliament had not chartered a single American colony. It had usurped the king's prerogative as "King of *America*," for it was only the sovereign who could "direct the fire down upon our heads." Left undetermined, the fate of America rested on an appeal to George III. "A brave nation is always generous," Lovell reminded his audience.[42]

The following year on March 5, prominent physician and Son of Liberty Joseph Warren gave the address. He reiterated the essential constitutional issues, distinguished again between slaves and freemen, and spoke of the "ruinous consequences of standing armies to free communities." With what one must imagine to have been a sonorous summons, he declared:

> The FATAL FIFTH OF MARCH, 1770, can never be forgotten—the horrors of that dreadful night are but too deeply impressed on our hearts—Language is too feeble to paint the emotions of our souls, when our streets were stained with the blood of our brethren,—when our ears were wounded by the groans of the *dying*, and our eyes were tormented with the sight of the mangled bodies of the *dead*.—When our alarmed imagination presented to our view our houses wrapt in flames,—our children subjected to the barbarous caprice of the raging soldiery,—our beauteous virgins exposed to all the insolence of unbridled passion,—our virtuous wives, endeared to us by every tender tie, falling a sacrifice to worse than brutal violence, and

perhaps, like the famed Lucretia, distracted with anguish and despair, ending their wretched lives by their own fair hands.

The depth of the moral crisis perceived was clear in the fearful images of Dr. Warren's nightmare: the cataclysmic degeneration of a virtuous community (beset by a fiendish, uncontrolled, and libidinous army) into a cruel and depraved place of vice and wickedness. Surrendering liberty was equivalent to surrendering one's wives and daughters. This was why "our hearts beat to arms" on the night of the massacre, why "we snatched our weapons and almost resolved, by one decisive stroke, to avenge the deaths of our slaughtered brethren, and to secure from future danger, all that we held most dear." This was a sentimental novel magnified, the saga of an entire city's moral sanctity threatened.[43]

Dr. Warren's expressions of pride and anxiety heightened the emotional state of patriotic resistance. Despite "repeated attacks made upon our freedom" and the astonishing "infatuation which hath seemed, for a number of years, to prevail in the British councils," resilient Americans had so far maintained patience along with principle. "Propitious heaven" had stayed the hand of armed resistance to this point; "calm reason" had prevailed. But "calm reason" would not stifle this orator's voice. "My sons scorn to be SLAVES!" Dr. Warren exclaimed, as he launched into his dramatic conclusion. "In vain we met the frowns of tyrants—in vain, we crossed the boisterous ocean, found a new world, and prepared it for the happy residence of Liberty," in vain bled on King Street—unless the present generation succeeded in its "valor to repel the assaults" of the "invaders." For the sake of their "worthy ancestors," he urged, never "part with your birth-right; be wise in your deliberations, and determined in your exertions for the preservation of your liberties." This most passionate of speakers then implored his audience again to follow "not the dictates of passion, but enlist yourselves under the sacred banner of reason." Only then would America claim its destiny as "a land of Liberty, the seat of virtue, the asylum of the oppressed," to remain so until "the last shock of time shall bury the empires of the world in one common undistinguished ruin!"[44]

This kind of hyperbole suited the taste of Dr. Warren's listeners. They did not embrace reason without an emotional cause to publicize or protect. Reason did not make one impervious to feeling, or society mute. Reasonable individuals evidenced emotion, and a reasoning society could take concerted action without constituting a mob. Passion had its place in the age of reason; civilization could not advance without it. The American Revolutionaries distinguished between healthy and base passions, the "bright" passion of decent citizens who cherished freedom versus the "unbridled" passion of the "raging soldiery." The language of sensibility was never absent from the patriots' appeals. For them, historical change demanded a moral catastrophe, a universal lesson. And so tiny Boston, with a population of approximately 15,000, preached emotionally to the world without sensing either destructive passion or unmerited arrogance in the tone of its spokesman.

According to the *Boston Gazette*, that evening after Warren's oration, "a select Number of the true Friends of Liberty, met at Mrs. Clapham's in King-Street," and exhibited on her balcony a decorative translucent lantern, which featured in front "a lively Representation of the bloody Massacre which was perpetrated near that Spot." Over the lantern were transcribed the words: "The fatal Effect of a standing Army, posted in a free City." There also stood a monument listing the names of the five who died and the six who were wounded. Thousands of citizens passed by in the course of the evening, their hearts "deeply affected with the Retrospect of so horrid a Transaction."[45]

## THE TEARS OF MULTITUDES

The spirit of sacrifice had already spread through the colonies but was viewed more intently now. A boycott of British goods, nonimportation, signaled a widespread effort to display solidarity and to register peaceful protest. Commentary inevitably focused on the warm, self-affirming feeling such actions brought about. "Recovery of our ancient Liberties," wrote a South Carolinian, required a self-sacrifice "in which we glory." The writer then blasted those who were too weak or selfish to comply:

That Individuals will be found in every Colony, who, dead to all the warm Emotions of the Heart, even when Liberty is at stake, will sacrifice the only Blessings, which make Life comfortable, to the dirty Consideration of present Emolument, is nothing extraordinary. Worthless Men are the Produce of every Climate: They serve only as a Foil to set off the Cause: And unless we become Traitors to our own Liberties, we have little to fear.

The article concluded with an apocalyptic vision:

Let us suppose that the worst can befal us, that the Iron Hand of Power will at last prevail, and trample upon every Right of American Liberty; yet we think it an indispensable Duty, which we owe to our Country and Descendants, inflexibly to persevere to the last, and let Posterity record, FORCE *obtained a triumph over* PUBLIC VIRTUE; and though we fell, we fell with a Dignity and Spirit becoming the Sons of GREAT BRITAIN.[46]

All that survived in this vision was the memory of America's noble self-sacrifice.

The charitable nature of average Americans was heralded in a piece by "A Layman" who praised Pennsylvanians for contributing funds to the sick and infirm. Bright-spirited Americans as a whole were said to be "warmed with that Patriot-Glow of Freedom."[47] Self-denial was the subject, too, of a versified dialogue read at Commencement exercises for the College of Philadelphia on June 5, 1770:

Attend, ye Patriot Throng! ye noble Sons
Of Freedom, who, to save your Country's Rights
With rigid Self-denial, sacrifice
Your private Gain—O! be your Worth approv'd![48]

Still in England, and measuring his language carefully, Benjamin Franklin struggled vainly to rectify the problem of faulty communication. His article for *The London Chronicle* appealed: "I hope the great principle of common justice, that *no man should be condemned unheard,* will not by us [England] be violated in the case of a whole people." But he began to despair. Likening Anglo-American disharmony to a medical disease, he noted that "harsh treatment may increase the inflammation, make the cure less practicable, and in time bring on the necessity of an amputation; death indeed to the severed limb, weakness and lameness to the mutilated body." The metaphor disclosed Franklin's growing distrust of the state of political medicine.[49] With similar logic but less contrivance, the *Boston Gazette* proclaimed: "We are either a state as intirely independent of Great-Britain as any other on earth which makes use of her protection; or we are *her FREE* Colonies. In both these cases *her* conduct towards us should be *identically* the same."[50] Not long after, Franklin reached the point where he gave up on soft persuasion, and he told the Massachusetts legislature that England needed America more than America needed an "infirm" and "aged Parent": "We ask no more" than "the exercise of prudent Moderation on her part, mix'd with a little Kindness. . . . They think we may risque much by violent Measures . . . I do not presume to advise."[51]

The Sons of Liberty, the restless, forceful mechanics' organizations born of the Stamp Act crisis, had agreed after their initial spurt of growth to attract public figures of greater community stature and known reserve in order to unify the designs of their various local societies and build momentum under somewhat less threatening auspices.[52] Thus they transformed an action-oriented committee into a propaganda clearinghouse, somewhat less provocative in the original towns and cities until reignited by the sparks of 1773. Parliament's passage of the Tea Act in that year cleverly appealed to the colonists by substantially lowering the cost of their imported tea, retaining a very small duty, but American radicals construed this parliamentary measure as a means of seducing people into accepting Britain's power to tax them. One December night, refusing to allow East India Company tea to be landed on Boston piers, a motley group dressed themselves up as Mohawk Indians in old blankets, with dabs of paint or soot or burnt cork applied to their faces—a "disguise" meant to suggest a people who were free to act without constraint. These "Indians" drawn from the reconstituted Sons of Liberty took 342 chests of tea off the boats and tossed them into the harbor.[53]

Those present at the pier that night, speaking the American language of resistance to tyranny, consciously and dramatically perceived the need for a disturbance, a memorable act, a rite of rebellion. That is why they were at once disguised and acting in the open. They had witnessed over a few short but disputatious years the power of writing, oratory, and symbolic action in developing *"principles, opinions, sentiments, and affections"*—a new emotional identity. What John Adams meant in his 1818 letter to editor Hezekiah Niles was much earlier inscribed into his diary on the day after the Boston Tea Party:

> This is the most magnificent Movement of all. There is a Dignity, a Majesty, a Sublimity, in this last Effort of the Patriots, that I greatly admire. The People should never rise, without doing something to be remembered—something notable[.] And striking. This Destruction of the Tea is so bold, so daring, so firm, intrepid and inflexible, and it must have so important consequences, and so lasting, that I cant but consider it as an Epocha of History.

As if testing himself, Adams added two paragraphs later: "The Question is whether the Destruction of this Tea was necessary? I apprehend it was absolutely and indispensably so."[54] Or, as his Philadelphia friend Benjamin Rush was to recollect of his own commitment to the values of the Revolution, "the adoption of republican principles, had acted like a ferment in my mind, and had led me to try the foundations of my opinions upon many other subjects as well as that of government."[55] For the leaders of the Revolutionary generation, vigorous reflection mandated vigorous action.

Increasingly, London viewed the colonial resistance as childish confusion, the unpardonable disobedience of a minority. The Boston press continued to sound optimistic about the efficacy of protest, though intercolonial political union did not yet appear likely.[56] After the end of 1773, when radicals disposed of the tea which represented parliamentary power over them, the government of Lord North passed punitive measures known as the Coercive Acts—Americans dubbed them the Intolerable Acts—which included the Port Act, closing the port of Boston until payment was made for the destroyed tea. Thomas Gage, commander of the British Army in North America, became governor of Massachusetts in May 1774, hoping to isolate the rebellious province. Making an example of Boston would serve as a lesson to all thirteen colonies that the principle of parliamentary supremacy was nonnegotiable.

Despite the persistence of patriotic expression in the press and in public assemblies, sensitive, suspicious Boston radicals perceived a relaxation of vigilance among the people of their colony. Certain that liberty once lost could not be regained, they created the loose and informal Boston Committee of Correspondence to awaken slumbering patriots. Initiated in 1772–73 by Samuel Adams, Joseph Warren, and Thomas Young, a onetime New York Son of Liberty, the Committee publicized the Coercive Acts as "grievous and unheard of Impositions," "the Machinations of our Enemies here and in Great-Britain." Samuel Adams, who had discussed the possibility of uniting with other colonies in his correspondence with Virginia's Richard Henry Lee, was intent on making the Coercive Acts "a Cause so interesting to *all* America."[57]

At this point, intercolonial union began to take precedence above all else in the minds of American patriots. In March 1773, Virginia's patriot leadership in the House of Burgesses established a Committee of Correspondence and subsequently worked to increase understanding of the Bostonians' predicament.[58] Connecticut's Samuel Sherwood delivered a sermon to "the FREEMEN of the colony" in August 1774 in support of nonimportation of British goods, while urging financial and other contributions to the struggles of neighboring Massachusetts. If "the people in the several colonies are very considerably divided, we are undone," he prodded. "Nothing but the united efforts of America can save us: and if united, they must have that weight, which gives me the most sanguine hopes of success."[59] In New Jersey's Essex County, freeholders passed resolutions expressing "our most affectionate Sympathy for the cruel treatment of our [Boston] Brethren." One of these consolidated a language in circulation since 1765: "The Providence of God having cast our Lot in a Land of Light & Liberty, we enjoyed perfect tranquillity under a most wise & gentle Government, Brittain considering the happiness of America as inseparably connected with her own; and America looking up to Brittain as a dutiful Child to an affectionate Parent." Once Britain became an "Oppressive & despotic Power," the "happiness we have enjoyed in the rational & filial dependance on the Crown" led to "regret & mortification."[60]

This "regret & mortification" indicated a degree of shame at a time when, whether apparent or illusory, Americans' presentation before the eyes of the world mattered. The Boston Massacre orators and those who sank the chests of tea appreciated the sensation of public performance. Regarding themselves as a dignified people, the colonists were especially sensitive to anything that seemed a disparagement, or a reduction in stature, or that brought collective shame; the connection with an oppressive parent who held them in contempt was easily construed as a shameful decline in America's circumstance. And so patriots spoke out to resist this displacement. They saw no rational choice but to fight degradation. A historical moment was upon them, and they feared idleness in the face of the change it augured. As the Essex resolutions noted, a "long dreaded Era, too fast advancing" required prompt action in the name of reason and right, if the colonies were to return to the state of happiness and liberty they had previously enjoyed.

An open letter "To the Freeholders of the Colony" of South Carolina, signed by "A Carolinian," exuded what seemed an extreme euphoria in appreciation of the united sentiments of the First Continental Congress. That body had convened in Philadelphia during the autumn of 1774 to express sympathy for Massachusetts, list joint grievances, and announce a new boycott of British goods. Its main work was to organize and publicize. But to the Carolina writer much more had been achieved: "Our most sanguine expectations have been exceeded," he wrote. "The thick cloud breaks underneath, and here and there discloses an hard blue sky. Your hearts begin to be relieved, by the distant prospect of basking once more in the fair beam of Liberty." The natural metaphor aroused vital passions: How could George III reject the moderate pleas of this sentimental union, "firm" but not "rash," and "tempered with . . . tenderness"?[61]

In November 1774, Joseph Warren wrote to his lifelong friend, the lawyer Josiah Quincy, who had been the first to propose annual commemorations of the Boston Massacre and who was in England on a last-ditch mission: "Our friends who have been at the Continental Congress are in high spirits on account of the union which prevails throughout the colonies. *It is the united voice of America to preserve their freedom, or lose their lives in defence of it. . . . I am convinced that the true spirit of liberty was never so universally diffused through all ranks and orders of people, in any country on the face of the earth.*"[62] Rhode Island's Samuel Ward wrote to the moderate Pennsylvanian John Dickinson: "The Idea of taking up Arms against the parent State is shocking to Us, who still feel the strongest Attachment to our sovereign and the warmest Affection & Veneration for our Brethren in Britain. . . . But if We must either become Slaves or fly to Arms I shall not and I hope No American will hesitate one Moment which to chuse." Dickinson himself had recently acknowledged to a Virginian, Arthur Lee, that a "determined & unanimous Resolution animates this Continent, firmly & faithfully to support the Common Cause, to the utmost Extremity, in this great Struggle for the Blessing of Liberty, that alone can render Life worth holding."[63] His tone less decorous, John Adams noted in his diary the toasts led by his friend Robert Treat Paine at a dinner that season: "May the Collision of british Flint and American Steel produce that Spark of Liberty which shall illumine the latest Posterity." These patriotic exchanges spread the conviction that the investment of heart and belief in harmonious union would result in victory for the cause.[64]

Preparing for the coming war, Patrick Henry introduced a resolution at a Virginia convention called in the early spring of 1775 to combine the colony's independent volunteer companies into a provincial army. His contemporary Edmund Randolph later described Henry's eloquence as the orator spoke on behalf of the measure at St. John's Church, the largest building in the young town of Richmond:

> Henry was his pure self. Those who had toiled in the artifices of scholastic rhetoric, were involuntarily driven into an inquiry within themselves, whether rules and forms and niceties of elocution would not have choked his native fire. It blazed so as to warm the coldest heart. In the sacred place of meeting, the church, the imagination had no difficulty, to conceive, when he launched forth in solemn tones, various causes of scruples

against oppressors. . . . It was Patrick Henry, born in obscurity, poor, and without the advantages of literature, rousing the genius of his country, and binding a band of patriots together to hurl defiance at the tyranny of so formidable a nation as Great Britain. This enchantment was spontaneous obedience to the working of his soul.

Spontaneity and heartfelt emotion seemed to capture Americans' purpose better than orthodox learning. Thomas Jefferson spoke, too, "closely, profoundly and warmly on the same side" as Henry, Randolph said, adding that "Washington was prominent, though silent. His looks bespoke a mind absorbed in meditation on his country's fate."[65]

This was Patrick Henry's finest hour. According to Henry's early-nineteenth-century biographer William Wirt, the famed orator uttered "sentiments freely, and without reserve." The moment had been reached, Henry said, when there was "no time for ceremony." His subject was the intense dichotomy of freedom and slavery. The "slighted," "spurned" patriots of America could no longer hope for respect or reconciliation: "An appeal to arms and to the God of Hosts, is all that is left us!" An early Jefferson biographer, Henry S. Randall, similarly reported that Henry's final exclamation on that day, "Give me liberty or give me death!" was "like the shout of the leader which turns back the rout of battle. . . . Men looked beside themselves."[66]

New England militia units mustered and trained. At Yale College, in New Haven, a student wrote that "College Yard constantly sounds with, *poise your firelock, Cock your firelock* &c. . . . from which we may gather as great evidence, war will be proclaimed soon." A clandestine committee of mechanics, led by the silversmith Paul Revere, kept watch on the movements of regulars and Tories in and around Boston. Governor Gage, meanwhile, relied on intelligence from a highly placed spy, as he planned raids on several patriot arsenals storing gunpowder and small arms. New fears and anxieties were leading to acts of provocation.[67]

On Monday, March 6, 1775, Joseph Warren for a second time gave the annual Boston Massacre oration—the fifth anniversary. The pulpit of the Old South Meetinghouse was hung with heavy black cloth. "Our country is in danger, but not to be despaired of," he rallied. "Our enemies are numerous and powerful, but we have many friends, determined to be free, and heaven and earth will aid the resolution." At the conclusion of Warren's solemn speech, Sam Adams moved that the town give thanks to the orator. Idle British officers who had sat through the address—some invited to the front pews by Adams himself—tapped their canes on the floor and began to hiss. Thinking the soldiers' "Oh! Fie!" was the cry "Fire!" men and women panicked and ran for the door. British marchers playing fifes and drums happened to be out front, and the people pouring out of the meetinghouse thought they were under attack. Anxious moments passed before calm was restored.[68]

Similar incidents revealed the extent of popular discontent and the impossibility of reducing tensions. By early April most of the patriot leaders had slipped out of Boston and into hiding. Joseph Warren remained, as did "express rider" Paul Revere, whom Warren dispatched, along with a tanner named William Dawes, on April 18 to warn Sam Adams and John Hancock in Lexington of an impending British military expedition. Warren himself then turned over his medical practice to his student and boarded the ferry to take him from Boston. He reportedly told a Mr. Adan at boatside, "Keep up a brave heart! They have begun it,—that either party can do; and we'll end it,—that only one can do." He reached Lexington in time to participate in some of the hottest fire of that day; a musket ball grazed his head on high ground east of the town.[69]

After the fateful shots were fired at Lexington and the British regulars were subsequently routed at Concord, both on April 19, the news spread rapidly by prearranged patriot channels and by word of mouth. It reached Maine in one day, New York in three, Williamsburg, Virginia, in ten. Competing interpretations of the events were promptly dispatched across the Atlantic. It was "good news" to Isaac Hasey in Lebanon, Maine, who mustered "ye Minute Men" to march south on April 21. But it was a "hubbub as no truth goes" to the loyalist-leaning Ashley Bowen, a mere thirty miles from Concord.[70] A Salem printer, Ezekiel Russell, issued a broadside, several times reprinted, with tens of black coffins in two rows across the top of the page; the headline read: "BLOODY BUTCHERY, BY THE BRITISH TROOPS; OR THE RUN-

AWAY FIGHT OF THE REGULARS." The *Pennsylvania Gazette* printed eyewitness letters from Boston in its April 27 issue, emotional but not always accurate portrayals: "Yesterday produced a scene the most shocking NEW-ENGLAND ever beheld," one began. The Lexington militia had been attacked, it asserted, while "innocently amusing themselves with exercise." "The marching of the [British] troops to the water side was so sudden and silent," wrote another, "that few of the inhabitants [of Boston] knew of it till next morning."[71]

Assessing the British retreat from Concord in a letter to a former Mount Vernon neighbor who had returned to England several years before, George Washington indicated that "the once happy and peaceful plains of America are either to be drenched in Blood, or inhabited by slaves. Sad alternative! But can a virtuous Man hesitate in his choice?"[72] The Second Continental Congress had convened in Philadelphia by then and, "for the defence of American liberty," named the stoical Virginia planter commander-in-chief of the American forces assembling on the outskirts of British-occupied Boston. Accompanied by mounted servants and prominent aides, General Washington did not arrive at Cambridge until July 2, two weeks after the momentous Battle of Bunker Hill had been fought.

At Bunker Hill, as at Concord, ordinary "country people," as the British called the Americans (and they, in some instances, referred to themselves), held back repeated charges, fought with pluck and intrepidity, and repelled the cream of the British Army. People thronged the Charles River shore and gazed up at the spectacle on the hill, as British columns crept up slowly through the thick grass. Though the overmatched Americans were forced into retreat, it was not before they had shot more than a thousand of their attackers, including ninety-two officers.[73]

Here, too, Dr. Joseph Warren, fighting as a volunteer under a burning sun while he awaited his major general's commission, martyred himself for his cause. The high-spirited Warren, then thirty-four, had requested of another indefatigable Yankee, General Israel Putnam, to be directed to the place "where I can be most useful." A Bunker Hill survivor attested that "his whole soul seemed to be filled with the greatness of the cause he was engaged in." And another: "His heroic soul elicited a kindred fire from the troops." Jonathan Brigham later recalled the "immense volumes of flames illuminating the battlefield." Warren and his men met three advances on their position until "a forest of bayonets" appeared over the parapet of their indefensible redoubt. The physician engaged in hand-to-hand combat, sword upraised, but was shot in the head by a British officer who, it was said, recognized him. Abigail Adams wrote the next day, "The tears of multitudes pay tribute to his memory." Seeing God's hand in the terrible conflict, William Linn praised the American volunteers: "a comparative handful withstood the cleavage of two thousand of the flower of the British troops." Bunker Hill came to mean defiance—and the shining example of a moral victory.[74]

Warren's body was found under three feet of dirt just days after the British abandoned Boston eight months later, in March 1776, and properly interred. He became known in death as "the immortal Warren," a "matchless patriot" who had lived a life of integrity and generosity and died for liberty and union. Another orator recalled how at every moment of "eminent danger," Warren's fellow citizens sought his advice, and in giving it, he "dispelled their fears." Finally, "when he found the tools of oppression were obstinately bent on violence," he reluctantly but assuredly took up the sword, and "in his last agonies he met the insults of his barbarous foe with his wonted magnanimity, and with the true spirit of a soldier." No war had so peace-loving a hero, Americans thought, a healer compelled by justice and generosity to offer his life to the cause of "general liberty."[75]

The call to magnanimity was not confined to a Boston under siege. In June, far from the fighting, Thomas Jefferson's Albemarle County neighbor Lieutenant George Gilmer organized an independent company of volunteers. "Gentleman Soldiers!" he addressed the men. "This alternative is now before us, either to become the voluntary and abject slaves of a wicked administration, or to live free as the air we breathe." With "valor, prudence, and love for our country," and "divested of every self-interested motive," they were to "unite hearts and hands"— this was becoming a choice phrase—and "behold integrity as an inestimable jewel." As the Virginia volunteers marched off to the capital of

Williamsburg, Lucy Gilmer heeded her husband's words of patriotic selflessness and contributed her most valuable jewelry toward creating a more secure system of letter carriers, as the patriots conveyed their secret plans across the countryside.[76]

Timothy Hancock, a young and seemingly untutored New Hampshire farmer who volunteered after Lexington and Concord, kept a pocket diary as he waited out the long siege of Boston. Encamped just outside the town, he noted each time a British regular deserted to the American side. On July 25, 1775, two regulars stole across from Bunker Hill, and the next day "a Regular Desarted to Dorchester point with two guns and Sixty rounds." There was cause for optimism when several sneak attacks yielded prisoners and plunder, and on August 1 when "John Blake fired at the Regulars Abought 60 Rood and made them wink." When the British acted in like fashion, though, Hancock wrote that the "Avowed Enemy" was exhibiting "malace" and "mollatations [molestation]." "Behold their Spite full Spirit," the farmer narrated for himself and an as yet unimagined posterity.[77]

Long responsive to news from their distant sister colony, South Carolina patriots rankled at the abuse Bostonians were suffering. It was, a newspaper circular called it, "the Voice of America" that delivered to Carolinians the lurid details of the "unnatural war" begun at Lexington. "This year [1775] will be a GRAND EPOCHA in the History of Mankind." "Divine Providence has inspired the Americans with such Virtue, Courage, and Conduct, as has already attracted the Attention of the Universe." A self-sacrificing people, rich in sensory understanding but "deaf to the alluring calls of luxury and mirth," would not relax their vigil until final victory was achieved. In the most satisfying of visions, "the children of your most inveterate enemies, ashamed to tell from whom they sprang, while they in secret curse their stupid, cruel parents, shall join the general voice of gratitude to those who broke the fetters which their fathers forged." Conscience reigned in the minds of these morally secure Revolutionary writers.[78]

After the outbreak of the war, Continental bills of credit were issued that featured suggestive emblematic devices. One of these was a harp with the motto *"majora minoribus consonant"* ("the greater and smaller ones sound together"). The frame of the instrument was described as solid and its sound concordant, attributing substance and equanimity to the Continental Congress. An interpreter of the design noted: "The several colonies of different weight and force, or the various ranks of people in all of them, who are now united by that government in the most perfect *harmony.*" On another bill was "a wild boar of the forest, rushing on the spear of the hunter," with the motto "*aut mors, aut vita decora,*" translated as "death or liberty." The wild boar was said to symbolize "strength and courage," its tusks used in defense: "He is inoffensive while suffered to enjoy his freedom, but when roused and wounded by the hunter, often turns and makes him pay dearly for his injustice and temerity."[79] The victimized union had made its resolve clear.

## THE GARDEN OF OUR FATHERS

Between the Stamp Act and the outbreak of the Revolution, the Whig or patriot element in British America believed that their physical country was the repository of liberties they had long regarded as fixed and now they feared were fleeting. England at an earlier time had been the chosen home of liberty, but it was America's turn to succeed her.

In the heat of the Stamp Act resistance, the *Boston Gazette* reprinted a 1755 sermon on rights and privileges which retraced the historical flight of Liberty "from soil to soil." Nearly exhausted on reaching the British Isles, Liberty had rested comfortably while "our great FORE-FATHERS (whose memories be blest)" had migrated into "these remote regions." The earliest British Americans were patient but expectant, believing that America was meant to be the last protected home of Liberty, the sacred "corner" where God's glorious purpose rested. To the Revolutionaries, no wilderness could restrain a zeal that was informed by such a promise.[80]

A dialogue read at commencement exercises at the College of Philadelphia in 1770 contained verses recounting the same inevitable westward movement of Liberty and moral civilization from Europe to America:

> ... when Time was young,
> Fair Freedom first upheld her bloodless Reign
> With growing Glory, thence she stretched her Course
> Still westward ...
> O'er fair Britannia's Isles ...
> ... and ling'ring leap
> There on Europa's last, but noblest, Sons
> She beam'd her Noon-tide Blaze; and westward still
> Across the vast Atlantic shot a Ray,
> To gladden Britain's Sons, where'er retir'd
> In Regions new. And tho' by Clouds obscur'd
> Yet shall her Beams, with renovated Strength,
> Break forth, and pierce those awful Depths of Woods,
> "Till all America's untutor'd Sons,"
> Of every Language, and of every Hue,
> Rous'd and exalted by her genial Warmth,
> Enjoy by Turns their Day of social Bliss.[81]

For patriot promoters, history was reaching a climax in America. In humanity's timeless drama, Good had a fighting chance to endure. The commencement poet found a haven for people "Of every Language, and of every Hue." Free, harmonizing America, rescued from Europe's fate, would go on one day to enjoy "social Bliss." This verse was a more inclusive celebration than most, delighting in the primitive "untutor'd Sons" who were spread across "awful Depths of Woods." The woods continued to offer protection for Americans long accustomed to them, as the *South-Carolina Gazette* boasted in its confident challenge to Parliament after the Stamp Act repeal: "Would [a body of British troops] have no dangers to encounter in the woods and wilds of America?"[82]

Away from the tempest of political debate, the pioneer naturalist William Bartram recorded different thoughts as he traveled through the Georgia piedmont in 1773: "Continuing my ramble about these fruitful Hills and vales I descended down again to the Creek & traceing its winding courses through these fragrant Groves which led me to the foot of a hill, here a group of fine flowering Trees & Shrubs drew my attention. Approaching this joyfull retreat which decorated the banks of the Creek just by a cascade, this noble assembly of vegitable could scercely be parallel'd in America." In the next paragraph, Bartram used repeated superlatives: "majestic," "most exquisite," "first in magnitude," "most perfect whiteness." With surroundings that produced for the traveler a natural harmony and balance, the American vision remained pristine. "I listened, undisturbed," wrote Bartram, "to the divine hymns of the feathered songsters of the groves, whilst the softly whispering breezes faintly died away. . . . How melodious is the social mock-bird! The groves resound the unceasing cries of the whip-poor-will." As tuneful as the birds which animated him, Bartram promoted the wonders of the continent. Similarly, George Mercer, George Washington's friend since boyhood and principal aide during the French and Indian War, referred to America fondly in 1770, after his removal to England, as "the Land of Promise."[83]

Most Americans who wanted to recapture an extravagant, uncluttered, romantic engagement with the land would have to wait out the coming war. But that necessity did not detour those who subscribed to a vision of millennial history, which was steadily politicized during the tense decade 1765–75. Patriot clergy, blurring the boundaries between civil and religious liberty, helped to encourage the prospect of union. Timothy Dwight, a grandson of Reverend Jonathan Edwards and a future president of Yale, published "America: or, a Poem on the Settlement of the British Colonies" in 1771, which Ernest Lee Tuveson has termed the moment when America's destiny became "manifest." Dwight's poem suggested a historic destiny for the Revolutionary generation, following the "light" that had penetrated the dark upon Columbus's discovery of America:

> AMERICA'S bright realms arose to view,
> And the *old* world rejoic'd to see the *new*.

To the poet, freedom possessed "radiance"; America was the "Land of light and joy!" "Savage nations" would bend to its will, as American sailing ships, representing the commercial empire of the future, "stretch their canvas to the ASIAN gale." Again the metaphor of light and the allusion to empire:

> Round thy broad fields more glorious ROMES arise,
> With pomp and splendour bright'ning all the skies.

Dwight's was a vision of a better world under the reign of "white-rob'd Peace," with the blessing of God.

> Then, then an heavenly kingdom shall descend,
> And Light and Glory through the world extend.

Secular leaders were as willing as Dwight to invoke God's providence, as they raised apocalyptic fears in their written and oratorical polemics. Civil millennialism molded a new, stronger American identity for once loyal Britons now bent on justifying the act of separation.[84]

In providential drama, the march of time enlarged the cause of America. The *Boston Gazette* laid out a typical scenario: the Glorious Revolution of 1688, which had weakened the monarchy and strengthened Parliament, was the moment of reawakening for the tradition of British liberty; as arbitrary government fell, "the Sky brightened," and then, in its aftermath, America "rose and flourished." In biblical prose, the newspaper continued: the immediately preceding generation had seen this brightening sky and "rejoiced. They begat sons and daughters." Now, a new and critical generation was maturing, destined to witness the horrifying removal of British liberty: "lo! the storm gathers again, and sits deeper and blacker with boding aspect!" Their time was a test of biblical proportions: Would a sinful people "degenerate as to desert the sacred trust consign'd to us for the happiness of posterity?" Then, conjuring a still more odious sensation: "Shall we tamely suffer the pestilential breath of tyrants to approach this garden of our fathers and blast the fruit of their labours?"[85]

The "garden" was the most precious site that could be called up, the choicest language to describe earthly potential. The "garden" offered a familiar form of nostalgia, an imagined past of primordial significance, a symbol of loss (and a moral test besides) to animate Revolutionary acts of self-preservation. Glorifying the process of American settlement was key to developing an unassailable ideology. A subsequent article about military preparedness showed how cherished such

imagery was: "Only look back to your worthy ancestors, who first settled in this land, and see at what a dear rate they purchased the fair
towns, the pleasant gardens, the fruitful fields which you now enjoy."
Once the American "garden" was assaulted, despoiled, was there any
other place on earth where Liberty could travel? This was the writer's
ultimate question. "SPIRIT of ancient Britons!" he summoned.
"Where art thou? Into what happier region art thou fled or flying?
Return, oh return into our bosoms." If America was meant to be an
Eden, then might a collective indecision about protecting the land of
liberty be the equivalent of repeating original sin?[86]

The Boston Massacre introduced other metaphorical devices.
Streets "stained with blood" and "houses wrapt in flames" signified a
new view of the land as a scarred scene where a grand contest of wills
was taking place. The inhabitants of Boston described themselves and
their property as "insulted and much abused." Elsewhere, Bostonians
lamented "this *distressed* and *insulted* continent." If nothing were to be
done about the King Street killings, then it was in vain that "our Ancestors quit their native Land, and encountered numerous perils and
dangers, in settling this Country, to enjoy the Blessings of Freedom,
and to transmit the same to their Posterity." The "perils" endured over
two centuries of hard-fought, industrious settlement and expansion
made the land precious, and made hardy Americans experience the
"crimes" of unfeeling redcoats all the more profoundly.[87]

While having eclipsed Boston as the most populous American city,
Philadelphia shared with it a sense of suffering and fear of pending
destruction. "Amicus Publici" (Friend of the Public) wrote that Philadelphia, "the Flower of America, if not of the World," was in danger
of decline. The viability of the garden landscape, the survival of the
idea of America, was uncertain. "This the Land of my Nativity" seemed
destined for a rhetorical if not real conflagration: "Solomon says, 'behold what a great Flame a small Spark kindleth!'" "O Libertas! O
Patria!" the pseudonymous writer cried, fearing for the loss of all from
a perversion of the passions.[88]

The moral crisis had a physical dimension. In the course of his 1772
oration, Joseph Warren had identified the natural wealth of the American landscape while he noted Britain's covetousness. London had con-

sistently enjoyed a "smooth channel of commerce" and real prosperity because of the contributions of America, he observed. The "amazing increase in riches to Britain, the great rise in the value of her lands, the flourishing state of her navy are striking proofs of the advantages" voluntarily offered her by the colonies. "It is our earnest desire that she may still continue to enjoy the same emoluments, until her streets are paved with AMERICAN GOLD; only," he underscored sharply, "let us have the pleasure of calling it our own, whilst it is in our hands."[89]

In 1771, two young scholars, Philip Freneau and Hugh Henry Brackenridge, of the College of New Jersey, together wrote a proud poem, "On the Rising Glory of America." In it they projected an American empire greater than the British and anticipated what it was that patriots would soon give their lives to protect. A lush and promising landscape was inviting a virtuous, pioneering people to develop it. To these young Princetonians, the growing colonies were to become a "seat of empire" and "not less in fame than Greece and Rome." The historian Joseph Ellis has in modern times said much the same: that American cultural energy was about to "explode onto the world." A place so grand needed its own self-constituting epic, the poets surmised, and they wished to be the ones to chart a path for American poetry, claiming "E'en now we boast / A *Franklin*, prince of all philosophy, / A genius piercing as the electric fire," the rival of Britain's giant, Sir Isaac Newton. "This is a land of every joyous sound," they crowed, where "liberty and life, sweet liberty!" would continue to promote discovery. America was not yet in any real sense a nation, but they viewed it as a land waiting for momentous events to reveal its full epic message. Fears of dissolution dramatically mixed with boasts of dominion.[90]

America had once been rhapsodized as the continent where Britain's empire could be seen in its most resplendent glory. After the Stamp Act, the mass and extent of the land rather quickly became Americans' exclusive prospect. With its usual flair for bold expression, the *Boston Gazette* contended in 1771 that it was

> impossible in the nature of things that a people situated as the Americans are, should ever be enslaved by a foreign power; if they fall it must be a tyranny among themselves. The wildest

imagination can hardly suppose this great continent of British America, which is more than three thousand miles long, . . . and possessed of all the natural advantages for wealth, power and independency, should long be subjected and oppressed by an Island not one hundredth part so big![91]

The young Alexander Hamilton extended the boast in early 1775. England's "oppression" masked "a jealousy of our dawning splendour. . . . The boundless extent of territory we possess, the wholesome temperament of our climate, the luxuriance and fertility of our soil, the variety of our products, the rapidity of our population, the industry of our country men and the commodiousness of our ports, naturally lead to a suspicion of independence."[92]

Hamilton was born on the West Indian island of Nevis and arrived in New York City as a teenage student only late in 1772. Little more than two years later, he was advertising the harmonious possibilities to be obtained by joining America's parts together. Evidence showed that nature had "disseminated her blessings variously throughout this continent . . . some colonies are best calculated for grain; others for flax and hemp; others for cotton; and others for live stock of every kind: By this means, a mutually advantageous intercourse may be established between them all." Hamilton favored, at this time, a self-sufficient America, promising "more lasting prosperity" through stimulation of its internal connections rather than yielding to the "luxury and vices" acquired through foreign commerce. He proudly determined that America's wealth of resources made trade with England unnecessary. Anyone put out of work for any reason "may be employed in cultivating lands. We have enough, and to spare." And therefore, "Great-Britain can never force us to submission." The young immigrant seemed to be identifying the boundless continent with a newcomer's ambition for career opportunity and social mobility. It would be best, he warned, for London to acknowledge the "natural intrepidity, and that animation, which is inspired by a desire of freedom, and a love of one's country" that was possessed by the fortunate American people. They knew their land and could resort to the byways of a varied topography to "evade a pitched battle" with any invader from across the Atlantic.[93]

Though patriot newspapers, their language rich in sensation, described the British government as ever more monstrous and ravenous, they predicted victory in terms of civilizing progress—if one was inevitable, so was the other. With Boston in enemy hands in the autumn of 1775, the *Essex* (Massachusetts) *Gazette* addressed American soldiery: The "extensive country we inhabit" had matured from "a state of savage barbarity," "dreary wastes," to "pleasant fields . . . elegant buildings, and beautiful landscapes." Liberty's great trial had to result in "the future grandeur of the western world." To compatriots in Ireland, delegates from the United Colonies wrote: "We already anticipate the golden period."[94]

Old World thinkers had long regarded America as an inferior place, the most revealing example of a primitive state of society aiming to rise to European levels of refinement and civilization. Now the Revolutionaries were announcing to the world that they had indeed risen, just as the Old World was growing more critical of the persistence of its own pauperism and injustice. European men of letters were beginning to waken to the Americans' proud assertions and look admiringly at their prospects. The inhabitants of the New World were becoming, to the European mind, a more competent people, and this idea no doubt ricocheted, boosting an already growing self-regard.[95]

# CHAPTER FOUR

# THE AMERICAN DREAM: 1776

THE BRITISH GOVERNMENT did not appreciate the moral energy that lay behind the actions of America's patriots. And so it flatly rejected the logic of the emerging colonial leaders who justified their Revolutionary speech on the basis of "natural laws." The Continental Congress would declare independence first and foremost on immutable grounds: nature could not be altered for mere political opinions, but governments could be altered because the people of the earth were by nature separate and equal.[1] After claiming their natural rights, the Revolutionaries accentuated what they identified as a public *feeling* (majority will), as they in fact manipulated a public *mood*. And believing themselves touched by benevolence, they defended their acts amid social turmoil with words that reflected the culture of sentiment and sympathy—in Jefferson's words, "agonizing affection."

As a ritual performance, the American Revolution was a high-spirited spectacle befitting what was both an age of civility and an age of contentiousness. By 1776 there was nothing capricious in either the ideology or the public actions of the Revolutionaries. They promoted a sense of themselves as stouthearted, mindful men of affairs—republicans—and as women of sensibility who mirrored the Revolutionary consciousness and expressed political convictions within the family, while publicly assuming a nonpolitical role.[2] Carefully constructing their Revolutionary republican identity, even those Americans who were trained in England before the outbreak of war were now concluding that provinciality by no means implied moral inferiority. Commonness did not connote meanness.

Neither did a recognition of their provinciality mean that Americans should rely on British literary magazines for an informed sense of taste. In the introductory issue of *The Pennsylvania Magazine*, Thomas Paine accused British journals of having "sunk to simplicity, from simplicity to folly, and from folly to voluptuousness." What was British, he insisted, had grown "dissolute." As magazine culture was the "nursery of genius," young America should advance its creative spirit and replace effete British forms with bright examples of the New World's virtue and freshness.[3]

As eager readers of politics, science, and literature, this sociable generation of American thinkers judged that they had outgrown England's pompous history and had a history of their own to construct—a nation, both politically and culturally speaking, to fashion. As communicative writers already identifying with an enlightened republic of letters, they defined natural rights and self-evident truths for their age, and dramatized their interpretation of such concepts as liberty and happiness. They looked for cohesion and found security in the notion that nature was their teacher. Nature could liberate them from a past that had taught them to feel inferior. Americans believed, as Franklin did, in "improvement"; their projected independence, once they woke to the inevitability of it, would be an obvious improvement on political and cultural subjugation. Centering on the possibilities of the present and on dreams of the future, they prized change. They conceived an optimistic order and tried to convince themselves that they could sustain it.[4]

## THE IMPRESSIONABLE REVOLUTIONARIES

In the momentous year of America's birth as a union of states, a good many writers took as their subject the American dream—literally, the dream state. In February, for instance, the inventive and patriotic *Penn-*

*sylvania Magazine* published "The Dream of Irus," which set its scene in the remote past.⁵ Here was where great happenings could be chronicled and a time-bending destiny pursued in the guise of a literary exercise.

"O Happiness!" the unsigned piece began, in the stylized sentiment familiar in magazine columns for several decades, "thou object of universal desire, thou unknown deity, whom all men ignorantly worship; where shall I find thee, and in what temple art thou manifest to the children of the earth? Dost thou shine in the palace? Dost thou hide thyself in the cottage, or dost thou associate with mediocrity?" The quest for happiness was, of course, about purity of heart and, as always, coupled individual virtue with larger social virtues; the worth of America was an extension of the character of the people.

Irus conjures in his dream "a mighty prince" surrounded by nobles who "filled the air with acclamations of praise." He says to himself, "Surely this is a happy man," being as he is the beneficiary of constant attention and adulation. Depicting civil society in both intimate and august terms, Irus observes: "If one tender and faithful friend, can soothe the infelicities, and heighten the enjoyments of life, how happy he must be, who hath thus won the hearts of a whole nation! . . . Surely this good prince deserves a happiness that is unmixed."

In the next dream scene, another princely person, an "Asiatic sovereign" of handsome features, sits surrounded by "whatever could administer delight." Though a charming lady is by his side his countenance shows a gloom which neither love nor music can dispel, and a "nameless kind of wildness" in his eye suggests a restless mind. Suddenly an armed man rushes in and slays the sultan. "Alas," says Irus, "this man must certainly have been a monster of wickedness. Happiness can never be the portion of guilt!"

Then, an old woman, shriveled and emaciated, appears before his mind's eye. Insisting that she represents happiness itself, she relates the story of her life, of having dealt capriciously with her husband in her youth, inheriting his wealth but loving little or nothing in the world. Irus terms her happiness that of a "tyger or wolf." Then one vision melts into another, and Irus conjures up a pastoral village fed by a "chrystal stream" with a betrothed young couple beside it, "animated by a native and unaffected chearfulness," their marriage bed but a "thatched hovel." At first Irus imagines them happy, but their destitution proves him mistaken. Poverty cannot breed happiness.

Eventually the dreaming Irus sails through a cloud into a court of justice. A "celebrated pleader" moves the court, but Irus is able to discern that at that moment the orator's wife is in bed with another man. "How happy is this man, said *Irus*; he is deceived, indeed, but he derives from falsehood the same enjoyments as he could receive from truth." A recluse next appears, who allows that if "life is long with respect to pain, it is short with respect to pleasure." Now Irus is transported back to the city of the first prince. An androgynous flying creature settles above him, a phantom who, without warning, returns to the uncomplicated opening sentiments of the tale in order to pronounce its moral: health, virtue, moderation, and a conscience at peace are "never long, the lot of man." And so, if happiness is but an occasional thing, "he risks the loss of all, who departs from the simplicity of nature."

Irus's unfaithful visions were meant to remind readers that only nature provided self-evidence of truth. If they were disheartened by human complexities in such heated times, the bewildered and doubtful people had yet one recourse: to return to nature, to sample its curative power. Nature's laws of balance coincided with pure reason and revealed changeless moral properties. Only nature was perfectly effective and productive of happiness. Its consonance was the source of all goodness and beauty and purity and sympathy in the world, and inseparable from the individual's quest for knowledge.[6]

The search for happiness in this parable is a search for truth by way of discernment. In fact, though, Americans were uncertainly seeking consensus among themselves as they struggled to clarify their expectations with regard to Great Britain. When they labored over petitions and pamphlets in appealing to London, they divided their moral universe into terms of consistency and inconsistency, into what was real and what was chimera. Their common object was to know what conditions equated with justice and reasonableness. But this was extremely hard to do. In his fantastic travels Irus observes praise that is unreliable, charms that do not satisfy, a mind "not at rest," a "phantom," a lover's deception. Things are rarely as they seem.

The search for happiness and political harmony under existing circumstances required, of course, that language be understood. There was something almost surreal at times in Americans' perceptions of British intransigence. Experiencing repeated frustrations, Irus learns that understanding is elusive, that human communication is inevitably bent or flawed and that only self-discipline is rewarded. In the summer of 1775, when everything seemed to project frustration, Thomas Jefferson appealed to a loyalist he had grown up admiring: Virginia's attorney general John Randolph was about to return to England, and Jefferson urged him to talk sense to Britain's leaders. Looking with fondness toward a projected day of reconciliation, he hoped that London, even at this late date, would recover its wisdom. He bade Randolph contribute toward "expediting this good work" by outlining the way in which Crown appointees in the colonies had misrepresented the truth ("for what purposes I cannot tell") about American attitudes and intentions. Randolph should "undeceive" London and do "service to the whole empire." The letter appears in retrospect either a fanciful (and thus fruitless) stylized entreaty or else a telling example of misplaced optimism about the gulf separating Britain and her colonies.[7]

Jefferson thoughtfully applied Enlightenment principles to his optimistic American vision. This was a world governed by a generous nature. To realize its potential, people should strive to unite in celebration of eclecticism, tolerance, and pacifism, to defy absolutes and promote individuality and cosmopolitan values.[8] Ironically, while awe and power in nature excited the *philosophes'* nerves (to borrow language from the culture of sensibility), dreams were as unpalatable to them and to their investigative purpose as was religious faith. Classical Romans, who delighted eighteenth-century rationalists, had mocked the early Christians as fanatics but had responded to messages that came to them in dreams.[9] Could dreams, or parables related as dreams, or stylized delusions like Jefferson's in the letter to Randolph lead to self-knowledge and truth? Jefferson's fantasy of reconciliation, his prescription for social harmony, was a version of *The Pennsylvania Magazine*'s dream-borne literary fantasy wherein conflicts could be worked out without adverse consequences. The sentimental mind often yielded to wishfulness, as Jefferson did here, imagining that Randolph could influence the government in London to wake from its own distorted dream. He wrote to relieve his anxiety about war and, in his wishfulness, expressed the desire to know in advance how the story would play itself out, which, as Freud instructs, is a common feature of dreams.[10]

The Revolutionary American mind, then, exhibited a strikingly optimistic component that coexisted with tremendous (and not always exaggerated) fear. To Americans, Toryism was a perversion of moral principle that had to be reckoned with because it commanded a broad respect. The dream mode in the quest for happiness was one place of removal on which to stage drama that spoke to the human condition, that might narrow the gap that kept patriot and loyalist from understanding each other. In dreams the classical ideal of *humanitas* could be satisfied: the cultivated decency and refined aestheticism of the informed citizen, resolving to aid society through political activity. The practice of *humanitas* alone—the elevation of human endeavors to an unprecedented level of compassionate commitment—might make a person godlike. For enlightened thinkers, to attempt the same through mere reliance on faith in the deity was less pragmatic and perhaps even self-deceptive.[11]

In fact, though, by repudiating Britain's authority and withdrawing allegiance, the Revolutionaries presented an exacting majority will. They recognized the principle of an individual volitional allegiance (loyalism), but this did not make them merciful. The need to control enemies of the patriot cause prevailed in a host of legal cases; residents of the colonies subject to independent America's laws who dissented from them or levied war or committed espionage against the newly declared nation were prosecuted. Penalties ranged from fines to confiscation of property to execution for treason. Oaths tested citizens' loyalty.[12]

In 1776, a year of war in New England and the mid-Atlantic states, reality was all too menacing. Activity and passivity, perceptions of robustness and frailty, spirited generosity and obnoxious self-indulgence, each pair of opposites were invoked in military recruitment and training and in general political discourse, as in the dream quest.[13] It is not surprising that patriot leaders constantly urged fortitude upon their fellows, reminding all to attend to their moral duty and sacrifice private pleasure to the good of the community. At the heart of it all was feeling, assigning characteristics to the People of Feeling—that is, to a constructed American character.

There is no better parable to illustrate this keen consciousness than the enduring tale of a Connecticut captain. In 1776, twenty-one-year-old Nathan Hale, athletic and easygoing, was hanged by the British as a spy. Five of Hale's brothers had joined the Revolution with him, but only Nathan went on to martyrdom as the ideal of a patriot. Having been educated at Yale just before the war, he had taught school in New London, Connecticut, where he once gave an impassioned speech in favor of liberty and in support of the farmers who fought at Lexington. A short time later he joined Washington's army in Cambridge and took part in the siege of Boston; after the British abandoned that town in March 1776, he sailed with his comrades to New York, where fighting was next expected. Following the catastrophic Battle of Long Island in the summer, which nearly sank America's cause, Hale volunteered to serve as a spy, to ascertain British designs. He crossed lines, posing as an innocent schoolmaster, only to be captured at a guard post within a mile and a half of the American position after nearly fulfilling his mission. Possibly betrayed by a loyalist cousin, Hale was brought before General William Howe, whereupon he promptly acknowledged his role and his rank in the Continental Army. The following morning, he was executed. Composed, the onetime Yale debater "bore himself with gentle dignity" and went to the gallows after what a witness termed a "sensible and spirited speech," uttering as his final words: "I only regret that I have but one life to lose for my country." His body was left hanging, as a warning to the rebels.[14]

The committed and unselfish spirit of 1775–76, though far from secure, gained enough adherents to field an army. Patriots, as builders, found a place in their texts for every moral-historical moment. They wanted their majority to believe that as a distinct people they had attained a level of virtue previously unknown—or at least unknown since antiquity, a time that was almost dreamlike and from which they drew their models of public performance. Like Greek Stoics and Roman republicans, they might glean knowledge as they prized selfless deeds and moderated desires.

Another piece in *The Pennsylvania Magazine* subsequent to "The Dream of Irus" chronicled the history of dreams from the Old Testament to the present. It cautioned against falling prey to the ancient superstition which told that extraordinary visions in the sleeping state revealed truths to pious persons and were meant to be adopted by government. In the Enlightenment age of science and reason, enigmatic events had to be unraveled logically. A dream concerning fire related to a "redundancy of yellow bile." A dream of "stenches" connected to "some putrid matter in our bodies." A dream of falling predicted a bout with vertigo, "or other disorders in the head." And one who had overindulged at dinner could be expected to dream that "some heavy weight or animal is lying upon that part." In an age of self-evident truths, medical professionals discerned the "intimate connexion" between mind and body. Scientific observation of nature predominated as mysticism declined. Dreams could foretell, "without presupposing them to be sent from heaven."[15]

Another article, adjacent to this tribute to skepticism, bore a religious character, declaring that the "multitudes flocking to the formidable standard of the Thirteen United Colonies" needed to couple their armed crusade with proper Christian values. America was fighting for "the rights which God and nature have granted us." Already ragtag militiamen had embarrassed the world's greatest fighting force at Concord and Bunker Hill, and the new Continental Army led by General Washington had withstood the long siege of Boston. Was this not evidence that America's cause was the cause of God? "Yea heaven has given it the sanction of its approbation, by the amazing success which hitherto has attended it." It followed that only God-fearing behavior by each and every soldier would ensure complete success.[16]

American patriots, prudent, moderate people as they described themselves, would have seen nothing incompatible in these two magazine articles. Both expressed the calm, deliberative self-image of the Revolutionaries. A rational approach to dream interpretation assumed that the mind was not strictly mechanical, that the truth lay somewhere between ancient superstition and total skepticism. The Revolution, too, required faith and effective propaganda to unite sentiments. That is why, in need of support from all available sources of aid, patriots asserted that their cause was blessed by the ultimate arbiter of right.

Two years later Henry Laurens of Charleston, South Carolina, while serving as president of the Continental Congress, related a dream to the *Pennsylvania Packet*: "I have very little faith in dreams, but whenever those unaccountable visions of the night make such strong impressions upon the sensorium as to leave whole pages of what I dreamt I had read or heard, it is my practice to commit them in writing early in the morning." Attesting to the importance of newspaper reading in framing his opinions, he noted that he not only amused himself this way, "conversing with my neighbours about the times," but was capable of going into "deep reflection" while sitting evenings with his pipe and the news. Once, he reported, he fell asleep contemplating "the conduct of each of the United States, and of their representatives in Congress." In the dream he was visited by "a little fairy maid," who said to him, "Old Man, Virtue is its own reward," and vanished, leaving a detailed memorandum on the state of the ongoing war. As he imagined himself having finished reading this paper, the dozing Laurens let go his pipe from his hand. Its "clattering upon the floor" startled him, and he awoke. The conscious writer went on: "Now I am awake, let me, Mr. Printer, say what I should probably have dreamt had not the breaking pipe disturbed me." It was that Congress, "those who are appointed guardians of an infant empire, and with the most profound respect for the FREE CHOICE OF THE PEOPLE," should heed that its proceedings were being scrutinized by (signed) "An OLD MAN."[17]

Laurens's "pipe dream" was succeeded, in a sense, by another Revolutionary's impressionable encounter. Upon recovering from "break bone [mosquito-borne dengue] fever" in 1780, Dr. Benjamin Rush recorded that he had dreamt that a poor woman visited him to say that he should never lessen his commitment to his needy patients. The dreaming Rush was "worn out in attending poor people," and was counseling the woman to take her concerns to another doctor, when, lifting up her hands, she exclaimed, "O! Sir . . . you don't know how much you owe to your poor patients. It was decreed that you should die by the fever which lately attacked you, but the prayers of your poor patients ascended to heaven in your behalf, and your life is prolonged upon their account." This revelation, Rush insisted, "affected me so much that I awoke in tears. I have been as little disposed to superstitions as most men, and have often exposed the folly of being influenced by dreams, by explaining their cause by obvious physical principles. The dream I have related left a deep and lasting impression upon my mind." As a highly sensitized Revolutionary Man of Feeling, Rush represented this "impressionable" generation. Underlying moral causes and moral messages abounded.[18]

A final example of the wartime fantasy appealing to frightened but determined patriots was "Vision of the Paradise of Female Patriotism." Reminiscent of others' historically staged dream-borne projections, the female author of this 1779 article employed "the power of fancy, or perhaps it might have been a vision from above," to find strength. In the moonlit sky she conjured an awe-inspiring mountain, lifted her eye, and encountered a "winged youth, like a stream of light descending to the plain whereon I stood." This youth said to her, "I am the angel of *the paradise of female patriotism*," and bade her follow to "the abode of sisters." Making the difficult ascent, the dreamer found "a new day" in a garden (no accidental symbol) busy with "all the choice and refined souls that have burned with the love of country." They were queenly figures from the ancient world, Jewish, Greek, Spartan, and Roman. To the rising hill west of this garden, the angel explained, were "your country-women the Americans," from the "several states in the union of the empire." A "rapture" gripped the writer-dreamer's heart as she viewed this assembly, destined to join history's great and successful female patriots. It was just as "Mrs. John and Samuel Adams had advanced to me and I reached out my arms to embrace them" that the "strong passion with which I was agitated" woke her from her powerful reverie.[19]

Why should all this be important? By transcribing their dreams (as well as dreams that were not really dreams) the Revolutionaries found not only a guide to behavior but a realm of imagination in which to liberate themselves. They needed to remain convinced not only that their republican cause was defensible but that it was destined to capture the hearts of all those in the world who cherished human freedom. Their cause balanced reason with faith, the objectivity of philosophy with the subjectivity of politics. It ushered in the American notion—or expanded the myth introduced by the promoters of early English exploration and extended by the Puritans—that equated the idea of America with the promise of universal good. Dreams, in this manner, left "a deep and lasting impression," as Rush put it, making them more meaningful than vague meditations. Dreams contributed to Revolutionary faith. Patriots whose writings built a case on legal and social principles at the same time demanded an acceptance equal to and indistinguishable from religious conviction.

## FERVENCY OF SPIRIT, PROMPTITUDE OF ACTIONS

One contributor to *The Pennsylvania Magazine* new to American shores but bold in his prescription was Thomas Paine. The polemicist, a virtual unknown in his native England, bore a letter of introduction from Benjamin Franklin when he arrived in Philadelphia in the months before Lexington and Concord. In January 1776 his pamphlet *Common Sense* was printed, urging independence on what he assessed was a too cautious people, and it quickly became a best-seller across the colonies. Calling any connection between Great Britain and her colonies in essence a lie, Paine stated baldly what Jefferson in his letter to John Randolph danced around for apparent purposes of artfulness and civility: no dream could mask or reconfigure the truth. "Reconciliation is *now* a fallacious dream. Nature hath deserted the connexion, and Art cannot supply her place." It was "repugnant" to Paine to suppose that America stood to profit from subjection to an external power.[20]

Paine's ebullient prose was calculated to take patriots to a new level of commitment. Praising Americans' innate virtues, he declared in his opening section: "The cause of America is in a great measure the cause of all mankind." He invoked the metaphor of light to convey virtue and power at once: "The sun never shined on a cause of greater worth." Asserting that faith and honor prevailed among the American people, he showed that he trusted in affections: "Society . . . promotes our happiness *positively* by uniting our affections." And he associated Britain with an abandonment of all that was productive of affections, that nation having proved itself "false, selfish, narrow and ungenerous," neither a legitimate parent nor a creature of refined sensibility.[21]

Josiah Quincy, Sr., of Massachusetts had chosen similarly potent words some months earlier in a letter to Benjamin Franklin, not knowing that his own son and namesake, who had met Franklin while on a fruitless mission to England, would succumb to illness at sea en route home.

> As a dutifull Son, settled at a Distance from his Father's House considers it his *Home*: Have not the Colonies, in like manner considered England as their *Home*; and behaved towards the Parent State with most cordial and filial Affection? . . . Are we Bastards, and not Children, that a Prince, who is celebrated as the best of Kings, has given his Consent to so many and such unprecedented and oppressive Acts of Parliament, as if carried into Execution must eventually render the Condition of his *American Subjects* no better than the *Slaves* to his *British Subjects*?[22]

Quincy's poignant remarks demonstrate that affectionate memories, like wish-fulfilling dreams, informed the patriot community's current understanding of their hold on moral order, properly directed faith, and a germinating national honor.

What confusion persisted in the Anglo-American relationship was, to Paine, merely the result of kingly rule, which poisoned, which impoverished. "Of more worth is one honest man to society and in the sight of God," he wrote, "than all the crowned ruffians that ever lived." The king's title "FATHER OF HIS PEOPLE" was a "pretended" one, for no father could so "unfeelingly hear of their slaughter, and composedly sleep with their blood upon his soul." But unlike Quincy's gloomy recollection of the course of America's humiliation and the denial of affection from the unfeeling parent, Paine in *Common Sense* pursued the familial metaphor to project America's ultimate growth and health. It was "*now* the interest of America to provide for herself. She hath already a large and young family." And what of America's "infant" state? Far from being an argument against independence, "Youth is the seed time of good habits, as well in nations as individuals."[23]

For Paine, the "birthday of a new world" was at hand. America was to be the place of "asylum for the persecuted lovers of civil and religious liberty from *every part* of Europe." As soon as the legal voice of the people in Congress spoke honorably and firmly, the healthy infant would rise to its feet. The time had come, the pamphleteer prodded, to break free from that system ("monarchy and succession") which had only "laid . . . the world in blood and ashes." American independence was "the only BOND that can tye and keep us together" and banish "the schemes of an intriguing, as well, as a cruel enemy." Opportunity was embedded in bonds of affection and only awaited united action.[24]

Despite Paine's observation that the Continental Congress had been too polite to act on the "unexampled concurrence of sentiment" that united the colonies, not all Americans held their emotions in check. One member of Congress, the energetic planter and merchant Christopher Gadsden, returned home from Philadelphia and appeared at the South Carolina Provincial Congress in February 1776 carrying with him a bright yellow flag of his own design that featured a coiled rattlesnake poised to strike, with the motto below: "Don't tread on me"; and also a copy of Paine's freshly printed *Common Sense*. Gadsden placed the flag beside the chair of the president of the Provincial Congress, and he read from *Common Sense* after triumphantly (and prematurely, in the minds of most delegates) declaring for independence. One Charleston loyalist observed, "Gadsden is as mad with [*Common Sense*], as ever he was without it."[25]

Gadsden, educated in England, had always been more restless and more radical than most of his compatriots. During the Stamp Act crisis, he had befriended activist mechanics, and in 1766 he had written under the pseudonym "Homespun Free-man" advocating nonimportation. He had called for "Liberty or Death" well before Patrick Henry captured the popular imagination with that phrase. A 1770 Charleston broadside composed by "Rusticus" heralded Gadsden as a man of truth and a lover of liberty. His generous and sympathetic spirit emerged after Britain closed the port of Boston in 1774, when he contributed a shipload of rice to the beleaguered New England colony, cursing the "damned Machinations" of Parliament in a letter to Sam Adams. Now in 1776, the emotional South Carolinian ushered his reluctant neighbors along the road to independence. Even Henry Laurens, soon to be president of the Continental Congress, considered Gadsden a troublemaker and could not match his Revolutionary fervor. Gadsden was a particular kind of American—a brash man, a risk taker, lacking the appearance of moderation that most Revolutionaries cultivated. He spoke and wrote without reserve, schemed for private commercial success, and applied his natural passion to the cause of liberty. He believed in the spirit of 1776 with utter consistency, and he seemed to generate excitement wherever he went.[26]

Zealous John Adams was in his own way equally emotional. In diary entries of early March, as the British siege of Boston neared an end, he wrote:

> The Colonies are now much more warlike and powerfull than they were, during the last War. A martial Spirit has seized all the Colonies. They are much improved in Skill and Discipline. They have a large standing Army. They have many good officers. . . . Resentment is a Passion, implanted by Nature for the Preservation of the Individual. Injury is the Object which excites it. . . . It is the same with Communities. They ought to resent and to punish.

For Adams, an astute observer of human nature, passion spoke the language of reason. To receive "satisfaction" by contesting those who deliberately caused injury—a recourse dictated by the passions—was what secured liberty.[27]

The positive passion of patriotism found expression in many ways during the trials of this year of British advance and American military reverses. Lieutenant Joseph Hodgkins wrote to his wife during Washington's retreat from New York in the fall of 1776, "This was the first Time we had any chance to fite them and I doubt not if we should have another opportunity, but we should give them another Dressing." Exaggerating enemy casualties, he thanked "gods goodness" for carrying his comrades and him through the peril. After the same battle, the New York patriot and later U.S. Vice President George Clinton insisted that the "choicest troops" of the British were less brave than the Continental Army. He wished he had shot "a puppy of an Officer I found slinking off in the heat of the Action." An infantryman, Timothy Hancock, noted tauntingly, "Some of the Regulars Landed by Elezebeth Town to plunder and our men gave them a kind Reseption and killed and wounded several." The troops were emboldened.[28]

In an anonymous "Dialogue on Civil Liberty," very possibly written by Paine, three citizens debate: The first is so set afire by the unfolding Revolution that prudence and moderation are, to him, akin to treason. He admits that a "fervency of spirit" led him to a "promptitude of actions," but he equates his strong feelings with "first rate virtues" and happiness with patriotism: "A real patriot appears to me the most illustrious character in human life. Is not the interest and happiness of his fellow creatures his care? Can any thing be more noble? Is he not ready to sacrifice ease and indulgence, the sweetness of family connections, nay even fortune and life to the public good?" As in "The Speech of Logan" and Mackenzie's tale of Old Edwards's son, sympathy and generosity for one's fellow creatures sometimes make extreme actions excusable.[29]

The debater pursues his argument with relish. Civil liberty rests upon "the dignity of human nature" and the Lockean premise that human beings are born free and equal. "To usurp dominion over others, and reduce them to a state of dependence on absolute will, is a perversion of the order of providence, and high treason against the *majesty of human nature*." Because civil liberty stands as "the foundation of all earthly happiness," rebellion for the end of human happiness is not only good but necessary. The sanctifying example of antiquity underscored this reasoning: "What a difference between the carriage and language of a free citizen of Athens, or an austere and hardy Spartan, and that of a trembling and obsequious slave of the Persian monarch?" A catechism results: "Virtue and liberty go together." (Indeed, as Josiah Bartlett, signer of the Declaration of Independence from New Hampshire, put it on July 1 of that year: "The time is now at hand, when we shall see whether America has virtue enough to be free, or not.") Americans knew civil liberty as happiness, for they had been raised to it and called it by the name of English liberty. As the earnest citizen concludes, it is only "the prevalence of a mean self-interest" on London's part that has subverted that liberty and happiness and dictated a heated response.[30]

The second debater in the dialogue opposes these "pompous encomiums upon civil liberty," and urges more sense, less ardor. Virtue and happiness, he insists, do not equal civil liberty but merely "personal and internal" liberty. According to the great moralists, virtue "shines with the greatest lustre in, a suffering state." Liberty, alas, is not necessary for happiness, because virtue is possible for a slave: "Are the subjects of free governments generally happy and those of despotic governments miserable?" he asks rhetorically. Most subjects of arbitrary government are, in fact, no less pleased with their lives than any freer person.

The third debater smiles at the "warmth" of the first and the "ingenuity" of the second, then demonstrates that virtue and happiness are easier to obtain under freedom than under coercive rule. Returning to the familial metaphor so as to highlight natural growth processes and celebrate America's health, he observes: "Liberty is a fruitful parent, teeming with her countless offspring; slavery is the savage and barren mother, followed by a thin and meager progeny." The panicky language of the Stamp Act crisis may have continued to sound alarm, but in light of the patriots' towering commitment to the ideal that human dignity must endure, their language was by now more confident and cleverly presented. They had premonitions as well as dreams to guide them to decisions.

Given the intensification of debate concurrent with the escalation of armed conflict, independence appeared inevitable. In April, not yet knowing the task his friend would soon be given, Jefferson's closest confidant from youth, John Page, wrote to him in Philadelphia: "For God's sake declare the Colonies independent at once, and save us from ruin."[31] Benjamin Rush recorded that the seventy-year-old philosopher-statesman Benjamin Franklin was as dismissive as Paine of the notion that cooler heads were needed to recover the once comfortable attachment to the Crown: "He was a firm Republican, and treated kingly power at all times with ridicule and contempt. He early declared himself in favor of Independance."[32] On June 7, Richard Henry Lee of the Virginia delegation submitted a resolution for action by the Continental Congress, proposing that "these United Colonies are, and of right ought to be, free and independent States, that they are absolved from all allegiance to the British Crown, and that all political connection between them and the State of Great Britain is, and ought to be, totally dissolved." Lee then returned to Williamsburg to tend to his ailing wife, and his thirty-three-year-old colleague Jefferson was selected to put Lee's resolve on paper.[33]

On June 14, as Jefferson was laboring over his solemn Declaration in Philadelphia, the Pennsylvania Assembly met. It was on the eve of its own extinction, to be replaced by a convention called to form a new state constitution. Under these hazy circumstances, the Assembly issued a declaration of its own, rhetorically still hoping for a "secure and honourable peace," but putting happiness before reconciliation: "The Happiness of these Colonies has, during the whole Course of this fatal Controversy, been our first Wish. Their Reconciliation with Great-Britain our next." The impending step was a foregone conclusion.[34]

Echoing the noble spirit of that season, the even-tempered Henry Laurens dispatched a letter to his son John, then in London but due to forsake a comfortable life in order to return home and serve as an aide to General Washington. "God grant that our success may work the happiness of both parties," he wrote with generosity, "that out of seeming Evil, solid good may grow. I triumph not, in Britain's blushes; when an Englishman bleeds, I feel the blow; when my Mother Country, my old friend suffers disgrace, I droop." One paragraph later, touched by his son's previous "declarations of affection & Duty," the elder Laurens assured the young man that his patriotic "Piety" would "yield a luxury of happiness, of which you can now form but imperfect Ideas." He allowed that he "would rather Die or even hear of your Death, than, from tenderness or from any motive, command you basely to shun danger by refraining from your Duty, . . . Duty to yourself, to your Father, to your family, to your Country." Pleased with his son's determination, he avowed: "No Man loves his Country more than I do. . . . I would give up All, I think, I would give up my Children to save my Country."[35] Ironically, after succeeding John Hancock as president of the Continental Congress, Laurens was captured at sea and imprisoned in the Tower of London until the Battle of Yorktown convinced the British to give up trying to prevent American independence. John, the chivalrous son, helped to negotiate his father's return in exchange for the defeated Cornwallis, but then forfeited his own life in an undistinguished action against remnant British troops in his native South Carolina in 1782.


## THE PURSUIT OF HAPPINESS


Americans across the United Colonies read or were read the Declaration of Independence in the days following its adoption by Congress. There were parades, and, at least in New York's Provincial Congress, "animated shouts" accompanied the official reading. In Savannah, Georgia, patriots undertook four separate readings and the firing of cannon. In Philadelphia on July 8, bells rang out "all Day and almost all night." Bonfires lit the night sky and the windows of houses lined up illuminated candles. In Massachusetts, the provincial government directed ministers of every denomination to read the Declaration to their parishioners "as soon as divine Service is ended . . . on the first Lord's-Day after they shall receive it."[36] Timothy Hancock, the New Hampshire enlistee who had weathered the siege of Boston and was transported by sea to New York, noted dryly on July 8: "Nothing Very Strange only Heir I would remark that the fourth of this Instant it was Resolved and pased in Congress that Amarica is an independent State." On the evening of the 9th, he added, "the kings Immage was thrown Down and His Head Cut of[f] and Carred in A wheele Barrow to general Worshenton with A file of men round it."

Jefferson's Declaration of Independence,[37] a covenant containing America's most fundamental principles, was drafted to make the union of the colonies official and to explain separation in terms of the right of self-defense under the laws of nature. The document begins by announcing the determination of "one people," who are cognizant of their separateness "among the powers of the earth," to clarify a sense of their just rights. It ends by introducing a previously unused combination: "the United States of America."

The crux of Jefferson's argument is a people's right to government that ensures their "life, liberty, and the pursuit of happiness" and (in the same paragraph) "safety and happiness." After exhausting all reasonable efforts toward an amicable solution, Americans had found British cruelty and destructiveness insufferable. Whether their life-affirming truths were "sacred and undeniable" (as Jefferson marked in his original draft) or "self-evident" (as altered by a fellow committee member, presumed to be Franklin) it remained that life and liberty and safety and happiness were joined in a deliberate and binding fashion. Issues of physical and moral security resonated equally in the general hazard that British brutality posed. Intellectualization of Anglo-American conflict and revelation of Americans' most powerful sentimental assumptions were indistinguishable elements combining to proclaim the Declaration's expectations.

Life, liberty, and the pursuit of happiness: though each succeeding generation has understood the elements of this trio differently, the intriguing climax of the phrase has always seemed the most problematic. The phrase "pursuit of happiness" springs from Locke's *Essay Concerning Human Understanding*, a text the Revolutionary leaders knew well,[38] with its subsections titled "A constant Determination to a Pursuit of Happiness, no Abridgment of Liberty" and "The Necessity of pursuing true Happiness, the Foundation of Liberty." To Locke, liberty and "true" or "solid" happiness were fulfilled by each other; that is, a happiness built on "the highest Perfection of intellectual Nature" was "the necessary Foundation of our *Liberty*." Humans could construct a selfish "imaginary" happiness, but that would only be a happiness removed from nature. It was intellectual and moral judgment, rather than an intrinsic sense or the sympathetic imagination, that Locke associated with the pursuit of happiness. Minimizing the primacy of social affections or sympathetic connections in the mind's construction of happiness, he contended that the pursuit of happiness, "our greatest good," compelled individuals to address to the faculty of reason (the unemotional component of the mind) the question of whether "our Desire" was consistent with "our real Happiness." This is why, as crucial as his conceptions were, Locke could not have represented the sole philosophical basis of America's birth certificate.[39]

Regarding happiness as the "greatest good" in turn dated to Aristotle, who termed it a "higher good" than even virtue. Happiness was "prosperity" *combined with* virtue, and here prosperity suggests the health and wholeness of the polity without which happiness could not be nurtured. No faculty was so desirable to Aristotle as rational, scientific-investigative, or contemplative pleasure. He could write of happiness as something that contributed strength and nobility to the human condition ("activity of the soul in accordance with virtue . . . in a complete life") without sentimentalizing his description.[40]

To Locke even more than Aristotle, pursuing happiness or "true Felicity" was a restrictive process. It demanded "Caution, Deliberation, and Wariness," making certain that "the Satisfaction of Desire does not interfere with our true Happiness." One suspended desire in order to achieve happiness. Another way of putting it is that governing one's passions furthered the cause of liberty and happiness: "Forbearance of a too hasty Compliance with our Desires, the Moderation and Restraint of our Passions," allowed free examination and provided "Reason unbiassed" to reach those judgments on which "true Happiness" depended. In sum, to Locke and to the eighteenth-century mind, the pursuit of happiness rested on moral consistency, sound reasoning. In readily acknowledging their positive passion, America's Revolutionaries in 1776 added a new ingredient to this mixture.[41]

The Anglican clergyman and sentimental novelist Laurence Sterne, a confirmed Lockean whose influence on Jefferson as a humanist and moralist was profound, helped to define that positive passion. In the first of his published *Sermons*, titled "Inquiry After Happiness," he offered the following words: "The great pursuit of man is after happiness; it is the first and strongest desire of his nature;—in every stage of his life, he searches for it, as for hid treasure." (Trying to locate hidden treasure might be seen figuratively as the fulfillment of a dream quest, too.) Importantly, Sterne saw the pursuit of happiness in terms of good-humored, as opposed to rigid, morality. In his *Sermons* as well as his fiction, the value of human life derived from a combination of self-scrutiny, altruism, and public spirit, qualities that Americans since Franklin had been vocally promoting. Indeed, the only section of Locke's *Essay* he quibbled with was that asserting Judgment's superiority to Wit or Imagination; Sterne could not see absenting the heart from any deliberation on happiness. And Jefferson, revealingly, was to credit Sterne's writings as "the best course of morality that ever was written."[42]

There appears to be an even more immediate influence on Jefferson's particular phrasing in the Declaration. He may well have opted to reiterate the Lockean language only after reading a draft of fellow Virginian George Mason's Declaration of Rights. Mason's final draft was submitted to that state for consideration on June 12 and contained these words: "That all men are by nature equally free and independent, and have certain inherent rights, of which, when they enter into a state of society, they cannot, by any compact, deprive or divest their posterity; namely, the enjoyment of life and liberty, with the means of acquiring and possessing property, and pursuing and obtaining happiness and safety."[43]

Given that a relatively small circle of legal thinkers and philosophic writers, equally challenging and precedent-seeking, and all politically active, circulated their letters, pamphlets, petitions, and newspaper columns among friends and colleagues, repetition of this kind is to be expected. In any case, Jefferson's "pursuit of happiness," both Lockean and Sternean, understood the obligation that accompanied freedom. It demanded deliberation before delivering pleasure. It placed self-examination before self-realization. And it coupled an awareness of individual variation with preservation from that homogenization of personality which tyrannical regimes and other "lethargic" societies seemed fated to produce.

Thus Jefferson's "pursuit of happiness" implied a recognition of both human potential and human limitations. People were born equal but with noteworthy differences. While they shared a certain nobility of character, they achieved less or more on the basis of their individual self-cultivation. This process could not be merely an intellectual one, however. The acquisition of knowledge was, to use an expression of which he was fond in his personal correspondence, a "sublime delight."

To Aristotle, Locke, Sterne, Jefferson, and a host of others, happiness drew upon a bright and lively virtue. It was cumulative, active, conscious, and apparent. In Revolutionary America in 1776 it was meant to arise from a general commitment to the lives of others and to produce a proud, expansive, generous-spirited nation.

The shy but profoundly sentimental Jefferson was particularly suited to compose this document. Caught in a discordant haze of social unrest and grisly combat, the new nation required words that expressed faith in the future. Jefferson was imbued with a spirit of optimism beyond that of most of his peers. He regarded corruptibility as the lamentable tendency of an effete and selfish minority, to be checked by the virtuous feelings pouring forth from a more chaste, educable citizenry, nurtured by the morally uplifting climate of an easily fantasized America, a land and a society still under construction. To Jefferson, America remained fresh. He could express this confidence because he believed that its people were less encumbered by the weight of the bloody and monarchical European past and grounded in an enduring love of liberty. He believed in the power of his own words with an uncommon and contagious enthusiasm; again, it is important to remember that in Jefferson's original draft of the Declaration he called the pursuit of happiness one element of a truth that was "sacred," emotionally richer than the merely axiomatic "self-evident." Jefferson's secular catechism was designed to solidify his faith in a moral civilization, to give substance to the idea of America.[44]

That America had to be united in an unbreakable metaphorical band for victory to ensue. "A country poet" published in the *Virginia Gazette* a testament to the singular "voice" and wedded "sentiment" of the Virginia legislature:

> AMERICANS num'rous as sand
> And owners of a boundless land,
> While joined in unions golden band
> Can live without you* or your king.

*Virginia's royal governor, Lord Dunmore, and the British general William Howe.

Virginians spoke with one voice, doing their part to strengthen the circular band of union.[45] In 1776 the Continental Congress also issued paper currency that exhibited the bands of union. Worth one-sixth of a dollar, this bill featured a circle formed of thirteen interlocked rings, each with the name of a state printed on it.

The band of union required heart, affection, unselfish feeling. A short time after independence was declared, an unknown engraver produced a variation on this motif, a print consisting of thirteen chain-linked hands forming a circle. In the center of the print was a beating heart warmed by the glow of a slender candle. The verse inscribed below it restated what a people already invested in an armed struggle for over a year still believed—that the Revolution was heart-driven. Underdogs in a determined contest with the world's most ambitious power, Americans were "Warm'd by one Heart, united in one band." Strength of heart was more important than force of arms. To the personified Era (a "glorious Era" began with adoption of the Declaration on July 4), the anonymous versifier attested:

> With Virtue fir'd
> Thy injured Sons of America aspir'd
> to raise thy sinking Head.

The reverse of the engraving reads:

> The Thirteen States united in one Ring
> Join heart to hand and Independence sing.[46]

Standing up to Britain and standing apart from the rest of the world, Americans pronounced their principles and maintained that liberty was worth dying for. John Adams, who along with Franklin had at least an editor's hand in Jefferson's Declaration, wrote to his wife, Abigail, the day after its submission to Congress that this "Day of Deliverance . . . ought to be solemnized with Pomp and Parade" and include "Guns, Bells, Bonfires and Illuminations from one End of this Continent to the other from this Time forward forever more." Knowing the trials yet to come, aware of the "Toil and Blood and Treasure, that it will cost Us to maintain this Declaration," he nonetheless perceived "through all the Gloom . . . the Rays of a ravishing Light and Glory." The crusty Adams, who would not always express such confidence in the fate of his people, was sanguine at this point. In the end, he wrote, "Posterity will Tryumph," and the rays of a spreading glory—light and warmth—would preserve the virtues of the Revolution for future generations of Americans.[47]

Meanwhile, the euphony of the phrase "pursuit of happiness" was growing so infectious that the state constitutions of Pennsylvania (1776), New Jersey (1776), Virginia (1776), New York (1777), Vermont (1777), Massachusetts (1780), and New Hampshire (1784) all adopted it, borrowing either Jefferson's construction or Mason's language from the Virginia Declaration of Rights. Though irregularly retained in state constitutional conventions over ensuing decades, the comparable phrases "safety and happiness," "interest and happiness," "happiness and prosperity," and "protection, safety, and happiness" would be asserted as citizens' rights over the next century and beyond, in states from Mississippi to Montana.[48]

## INVASIONS FROM WITHOUT AND CONVULSIONS WITHIN

America could not be a "satellite," Paine asserted in *Common Sense*, when its territory was so much larger than the "planet" it was meant to orbit: "In no instance hath nature made the satellite larger than its primary planet, and as England and America, with respect to each other, reverses the common order of nature, it is evident they belong to different systems: England to Europe, America to itself." America's situation in 1776 was ideal, he said further. It was not so populous that its defense could not be easily coordinated: "The more sea port towns we had, the more we should have both to defend and to loose [sic]. Our present numbers are so happily proportioned to our wants, that no man need be idle." Land and people harmonized; America exuded health.

"It is not in numbers," Paine assured, "but in unity, that our great strength lies." For this recent immigrant to American shores, his personal asylum, the asylum for the "fugitive" freedom, was at the moment of "ripeness and fitness" for independence.[49]

Paine's extraordinary optimism masked the evidence, for the colonists' "great strength" was clearly not military. America's real challenge lay on the ground. As Liberty was a defenseless goddess requiring the vigilant care of a virtuous citizenry, so the continent of America was similarly passive, a land as "ripe and fit" for invasion as it was for independence. To personify a generous and yielding land as feminine was not new, but during the Revolution this came to represent more, given the very real possibility that invading armies would wreak devastation.[50]

On the eve of independence, the state of the war was unpromising. Early zeal exceeded discipline, and initial successes were followed by a train of defeats. After Lexington and Concord, Ethan Allen's hardy band of Vermonters were joined by Connecticut's Benedict Arnold, marching without long deliberation on Fort Ticonderoga, which they easily captured. From that strategic garrison overlooking Lake Champlain, ambitious fighters from New York and New England launched a hasty, somewhat overconfident expedition against Canada, led by General Richard Montgomery and Colonel Arnold. The preemptive attack, aiming to win French support for the Revolutionary cause, was halted at Quebec. The Americans' death toll was high, and included the loss of the general. Meanwhile, the redcoats occupying Boston were unable to break through Washington's encircling forces, which had been strengthened by the emplacement of cannon captured at Ticonderoga. They departed in March 1776, sailed for Halifax, Nova Scotia, and descended upon New York Harbor in late June, at which point they numbered some thirty thousand, including the fearsome Hessian (German) mercenaries. While the Continental Congress readied itself to proclaim the Declaration of Independence, Washington's army was divided between Manhattan and Long Island, preparing to face the invasion that finally came in late August. The Americans were routed at the Battle of Long Island, and the British continued to prove their armed superiority in a series of engagements. By October, Washington was driven completely from New York City and, disheartened by defeat, retreated to New Jersey. The volunteers who remained under his command slept outside in tents as winter blew in.

Timothy Hancock, who referred to the British regulars as "our cruel and unnattaral Enemy," feared the Germans even more. After skirmishing with Hessian mercenaries just north of New York City, he wrote in his diary: "the Hessians took three of our men and one made his Escape and by His acount they poot the other to Emedeate Death as their Custom is." Hancock's men were later able to recover some of what the Hessians plundered, only reconfirming the widespread belief that the invaders were pillagers who lacked conscience and humanity and bore no attachment to the land.[51] On British-occupied Long Island, predatory forces abused innocent citizens. A Connecticut militia commander, Gold Sellek Silliman, placed guards along the southern coast of his state to keep watch for Long Island-based raiders. He and his wife wrote her father that the British were anchored offshore, "to get something or other that is fresh to eat, for they have devoured every Thing that can be eat that is fresh on L. Island." Sharing her husband's concern that "deluded, infatuated, bewitched Tories," as brothers, fathers, sisters, and sons, were "so interwoven with Friends to our Cause," Mary Fish Silliman lived in fear of her loyalist neighbors, writing to her son that "we have so many Tory *Enemies* and we expect to be plundered."[52] Satirical John Trumbull, also of Connecticut, published the first canto of his mock-epic *M'Fingal* in 1776; his "Great 'Squire M'Fingal" was a loyalist and imagined scion of the ministerial corrupt breed back in England who would "Enslave th' American wildernesses, / And tear the provinces in pieces."[53]

The New York Mechanics organization asserted on May 29 that their "beloved continent" contained "fruitful fields" which had "made the world glad," in making Britain "rich by our commerce." Yet now, George III only took "pleasure in our destruction." The land was inviting to the long esteemed, lately perverted, mother country, suddenly identified as a predatory nation. Residents of Charles County, Maryland, noted: "Decent, dutiful, and sincere petitions . . . giving every assurance of our affection and loyalty," had only resulted in "an increase of insult and injury." Virginia's patriots bemoaned the "increased insult, oppression, and a vigorous attempt to effect our total destruction." In August, a North Carolinian taunted:

> That George is no more
> King of this fertile shore,
> From whence he drew his store,
> Completes our joy.[54]

The notion that the invader would consume the natural wealth of the land heightened resolve and found its way to prominent expressions of patriotic sentiment. The Declaration of Independence presents this potent image: "He [George III] has . . . sent hither swarms of officers to harass our people and eat out their substance." If the land and the body of the people were one, then the occupiers who came in hungry "swarms," who would "harass" (exhaust) a healthy place and "eat out" the "substance" that derives from that place, by definition denied to the residents a right to their plentiful exertions.

The Declaration lists additional examples of crimes against the people of the land. It accuses the king: "He has dissolved representative houses repeatedly, for opposing, with manly firmness, his invasions on the rights of the people." Here, with "manly firmness" against insensitive "invasions," Americans had sought to protect exposed sensibilities. Nature-given rights were threatened by physical attack. In the next paragraph the dominant metaphor is at once military and medical: Vulnerable states are said to remain "exposed to all the dangers of invasions from without and convulsions within." These "invasions" were literal, armed attacks from outside which contributed to strengthening the Tory disease festering within. The body of the country had to act to save itself.

From this point in the text there is nothing metaphorical anymore. Verbs are harsh and direct: "He has plundered our seas, ravaged our coasts, burned our towns, and destroyed the lives of our people." The euphonic phrasing has real authority as it proceeds to an almost dumb-founded tone of exasperation: "He is at this time transporting large armies of foreign mercenaries to complete the works of death, desolation, and tyranny already begun with circumstances of cruelty and perfidy scarcely paralleled in the most barbarous ages, and totally unworthy of the head of a civilized nation." Introducing onto the land foreign mercenaries who had no feeling for it was an obvious abuse, a barbarity further heightened by the king's willingness to compel a certain group of Americans to violate their own land: "He has . . . taken [them] captive" on the high seas and forced them to "bear arms against their country, to become the executioners of their friends and brethren. . . ." Whether or not it was the king himself who most demonstrably embraced such policies, Jefferson's rhetoric required this recitation.

The conspiracy against the land reintensifies: "He has excited domestic insurrection among us, and has endeavored to bring on the inhabitants of our frontiers the merciless Indian savages, whose known rule of warfare is an undistinguished destruction of all ages, sexes, and conditions." (This was a twisted recitation of the history of white-Indian combat, but useful propaganda. It assumed that the Indians had voluntarily surrendered any title they might have had to the land.) Despite having "reminded" Britain repeatedly of "the circumstances of our emigration and settlement here"—free, voluntary, and lawful possession of the land—these invasions, and the "long series of abuses and usurpations" listed earlier, had persisted. Destruction of the land contrasted plainly with the contemporary emphasis on progressive, constructive dreams. Revealing the intense emotion Jefferson intended the document to expose, he included a long paragraph on the slave trade, the "cruel war against human nature," that the king had sanctioned. The unfeeling monarch, giving sway to "piratical" merchants, easily violated the rights of "a distant people who never offended him" while inhibiting colonial legislatures from restraining commerce in human chattel. At the same time Jefferson unabashedly announced, without suggesting the virtue of emancipation, that the king was bribing America's slaves with freedom, if they took up arms against their rebellious masters. This section of Jefferson's Declaration clearly placed the ruling race of Americans on grounds that were morally suspect and so, ostensibly in deference to the sensitivity of less expansive-minded Southerners, Congress edited it out entirely.[55]

Declaring independence on Jefferson's terms (and as reworked by Congress) was not only designed to convince the world that America's cause was morally just. It was an essential act if the land was to be preserved for future generations of Americans, for whom the sanctity of the land and liberty and happiness were inseparable.

# CHAPTER FIVE

# ACTUATED BY A VIGILANT AND MANLY SPIRIT: 1777–88

THE WAR WAS GOING badly for General Washington's forces when sixteen-year-old Ebenezer Fletcher of New Ipswich, New Hampshire, joined the Continental Army as a fifer in 1777. The teenager was involved in the failed American attempt to prevent the British recovery of Fort Ticonderoga that year, when he was shot in the back, captured, and imprisoned. "Some of the enemy were kind," he noted, "while others were very spiteful and malicious." An "old negro" took his fife; a doctor gently sought to persuade him "to list in the King's service." Even when a pair of supercilious officers repeated this invitation, "telling me they were sure to conquer the country," the prisoner staunchly declined. It was shortly after this incident that, despite a painful wound, the fifer fled his captors and endured the trials of the northern New England forest: stalkings by wolves, possible starvation, constant fears of recapture. Recounting the dangers of his mini-odyssey over mountainous terrain was meant to highlight the independent spirit of the commonly courageous patriot soldier and to demonstrate that American purity must be reinforced through trials.[1]

There is something else of interest in Fletcher's brief narrative. Perilous navigation in an invaded land—"darkness of the night," bewilderment and loss of direction, the approach of "howling beasts"—frames an anxious morality tale in which principled republican conversation ultimately restores the prisoner to the world of his friends. He must preserve himself in the wild, convince others to spare him, and identify good and sympathetic as well as sinister and untrustworthy people. In telling his story, Fletcher relates informative encounters with "surly" Tories speaking an "insolent language," enemy-allied Indians who "abused me with their language," and "patient and mild" farmers who "received me kindly," who were "friendly and much concerned," and who proved themselves patriotic.[2]

Fletcher's obscure tale can be placed alongside the widely read narrative of the more distinguished Ethan Allen of neighboring Vermont. After dramatically capturing Fort Ticonderoga, the impulsive Allen was taken prisoner during the ill-conceived incursion into Canada. When he returned to Vermont, he wrote of his two and a half years' confinement in *A Narrative of Colonel Ethan Allen's Captivity* (1780), which went through eight editions before the 1783 signing of the Treaty of Paris, which acknowledged American independence. The *Narrative* was Allen's testament to the persistence of patriotism among prisoners of war; he asserted American valor and endurance and magnified British and Tory atrocities. In the words of his biographer Michael Bellesilles, he wrote "one of the war's most virulent denunciations of British character, a popular call for continued struggle against the British beast," pitting "a decadent, overcivilized culture against a natural, uncorrupted America."[3]

Language once again served to distinguish Americans' moral position and to point, more generally, to American excellence. Confirming plain Timothy Hancock's hostile impression, the emotional Allen charged in his *Narrative* that the Hessians who fought alongside the "merciless Britons" were "sent to America for no other design but cruelty and desolation." Gloriously, America's "injured little republic" was sustained thanks to camaraderie among prisoners. "Hollow groans saluted my ears," he wrote of their suffering. "I have seen whole gangs of tories making derision, and exulting over the dead, saying there goes another load of damned rebels."[4]

Ethan Allen's "barbarous captivity" softened once he was paroled from a New York jail to British-held Long Island, though his restlessness, his drinking, and his eagerness to retell the story of the capture of Ticonderoga led his captors to consider him mad. Like Fletcher, Allen had refused to switch sides, even with bribes of a colonelcy in a loyalist regiment and substantial acreage in his beloved Vermont. The leader of the Green Mountain Boys was proud, even boastful, of his rustic independence. Seen through the popular *Narrative*, Allen and his fellow prisoners expressed, according to Bellesilles, "a deep democratic conviction which persisted in the face of the harshest adversity." They were "bright, egalitarian, physically courageous, and graceful under pressure."[5]

In Ethan Allen's lexicon, as much as in Ebenezer Fletcher's perception and Thomas Paine's contemporary writings, the Revolution could no longer be seen as a mere family dispute. Patrick Henry wrote his fellow Virginian Richard Henry Lee that the enemy deserved to be "deluged with blood, or thoroughly purged by a revolution which shall wipe from existence the present king with his connexions, and the present system."[6] Americans were English no more.

## DAILY ACQUIRING STRENGTH AND CONSISTENCY

After the Declaration of Independence, the tone of public writing on the subject of happiness became more optimistic, less severe in its reminders of the elusiveness of earthly bliss. Happiness, in fact, was most readily associated with the privilege of being a Revolutionary American.

Propagandists for the Revolutionary cause were eager to provide tangible definitions and to characterize the immediate effects of Revolutionary commitment. In this ideal picture of life as a citizen of America, individuals of promise were elevated to desirable positions in the public service under a solid republican government. "We regard it as our great happiness in these United States," wrote Hugh Henry Brackenridge in the introduction to his *United States Magazine*, "that the path to office and preferment, lies open to every individual. The mechanic of the city, or the husbandman who ploughs his farm by the river's bank, has it in his power to become, one day, the first magistrate of his respective commonwealth, or to fill a seat in the Continental Congress." The magazine's "maxims for republics" related the essential truth that "we judge the *principles* of a government by our *feeling*"—the particular province of this people—while "men of education and reflection," by "*reason*," determined the "*form*" that government takes.[7]

Greatness could not be achieved in any polity until the people were happy. "A Citizen of C[hester] C[ounty]" wrote to the *Pennsylvania Gazette*: "The true greatness and happiness of rulers are inseparable from the greatness and happiness of their people." The smallest part of the citizenry cannot suffer, he said, but that the whole must be hurt as well. "Rulers and governors are called the fathers of their country, and may justly merit that glorious title, by never attempting to build their own happiness on any other foundation than the happiness of their people." "CATO," in the same newspaper, claimed that the patriotic impulse was rooted in a natural "passion" to preserve the human species: "There is in the souls of men a certain attractive power, which leads them intensely to associate, and to concert the plan of their common happiness."[8]

Life in the Continental Army presented temptations and tested that attractive power. The *Virginia Gazette* openly exhorted the volunteers, even before they saw battle, to resist vice for the sake of self and nation. Facing death, it explained, could cause a man to turn from religion to a "voluptuous life" that "not only loads the soldier's conscience with guilt, but makes the hardships he must undergo more grievous. . . . The dangers to which the soldier is exposed, makes a religious life the more necessary. His time of parading our streets, rioting in taverns, and enjoying the luxuries of our cities, will soon be over." And when he should prepare to march into battle, he faced the choice of finding his courage from "insensibility" like a "bull-dog" or from "rational motives," understanding "the worth of life." The general fear of the natural passions getting out of hand again elicited a profusion of cautionary texts.[9]

Significantly, this exhortation to soldiers was immediately followed by verse from the pen of an "unfortunate" young lady seduced by a "faithless lover"—a stock evocation of the Richardsonian model. She cries out her fate, an "endless infamy," and urges others of her sex to show care and discernment. "Sorrow and shame were written on my heart," she mourns pathetically. "Life from the great, the rich, the happy flies, / But grief's immortal, and it never dies." While soldiers were known to be drawn to wantonness, the exemplary Man of Feeling served as the alternative; Harley's virtuous character and generous spirit guide him and protect him from temptation; obliged to interact with "sharpers" in a lurid part of town, he does not become like them, nor can he ignore the plight of a miserable prostitute, instead reclaiming the worthy young woman with the power of his own goodness and self-restraint. Like the captivity narratives of Fletcher and Allen, printed admonitions to turn away from the "voluptuous life" told American soldiers what was expected of them if they were to live up to the model of Revolutionary fortitude.[10]

The unoccupied soldiers' morals aside, during the precarious years 1776–77 militiamen and Continental soldiers alike exhibited the stubborn individuality that long persisted in the character of rebellious young Americans. Officers who tried to enforce conformity in dress and appearance did not succeed. Difficult to discipline, the young patriots grew their unruly hair over their foreheads and wore "earcurls" rather than the short, straight look the army demanded; they did this in part because it appealed to young women. One soldier's tune went:

No Foreign Slaves shall give us Laws, No Brittish Tyrant Reign
Tis Independence made us Free and Freedom We'll
   Maintain. . . .
Each hearty Lad shall take his Lass all Beaming Like a Star
And in her softer arms Forget the Dangers of the war.[11]

These brash and increasingly rugged troops displayed a resistance to regimentation that bears out the later evolving myth of the pioneer hero. Yet, as Charles Royster has explained, the Revolutionaries had so propagandized Americans' inherent virtue that living up to the ideal amid war proved trying. They had to adjust through compromise: they pretended not to fear (their "natural" courage had been greatly exaggerated after Lexington and Concord), and they pretended to deserve independence purely on the basis of disinterestedness and benevolence: "They preferred to believe that they were achieving or would soon achieve . . . the fullness of their ideals."[12]

Despite corruption, desertion, and intersectional squabbling, not to mention persistent camp diseases, the Americans fought well and experienced some shining moments of battlefield glory. They trudged through snow and hail and mud to bring General Washington victories at Trenton and Princeton around New Year's Day 1777; the army's suddenly brightened prospects encouraged critically needed recruitment. The temporary loss of Philadelphia that fall was offset by decisive victories over the British (marching south from Canada) at Bennington, Vermont, and in the upper portions of New York State. Generals Horatio Gates and Benedict Arnold combined to force the surrender of British general John Burgoyne and some six thousand of his troops at Saratoga, New York, in October. This event convinced France to enter the war on America's side.

National loyalty felt real and palpable at even the most apprehensive moments. Lieutenant Colonel John Brooks wrote in his journal for January 1778: "Our poor brave fellows . . . bare-footed, bare-legged, bare-breeched . . . no men ever shew more spirit or prudence than ours. In my opinion nothing but Virtue has kept our Army together through this campaign. There has been that great Principle, the love of our Country, which first called us into the field, and that only to influence us."[13] This kind of sentiment was expressed at all levels. When Congress proposed that he go to France to negotiate peace in 1782, Thomas Jefferson told his friend Benjamin Rush, according to the latter, that "he would go to hell to serve his country." Just as revealing is Rush's characterization of the traitorous Benedict Arnold, hero of Saratoga, who in 1780 attempted to sell the Hudson River stronghold of West Point to the British. Rush had lodged with Arnold for three weeks in 1777 and presumed to know him well: "His conversation was uninteresting and his pronunciation vulgar. I once heard him say 'his courage was acquired, and that he was a coward till he was 15 years of age.' His character in his native State, Connecticut, was never respectable, and hence its vote alone was withheld from him when he was created a general by the Congress."[14]

Rush needed to vilify Arnold not only in order to promote a republican interpretation of American history but also to identify character with the inevitable triumph of good. In demonstrating his failure to embrace the proper sentiment, the traitor had lost or forfeited his moral connection to the community. His vulgarity and lack of respectability were (in retrospect) easily verifiable. Americans could see him as a "freak," an aberration of nature. Though Arnold initially had protested "the rectitude of my intentions," American patriots, to satisfy their own emotional requirements, needed to believe that he would feel remorse and suffer a life of guilt and dishonor for his betrayal.[15]

In the end, America outlasted British resolve by meeting the enemy's offensive in the South and bottling up the armies of Lord Cornwallis on Virginia's Yorktown peninsula. With essential French support on ground and at sea, Washington swiftly moved his troops from the vicinity of New York and cut off Cornwallis's possible retreat routes. Eight thousand men surrendered, forcing London to accept a western boundary of the new United States at the Mississippi River. Congress issued a proclamation congratulating those who fought in the "arduous and difficult war" for having displayed "every military and patriotic virtue." The commander of the Continental Army discharged the men with his farewell orders, taking leave with "an Heart full of love and gratitude."[16]

Such was Washington's standard profession of his devotion to the nation. His meditative circular letter of June 1783 to the governors of all the states, in disbanding the Continental Army, highlighted America's prospects. This important announcement symbolized a new genre expressing political happiness—the patriotic style which proliferated at war's end and tendered welcome sentiments relating to the blessings of peace. In categorizing the postwar order, the victorious general commented first on the favorable environment America came by naturally, and then he added comfortably, "Heaven has crowned all its other blessings by giving a fairer opportunity for political happiness, than any other nation has ever been favoured with." It was the character of the American people, their native educability and Revolutionary experience combined, which prepared them to greet the new age. Peace invited them to apply their improved knowledge of themselves to the particular genius of their time. In Washington's words:

The foundation of our empire was not laid in the gloomy age of ignorance and superstition, but at an epocha when the rights of mankind were better understood and more clearly defined than at any former period; the researches of the human mind after social happiness have been carried to a great extent; the treasures of knowledge . . . are laid open for our use, and their collected wisdom may be happily applied in the establishment of our forms of government; the free cultivation of letters, the unbounded extension of commerce, the progressive refinement of manners, the growing liberality of sentiment, and above all, the pure and benign light of revelation, have had a meliorating influence on mankind and encreased the blessings of society. At this auspicious period the United States came into existence as a nation, and if their citizens should not be completely free and happy, the fault will be entirely their own. . . . [H]appiness is ours if we have a disposition to seize the occasion and make it our own.[17]

Happiness, the commander insisted, was a choice, certainly not a guarantee; but nowhere else on earth was it more readily attainable.

In the year 1783 American independence was universally accepted. In Philadelphia, the Assembly authorized a "public demonstration of joy" in the creation of a fifty-six-by-forty-foot triumphal Roman wooden arch in the town center, adorned with paintings by the popular Maryland-born Charles Willson Peale, called in his day "a Politician by Birth, & a Painter by Trade." Peale was another modest American, after the model of a Franklin or Charles Thomson, who rose to prominence through peripatetic activity. He was the eldest son of an English schoolmaster with aristocratic pretensions who had been banished to the colonies for embezzling money. After his father's death, Peale's widowed mother worked as a seamstress, while young Charles was apprenticed to a saddler. In 1762, at twenty-one, he decided to take up portraiture, staving off debt through diligent cultivation of the popular taste and by extensive travel. He displayed his patriotic productions, a contemporary noted, "at the Corners of Streets to such audiences as can usually be collected at such Places."[18]

Peale's more elaborate work contained the dramatic neoclassical symbols common to his time: stark cloud contrasts, Roman columns, statuary poses—to patriotic minds, these expressed national glory. In a painting of 1768 William Pitt is dressed in a Roman toga and gestures to the goddess Liberty. Peale's 1772 portrait of a reflective George Washington wearing the Virginia regimental uniform is soft and emotive but does not deny his subject that manly spirit with which he would be enshrined in prose. A sash extends across the soldier's chest; a sword is suspended from his waist. Even more affectingly, Peale's 1779 full-length portrait *Washington at the Battle of Princeton* depicts the tall, unflinching general under billowing clouds, leaning on an artillery piece that is draped with a flag. In 1776 John Adams said that the expression of sentiment struck him most "prodigiously" in Peale's portraiture. But softness did not connote weakness. As an artistic subject from the moment it began, the Revolution was expected to bequeath sublime moral lessons to future Americans. The sentimentalism of this generation did not cause it to turn from epic tales of combat; rather the providential War for Independence was understood as a moral trial revealing courageous virtue, not unlike Homer's *Iliad*.[19]

At Washington College in Chestertown, Maryland, the first commencement exercises were held in the summer of 1783. A new graduate named Charles Smith read a valedictory oration in which an almost giddy happiness was expressed. For this graduate, something wondrous had just occurred to secure a patriotic union. The "sovereign and independent states," Smith announced, were fortunate to behold "TRUTH and PEACE, in CHERUB-FORM, descend from heaven to crown their labours, and conduct them from *scenes of blood* into the path of *happiness and glory*—while the fields laugh and sing with the prospect of *future plenty*, and nature, decked out in *vernal pride*, participates in the general joy." America had passed through a trial, much as Ebenezer Fletcher and Ethan Allen documented, and the successful issue now assured a continuation of expansion and progress. Purity was the reward for loving peace and virtue even when forced to kill to survive. Purity was recovered in the national act of bringing forth.[20]

To "hopeful youth," his classmates, Smith addressed his most flowery sentiments: "The eyes of the world upon you, the *rising* glory of your country calling for *rising* exertions of WISDOM and *Virtue*—Oh lose not, I beseech you, lose not your present golden opportunities." Atop the summit of learning and life stood "the GUARDIAN GENIUS of your *Country*." He and his classmates would find happiness in climbing that "HILL OF HONOUR" and pledging service to America. Every moral category seemed to apply; they had everything to look forward to: "We will consider LIBERTY as the *first* of blessings, the parent of VIRTUE, the *guardian* of INNOCENCE, and the *terror* of VICE. *Equal laws, security of property, true religion, wisdom, magnanimity, arts* and *sciences*, whatever can adorn or exalt human nature, are her lovely offspring!"[21]

Charles Smith's bloated rhetoric may seem unpalatable to modern readers, but it was part of a euphoria at war's end. Celebrants projected plentiful opportunities for Americans through an expanding system of education and political progress that, many assumed, would follow naturally. In the valedictorian's rapturous language, the young nation was graduating from a sense of itself as the "infant empire" Tom Paine and Henry Laurens had invoked in 1776 to the status of "rising empire" that many other writers would embrace over the next decades. The emphasis was on rising—here in Smith's valedictory it was "rising exertions," "rising glory."

The valedictory fit a genre that continued to develop over the next several years. Consistency of morals (made possible only with liberty) and public happiness (liberty's vibrant rhetorical partner) were the subjects of countless articles raising expectations from citizens of the republic, now poised to move ahead. They had been liberated from their inveterate enemy, the unfeeling British soldiery, as well as from their rhetorical enemies, rapacity and vice, and now they had to prove themselves worthy of the attributes patriot writers had strutted before the British for years in describing Americans' collective character.

Contained in these published pleas from 1783 on was the implicit directive that republicans adhere to the secular culture of sensibility. A distinctive statement appeared in the *Columbian Magazine*: "The real happiness of society consists in actions whereby men benefit one another; which are called moral. Morality does not, like matters of faith, promote animosities and persecutions; but heals the one and prevents the other. A fantastic happiness is founded on fantastic notions. . . . Virtue is the only means to promote social harmony." If less restrictive than religion, this was still a somewhat dour form of sensibility. "Morality is of the sober kind; on the preservation of it in our heads, hearts, and practice, depend all the happiness of society." Morality was comprehensive; it had "its root in the heart, and its fruit in actions; it includes the science of good politics; the art of governing nations, societies, families and each individual's government of himself." Thus nation building began with individual self-cultivation and extended to sincere public commitment, that mindfulness of cultivated decency the Greeks called *humanitas*.[22] Healing had to occur. The divisions among Americans that the war had brought on could only be treated effectively with renewed feelings of generosity. The people of Concord, Massachusetts, demonstrated this quality to a certain degree when they welcomed back to civic duties loyalist-leaning men like Dr. Joseph Lee, snubbed and fired at in 1775–76 and confined to house arrest, who now stood for election as a state senator, or the elderly, slave-owning merchant Daniel Ingraham, who had failed to side with the patriots but in 1782 spoke of "the Independence of *his* Country."[23]

Virtue as the "law of the heart" pervaded the oratory of the early postwar years and found free rein in public ceremonies. The Fourth of July celebration in Charleston, South Carolina, in 1783 presented a "spectacle equally awful and grand," heralding "the expulsion of tyranny and slavery, and the introduction of freedom, happiness, and independency, throughout the greatest continent in the world." Bell ringing was absent because the British had "wantonly and wickedly" made off with the city's bells during wartime occupation, but "the glowing and happy countenances of our patriot citizens and patriot soldiers, arising from a conscious dignity derived from perfect freedom," were fitting substitutes. Toasts, accompanied by artillery blasts (thirteen rounds for each toast), were raised to the new nation, to the state of South Carolina, to General Washington, and to the wish that "candour, truth, good faith, justice, honor and benevolence" might always be characteristic of the United States. Final toasts were then made to the "glorious" Fourth of July, to "a lasting and happy peace," and to "the supporters of liberty and the rights of mankind, throughout the world."[24] The words themselves were boilerplate, but the oratorical performance deserves attention. While seriously in debt to its own soldiers and to foreign bankers, the government had a need to voice, over and over, its certain impression of the purity and innocence of the new nation, the uprightness of its founding vision, and the world significance of its victory.

One of the most resounding and prophetic declarations of the early postwar period was a sermon by Yale's president, Ezra Stiles, *The UNITED STATES Elevated to GLORY and HONOUR.* Celebrating a civil polity made happier with "true religion," his "discourse upon the political welfare of GOD'S American Israel" coupled "the diffusion of virtue among the people" with a "secular happiness" never before known. "Liberty, civil and religious, has sweet and attractive charms," he testified. "The enjoyment of this, with property, has filled the English settlers in *America* with a most amazing spirit, which has operated, and still will operate with great energy. Never before has the experiment been so effectually tried, of every man's reaping the fruits of his labour, and feeling his share in the aggregate system of power." Stiles forecast that even those individuals accustomed to life under a liberty-less regime and reared to hold "arbitrary principles" would "at length become charmed with the sweets of liberty."[25]

He envisioned a democratizing nation, whose rapidly growing population would produce "a great people" of fifty million within a century on whom "the sun will shine." Indeed, he believed it possible that by the year 2000 Americans would outnumber the Chinese, "when the LORD shall have made his American Israel, *high above all nations which he hath made*, in numbers, *and in praise, and in name, and in honour!*" Though prepared to be called a "visionary Utopian" for his ideas, Stiles could not be restrained: "How wonderful the revolutions, the events of Providence! We live in an Age of Wonders: We have lived an age in a few years: We have seen more wonders accomplished in *eight* years than are usually unfolded in a century."[26]

Victory had been "sealed and confirmed," he said, when God blessed the "glorious act of INDEPENDENCE." Britain had boasted of its army and seemed to have cause to do so. But something had occurred to change history: "What but a miracle has preserved the

UNION OF THE STATES, the PURITY OF CONGRESS, and the unshaken PATRIOTISM OF EVERY GENERAL ASSEMBLY?" Note the intentional correspondence (and capitalization) of "UNION," "PURITY," and "PATRIOTISM." This ecstatic language again captures the historical moment. Purity was embodied in unity, and sealed with the moral fastness of those who directed the nation to independence, who had not rested until their goal was achieved. Now generous America would go on to consolidate its commitment to happiness and liberty, not wallow in hate: "Here will be no bloody tribunals, no cardinal inquisitors-general, to bend the human mind, forcibly to control the understanding, and put out the light of reason, the candle of the LORD, in man." Stiles was content to fantasize unity in politics and faith alike, projecting an America that would naturally arrive at "one language," "harmoniously" concurring in "one holy faith," as it awaited divine destiny.[27]

Benjamin Rush mirrored Stiles's enthusiasm for the possibility of universal good arising from republicanism in America in a letter he wrote to the Scottish Reverend Charles Nisbet, inviting that gentleman at war's end to assume the presidency of Dickinson College:

We have not toiled and bled in vain. Our governments are daily acquiring strength and consistency, and our people become every day more subject to law and order. Europe in its present state of political torpor affords no scope for the activity of a benevolent mind. Here everything is in a plastic state. Here the benefactor of mankind may realize all his schemes for promoting human happiness. Human nature here (unsubdued by the tyranny of European habits and customs) yields to reason, justice and common sense. . . . America seems destined by heaven to exhibit to the world the perfection which the mind of man is capable of receiving from the combined operation of liberty, learning, and the gospel upon it.[28]

Imported "benefactors," men of enlightened minds held in check by the "torpor" of Europe, were meant to bring sentiment and sympathy, along with rational understanding, to the energetic people of America.

The newly independent union of states was primed to reconstitute the world on a sounder, more godly, and more humane basis. It was open country, its people endowed with open minds and common sense, receptive to sensible persuasion. "Plastic" and "unsubdued," yet law-abiding, Americans awaited unselfish teachers. This was the kind of place that would suit the Man of Feeling, Scottish or otherwise.

Like these influential treatises of the early postwar period, the iconography of the times also reveals the ideal national self-image being constructed. The ten-year path that the Great Seal of the United States took before its final adoption (it is now seen most commonly on the reverse of the one-dollar bill) illustrates how American virtue, national unity, and imperial ambition were all imagined. On July 4, 1776, the Continental Congress named a committee of three—Benjamin Franklin, John Adams, and Thomas Jefferson—to prepare, in Adams's words, "Devices for the Great Seal of the confederated States." Franklin proposed a biblical scene, that of Moses "lifting up his Wand, and dividing the Red Sea, and Pharaoh, in his Chariot overwhelmed with the Waters." Here was another example of the captivity narrative in which a people are reborn after enduring great hardship on their actual or metaphorical journey. The motto beneath the scene was to read: "Rebellion to Tyrants is Obedience to God." Jefferson, Adams reported, offered a nearly identical biblical vignette, "the Children of Israel in the Wilderness." Adams himself suggested Hercules surveying his choices: "Virtue pointing to her rugged Mountain" (compare the purifying "Hill of Honour" in Charles Smith's valedictory oration) urges the hero to ascend, while "Sloth, glancing at her flowery Paths of Pleasure," tries to charm Hercules into the way of vice. The common focus was on the historically charged and divinely guided mission for which America was cast.[29]

The Great Seal project went through two more committee assignments after 1776 before it was turned over to Charles Thomson, secretary of the Continental Congress, in 1782. The learned Thomson, rejuvenator of Franklin's American Philosophical Society, combined the fruits of the work of the first committees and modified the devices, highlighting the American bald eagle. Congress finally adopted his version of the Great Seal which, with minor alterations, still identifies the nation. The *Columbian Magazine* introduced citizens to the final design in the autumn of 1786. The emblazoned eagle was, it explained, "a symbol of empire." The shield on its breast contained a total of thirteen red and white "pieces," or stripes, representing "the several states in the union, all joined in one solid, compact *entire*." The motto *e pluribus unum* ("out of many, one") "alludes to this union." Insofar as the shield was not affixed to anything but was suspended loose from the eagle, the united states were "to rely on their own virtue" to preserve their independence and their healthy liberty. Over the head of the eagle "a glory, or breaking through a cloud" loomed amid a constellation of thirteen stars on an azure field. Finally, the national colors were assigned national traits: red denoted "hardiness and valour," white was "purity and innocence," and blue "vigilance, perseverance, and justice."[30]

The reverse of the Great Seal was also explained. The pyramid signified the "strength and duration" of the American nation, aided by the overseeing eye which represented "the many signal interpositions of providence, in favour of the American cause." The motto, too, *annuit coeptis* ("He has favored our undertakings"), referred to this trust. The Latin date at the base of the pyramid was 1776, "the beginning of the American aera," amplified by the motto *novus ordo seclorum*, "a new order of the ages." So not only was the Revolutionary era seen as an age of wonders; it ushered in a new moral order combining transcendent ideals of valor, purity, and wakeful justice.[31]

The iconography of the Great Seal symbolically took Revolutionary American identity to a new stage of confidence. Early in the Revolution, a Continental bill had featured an eagle "pouncing upon a crane, who turns upon his back, and receives the eagle on the point of his long bill, which pierces the eagle's breast." The motto read: *exitus in dubio est*, or "the event is uncertain." In this instance, the eagle had represented Great Britain and the poised, graceful crane America. The eagle was warned "not to presume on its superior strength, since a weaker bird may wound it mortally."[32] It seems ironic, then, that within a decade the resurgent, independent American state came to identify with the symbol of national strength and empire, inheriting Britain's expansive purpose without perceiving in it a predatory identity.[33] The eagle on the Great Seal may have been meant as well to conjure the biblical imagery that Franklin and Jefferson seemed predisposed to feature in their initial effort. If America was often depicted as wilderness, then the passage from Jeremiah of the Israelites being carried out of Egyptian bondage on eagles' wings powerfully commemorated both the introduction of civilized progress to the wilderness of the New World and American independence from the darkness of British rule.[34]

## A MORAL VACUUM

Patriotic writers stressed a unique quality of life in an open and tolerant society. America was happiness; America was hope. But, of course, union could not be so simple or consistent. While the Articles of Confederation loosely governed the former colonies, a debate over political society intensified as the 1780s proceeded. States conferred with each other, but union was tenuous. There were no federal taxes to accord power to the central government, no separate executive, and a unicameral legislature. Despite harmonious representations, social divisions were in fact quite threatening in postwar America: the now thriving patriot elite, concentrated along the east coast, was reluctant to welcome less affluent, less accomplished backcountry citizens into the ranks of policy makers. Independence redirected power and promoted intrastate and interstate jealousies.

First of all, independent states flexed their muscle and were loath to cede lands to the national government.[35] Separatists from the more remote parts of several states, feeling unrepresented, tried to constitute themselves as self-governing republics (unsuccessfully, except in the case of Vermont's separation from New York). Governmental authority was questioned routinely, and people disobeyed the laws they found oppressive. This was most fearfully displayed in Shays's Rebellion in western Massachusetts in 1786, where beleaguered veterans disrupted court proceedings and threatened widespread violence if their farm mortgages were foreclosed upon. Writers described the rebellion in varying terms, as a "fire" or "conflagration," a "contagion" that might spread south. As great as popular discontent appeared to be, however, the participants identified themselves as "American citizens" belonging to a political community greater than their respective states. The symbol of Daniel Shays and his band capped the nervous years when many shared second thoughts about the virtues presumed common to the American character. Self-interested groups, ambitious demagogues, and dark motives were located and exposed in sermons and in newspapers.[36]

In the South as well, doubts about American virtue were quite explicitly sounded. In the heat of the war's Southern campaign (1780–81), patriots and loyalists alike had terrorized the South Carolina backcountry, "butchering one another hourly," as General Nathanael Greene reported at one point. The invading British acted as catalysts for the desertion of slaves and the arming of some (which alarmed loyalists as much as rebels), but they did not take full military advantage of the opportunities that regiments of outfitted runaways might have afforded. As a bonus for militiamen who served the Revolutionary cause American commanders conferred slaves on them, and when the war ended, white South Carolinians indiscriminately snatched as many slaves as they could get their hands on for their ravaged plantations. Because Southern planting made slaveholding profitable, owners were learning to make the deprivation of freedom a matter of "special circumstances." *Their* ordered liberty, *their* private peace and harmony, seemed to require it.[37]

A moral vacuum existed. Under a suffering economy created by the disappearance of slaves, lost markets, and crop failures, unhealthy numbers among South Carolina's dislocated populace turned to vagrancy and vice, according to records of the state justice system. Desperadoes hiding in the swamps plundered vulnerable settlements. Patriots and Tories alike stood accused, and public executions called attention to the pervasiveness of crime. Under these conditions, the prospects of peace were difficult to gauge; estates were returned to loyalists despite a Confiscation Act officially in force, and British merchants continued to conduct a brisk business in Charleston, reestablishing credit for a variety of war-weary citizens. The most ardent patriot merchants protested the British presence and influence, but the best they could effect as the uncertain decade ran its course was a legislative stalling of prosecutions against debtor planters. The interior of South Carolina was not exactly fertile ground for national pride.[38]

A comprehensive (and symptomatic) expression of concern about the perils of independence passed through the mails in 1784. Jeremy Belknap and Ebenezer Hazard were both born in 1744; the former was graduated from Harvard in 1762, and the latter finished Princeton the same year, each trained in religious and classical texts. Belknap had settled at a parish in Dover, New Hampshire, and become a distinguished man of letters known for his monumental history of that state; Hazard performed as a surveyor in charge of the post roads during the war and afterward was appointed U.S. postmaster general. Both men had knowledge of diverse landscapes and of the variety of Americans settling new places, and they were regular correspondents.

What kind of government suited this people? asked Belknap of his friend in 1784, fresh from exploring the White Mountains. Before the war, union of the colonies had been thought "impracticable," he began. Only "the pressure of a common calamity" had produced a continental union: "The waves do not rise but when the winds blow." Tempestuous seas, it seemed, were needed to achieve emotional concord. Now, with "grievous" tyranny removed, the chance of preserving union appeared slight. "Thirteen *equally free, independent, sovereign* States are confederated for their mutual defence and security," just as Franklin had wished thirty years before; but with "each one retaining its own *sovereignty* (a darling word, but highly intoxicating)," a less generous America seemed inevitable. The confluence of liberty and happiness, so poetically realizable in past exhortations, was being succeeded by a stark new reality—a government "inadequate" to tap the citizens' potential to act charitably. This is what struck Belknap.[39]

It was less a lack of virtue among individuals than the unwieldy Articles of Confederation that demanded reexamination. Belknap offered the familiar metaphor of government as a machine whose wheels moved slowly: "Imagine, my friend, thirteen *independent* clocks, going all together, by the force of their own weights, and carrying thirteen *independent* hammers fitted to strike on *one bell*. . . . The plain English of all this is that our present form of federal government appears to be inadequate to the purpose for which it was instituted." The worn mechanism had to be put back into working order.[40]

Belknap went on: "[I]s it not a pity that such a machine as we have been at the pains to construct should fail in its effect? What fitter place can there be for a republic than America, where liberty is so well understood and the rights of human nature so clearly defined?" He was heartened in recalling the ideal of the Puritan ethic and the Revolutionary language of disinterestedness. These generous emotions animated him. He envisioned a society that promoted simple tastes and did not encourage private monetary ambition. But as his pen moved ahead, Belknap teetered between encouragement and discouragement. "Equality is the soul of a republic," he posed elegantly. "Where, then, is our soul? . . . The yeomanry of New England are, in point of *equality*, the fittest materials for a republic; but they want another grand perquisite, public virtue." In the suspect South, "every white man is the lordly tyrant of an hundred slaves," but this did not exonerate New Englanders: "They are as mean and selfish as other people and have as strong a lurch for territory as merchants have for cash. From such premises is it any forced conclusion that the people of this country are not destined to be long governed in a democratic form?"[41]

Belknap shifted to classical republican ideas of government to salvage his faith: "But all men are by nature free and independent, and therefore there should be no power but what is derived from the people and exercised by their consent and for their benefit. Granted. It is a good principle and ought to stand." Yet, since primitive emotions ruled most human actions, government was needed to check the predatory impulse, which he perceived everywhere: "Do we not see in fact that the wolf devours the lamb, the vulture the dove, and the whale will swallow a whole shoal of mackerel? And is there not as much inequality among men?" America's moral ideal appeared to be as hopelessly vulnerable as the lamb and the dove, symbols of purity and innocence. The answer Belknap arrived at was strong parenting, a superintending authority suited to America's soil and temperament which replaced the paternalistic king and mother country. As a child is "necessarily under the dominion of his parents," the ordinary citizen "will be a miserable creature" without those to look up to. "Let it stand as a principle that government originates from the people; but let the people be taught . . . that they are not able to govern themselves. . . . Should even a limited monarchy be erected, our liberties may be as safe as if every man had the keeping of them solely in his own power." It was now appearing to prominent Americans that liberty and happiness required a mighty government that educated as it comforted its citizens and stood ready to restrain their excesses.

When Shays's Rebellion was heating up, Belknap wrote to Hazard again. "Oh! my country! To what an alarming situation are we reduced." A toothless Confederation Congress continued in vain "advising, exhorting, and remonstrating" with a recalcitrant people. The states were "determined to do as they please, and to mind the counsels of their fathers only when their interest or passions do not urge the contrary." There was not enough public virtue. The too independent states were "giddy, unrestrained youth, bidding defiance to the admonitions of age and experience." Once again, "we want some imminent common danger presented pressing hard upon us, to make us feel our need of union."[42] George Washington was equally worried. In writing Virginia governor Benjamin Harrison, he reneged on his hopeful 1783 circular and spoke instead of his profound distrust of the instincts of the people: "Like a young heir, come a little prematurely to a large inheritance, we shall wanton and run riot until we have brought our reputation to the brink of ruin." The persistence of local self-interest oppressed him: "We have opposed Great Britain," he wrote, "and have arrived at the present state of peace and independency, to very little purpose, if we cannot conquer our own prejudices."[43]

A similar tone was expressed in newspapers. The *Pennsylvania Gazette* printed a Bostonian's parable: "A sage American, on being asked by his son, when he thought America would be a great people? replied, when they are a virtuous people. And when, continues the son, do you think they will become a rich people?—when they become an honest people. And when shall America be respected by the nations of Europe?—when they pay more attention to their public faith and less attention to trifle." The writer went on to deplore recent changes in the country's mood:

Lately took his departure from this country, Mr. Public Spirit, attended by Real Patriotism and Public Faith: . . . He was of eminent service in extirpation of tyranny, and in erecting the temple of liberty . . . [H]e promised himself much happiness. But, sad reverse—ingratitude indeed! Having received several marks of contempt from some who were his proffered friends, and seeing Mr. Self-Interest, a man, obnoxious to his feelings, caressed by all ranks, . . . he determined to leave this country for a clime more grateful—this he has put into effect—and is gone—we fear for ever.[44]

A nostalgic "Primitive Whig" of the *New-Jersey Gazette* castigated Americans for ceasing to conduct themselves with dignity. The war's legacy had been "marred, obscured, contaminated, and trampled in the dust" by a people who had once promised to risk their lives and fortunes and now were grumbling about taxes. "Ingrates! To see a lazy, lounging, lubberly fellow sitting nights and days in a tipplinghouse," squandering his earnings "in riot and debauch," proved that former patriots had devolved into a soulless, helpless race. Something had to be done to recover American virtue.[45]

These emotional issues raised profound questions: What was the people's proper power in a republic? Who could be trusted? What size should a state be in order to govern fairly and efficiently? How could national territory be carved from existing (and often overlapping) frontier claims? The Confederation Congress could claim this one success: After the states ceded their frontier lands to the national government, the 1787 Northwest Ordinance determined how western territories would be bounded and republican government instituted.[46] But confidence in the decentralized Confederation had obviously waned. A convention of the states to deal with the existing uncertainties was called in the spring of 1787 in Philadelphia. The republic had yet to constitute an effective national authority.

On the eve of dispatching its delegates to the Philadelphia convention, the Connecticut Assembly met in Hartford, and a distinguished religious scholar and amateur mathematician-astronomer, Elizur Goodrich, gave a sermon subsequently published under the title *The Principles of CIVIL UNION and HAPPINESS*. Like Belknap's model of social relations, Goodrich's projection was in no way egalitarian. He valued those people most who venerated their rulers, who elected those of a superior character—men bearing "knowledge, wisdom, and prudence, courage and unshaken resolution, righteousness and justice." The ideal citizen possessed "the wisdom to discern the true patriot of superior abilities." It was the presence of a "natural aristocracy" (made apparent to the people by God), and a people wise enough "to shew a fixed and unalterable regard to merit" in their choice of rulers, that promoted "happiness, union and strength of a people."[47]

The pastor's prescription reflected the federalist majority that emerged in the autumn, when the Constitutional Convention finally adjourned after four months and the persevering delegates took their compromise document to the states for ratification. Meeting behind closed doors and keeping their deliberations secret during the long summer, they had thrashed out issues of emotional as well as political significance to the meaning of American nationhood.

As the fifty-five delegates wrangled over matters of structure and balance, many, including the intellectually vigorous James Madison (who took copious notes at the proceedings), were preoccupied with the mutability of language. Even minute alterations of text had to concern the framers, if they were to translate their definition of the republic to the people at large. Words demanded agreement—indeed, obedience—if this innovative government was to succeed. For example, Virginia's George Mason had certain ideas about national character that he wished to see made part of the final document. Though one of the few delegates who in the end refused to sign, he praised the American people as peace-loving and argued successfully that, in a government of the people, *make* war should be changed to *declare* war. In Madison's words: "He was for clogging rather than facilitating war; but for facilitating peace." Playing with words in a most serious way, the octogenarian Benjamin Franklin judged the issue of whether the President should be popularly elected or elected by the legislature: in free governments, he said, "the rulers are the servants." It was apparent to these men that national identity could only be shaped by reaching emotional consensus on established principles.[48]

The improved system had to present the federative principle—a clear-cut formula for the sharing of power—in language that erased any and all confusion. To the eloquent parliamentarian Rufus King of Massachusetts, the oft-used words *states, sovereignty, national,* and *federal* were applied "inaccurately and delusively." To Pennsylvania's James Wilson, whom a contemporary credited with an understanding of "all the passions that influence," separation from Great Britain implied two legal essences: first, that the states were independent of each other, and second, that they chose to become "unitedly" free. If in constitutional terms, liberty required law, then in emotional terms (in shaping a national identity), prose required consistency and purity of expression.[49]

The Constitutional Convention, in a sense, was a tribunal measuring and judging the moral capabilities of all citizens, rulers and ruled. Always the subtext of debate referred to a conception of "the people" and how they could exercise power in the republic without overturning order. After Gouverneur Morris of Pennsylvania suggested that enfranchising the propertyless would merely allow such people to sell their votes to the rich, Franklin urged restively, "Do not depress the virtue and public spirit of our common people." James Wilson, in Madison's words, "with regard to the sentiments of the people, conceived it difficult to know precisely what they are. Those of a particular circle in which one moved, were commonly mistaken for the general voice."[50]

To Madison, writing in later months to promote the federal Constitution as adopted by the convention, the question "Who are the people?" was compressed into a factual statement about the electors of national representatives: "Not the rich, more than the poor," he offered, "nor the learned more than the ignorant; not the haughty heirs of distinguished names, more than the humble sons of obscurity and unpropitious fortune. The electors are to be the great body of the people of the United States." They were "actuated" by a "vigilant and manly spirit" which prevented their representatives from taking advantage of them. Indeed, recognizing this quality in those who elect them, congressmen were "bound to fidelity and sympathy with the great mass of the people" by "cords" of "duty, gratitude, interest" and even "ambition." Madison hoped the republic would be held together by promoting men of enlightened sympathy.[51]

One who slowly grew in his federalist faith over the year 1787–88 was Dr. Benjamin Rush of Philadelphia. Amid the debate over ratification, this signer of the Declaration of Independence was not immediately at ease. Writing to Jeremy Belknap, he cautioned against preaching too much optimism about the integrity of the American people: "What is the present moral character of the inhabitants of the United States? I need not describe it. It proves too plainly that the *people* are as much disposed to vice as their rulers, and that nothing but a vigorous & efficient government can prevent their degenerating into savages, or devouring each other like beasts of prey." Typical of the writers of his generation, Rush recurred to a sea metaphor to express the dangers he still perceived and his yearning for that release by which personal happiness could now be defined:

> I pant for the time when the establishment of the new government . . . shall excuse men who like myself wish only to be passengers, from performing the duty of sailors on board the political ship in which ou[r all] is embarked. . . . As soon as the storm is over, and our bark safely moored, the first wish of my heart will be to devote the whole of my time to the peaceable pursuits of science, and to the pleasures of social and domestic life.

Rush was cautious in his optimism. He hoped, like so many others, that the Constitution would be a catalyst for genuine peace and contentment. Elsewhere he had written that perfecting republican government was only the first stage in America's development, and that revolutionizing opinions and manners among a generally vice-prone people was the essential next stage. Rush was not one to wallow in despair, and he devoted his mind and his pen to the cause of republican education for the next two decades.[52]

The federalists were proud of the body of laws they had fashioned and believed it to be a proper culmination of the Revolution. The young

John Marshall put it forthrightly at the Virginia ratifying convention: the Constitution's supporters, far from fearing the people, "idolize democracy." But what did this most elastic word mean? The Constitution, he said, outlined a "well-regulated democracy." Though he would not have known it at the time, the future jurist had hit upon the key to comprehending the emotionalism of post-Revolutionary politics—the malleable meaning of democracy for the People of Feeling.[53]

## DEMOCRACY

The word *democracy* resonated with both a historically neutral and a contemporary discordant and troublesome meaning. In Montesquieu's *Spirit of the Laws*, democracy was a form of popular government present in the ancient world and relegated to small-scale societies (also called "simple democracy"); or, because it supposed the dissolution of that line separating rulers and ruled, it could connote the breakdown of authority and its replacement with lawless violence—what those who feared it commonly termed "democratic despotism."

At mid-century Montesquieu had divided governments into republican, monarchical, and despotic, stating succinctly: "In a republic when the people as a body have sovereign power, it is a *democracy*." His work made clear to the intellectual leaders of the American Revolutionary generation that greater virtue was needed in a popular government than in a monarchy, because all were equally subject to the laws. He noted further that a love of the laws of the land, "requiring a continuous preference of the public interest over one's own," was "singularly connected with democracies. In them alone, government is entrusted to each citizen." In a republic, he likewise observed, "everything depends on establishing this love." The material was now present for defining a *democratic republic*.[54]

In the decade before the Revolution, the influential pamphleteer James Otis had elevated the moral value of democracy, claiming that "in the order of nature it came immediately under God." Yet in 1772, Sir Thomas Gage maligned the colonists for their "democratic" impulses: "Democracy," he charged, "is too prevalent in America, and claims the greatest attention to prevent its increase," by which he meant disorder, which he associated, at least in part, with the movement of population away from the coast to inland areas unresponsive to a central authority. To the substantial loyalist communities of Massachusetts and New York, the rebel colonists' democracy was pure lawlessness, an artful cabal rooted in envy and ambition, and nothing more principled than a vengeful quest by unscrupulous demagogues to seize power from dedicated public servants.[55]

The Revolution enlarged the positive meaning of *democracy* but did not dispel the negative possibilities inherent in it. In 1777, predating the later conflation of *democracy* and *republic*, the *Providence* (Rhode Island) *Gazette* explained that "by a *democracy* is meant, that form of government where the highest power of making laws is lodged in the common people, or persons chosen out of them. This is what by some is called a republic, a commonwealth, or free state, and seems so the most agreeable to natural rights and liberty."[56] Though he recognized the possibility of democratic despotism, John Adams wrote decisively for a British newspaper in 1780: "It is very true that there is no strong attachment in the minds of the Americans to the laws and government of Great Britain. . . . There is a deep and forcible antipathy to two essential branches of the British Constitution, the monarchical and the aristocratical." In a subsequent letter (never published), Adams put it even more strongly:

> The predominant Spirit then of every Colony has been from the Beginning democratical. . . . The people ever stood by their Representatives, and what is more remarkable, the Lawyers and Clergy have almost universally taken the same side. This has been the popular Torrent, that like a River changing its bed, has irresistably born away every Thing before it. The Sentiments of this People therefore are not to be changed.[57]

He was talking largely about emotional harmony accompanying political stability, implying the existence of a folk element that did not contest the actions of representatives, and whose democracy was indirect.

In 1787–88, as the Constitution was presented to the people of

America, the two divergent meanings of democracy—its liberty-preserving and disorderly qualities—had been played out in debate, and ultimate agreement among the framers was now presumed in the sound construction of "We the people." Democracy was meant to indicate a constitutional delegation of power that technically belonged to the people—the meaning of the term "popular sovereignty."

But antifederalists, those who were less afraid of people power and openly opposed ratification of the Constitution, were not convinced by the sweet logic of federal language. They saw the federalists' terminology as the elitists' cover for reducing the liberties of their less privileged fellow citizens, which is why some historians have regarded them as similar to later populists. Prominent among them was the highly respected George Mason, age sixty at the time of the convention, who pointedly wrote to his son from Philadelphia of the antidemocratic mood he observed among people who were "soured & disgusted with the unexpected Evils we had experienced from the democratic Principles of our [state] Governments." The federalists, he perceived, wished to keep the people in check more than they wished to give the people a voice. Mason knew how critical this convention was not only to national self-definition but to the popular temper: "The Eyes of the United States are turn'd upon this Assembly, & their Expectations raised to a very anxious Degree," he noted impatiently. "The Revolt from Great Britain" was "nothing compared to the great Business now before us." At stake was "the Happiness or Misery of Millions yet unborn," an "Object of such Magnitude, as absorbs & in a manner suspends the Operations of the human Understanding." Under such apprehension, Mason argued, a general fear of excessive democracy had risen, so that the Constitution he refused to sign did not expressly protect individual rights.[58]

The "Federal Farmer" was an antifederalist pamphleteer more representative of modest Americans than a wealthy Virginia landowner like Mason. Writing at the end of 1787, this anonymous critic warned that the Constitution was being thrust on the community without adequate reflection. If adopted too "hastily" and "blindly," the new system of government might be as hastily and blindly scrapped later on. He wrote, "Nothing but the passions of ambitious, impatient, or disorderly men,

I conceive, will plunge us into commotions." He was every bit as interested in stability and order as the federalists, but less convinced that the convention delegates had thoroughly understood the popular will; the ambitious, impatient, and disorderly could come from any social class. He felt that small was better than big, that the people's happiness was best secured by keeping the states "independent republics" in closer touch with citizens' needs, rather than to oblige the people to surrender too much authority to a distant, "consolidated" national government. The problem he foresaw lay with the proposed system of representation: "it is impossible for forty, or thirty thousand people in this country, one time in ten to find a man who can possess similar feelings." "Feelings" and "sentiments" were important to him; thus he preferred a more democratic delineation of power than the federalists offered. Just because "we have sometimes abused democracy, I am not among those men who think a democratic branch a nuisance." The delegates in Philadelphia, he wrote, had met "without knowing the sentiments of one man in ten thousand in these states." He placed himself between the two extremes that Americans of the mid-1780s could identify: "little insurgents, men in debt," like the desperate Shaysites, "who want no law"; and "aristocrats," who supported the Constitution because they believed it guaranteed them "power and property."[59]

At least the state ratifying conventions, just then in planning, promised to draw larger numbers of delegates from "all parts of the community and from all orders of men," the "Federal Farmer" observed. He had equal confidence in the deliberations of "fishermen, mechanics and traders" as in the talk of the traditional elite; in any event, "the aristocratical, and democratical, with views equally honest, have sentiments widely different," and everyone needed to be heard and respected. Given their different perspectives and the passions naturally aroused, "men, elevated in society, are often disgusted with the changeableness of the democracy," and ill-equipped to "sympathize" with their less order-oriented constituents. In any event, all would agree that the "great object of a free people" had to consist of "a government of laws ... [to] induce the sensible and virtuous part of the community to declare in favor of the laws, and to support them." To the "Federal Farmer," the sensible and virtuous were a large community who needed to be faithfully represented—more than just symbolically, as the federalists had in mind when they constituted the "democratic" part of the legislature, the House of Representatives.[60]

Another prominent antifederalist, publishing under the name "Brutus," took a similar tack in a series of newspaper essays, predicting that the "well born, and highest orders in life, as they term themselves, will be ignorant of the sentiments of the middling class of citizens, strangers to their ability, wants, and difficulties, and void of class sympathy, and fellow feeling."[61] Recalling the pattern of miscommunication between the British ministry and colonial subjects that caused an irreparable emotional rupture before the violent political one, antifederalists wished to ensure that the sentimental distance between the people and their representatives would not be too great.

As one scholar has put it: "If the Antifederalists desired a *popularly* limited government, the Federalists advanced the idea of a *limited* popular government [italics supplied]." At this juncture, invoking the patriotic but abstract phrase "pure republican principles" seemed the best way to designate the American vision without employing the confusing word *democracy*. It would be some time yet before *democracy* ceased to arouse fears of "democratic" tyranny. In the factionalized 1790s, the "disorderly" in *democracy* would intensify again in its threatening aspect and only gradually lose its fearful connotation of mob rule over the ensuing decades.[62]

In the same issue in which it printed the Constitution, the *Columbian Magazine* uncomfortably analyzed the word *democratic* in the context of its meaning an all-encompassing social equality. Did Americans have "a real affection for democracy"? If, in decrying aristocracy, "they have wished all men to be equal," was it merely because they were already "nearly in that situation"? Americans seemed to this unnamed writer to be blind to their future, which he painted bleakly: The workforce would not always live as well as it did now; the class of artisans were likely to be reduced over time to the same level of distress as their European counterparts. Cautiously, then, because "men must be moved by some fixed principle," society ought to require that "grandeur" and "dignity" be conferred on its leading citizens. The strong "love of country" palpable at this time ensured only momentary peace and could not long continue to motivate Americans.[63]

Madison, however, stuck to his federalist maxims. He clarified in Federalist #10 the sound basis on which the new government was meant to stand: the just desires of the people would be expressed through "the medium of a chosen body of citizens, whose wisdom may best discern the true interest of their country." That is, the public voice was regulated by representatives who were likely to discern the public good more readily than the people themselves, amassed in a large convention, could. "Pure democracy" (or simple democracy)—"a society consisting of a small number of citizens, who assemble and administer the government in person"—was as turbulent as it was impractical in America; and so the federal republic as constituted altered the meaning of democracy to *that government which served the people best.*[64]

Benjamin Rush concurred, though he was as emotional as Madison was unemotional. He liked Fisher Ames's characterization of simple democracy, "a volcano that contained within its bowels the fiery materials of its own destruction," and was comforted by the Constitution's balance, the "political happiness," which the three interacting branches—executive, legislative, and judicial—would insure. He had witnessed the workings of a unicameral state legislature in his home state of Pennsylvania, which he termed for John Adams "below a democracy. It is *mobocracy*, if you will allow me to coin a term." It was like a balloon, "one of those air vehicles without sails or helm." So he welcomed a new, more vigorous, more efficient federal government that prevented the people from "degenerating into savages," and he anticipated that it would advance virtue and justice: "Think then, my friend," he wrote the South Carolinian David Ramsay, "of the expansion and dignity the American mind will acquire by having its powers transferred from the contracted objects of a state to the more unbounded objects of a national government! A citizen and a legislator of the free and united states of America will be one of the first characters in the world."[65]

The roots of the federalists' democratic theory can be traced to late-seventeenth-century England and the opposition ideology known as Whiggism. The Whigs were outsiders to the ruling circle who centered their criticism on unfair influence and corruption in government. The people had to remain virtuous, given the ever-present possibility of subversion by ambitious men, and had to unite to preserve their liberty. This is what the American Revolution had been fought to guarantee, and after Philadelphia it seemed, to most, realizable.[66] The Constitution now conferred a check on the power to oppress, restrained the rulers, ensured liberty, and moderated popular unrest by channeling it into regular electoral contests. Federalists could claim that the people were their own governors.

So with ratification of the Constitution by the states (eleven of the thirteen concurred as of July 1788; tiny Rhode Island held out until May 1790), the federalists succeeded in drowning out the voices of the antifederalists, or at least overawing them with their prolific printing presses, and ultimately they defined the terms of American republican society. The antifederalists continued to fear that the victorious federalists had abandoned the democratic impulse of 1776 and perhaps even turned their backs on Whig principles. Their challenge, if quieted somewhat with the passage of the Bill of Rights by both houses of Congress in September 1789, stood as a reminder that a *rhetoric* seeking harmony did not naturally produce uniformity. Philosophic differences led to political contentiousness, sometimes quite deadly—and the inevitable obverse of the boast that America might somehow remain morally aloof in an otherwise troubled (and unsentimental) world.

The language of liberty no longer was fraught with the fearful connotations it had had in the Stamp Act season, but the debate in Philadelphia did involve a major, continuing difficulty: its simultaneous understanding of individual rights for the white majority and the persistence of African-American slavery. Gouverneur Morris was most outspoken in his opposition to the uneasy three-fifths compromise, which mollified Georgia and Carolina delegates who wanted their human property to count toward representation in Congress. Invoking "the most sacred laws of humanity," he cursed a system that would not only countenance "the most cruel bondages" but reward the slaveholding states with more votes. Still the politics of compromise prevailed, and the desire to reach agreeable terms took precedence over moral obligation. "Great as the evil is," wrote Madison, "a dismemberment of the union would be worse." Indeed, as if to hide the republic's embarrassing problem, the word *slavery* was not used in the final document, describing instead "persons held to Service or Labour."[67]

Celebrations of political happiness, of nationhood, recalled the ecstatic public spectacles after the Treaty of Paris in 1783. Pennsylvania, in particular, timed its ratification to coincide with the twelfth anniversary of the Declaration of Independence. On July 4, 1788, Philadelphia orchestrated a great display, highlighted by a three-hour Grand Federal Procession, at the head of which stood the organizer of the day's activities, the Revolutionary satirist Francis Hopkinson, a signer of the Declaration and an energetic friend of Franklin and Jefferson, among others. The day opened with cannon blasts from a ship named the *Rising Sun* moored off Market Street.[68]

Printers distributed Hopkinson's ode:

> Oh! for a muse of fire! To mount the skies,
> And to a listening world proclaim;
> Behold! Behold! an Empire rise!
> An Aera new, time as he flies,
> Hath entered the book of fame.
> On Allegheny's towering head
> Echo shall stand; the tidings spread,
> And o'er the lakes, and misty floods around,
> An Aera new resound.[69]

Floats drawn by horses moved past a crowd of thousands. Confident for the moment about the government's ability to restrain popular excess through education, Dr. Rush, stern critic as he might have been, described the event as "a triumph of knowledge over ignorance, of virtue over vice, and of liberty over slavery. It was to celebrate the birth of a free government." He was exultant about the Federal Procession, and his words to Elias Boudinot of New Jersey encapsulated the patriotic moment:

Perhaps a greater number or a greater combination of passions never seized at the same time upon every faculty of the soul. The patriot enjoyed a complete triumph, whether the objects of his patriotism were the security of liberty, the establishment of law, the protection of manufactures, or the extension of science in his country. The benevolent man saw a precedent established for forming free governments in every part of the world. The man of humanity contemplated the end of the distresses of his fellow citizens in the revival of commerce and agriculture.[70]

Other cities celebrated, too, with their own symbols heralding union and a new beginning. Charles Willson Peale unveiled a new Washington portrait at an Annapolis tavern as the general was toasted. His *Genius of America* featured the female symbol of Genius dismissing Anarchy with one hand and pointing to science, commerce, agriculture, and the arts with her other. Trumpets announced the new Constitution. In New York, thirty-year-old Noah Webster, editor of *The American Magazine*, who had been lecturing on the English language since 1785 and whose reformation of English spelling was soon to be published, and twenty-two-year-old William Dunlap, who would become known one day as the father of American drama, marched triumphantly with the Philological Society, whose secretary held a scroll containing "the principles of a *Federal* language."[71]

Federal English, so called, was the new language of American union; it combined glowing words and good tidings with an unmistakable moral standard that supposed an inevitable advance over other existing governments. It has been characterized as "an American language independent of its origins . . . , a language in which the laws and literature of the new nation could be inscribed." It was meant not only to be a "perfect reflection of the American character" but to become "the next universal language." The Marquis de Chastellux, fluent in English and traveling across America in the early 1780s after having fought for its independence, noted that no one had said, "You speak English well," but invariably "You speak American well; the American is not difficult to learn." Americans were in the process of expropriating the mother tongue, retaining earlier elements already disappearing in England while making adjustments and inventing neologisms in order to transform the present; it was part of what Chastellux called "a sort of national pride." In 1789 a French official predicted that American English was destined to replace diplomatic French as the world language because Americans had been "tempered by misfortune" and were thus "more human, more generous, more tolerant, all qualities that make one want to share the opinions, adopt the customs, and speak the language of such a people." This was one instance in which others outdid even proud American republicans in praise.[72]

Republicans were proving their heart as well as their stamina. Thomas Jefferson wrote his teenage daughter in 1787: "It is part of the American character to consider nothing as desperate; to surmount every difficulty by resolution and contrivance. . . . Remote from all other aid, we are obliged to invent and to execute; to find means within ourselves, and not to lean on others."[73] Noah Webster used perhaps the most aggressive language to exhort his countrymen to grasp their inheritance: over six installments in his *American Magazine* in 1787–88, he prescribed an America-centered education that would improve the design of moral government, coupling awareness of "the history of the late Revolution" with the necessary fortitude to be instilled in American youth. He concluded his essay thus:

> Americans, unshackle your minds and act like independent beings. You have been children long enough, subject to the control and subservient to the interest of a haughty parent. You now have an interest of your own to augment and defend: you have an empire to raise and support by your own exertions and a national character to establish and extend by your wisdom and virtues.[74]

To Webster as to Jefferson, national character was the result of maturation, of a unifying education, of a mutual respect shared by the people of the various states, and of a knowledge of America's variety from intensive study *within* the country and not abroad. The American people already understood the underlying message of recovered purity after a journey of hardship—so well expressed in the characteristic literary form of the captivity narrative. Now they had to realize that their cultural and intellectual independence was a journey as well, and that it required their escape from captivity within "haughty" British English.

## THE FARMER OF FEELINGS IN THE RISING EMPIRE

The Connecticut wit John Trumbull published his mock-epic *M'Fingal* in 1782, a little more than a decade after having declared that American poetry ought to "Wake from nature's themes the moral song" and equal England's heroic output. The Yale College prodigy opted for the burlesque and chose a ridiculous Tory for his protagonist. Trumbull's verse, while playfully skeptical of patriotic ritual, honored his country by lifting American empire above the defeated and diminishing British. "States, like men, are doom'd," he warned, the "infirmities of age to feel." In Great Britain's case, a "deep distemper" of the emotions arose as a result of both moral and economic ills:

> Thus now while hoary years prevail,
> Good Mother Britain seem'd to fail;
> Her back bent, crippled with the weight
> Of age and debts and cares of state.

After long years of greatness, "Conceit and pride alone remained." The North American continent shone brightly beside the tarnished image of England.[75]

In Canto Four, the final section of the epic poem, Trumbull expresses his astonishment at the majesty of his own country. "The Continent ascends in light," he sings, rejoicing in the performance of the Revolutionary armies:

> Thro' all the land in various chace,
> We hunt the rainbow of success.

Still the poet is announcing the end of an era more than he is heralding a new beginning. He gloats over arrogant Britain's demise more than he celebrates America. But as Britain resigns American shores, with "ev'ry rebel fife in play" to the tune of "Yankee Doodle," the land of America is now of and for Americans.[76]

In *M'Fingal* the gyrations of the war and the eventual American victory are likened to the revolutions of heavenly bodies. The peevish General Henry Clinton, like a phase of the moon, "wanes" when British troops lose in battle; he is "Eclips'd in many a fatal crisis / And dimmed when Washington arises." The "antient" course of nature "inverts"; manners and tempers, like the climate, change "to suit the genius of the times." The classical personifications of "Victory" and "Fame" precipitously abandon Britain for America and "fir'd with love of colonizing, / Quit the fall'n empire for the rising." Trumbull concludes with a prophecy:

> To glory, wealth and fame ascend,
> Her commerce rise, her realms extend.
> Where now the panther guards his den,
> Her desert forests swarm with men,
> Her cities, tow'rs and columns rise,
> And dazzling temples meet the skies.[77]

It was indeed a time when prophecy seemed appropriate. More than a year before Yorktown, America's rising empire had been anticipated by Jonathan Mason, the twenty-four-year-old son of a Son of Liberty, who had read the law under the guidance of John Adams and who delivered the tenth anniversary Boston Massacre oration in 1780. "The important prophecy is nearly accomplished," he said on that occasion. "The rising glory of this western hemisphere is already announced, and she is summoned to her seat among the nations." Dr. Thomas Welsh, who delivered the 1783 oration—the last before the annual event was replaced with Fourth of July oratory—made the same point, stressing America's "dignity and importance." The rising empire recognized itself to be geographically favored as it pronounced itself providentially secured.[78]

Welsh's projection linked America's physical blessings with its people's development of a naturally sympathetic spirit, sympathetic even to Great Britain. "The situation of our country, with respect to other dominions, is so secured by *nature*," and by nature so prosperous, that the time was approaching when "we even weep over our enemy, when we reflect that she was once great," her commerce predominant, her name "revered," and America "her friend." A momentary calm at war's end allowed the orator to appreciate the effect of severing the emotional connection: "Cast off from the bosom and embraces of her pretended parent," independent America had emerged, "manly and fortunate," having "waded to freedom, through rivers dyed with the mingled blood of her enemies and her citizens." Americans could claim, after a bloody, righteous quarrel, that they had fixed a "manly" purpose, one that elicited "manly" sympathy, and had properly inherited the North American garden from an infirm, pitiful, even deranged parent. The concluding line of Welsh's colorful address read: "Henceforth shall the American wilderness blossom as the rose, and every man shall sit under his vine and under his fig-tree, and none shall make him afraid."[79]

Commentators on the rising empire assessed the land and the waterways, which few dissociated from the character of the people who sought to master them. In his 1783 sermon Ezra Stiles stressed the role of agriculture and commerce. Rather than privilege one mode of economy over the other, he noted that "both seem abundantly sufficient. . . . The whole continent is activity, and in the lively vigorous exertion of industry." Abundance and vigor went hand in hand. America was bound to surpass Europe with the "enterprising spirit of Americans for colonization and removing out into the wilderness and settling new countries." He perceived emigration from Europe as fulfillment of the prophecy of Noah: "Our population will soon overspread the vast territory from the *Atlantick* to the *Mississippi*, which in two generations will become a property superiour to that of *Britain*."[80]

Whereas Dr. Welsh had retrospectively described American independence as a natural and necessary separation, Stiles could not soften his sense of a titanic natural event: a "political earthquake through the continent hath shook off *America* from *Great-Britain*." But like Welsh and like Trumbull, he marveled at the meaning of the "long farewell" to an old association. He, too, seemed almost sympathetic: English liberty had failed, but it had been resurrected in America, and in similar fashion America's commercial fleet would compete on all oceans and prosper over the former mother country, now "wearied out with the insolence and haughtiness of her domineering flag." As a "well regulated state," the new republic would extend outward from every community "transfused with the efficacious motives of *universal industry*."[81]

There was no more dramatic portrayal of America's chaste inheritance than that found in the work of the French-born J. Hector St. Jean de Crèvecoeur, naturalized in New York in 1764. The persona Crèvecoeur adopted in his *Letters from an American Farmer* (1782) was that of a humble planter, "a simple cultivator of the earth," a "farmer of feelings," as he termed his model American. The farmer typified a modest but morally secure people drawn from European stock but molded into an excitingly different and most promising breed. In Crèvecoeur's Letter #2, "On the Situation, Feelings, and Pleasures, of an American Farmer," he recognized certain material distinctions between the lot of the English and American, but asserted the latter's "privileges": a relatively simple, debt-free farm and a peaceable domestic existence, a wife who might sometimes "sit under the shady trees, praising the straightness of my furrows," and "felicity," defined in quintessentially American terms—"freedom of action, freedom of thoughts, ruled by a mode of government which requires but little from us." Indeed, it was owing to mild government that pure family feeling predominated in the farmer's thoughts. He could always rely on his family to produce "some pleasing emotion." English readers might laugh at his portrait of the "artless countryman" that Crèvecoeur offered with artfulness and affectation, but what nourished the American farmer was "precious soil," "independence," and ample dignity to feed his spirit.[82]

In Letter #3, "What Is an American?," Crèvecoeur characterized the egalitarian ideal more fully. "We are all animated with the spirit of an industry which is unfettered and unrestrained because each person works for himself.... A pleasing uniformity of decent competence appears throughout our habitations." Like Stiles, Crèvecoeur seemed to remove all causes for social disharmony and suggested that a consensus of feelings could be permanent. "We are the most perfect society now existing in the world. Here man is free as he ought to be; nor is this pleasing equality so transitory as many others are." Americans were adaptive, new and improved moral actors, for whom pleasure lay in a condition of selfhood unknown elsewhere, a personality type in contrast to the false pride of the Old World.[83]

Propertyless people once scattered across Europe came to the New World and were "regenerated." Americans, to Crèvecoeur, did not stagnate; they were always emerging. Adding to his fertile land, to his stock of knowledge, to his circle of friends, the "farmer of feelings" remained generous and optimistic. "The American is a new man, who acts upon new principles; he must therefore entertain new ideas and form new opinions." Nothing bound him any longer to the Old World, where only language had once identified him with a former country: "*He* is an American who, leaving behind him all his ancient prejudices and manners, receives new ones from the new mode of life he has embraced, the new government he obeys, and the new rank he holds."

Crèvecoeur portrayed, in pacifist terms, a revolutionary social concept—to feel one acquired "consequence" and "rank" simply by working the land. Ideally, Americans' power was meant to transform humanity without muscle, through a common adaptation to the land, which would produce a sentimental consensus. So it was Crèvecoeur who led the way in romanticizing the life achievable within American empire. "Here individuals of all nations are melted into a new race of men," he wrote, "whose labours and posterity will one day cause great changes in the world." The simplistic "melting pot" archetype inaugurated here was destined for a long run among the well-intentioned majority who embraced it, though Euro-Americans were ultimately to be regarded as a self-satisfied, homogenizing people overlooking the injurious effects of their aggressive impatience with unyielding ethnic traits—of course, this was beyond Crèvecoeur's view.[84]

He conceived America as an "asylum" or "refuge" for the people of Europe of modest means and decent aspirations who, like himself, could be directed to achieve happiness in their adopted land. America was where strangers were welcome, where the concept of "stranger" in fact could hardly be said to exist; for every newcomer to the land was accepted and would become assimilated as easily as his illustrative farmer. Crèvecoeur's composite citizen pursued happiness so plainly and so routinely that he could reserve the time to identify sentimentally with the land he owned, to inspect and admire even the tiny insects "dancing in the beams of the setting sun" and the bees, industrious "tenants" on his farm, that formed a quaint militia. Quails offered "a great fund of pleasure." The farmer saw that the birds were fed, and in return for his "inviolable hospitality, . . . they abundantly repay me, by their various notes and peculiar tameness." And "who can listen unmoved to the sweet love tales of our robins, told from tree to tree? Or to the shrill cat birds? The sublime accents of the thrush from on high always retard my steps that I may listen to the delicious music." The "peaceable swallow" and the "passive Quaker" were alike to him. Nature and the well-disposed American personality were each productive of the farmer's harmony and ease.[85]

In Crèvecoeur, nature metaphors often recur. "Men are like plants," he wrote, "the goodness and flavour of the fruit proceeds from the peculiar soil and exposition in which they grow." If the air influenced both forms of government and religion, this did not mean that life remained static or communities insular. Extending the melting-pot image, he added that what was dividing people at present, their zealous religious practices, would "cool for want of fuel." Just as Englishman or Frenchman melded into American, so the "medley" of religious sects would unify over a few generations. The absence of religious persecution would loosen systems of belief.[86]

The "venerable woods" of the American frontier suggested to Crèvecoeur a monumental contest in which the natural elements influenced character formation. Of course, given the author's cosmic optimism, "good conduct and temperance" were meant to prevail over rudeness and licentiousness, and the "smiling country" purged of all barbarity to feature "a general decency of manners." Before finally exhausting his fund of prophecies, the naturalized American introduced a Russian visitor, representative of another people with a continent to tame, "new . . . in knowledge, arts, and improvement." Crèvecoeur's Russian decisively concurs: "I view the present Americans as the seed of future nations, which will replenish this boundless continent."[87]

The author dedicated his work to the French Enlightenment figure

Abbé Guillaume Raynal, whose Catholic piety was less pronounced than his penchant for writing philosophical history. It was Raynal's overall appreciation for the meaning of America that Crèvecoeur delighted in: "You viewed these provinces of North America in their true light, as the asylum for freedom; as the cradle of future nations, and the refuge of distressed Europeans." There was, Crèvecoeur imagined, "a secret communion among good men throughout the world; a mental affinity connecting them by a similitude of sentiments." His was the vision of a Sternean world, a sentient world, if ever there was one.[88]

Another toiling sentimentalist and patriot spent the mid-1780s trying to convince the European literati of America's virtues. Jefferson largely composed his encyclopedic *Notes on Virginia* in the library of his Monticello estate before the war's end, but he painstakingly revised and eventually published it in Paris in 1785 and London in 1787. The *Notes* catalogued Virginia's Indian tribes, bird species, income and expenses, weights and measures, and other miscellaneous subjects of science and general knowledge. It also endeavored to define the progressive eighteenth-century scholar-statesman's social and ethical outlook. Or, as Leo Marx has put it, Jefferson's *Notes* alternates between mathematics and reverie, fact and feeling.[89]

Jefferson's America (a transformative Virginia writ large) was a place that heralded human achievement and would supplant European civilization, especially an unwholesome Great Britain that he now presumed to be "passing to that awful dissolution," the final resting place of which no one could yet project. For Jefferson, at least, "the sun of her glory is fast descending to the horizon," while America, he claimed, had produced "a Washington, whose memory will be adored while liberty shall have votaries," and inventive scientists like Benjamin Franklin and the self-taught Philadelphia astronomer David Rittenhouse. America, he went on, "though but a child of yesterday, has already given hopeful proofs of genius" and those aesthetic and intellectual pursuits "which arouse the best feelings of man, which call him into action, which substantiate his freedom, and conduct him to happiness." Private morals and social responsibility—what Jefferson termed "the best feelings of man"—once again assumed liberty and happiness to be not mechanistic principles but active pursuits.[90]

Jefferson believed strongly in the suitability of the American landscape for republican manners and public harmony. On the other hand, unlike Franklin in his early population study and unlike the ecstatic Crèvecoeur, he ruminated about engineering political harmony by aggressively monitoring the character of the people over time. Jefferson expected pollution to enter America as European immigration increased—that is, unless none but the "useful" were granted citizenship. Welcoming people who had had an enlightened education and who possessed agricultural enterprise would improve the nation, but unrepublican immigrants would eventually, if their numbers and representative power grew, "warp and bias" legislation "and render it a heterogeneous, incoherent, distracted mass." In the interest of social happiness, a coherent sense of national principles had to be preserved, in which case "the importation of foreigners" nursed under monarchical systems only threatened to make America "more turbulent, less happy, less strong." For the generally optimistic Jefferson, the moral-political spectrum ranged from absolute monarchy to "unbounded licentiousness." America's "temperate liberty," the middle ground, still stood a chance of being tainted with Old World moral weaknesses. The Virginian did not share completely in Crèvecoeur's bliss. He did not assume balance.[91]

Jefferson also assailed the "great political and moral evil" of slavery that scarred the land, yet, notably, he praised the "mild treatment" accorded to African Americans in bondage. The eradication of slavery, an institution inherited from colonial British rule, would be far from simple, he thought, and interracial harmony utterly impossible: "Deep rooted prejudices entertained by the whites; ten thousand recollections, by the blacks, of the injuries they have sustained . . . [will] produce convulsions which will probably never end but in the extermination of the one or the other race." Even allowing for social inequity, for the different "sphere in which they move," and the fact that their white masters denied them education, Jefferson also believed that blacks were inferior in reasoning ability: "their existence appears to participate more of sensation than reflection." The Native American Indians, whom he found a physically attractive people, brave, affectionate, honorable, and capable of "sublime oratory," needed only "cultivation" to raise them to parity with whites; but blacks were less gifted, less original—capable of arousing sympathy but not admiration. No black, Jefferson claimed, "had uttered a thought above the level of plain narration." What he regarded as inelegance and lack of physical appeal, combined with the animosities engendered under long enslavement, led Jefferson to suggest that America's blacks should be recolonized abroad, "beyond the reach of mixture."[92]

As Peter Onuf has recently argued, Jefferson viewed African Americans as a captive nation, like America the product of British despotism requiring and deserving *national* independence. But as a captive nation, Africans could not combine or coexist on an equal basis with the white majority, even without their deep resentment for having been enslaved by these people. Therefore, in Jefferson's thinking, white America (comprised of a variety of European emigrants) had become a distinct people—*one* people—while the captive African population loomed as a potent, if presently powerless, alternative to this *one* people dominating the eastern half of the North American continent. The dwindling population of the Native American nations, alone in not being identifiable with a people residing elsewhere, would be either resettled west of the Mississippi or assimilated into white society. But for Africans to achieve liberty in America, Jefferson surmised, a war for control of the continent must ensue, a bloody contest for space destined either to whiten or to darken. He thought blacks lacked historical motivation to give their loyalty to any country but one they established on their own, and as a believer in national harmony, he felt certain that the only happy outcome could occur through assisting the captive Africans to get a fair start elsewhere before a geometric rise in the enslaved population made the cost of recolonization prohibitive. Otherwise, the chronic state of conflict that slavery already represented to him, with the morals of both peoples suffering under the facts of inequality, would provoke an open and destructive war for dominance.[93]

On the other hand, like Crèvecoeur, Jefferson idealized the independent white tiller of the American soil. His emblematic statement in *Notes on Virginia* compresses Crèvecoeur's theme nicely: "Those who labour in the earth are the chosen people of God, if ever he had a chosen people, whose breasts he has made his peculiar deposit for substantial and genuine virtue. It is the focus in which he keeps alive that sacred fire, which otherwise might escape from the face of the earth. Corruption of morals in the mass of cultivators is a phaenomenon of which no age nor nation has furnished an example."[94]

Of all the romances with the American landscape, none perhaps has had the same enduring appeal as the story of Daniel Boone. It was John Filson's 1784 biography that first lauded Boone's accomplishments as the prototypical American pioneer-patriot, but Boone would have been nothing without the inviting landscape. As the historian John Mack Faragher put it: "Filson's Boone deems the greatness of Kentucky itself sufficient reward for his sacrifices and is content with the virtuous satisfaction of a job well done." Modesty became the great man, and Boone, notoriously a man of few words, fit the mold of the deserving hero as an independent man of principled action. A celebrity among the recent emigrants to the backwoods who read Filson, Boone lived in a cabin built from an old boat and did his best to eke out a living as civilized dominion caught up with him.[95]

Filson had been a schoolmaster in Pennsylvania, and so his reflective account of Boone's life ranged from dispassionate chronicle to moral lesson. It was written as if narrated by Boone, who was in fact unschooled, but in this way the pioneer hero appealed successfully to a readership intent on feeling closer to the idealized American character through the moral bearing of their hero. In his preface, Filson tells us that, "from the top of an eminence, with joy and wonder," North Carolina's Daniel Boone first looked upon Kentucky in 1769. Though his fellow explorers were all killed by Indians, the survivor Boone remained in the wilderness for two more years before returning east and bringing his wife and children and five other families back across the mountains to Kentucky, "which I esteemed a second paradise." In 1775, at the head of a party of "enterprising men, well armed," Filson's vigorous pathfinder "undertook to mark out a road in the best passage" through the Appalachians and erected the fort of Boonesborough. In mid-July 1776, after Indians kidnapped his daughter, Boone tracked them down and recovered her. But he himself spent a much longer time in captivity in 1778, when Indians operating at the behest of the British in Detroit overpowered his Virginia-based force; they "entertained me well," he said with apparent nonchalance, and their affection was so great that Boone found himself adopted as a "son" in an Indian family. They took him hunting and the resourceful American earned their trust before finally escaping. Resettling his family in Boonesborough in 1780 (believing Boone dead, his wife had returned to North Carolina), Boone concluded, "I now live in peace and safety."[96]

Filson was not the only wilderness enthusiast at this time to use rapturous language. A North Carolinian who had accompanied Boone but later returned home, wrote happily to a friend in 1782 of his frontier life: "if you did not live so far out of my road I would call on you where I could once more take you by the hand and take a Harty Drink in the Fear of God, and talk all our old affairs over. . . . Yet Sir I can inform you when I set down Coolly and reflect on that delightful Country and the Benefits I one day promise myself from its Beauty and Fertility that all my Loss Vanish and then Sir am Rich as my Lord."[97] And John Marshall, twenty-nine years old, wrote in 1784 of the "happiness of the western country . . . the New world," where "no people on earth possess a fairer prospect of political happiness." His reasoning was simple: The people of the thirteen original states had grown "entirely under a Monarchy" and could not resist the inherited need of "guarding against the influence of a crown where no crown exists." The people of Kentucky, on the other hand, were unencumbered by such a past, and their state would be "formed with more experience & less prejudice." Kentucky society would draw from Virginia and neighboring states "a few of the wise & virtuous," to develop a flourishing commerce and society, already in 1784 "improved beyond the hopes of the most sanguine."[98]

Filson was a promoter of Kentucky settlement who saw curative power in the frontier landscape and a morally regenerative purpose in adding white population to it. Filson-cum-Boone sounded much like Crèvecoeur in attesting to the "diversities and beauties of nature I met with in this charming season, expelled every gloomy and vexatious thought . . . Not a breeze shook the most tremulous leaf." At the time of this writing, as the Revolution reached its happy issue, Kentucky already had, as Filson put it, "by accurate account" upward of thirty thousand white inhabitants. These people were "polite, humane, hospitable," while diverse in their geographic origins. "We behold Kentucke, lately an howling wilderness, the habitation of savages and wild beasts, become a fruitful field . . . , the habitation of civilization." The "beautiful River Ohio, bounds Kentucke in its whole length . . . and in its course it receives numbers of large and small rivers, which pay tribute to its glory." Filson issued a promise, that "the reader, by casting his eye upon the map . . . may view . . . the most extraordinary country that the sun enlightens with his celestial beams."[99]

Like the botanist William Bartram a decade earlier, Filson was paying homage to a definition of sublime nature as that tendered by the Scottish arbiter of style and eloquence, Professor Hugh Blair, whose *Lectures on Rhetoric and Belles Lettres* (1783) emerged toward the end of its author's distinguished career at the University of Edinburgh and proved tremendously successful in America from its date of publication to the middle of the next century. "The simplest form of external grandeur," wrote Blair under the heading "Sublimity in Objects," "appears in the vast and boundless prospects presented to us by nature; such as wide extended plains, to which the eye can see no limits; the firmament of heaven; or the boundless expanse of the ocean. All vastness produces the impression of sublimity." What elevated the mind "in the highest degree" were scenes such as Bartram, and now Filson, tried to record: "the hoary mountain, and the solitary lake; the aged forest, and the torrent falling over the rock." Writing in the same tradition, Jeremy Belknap in his *History of New-Hampshire* (1784) highlighted the sensuality of nature found in the accounts written by earlier explorers of his state: "goodly forests, fair vallies and fertile plains . . . rivers well stored with fish, and environed with goodly meadows full of timber-trees." As Belknap construed: "No one who is acquainted with the interior part of the country in its wilderness state, can forbear smiling at this romantic description, penned in the true style of adventurers." New England summits revealed "vapor like a vast pillar, drawn up by the sunbeams, out of a great lake into the air." While attempting a data-rich compilation, Belknap as natural scientist identified past worshippers of the sublime as he previewed an appreciation of the mysteries of nature that would absorb romantic poets to come.[100]

George Washington was less given to the sublime. He had seen the land in a different light—scarred by battle, yielding marginally sufficient food. And he saw America's future in the spotted character of his often contentious troops. Enterprising western agriculturalists could drift from their identification with eastern settlement and, instead of strengthening union, might become "a formidable and dangerous neighbour." Leaders in the early postwar period recognized different interests among manufacturers, merchants, and farmers that, in Peter Onuf's words, "could not always be concealed by fulsome rhetoric, or by imaginary abundance."[101]

Washington's recommendations to the Confederation Congress should be understood in this context, when he proposed that the frontier West should be settled by demobilized soldiers already promised land as part of their payment for enlisting: "it cannot be so advantageously settled, by any other Class of Men, as by the disbanded Officers and Soldiers of the Army, to whom the faith of the Government hath long since been pledged." Washington intended that they should "connect our Governments with the frontiers, extend our Settlements progressively, and plant a brave, a hardy and respectable Race of People, as our advanced Post" to check "incursions" by "savages." Such men would "awe the Indians" and induce them to relinquish even more territory for white settlement. Manliness, he believed, "*Competence and Independence*," could be used to inspire patriotism on the frontier.[102]

From the seeds of settlement to expressions of political longing, republican mission found a voice. On July 4, 1787, as the delegates to the Constitutional Convention were giving birth to a federal republic, Joel Barlow, son of a modest farmer and orphaned young, yet a 1778 graduate of Yale, delivered an oration in Hartford. "Every free citizen of the American empire," he announced, "ought to consider himself as the legislator of half mankind." Proud to be an engine for progress in the arts, commerce, and manufactures, proud to be creating a "rational political system" designed for "the general happiness of mankind—his mind, dilated with the great idea, will realize a liberality of feeling which leads to a rectitude of conduct." Barlow's extravagant assignment for a new, responsible empire was to combine "rational" government with "liberality of feeling."[103]

Barlow's common denominator was boundlessness, endless promise; it came from the mind—"dilated with the great idea"—and was sensorially interconnected with the land's assets, America's imperial dimensions: "The natural resources of this country are inconceivably various and great; the enterprising genius of the people promises a most rapid improvement in all the arts that embellish human nature." Unquestioningly, the patriot assumed that the idea of a self-liberated America, purified through Revolutionary trials and then improved upon with governmental reconstitution, offered hope to the entire globe: "the example of political wisdom and felicity here to be displayed will excite emulation through the kingdoms of the earth, and meliorate the condition of the human race." American preeminence seemed as certain to Barlow as the happiness projected for all those who would gravitate into America's moral-political orbit.[104]

The new nation was onstage, on display to all humanity. In 1789, as the First Congress of the United States prepared to assemble in New York City, only a few years earlier headquarters of the British invasion force, America was in a novel position in the world and in world history; it felt it had no peer. This is what Thomas Jefferson was no doubt thinking when he wrote proudly, if fancifully, to Angelica Schuyler Church, daughter of one of New York's wealthiest patriots and the wife of an Englishman. What was happening in America was the model of the future, he assured her: "I know nothing so charming as our own country. The learned say it is a new creation . . . made on an improved plan. Europe is a first idea, a crude production, before the maker knew his trade, or had made up his mind as to what he wanted."[105]

America and the Old World were in the process of disjoining. Ironically in the 1790s, as it continued to invent itself, America would become newly embroiled in the disputes of Europe, further challenging citizens' confidence in the superiority of their collective character.

# CHAPTER SIX

⋘≫⋅◊⋅⋘≫

# TORMENTED BY PHANTOMS:
# 1789–1800

NOAH WEBSTER PUBLISHED his *Dissertations on the English Language* in 1789 and dedicated it to that "illustrious defender of American freedom" Benjamin Franklin. His goal was a unifying American language, and in its pursuit, in the interest of refining the *"general custom of speaking,"* he saw no point in copying British phrases and pronunciation. To look abroad only served to widen differences "between the language of the higher and common ranks; and indeed between the *same* ranks in *different* states." Arbitrarily following British standards would be "both *unjust* and *idle*," he declared, unjust for "abridging the nation of its rights."[1]

As George Washington took office, America was intent, no less than before, on obtaining satisfying definitions of individual and national moral progress. The republic was not yet liberated from the colonial past enough to chart progress other than in relationship to Britain. The word *progress* itself was wrapped up in transatlantic cultural conflict. The British took offense in the 1790s at Americans' introduction of *progress*, an acceptable noun, as a verb. Altering English orthodoxy, the upstart former colonies were developing a new way of life by refusing to submit to the authority of their inherited tongue. Webster wished to standardize the American language in such a way that new words, usages, and spellings would fulfill the Revolution, codifying America's separation from the British model to become itself.[2]

Between 1785 and 1830, the United States produced more than one hundred different school readers, some adapted directly from British texts, others, like Caleb Bingham's *Columbian Orator*, designed to inculcate patriotic ideas as well. From 1794 (and at least through the 1818 edition), Bingham included in his reader the 1793 Fourth of July address of young John Quincy Adams, which earnestly called on Americans to retrieve the "rapturous glow of patriotism" that illuminated the year 1776.[3] He also featured a 1796 Fourth of July oration given in Worcester, Massachusetts, projecting the overthrow of tyranny in the world: "The grand POLITICAL MILLENNIUM is at hand; when tyranny shall be buried in ruins; when all nations shall be united in ONE MIGHTY REPUBLIC!" And, from Dartmouth College, Bingham's alma mater, a 1795 commencement poem:

> Hail happy States! Thine is the blissful seat,
> Where nature's gifts and art's improvements meet . . .
> Columbia's genius shall the mind inspire,
> And fill each breast with patriotic fire . . .
> Plenty and peace shall spread from pole to pole,
> Till the earth's grand family possess one soul.

Bingham ended his reader with an excerpt from Jonathan Mason's 1780 Boston Massacre oration taking pride in the "land of liberty" where "public spirit and the love of virtue for our social happiness" were destined to "throw smiles upon the brow of individuals."[4]

The American reading public may have been only just emerging from its colonial bounds, but the nation as a whole was already more literate than the general population of Europe. New England led the way, yet the revolution of the word was by no means a fluid process. The cost of books was prohibitive for many (three or four times the comparative cost of today's books), which limited their distribution. First printings usually numbered in the hundreds, not the thousands. Even newspapers were scarce, though they were read respectfully, until the Post Office Act of 1792 set up a national postal network and for the first time allowed all newspapers (instead of just a favored few, as before) to be sent by mail at subsidized rates. Even before the act, New England presses were printing "not less than thirty thousand" copies of newspapers every week.[5]

When in 1793 Webster printed the inaugural issue of his New York-based paper, *American Minerva*, he announced on the front page the ways that newspapers "may be rendered useful." Like schools, he said, they ought to be encouraged by the government "and placed on a respectable footing" as "heralds of truth," because, to this socially conservative publisher, afraid of misrule and disorder, "it is an important fact in the United States that the best informed people are the least subject to faction, intrigue and a corrupt administration." Hope for national progress moved Webster's pen. It was axiomatic for him at this time that the "foundation of all free governments, seems to be, a general diffusion of knowledge. People must know they have rights, before they will claim them." As Secretary of State, bibliophile, and avid newspaper reader, Thomas Jefferson mapped out a plan to improve efficiency of delivery while extending postal routes westward across the Appalachian range.[6]

The changes were far-reaching. In the 1740s and 1750s, Franklin's *Poor Richard's Almanack* had sold approximately ten thousand volumes a year. It was extraordinary when Paine's *Common Sense* sold 150,000 copies in 1776, and yet Webster's comprehensive speller, first published in 1783, sold (according to the author) three million copies in its first twenty years on the market. Subscription sales, attracting advance buyers, continued to be the primary means of generating new works, but beginning in the 1790s, opinion-shaping traveling book salesmen reached out to more small towns and stimulated general interest. Cheap circulating libraries also expanded in post-Revolutionary America, though it was not until the 1820s that American publishing really developed into a profitable, mass-market enterprise.[7]

## THE FRANKLIN FACTOR

Benjamin Franklin, writer, printer, and discoverer, who had personified the best in the American character to people on both sides of the Atlantic, breathed his last in the spring of 1790. He was eighty-four. As a thunderstorm rose up in Philadelphia, William Smith, clergyman and longtime provost of the College of Philadelphia, reportedly intoned that this tempest was but the clouds announcing that their master—he who could redirect the lightning—was dead. Recalling the incident some years later in a solicitous letter to Smith, Benjamin Rush put this event into verse:

> What means that flash! The thunder's awful roar!
> The blazing sky! Unseen, unheard before?
> Sage Smith replies, "Our Franklin is no more;
> The clouds, long subject to his magic chain,
> Exulting now, their liberty regain."[8]

Smith's eulogy of Franklin (which Jefferson and Rush helped him to prepare) was published in 1791 by Franklin's grandson Benjamin Bache, who had been present in the room when his grandfather expired. Smith's theme was the multidimensional personality of the sagacious patriot, an "original and universal genius" who was "capable of the *greatest* things, but disdained not the *smallest*, provided they were useful. With equal ease and abilities, he could conduct the affairs of a Printing-Press, and of a great Nation." Comfort in dividing oneself between the simple and the grand was the model for American character.[9]

But humility did not dictate modest goals, for "the desire of Fame and posthumous Glory is also the most powerful incentive to moral excellence in this world." This was how Smith regarded the canny Franklin. The American republic needed citizens who were as ambitious as they were civic-minded, so that the nation's ascent did not have to wait long to become measurable. The rationale for commemorating "illustrious characters," America's founders, was to complete "the glorious fabric of American Empire and Happiness."[10]

Franklin's worth could be seen in his projection of American greatness. He rose because he was never satisfied. In celebrating friendship and improvement—whether cleaning and lighting the city streets or establishing the American Philosophical Society—he displayed charity amid a quest for knowledge and shared growth. Franklin's "schemes for the public good" brought him deserved fame and popularity; equally, his embassies to Great Britain showed his strong commitment to the country he loved, feelings that transformed him into "the bold Asserter of the rights of America in general." Smith consciously emphasized Franklin's "workman" character in the cause of independence, in establishing America's "empire and renown."[11] Most important, then, was his lifelong love of liberty. As he aged, Franklin elevated the cause of African Americans held in bondage. Liberty, justice, and humanity were one, and he looked forward to the day when there would not be "a *Slave* nor a *Savage*, within the whole Regions of America." Smith went on to assert that Franklin believed "this sublime Aera had already dawned."[12]

Franklin's death, America's loss, was seen as symbolic. He had been the spirit of the age, the embodiment of American potential. He was his fledgling nation, humble in itself but inspired by its own growth to be bold in presenting its mission, to share its presumption of a realizable affinity with the larger world. If America was, from the beginning, about discovery and improvement, then Franklin enriched the notion that the creative imagination gave generously. He understood the value of sympathy. To his countrymen, his pedigree of commonness, more than any other single life, demonstrated how an extraordinary mind required only the soil of America to present new possibilities to the world. Thus, if in life he represented the pursuit of harmony, in death he was a powerful reminder of how elusive harmony—friendship and equanimity—was in society.

The symbol of Franklin as the guide to social harmony stood as a poignant reminder of what America under George Washington's virtuous eye still could not attain. Through the 1790s, Franklin's memory was kept alive in countless hopeful odes to happiness and liberty. A typical one urged that citizens internalize his wisdom:

His lib'ral soul, his worth, his actions scan:
Go, Reader, go, and imitate the man.[13]

In a 1792 poem by the pseudonymous "POPULUS" titled "LIBERTY
FIRE," Franklin's most heralded discovery evoked a larger inspiration:

> Latent long, and undetected,
> Lay this heav'nly fire electric:
> *Franklin* drew it from the skies,
> Flashing Freedom in our eyes.

> Through all nations now excited,
> Fly the sparks of minds *ignited*. . . .

Freedom, given divinely to humankind, was an energy harnessed like
Franklin's lightning bolts:

> Loose from *despots* and their *minions*,
> Loose from *Priests* and their opinions . . .

In an almost magical way, the inventor of the lightning rod had connected America to "heaven's ethereal fire." The natural right to liberty
was as unstoppable as the heavenly bodies:

> Blow, all ye winds! the rising flame!
> Let it be a fire of fame,
> Blazing, rolling round the *Ball*,
> Like the *Sun* rejoicing *all!*[14]

Metaphors of light and heat now excited notions of liberty's permanence.

Yet the 1790s were a decade when America rumbled once again
with fears of conspiratorial threats to liberty and order. The republic
had new legitimacy with Washington's accession to the presidency, but
the people were contentious. Even as factionalism was decried at both

ends of the political spectrum, two distinct parties formed, one agonizing over the country's apparent reversion to the discredited ideology of elitist privilege, the other obstinately resisting the threat of an intemperate democracy.

In Washington's cabinet in 1791–93, Secretary of State Jefferson and Secretary of the Treasury Hamilton clashed repeatedly over principles. Jefferson accused his opponent of plotting to consolidate power among the few, the wealthy, surreptitiously transforming the United States government into an aristocratic or monarchical regime. Hamilton wished to strengthen America's economic position in the world by profiting from the British model of growth, and he thought that under dynamic, creative leadership and investment by citizens who could afford to place their confidence in the new government, there would be prosperity; he wrote to Vice President John Adams in 1792 that Jefferson's fear for the sanctity of republican government under such a policy was absurd: "Were ever Men more ingenious to torment themselves with phantoms?" But to an anxious Jefferson, the Hamiltonians were betraying their obligation to the people as set forth in the Constitution and, more emotionally, betraying the sacred memory, the hallowed spirit, of '76. The administration party had become in effect "the British party," a new incarnation of a banished phantom.[15]

Taking their quarrel to the newspapers while the President attempted to stay above the public fanfare, the two main disputants in an attention-getting drama galvanized support among legislators, as they became the respective heads of the first two competing political parties: Hamiltonian Federalists and Jeffersonian Republicans, or Democratic-Republicans, as it officially listed itself in national elections from 1796. In essence, Jefferson tried to convince the American people that his party had inherited the Revolutionary republican mantle—sympathetically representing the interests of the many—while errant Federalists had abandoned the spirit of the Constitution in a misguided, self-interested restoration of Toryism. Republicans in South Carolina, for example, characterized the High Federalists as "aristocrats under the name of *moderate* men," who perversely considered that "wealth makes power and right."[16]

Jefferson had, in a sense, stepped up the controversy in 1791 by associating himself with the explosive first volume of Thomas Paine's *Rights of Man*, a pamphlet that seemed to welcome social revolution and threaten the forces of order.[17] Hamilton fixed on this "evidence" of Jefferson's secretiveness and unpredictability, hinting that the Secretary of State was looking for every opportunity to court popular favor, disingenuously associating his own name with "that *republican firmness* and *democratic simplicity*, which ought to *endear him* to every friend of the 'Rights of Man.' "[18] What Jefferson strove to embody, "firmness" and "simplicity," mirrored Americans' composite memory of the mind and spirit of Franklin. Hamilton saw this presumed affinity as an obnoxious charade.

In very personal terms, Hamilton wrote as "An American" for the *Gazette of the United States* that Jefferson acted in an undignified manner by establishing Philip Freneau as editor of the antiadministration *National Gazette*, supporting those in the country who preferred "National insignificance, Public disorder and discredit" to "National Union, national respectability, Public Order and public Credit." How, Hamilton asked, could Jefferson be right in asserting that the members of the national government, "men whose abilities and patriotism were tried in the worst of times, have entered into a league to betray and oppress" the people? As "Metellus" (not inconsequentially the name of a general allied with the aristocratic element in the Roman republic), Hamilton charged that, while in France in 1787, Jefferson had opposed the federal Constitution, his subsequent comments revealing "fluctuations of sentiment" and fallible judgment; he disguised himself as "the disinterested friend of the people" while behaving as "the intriguing head of a party."[19]

Jefferson defended himself to President Washington, stating that he was known to the people "not as an enemy to the republic, nor an intriguer against it . . . as the American [the pseudonymous Hamilton] represents me. . . . No cabals or intrigues of mine have produced those in the legislature," as he alleged Hamilton's activities had. Intrigue and conspiracy preoccupied the anxious contenders. Defending Jefferson publicly was his fellow Virginian and protégé James Monroe, who wrote that Hamilton would subvert the "free and manly spirit of enquiry" (the Franklinian method of rational persuasion) in order to advance his partisan political aim of consolidated power. To Republicans, Hamilton represented the breakdown of Franklin's ideal of harmonious science and politics, and the corruption of America's national innocence and purity. Predictably, amid their dispute, Hamilton and Jefferson both insisted that difference of opinion was natural in a republic but that vicious temper and ill humor designed to excite dissension were inexcusable. Reason was ever the watchword.[20]

What Federalists feared and what Hamilton specifically identified as Jefferson's design was social "innovation and change" (as opposed to sound commercial development). War between England and France had once again broken out in 1793, and Americans were divided. Some Federalists thought the radical language of the French Revolution was a potentially anarchic influence on America's misguided masses; this brought the administration party closer to England, on which it also depended for revenues collected on all-important Anglo-American commerce. The Jeffersonian Republicans, meanwhile, held out hopes for the French republic and were also irked by Britain's continued military presence on American soil below the Great Lakes, in violation of the 1783 Treaty of Paris. Stern moralists in their resentment of British haughtiness, they judged themselves generous and flexible in their sympathetic understanding for momentary excesses occurring in the revolution the Federalists so abhorred. They equated their sympathy for France with an optimistic appraisal of the capacity of any people to resist monarchical tyranny and to create a responsible government. Fourth of July toasts in Philadelphia in 1793 emphasized the perceived link between the French Revolutionary spirit and American patriotic sensibility: to "The Republic of France—Sympathy to her misfortunes, praise for her virtues"; to "the human race—may the great family of mankind, without distinction of countries or colours, be united by charity"; to "the times—may the 18th century, which has elevated the philosophy . . . restore the rights of man."[21]

Republican-leaning clergymen said the French Revolution was the successor of America's own revolution in inspiring millennial hopes for a regenerated world where civil and religious tyranny would be overthrown.[22] Indeed, the Republican worldview feared social upheaval from below less than tyrannical elites above. Jefferson translated the situation in France into a new call for the active expression of enlightened sensibility. And the Republican Hugh Henry Brackenridge spoke in Pittsburgh to the issue of America's support of Revolutionary France:

> That we are bound [to France] by treaty, and how far, I will not say; because it is not necessary. We are bound by a higher principle, if our assistance could avail; the great law of humanity. . . . Shall kings combine, and shall republics not unite? We have united. The heart of America feels the cause of France. . . . [S]he is moved, impelled, elevated, and depressed, with all the changes of her good and bad fortune; she feels the same fury in her veins.[23]

It was not that America should support the French because they were always right, for indeed their revolution had gone awry, but because of a sympathetic responsibility to act to promote political good wherever republican sentiment had in some measure taken root. This Jeffersonian language of feeling gave the culture of sensibility an enhanced political flavor, though not, as we shall see, an exclusive political identity.

In correspondence, Jefferson and his allies consistently identified their interest as "republican" rather than "democratic," but "democratic societies" began to form in 1793. The first sprang up in Philadelphia and others developed in Virginia, New York, New Jersey, Vermont, Kentucky, and South Carolina, popular organizations critical of pro-British policies. These "Democrats" came from various professions: printers, cabinetmakers, bricklayers, grocers, doctors, innkeepers, marine captains, teachers, lawyers. Here is how Philadelphia's Democratic Society offered its founding rationale:

> THE RIGHTS OF MAN . . . have been clearly developed by the successive Revolutions of America and France. Those events have withdrawn the veil which concealed the dignity and the happiness of the human race, and have taught us, no longer dazzled with adventitious splendor, or awed by antiquated usur-

pation, to erect the Temple of LIBERTY on the ruins of *Palaces* and *Thrones*.

The society promised to be vigilant, to take "every proper precaution" not to forfeit the "prize" of providential blessings only recently won. Members would cultivate knowledge of "rational Liberty" and attend to the "public good." Above all, they would defend republican government, "the most natural and beneficial form, which the wisdom of Man has devised."[24]

A circular to "fellow citizens" of various Pennsylvania counties warned of present dangers: "The seeds of luxury appear to have taken root in our domestic soil; and the jealous eye of patriotism already regards the spirit of freedom and equality, as eclipsed by the pride of wealth and the arrogance of power." The societies doubted that the Congress was truly representative and suspected the U.S. Senate in particular, because it was not popularly elected, of becoming an "established Nobility."[25]

These post-Revolutionary activists, rekindling the Revolutionary spirit of protest, tended to be blunt and aggressive. The Democratic Society of Chittenden County, Vermont, which had modeled itself on the Philadelphia group ("we believe they speak the general language of the people"), opposed Federalists who did not seem willing to stand up to continued British pressure—to British incitement of Indians on the western frontier and bullying and impressment on the high seas. They were manifestly defiant: former subjects of the king, now called "our best citizens," had best not "thwart the inclination of the great body of the people. . . . Let our generosity to others be great and extensive, but bounded by the necessary line of safety to ourselves and our dear bought rights." Americans were "generous" and "unsuspicious," but never again to be "dupes" of the nation that had held her "faithful children" in contempt and only recently termed her sons "stubborn, perverse and rebellious." Emboldened by the success of the Revolution, they scorned that government which had "lost thirteen flourishing colonies, after sinking one hundred and twenty millions in the equally vain as wicked pursuit of bringing them to acknowledge their obedience in all cases whatever." In contrast, Revolutionary France was "a nation who is gloriously, zealously, uniformly, and perseveringly (beyond example) wading through *oceans of blood*, for the mere purpose of obtaining permission to establish a government for herself, upon the same plain, simple, and immutable principles of truth, on which the whole system of ours is founded."[26]

Judge Nathaniel Chipman of Vermont framed a thoughtful response to the outpourings of the Chittenden County Democratic Society. He had written the well-read *Sketches of the Principles of Government* in 1793 (Jefferson owned a copy), which had been cited by the Chittenden organizers in their March 1794 "Principles of Formation and Regulations," and so this staunch Federalist judge wanted to be sure to disassociate himself from them. The Democratic Society had quoted Chipman: "The Governments of the several American States, as well as that of the Union, are of the *Democratic* Republican kind." In his response, published in *The Herald* of New York, he tried to introduce calm reason into a fiery situation, suggesting that the members of democratic societies needed to reassess the workings of the Constitution. In being a "representative democracy," he stressed, the national government was designed to prevent both the tyranny of the few and the tyranny of the many. For every violation of trust there was a constitutional remedy. So the fears of Chittenden County were unreal and—now he hardened his position—the democratic societies themselves "not merely useless, but mischievous." They resembled "all the heat and ungovernable passions, of a simple democracy." Ill equipped to investigate matters thoroughly, they acted rashly, even assuming a "dictatorial style." Distinguishing healthy from unhealthy distrust of rulers, Chipman repeated: "Like the demagogues of a simple democracy they have applied wholly to the passions and jealousies of the people," incongruously making jealousy "a species of virtue." They were in fact an "inconsiderable minority," deceptive, presuming to speak for America while in fact standing in the way of the people's true happiness.[27]

The Chittenden County Democratic Society continued to challenge, insisting on a positive meaning for the name of democrat. In a response to Chipman, one member referred to his fellows warmly as "the sensible, the thinking, the judicious freemen of Vermont," resentful of being called dictatorial. The society also issued brusque denunciations of a Federalist congressman, Fisher Ames of neighboring Massachusetts, whose "supercilious vanity" exhibited itself in insulting remarks about the societies he called mere "clubs." The Vermonters reasserted their valid censorial purpose, stating that if their warm statements were in fact "contradictory to those of the great body of the people, we must as naturally as deservedly fall into contempt, and dwindle into insignificance." But that had not happened. Because the Federalist "gentlemen" who sought to silence them did not "merit the appellation of *'real friends of the people'*; we can be but little surprised, that [they] . . . have endeavored to crush us." The indignant Vermonters took on "Tory-connected" Ames and others in Congress who had "indecently abused" them: "We shall ever glory in intermingling our sentiments, our friendship, and our love, should you and every King on earth continue to lash them with all the malevolent virulence which vindictive impotency never fails to inspire." Organizing public celebrations, parades, and discussions, proclaiming the right of citizens to assemble and make their criticisms known, these spirited societies, comprised equally of well-to-do and ordinary working people, claimed to embody the true voice of the American people.[28]

By 1794, President Washington himself began protesting what he called "self-created" societies. He believed they were bent on violence. That year, thousands of disgruntled frontier folk in western Pennsylvania became part of the Whiskey Rebellion, a period of agitation vaguely resembling the 1765 Stamp Act (in miniature), when hard-pressed farmers protested an excise tax imposed by Congress on the whiskey they produced. They may have groped for a sense that government could be more palpably democratic, that Madisonian federalist language was not empty rhetoric. Indeed Madison himself warned in a speech before Congress that "the censorial power is in the people over the Government, and not in the Government over the people." Though Madison did not subscribe to the democratic societies or support the Whiskey rebels, he greatly suspected the Federalists (though not Washington himself) of looking for an excuse to assume despotic power.[29]

The Southern states and Kentucky and Tennessee joined in the resistance, but it was to more accessible western Pennsylvania that Washington dispatched 15,000 troops, with his trusted Treasury Secretary and former wartime aide Hamilton along to conduct interrogations. He meant to demonstrate that unlawful behavior would be severely punished, but Washington had exaggerated the Whiskey rebels' disloyalty as well as their organization, and the insurgency quickly melted away. Efforts to round up the leaders yielded but twenty arrests of insignificant men; no conspirators were clearly identified. Though the democratic societies had been silent about the excise tax and scrupulously avoided making incendiary remarks, the President suspected that they had had a hand in fomenting the antigovernment agitation. He worried about lawlessness disguised as liberty and feared the ruin of constitutional controls in the Republican challenge to Federalist rule.[30]

Thus the language of Federalist-Republican debate continued to be explosive, both sides in effect calling the other traitorous without actually using the word. Federalists emphasized the legitimacy of Washington's administration and decried the rise of an opposition. They argued that the groups aligned with Jefferson had put themselves above the law: "Those who represent the people support the laws and are protected by them; those who are in opposition have need of aid and support from other quarters: They naturally have recourse to secret influence and intrigues . . . they form clubs, corresponding committees, and societies of various descriptions." Once again, the Federalists seemed unwittingly to be criticizing Franklin's legacy, for clubs, committees, and societies were the forms around which he had ordered his own rise from obscurity to prominence and respectability. In the phantom-tormented language of the 1790s, even civic improvement according to Franklin's model could appear conspiratorial. Political equality, by the Federalists' definition, was meant to coexist with personal inequality: "It is not only compatible with, but essential to a system of equal rights, that a man should enjoy the fruits of his talents and industry." For this reason, an elite class of Federalists ensured social and political stability.[31]

The Republicans went on calling the Federalists pretentious, or, as one Republican writer acidly labeled them, "incorrigible aristocrats" and "gaudy insects." "They are in general the sons or relatives of wealthy individuals. Pride naturally accompanies good fortune. . . . The fondness of parental folly hails them as the patricians of the country." Jefferson portrayed his Anglophile opposition as a body set up by "old Tories" (magnanimously accepted back into republican society after the Revolution), duplicitous merchants whom he called "foreign & false citizens" profiting from their British connections, and "stock dealers & banking companies . . . enriching themselves to the ruin of our country." He feared lest the British gain such a hold that the new American republic might yet be reeled back in to the island that had formerly captivated it. To his erstwhile ally Aaron Burr he wrote that he feared America was "but a sturdy fish on the hook of a dexterous angler, who, letting us flounce till we have spent our force, brings us up at last."[32]

In the terms of sentiment and sympathy, the Federalists considered themselves advocates of the civic generosity that wise and authoritative leaders should show toward the less privileged when public order made such behavior possible. They trusted in their own deliberations and consciences and feared "unqualified" people who would selfishly wrest government from the reasoning elite. For the Republicans, sympathy and generosity flowed when all fellow citizens felt morally (if not yet socially) equal and recognized the same potential for enlightenment. This moral calculus related to citizenship: If the public-spirited Franklin had been America's model citizen, avaricious, pro-British Federalists were the "false citizens" whom Jefferson berated.

## Where All Hearts are Engaged

Both groups believed that faction or "party spirit" was fraudulent, that it reflected not just one-sidedness but a corrupted nature. As much as both believed in reason and candor, they were certain that the opposition was uncompromising, covetous of office, and arbitrary in its methods to obtain it. Perhaps because this tone of desperation permeated political society, the 1790s in America were a time when the call for sensibility remained strong. The first two American editions of Mackenzie's *The Man of Feeling* were published in the 1780s, and further editions were published in Litchfield, Connecticut (1790), Philadelphia (1791 and again in 1794), and Worcester, Massachusetts (1795). In 1792, America's first professional novelist, Charles Brockden Brown, wrote his sketch "The Story of Julius," meant to highlight, in a touching way, human responsiveness to an altruistic passion. Susanna Rowson's enduring *Charlotte Temple* was printed in Philadelphia by the entrepreneurial Mathew Carey in 1794 (there were two more editions by 1797); the compassionate author exulted in her text: "Content, my dear friends, will blunt even the arrows of adversity. . . . If I have been so lucky as to find the road to happiness, why should I be such a niggard as to omit so good an opportunity of pointing out the way to others. The very basis of true peace of mind is a benevolent wish to see all the world as happy as one's self."[33] Sensibility had struck a chord for many decades now, but the nation's leaders failed to use it to advantage. It had been tapped to contribute to social order, to a spirit of reconciliation among America's parts, and to draw out Americans' feelings so as to nourish a nationalistic language; but now passion was merely exposing the destructive sentiments of terror and panic instead of feeding sympathy and generosity.

This is ironic, because, of course, sensibility did not break down along party lines. One of the most constant of New England Federalists, Noah Webster, showed that one did not have to project an egalitarian ideal in order to highlight sentiment's function in the republic. The 1783 first edition of his famed "blue-backed speller" told the story of two brothers, Tommy and Harry. The first was pious and virtuous, the second "sullen," "perverse," and "disobedient." As Tommy grew, he urged Harry to be "steady and diligent," reminding "his wicked brother, with tears in his eyes, that if he did not reform . . . he would soon be ruined." It was Tommy's "tender feelings" that led him to care for the sinful Harry. On their mother's death, Tommy "burst forth in a flood of tears," but Harry did not grieve at all. Tommy came to exemplify a life of "industry, virtue, and generosity," marrying "a most lovely woman, whom he admires and treats with all possible tenderness." Harry landed in jail. The rewards of sensibility could not be clearer.[34]

In a 1795 sermon, *The True Means of Establishing Public Happiness*, the prominent Connecticut Federalist Timothy Dwight, who succeeded Ezra Stiles as president of Yale, equated the language of sentiment with a means of grace. Influenced by Scottish thinkers such as Adam Smith, Dwight believed that sentiment moved citizens to commitment and compassionate social actions, in pursuit of the common good. In conventional terms, he contrasted reason and good sense with passion and unhealthy appetite, to establish, in a nonpartisan way, the substance of American virtue and to undermine "shewy" self-interest and covetousness. While religious education had "given birth to just moral sentiments," it was secular practice, "general influence and example, united with public instruction," that Dwight identified as having "cultivated such sentiments into habit."[35]

Though their politics clashed, Dwight's practice of a virtue rooted in piety was compatible with Jefferson's Sternean sensibility. Both owed their political idealism to a belief in the activity of the moral sense, to the role of conscience in determining empathy with the lives and feelings of others. "Good-will to Mankind," Dwight offered, "accomplishes directly most of those desirable objects, at which the political Constitutions, and the Laws, of Society aim; it makes men honest, just, faithful, submissive to government, and friendly to each other, without restrictions or punishments; and renders magistrates equitable, public spirited, and merciful, without checks, factions, or rebellions." Jefferson, of course, would not have used such words as "submissive to government," nor invoked a contrast between "public spirit" and "checks, factions, or rebellions," but the underlying sentiment was alike. In Dwight's words: "The principal motives to virtue are evidently the pleasure found in the practice of it—the esteem, affection, and beneficence which it excites in our fellow creatures." "All things flourish," he asserted with a Jefferson-like cadence, "where all hearts are engaged."[36]

Dwight took the lead in promulgating an exclusive religious outlook suited to the politics of this probationary decade, hoping for persuasion of errant citizens. "Men of extensive political information, and sagacious forecast," he sermonized, "have frequently trembled for our national existence; and, notwithstanding some favourable interpositions of Providence in our behalf, they still wait anxiously to know what the end will be." Noting that "a family is, in some respects, a state in miniature," he explained (much like the Tom and Harry of Webster's parable) that there existed in families ill-mannered children of bad character and duty-bound children of good character. He urged the virtuous not to give up on their fellows. If virtue were taught and practiced and the human will restrained from the pursuit of selfishness and coarse pleasures, the resulting (responsible adult) character would enable government to consist in "mild and equitable measures, few and gentle interpositions of mere authority, united with argument and persuasion" to "establish domestic order, peace and happiness." Except for the selectivity underlying Federalists' social order, this was still republicanism—the Republicans' faith as well. Dwight added, "If the personal character of its citizens were perfectly good, there would be neither necessity, nor opportunity, of governing by force." He envisioned his virtuous citizens enjoying "free and rational government." "Man," he concluded, "may be as easily a Saint as a Savage; and Nations as easily enlightened with Millennial glory, as overcast with the midnight of Gothicism."[37]

Along with sensibility, the macabre was not unwelcome in America at this time, as gothicism, whether or not stimulated by political dissension, found its way into the literary imagination. Charles Brockden Brown's *Wieland, Or the Transformation: An American Tale* (1798) presented personal phantoms—madness, secrecy, and self-destruction—to challenge the American dream and tempt readers to see in post-Revolutionary society prospects less harmonious and less affirming than those which enthusiastic pamphleteers and columnists had fixed upon.[38]

In *Wieland*, reason and faith contend, the senses prove unreliable, and at points in the novel the source of one's own thoughts becomes suspect. Narrator and heroine Clara Wieland faces the manipulations of Carwin, who uses ventriloquism to intrude into her privacy, while she reacts to her grave, impressionable brother, who hears voices and believes that God has commanded him to kill his wife and children. Clara announces the ideal of the age early on: "Self-denial, seasonably exercised, is one means of enhancing our gratifications." Her own attraction to religion was deistic, measured to provide balance: "the product of lively feelings, excited by reflection on our own happiness, and by the grandeur of external nature." But throughout the tale she is tormented. "Ideas exist in our minds that can be accounted for by no established laws," she reports after dreaming that her brother "tempted" her to her own destruction. "Surely it was frenzy," she attempts to rationalize, that brought on such a dream. (The word *frenzy* is used repeatedly throughout.) She meets increasingly with "invisible" powers that raise questions about human nature: "conspiracy," "whispers," "images," "impulses," "shadows," "hellish illusions," and "tempestuous commotion." She wails, "I have lost all faith in the steadfastness of human resolves." Her uncle explains to her after the murders, "The phantom that has urged him . . . is not yet appeased." The mischievous Carwin, in apologizing later for his lack of openness, suggests to Clara that her present torment resulted from having grown up perfectly innocent: "You held apparitions and goblins in contempt." Passion was real and constant, and so, the ventriloquist admitted, he could not stop himself from pursuing his perverse gratification until "I had filled your mind with faith in shadows and confidence in dreams." The captivation, frenzy, and deceptions of the novel mirrored the troubled decade in which it appeared. Language heightened fear.[39]

Under conditions of spiritual disorder, the vision of Dwight and his fellow Federalist clergy grew self-defensive. As much as they wished for evidence of virtue to facilitate mild government, they were anxious moralists who equated Republicans' ridicule of church pronouncements (and the high society it protected) with a crumbling of society. Jefferson did not reveal his private faith to any but trusted friends such as the philosophical Benjamin Rush or the Unitarian English émigré and political liberal Joseph Priestley. But he did make it clear that he believed morality did not have to be founded on religion. And so, based in part on evidence gleaned from the pages of his *Notes on Virginia*, the Republican leader was conveniently targeted as a morally lax atheist, unworthy to lead a pious Christian nation. Federalist clergy presumed correctly that Jefferson belittled biblical explanations for great events and that he denied revelation. They looked harshly at his lack of interest in the Bible as a teaching tool for the young.[40]

The Virginian's tenacity on this subject was well known and Federalists did not take kindly to it. In the *Notes*, Jefferson most strongly advocated religious freedom: "Difference of opinion is advantageous in religion. . . . Millions of innocent men, women, and children, since the introduction of Christianity, have been burnt, tortured, fined, imprisoned; yet we have not advanced one inch towards uniformity." Jesus had never claimed to be divine, and to Jefferson one could be a moral Christian without being a Trinitarian. Dwight and like-minded Federalists panicked. They imagined that Jefferson would dismantle the Christian church in America. Though both Jefferson and Dwight preferred to think that (here quoting Jefferson) "reason and persuasion are the only practicable instruments," the rhetoric of harmony seeking was ineffective. Phantoms of the mind produced dreaded images. Dwight personally predicted that if Republicans gained power they would burn Bibles and unite children in "chanting mockeries against God." Jefferson's politics were equated with French Revolutionary terror, his religion indistinguishable from French philosophic atheism. Anguish and frustration made "reason and persuasion" as abstract a standard as virtue. Just as Dwight saw the spirit of the American republic in religious terms that he believed American Francophiles would extinguish, offended Jeffersonians referred to Dwight as the "Connecticut high priest." And Jefferson himself, before the century was out, would make one of his most ardent declarations with respect to clerical narrowmindedness. Employing unmistakable imagery, he wrote to Christian Republican Benjamin Rush: "I have sworn upon the altar of God, eternal hostility to every form of tyranny over the mind of man."[41]

The sentimental vision of America suffered as the rift between "French" and "English" principles deepened amid the conflict over religious scruples. Together these assumptions about partisan characteristics blurred Americans' sight. And yet, the doctrines of sensibility and Christianity remained compatible. The 1794 sermon of Peter Thacher, preached at the First Baptist Church of Boston, offers persuasive evidence that notions of individual self-cultivation and millennial visions for a morally triumphant America, if dormant, continued to exist in the fractious 1790s.

Sterne himself, it must be recalled, was an Anglican minister and author of a collection of sermons, even if his popular fiction tested the limits of social acceptance for the expression of men's sensual appetites.

Recalling the story of Job, Thacher was moved to observe in the Sternean fashion: "These are the deep lamentations of a man greatly afflicted, and they paint a scene of woe which must be affecting to every humane and sensible heart. . . . The heart which is not melted by another's woe, the heart which does not bleed when it beholds misery and death, hath never yet felt the power of the gospel, nor can it be acceptable to the God of compassion." Thacher emphasized "the sensation of pity and sympathy . . . founded on the social nature of man," whose happiness depended on the happiness of others. "It is not fit," he cried out, "that our hearts should remain hard and callous, when those of our friends are breaking around us. . . . The gospel requires us 'to weep with them that weep,' to mingle our tears with the afflicted and discover to them what we really feel for their calamities." (His words nearly matched Jefferson's to the artist Maria Cosway in the 1786 dialogue "My Head and My Heart": A "sublime delight" arose when an individual was able to "mingle tears with one whom the hand of heaven hath smitten.") The sensible Thacher credited God with having given human beings "an heart of flesh, an heart not only susceptible of all the impressions of virtue and religion, but of those exquisite sensibilities which humanize our souls, and cause them to vibrate with pity and compassion whenever a tale of woe reaches our ears, or our eyes are pained with the view of the distress or anguish of our fellow men." The pastor's understanding of compassion, consistent with the physiological basis of sensibility, was "the spontaneous effusion of the moment," and at the same time "a steady principle, which . . . will lead us to constant acts of kindness, charity, and compassion. It will irradiate the whole path of our life." The position of sensibility, it appears, had not been dislodged.[42]

And yet fear of tyranny and fear of anarchy rent America in two. The chasm enlarged during Washington's last years in office and throughout John Adams's presidency. While envoy James Monroe was embracing French Revolutionaries in Paris and describing the union of spirit which bound the two "sister republics," Chief Justice John Jay negotiated a treaty with England. Passed by a reluctant Congress in 1796, it recognized British control of the seas in order to reduce Anglo-American tensions.[43]

The Jay Treaty was regarded as a lesser of evils by most Federalists but was detested in many corners of America, contributing to political polarization. The pro-French Philadelphia newspaper *Aurora* remarked that while America continued to suffer British "indignities," the Jay Treaty had inflicted *"national injuries* and *national insults."* According to a column in the *Independent Gazetteer* reprinted in the *Aurora*, snubbing France through a treaty undertaken with *"excess secrecy"* suggested that the Federalists viewed France as "an *ideot*, who would not resent any engagements which we might enter into, however injurious to herself;— but are we certain that France will be passive when she is dishonoured?" On July 4, 1795, when the terms of the treaty were presented to the American public, the *Aurora* editorialized:

> This whole transaction has been conducted with a studied parade and ostentation of contempt for the sentiments of the people at large. . . . One would have imagined that America was to turn with loathing from the embraces of a foreign tyrant, to whom Nero & Caligula were but diminutive butchers, and who has perpetrated every outrage on this country which weakness can suffer or villainy can inflict.[44]

Jefferson had retired to Monticello in January 1794, but his pen was still active. He railed that the Jay Treaty was designed by the Hamiltonians to reduce America to semicolonial dependency and ensure that it was transformed into a state patterned on ministerial corruption. The year 1796 was destined to witness the first contested presidential election. Republicans in Congress led by James Madison put forth Jefferson's name, well before the candidate knew he was one. The *Aurora* defined the contest between Jefferson, "steadfast friend to the Rights of the People," and Adams, "an advocate for hereditary power and distinctions," while to Jefferson's detractors his pronouncements revealed him to be a demagogue, a dissembling democrat of false refinement who would, if elected, preside over the breakdown of social order and the elevation of less "honorable" men, French-thinking men, to positions of public power.[45]

Although in the early years of the republic presidential candidates did not campaign, electoral politics was beginning to acquire a new complexion, foreshadowing the richly embellished and well-organized contests to come. Clerk of the House of Representatives John Beckley was the Republicans' most active campaigner in the 1790s, an ambitious former indentured servant from England who seemed to regard liberty and equality as personal tools of upward mobility. While he was excluded from Federalist society because of his humble roots, Beckley was given acceptance by the Republicans for his travels through the countryside, distributing pro-Jefferson literature and making zealous addresses. Beckley sought greater respectability through such efforts, but succeeded mainly in shielding the likes of Jefferson and Madison from active campaigning. True republicans were expected to be willing to serve in high office without seeking personal gain or unwarranted prominence, and so this early party organizer allowed the Republican standard bearers to retain an appearance of disinterestedness. As a contentious democratic canvasser, Beckley was ahead of his time. He held the as yet uncommon view that partisan politicking was an expression of republican virtue. Federalists in newsprint mocked Beckley's lower-class background, as Federalists in Congress saw to his dismissal from the nonpolitical clerk's position.[46]

President John Adams inherited an unstable world in the spring of 1797. The honest and independent-minded New England moralist had been a great Revolutionary. But he was somewhat of an eccentric who lacked the personal skills needed to navigate through the inflammatory politics of the 1790s.[47] Nevertheless, in his Inaugural Address, Adams assumed an admirable dignity when he said that American national pride was "justifiable" when it grew from "conviction of national innocence, information, and benevolence." By "innocence" he did not so much mean the opposite of guilt as the lack of artifice or deception.[48] By "information" he referred to the embrace of knowledge and a scientific spirit that could lead to broad progress. By "benevolence," of course, he wished to see a revival of generous conduct, the enlightened instincts Adams had witnessed when he was one of the leaders of the principled move in opposition to an unjust Great Britain in the 1770s. His sense of honor, personal and national, had carried him far. What the proud, temperamental New Englander did not anticipate on succeeding Washington was a sustained effort on the part of the dominant Hamiltonian wing of the party to manipulate him.[49]

American factionalism was not to be rerouted, nor political enemies appeased, during this ill-starred administration. By the end of Adams's term, hurt as much by a lack of appreciation within his own discomfited party as he was by his defeat by Jefferson and a more solidified Republican constituency, the embattled President would characterize his torment in a warm letter to a man like himself, Revolutionary firebrand turned Federalist Christopher Gadsden of South Carolina. After the Southerner commiserated with the President over his forced encounters with political "bedlam," the reactive but unmartial Adams replied that Gadsden's "friendly sentiments" had struck him "with a tenderness which was almost too much for my sensibility." John Adams identified strongly with America's longing for dignity and character, and the muddled state of affairs he presided over apparently stripped him of what hopes he had on taking the oath of office.[50]

The problem of interpreting European politics continued to preoccupy the nation. As Adams entered the presidency in the spring of 1797, France made it clear that it viewed the Jay Treaty as the announcement of an Anglo-American alliance and soured relations further by snubbing the new administration's envoys in what came to be called the XYZ Affair. In the fall of that year John Marshall, Charles Cotesworth Pinckney, and Elbridge Gerry were told that they needed to pay $250,000 simply for an audience with French Foreign Minister Talleyrand. The "quasi-war" that followed intensified anti-French sentiment in America, as the Republicans and their symbol, Thomas Jefferson, former U.S. minister to France and former Secretary of State, became even more obnoxious to Federalists and more readily associated with French immorality. In *The Federal Songster*, a book of blatantly anti-French verse, President Adams was portrayed as sage and savior:

> When we're insulted by the world,
> Our stripes and stars in wrath unfurl'd
> Shall guard our country's coast;
> We fear no tyrant, no, not we,

> For brave Columbia will be free,
> Since ADAMS is our boast.

The song "Five Headed Monster" told of "sly" Talleyrand, a "cloven foot Reptile." And a new version of "Yankee Doodle Dandy" was equally militant, equally cocky:

> Yankee Doodle (mind the tune)
> Yankee Doodle dandy,
> If Frenchmen come with naked bum,
> We'll *spank* 'em hard and handy.[51]

Like the Whiskey Rebellion that was blown out of proportion by Washington, the "quasi-war" was essentially bloodless, resulting only in the seizure of ships in the Caribbean and a series of militant speeches and editorials. The crisis, however, brought the Federalists a most effective revenge on their domestic opponents, in the form of the Alien and Sedition Acts, passed by Congress in the summer of 1798. The Alien Acts were deemed a war measure, designed to counter undue French influence over the American people by threatening expulsion or prison without benefit of trial to any foreigner suspected of agitation ("danger to the public peace or safety") within the United States. The Sedition Act was the more pernicious, declaring that *any* written or spoken statements in opposition to administration policy ("false, scandalous and malicious") or criticism of the President ("with intent to defame") constituted a crime punishable by fine and/or imprisonment. With Americans' First Amendment freedoms curtailed, the conspiratorial air thickened.[52]

As Hamiltonians clamored for war with France, the ever-optimistic Jefferson wrote political ally John Taylor of Caroline County, Virginia: "A little patience, and we shall see the reign of witches pass over, their spells dissolve, and the people recovering their true sight, restoring their government to its true principles." It was another reference to the illusory nature of truth, fixed and self-evident in the momentary harmony of 1776, but a mere phantom afterward. In Jefferson's vision, the High

Federalists were ghoulish hags and sorcerers preying on the rational mind, America caught in a trance in the year of Charles Brockden Brown's *Wieland*.[53]

During the "reign of witches," a number of prosecutions were undertaken and Republican editors hounded and some jailed. Federalist congressman John Allen of Connecticut complained of writers who were "vile assassins of our country's peace." His colleague Robert Goodloe Harper of South Carolina targeted Republicans in Congress as well as offensive newspaper editors whose "filthy streams" of "invective," if unrestricted, stood to "gain credit" with too susceptible citizens. Republican congressman Edward Livingston of New York countered the witch hunt forcefully by offering the Federalists an extension of their logic: "We have . . . nothing to do but to make the law precise, and then we may forbid a newspaper to be printed, and make it death for any man to attempt it!" A brazen newspaper editor tempted fate, calling President Adams a "mock Monarch," while a Federalist-allied newspaper identified "seditious" Republican congressmen and furiously pronounced that if Americans wanted to build the kingdom of Satan, "let them chuse democrats to Congress." Congressmen on both sides of the issue displayed their short tempers, speaking in terms of "irritation," "slanders," "calumny," "shameless falsehoods," and things "inflammatory." The verb "to excite" was invoked often, as in "to excite insurrection."[54]

One of the most absurd of the prosecutions was that of Luther Baldwin of Newark, New Jersey, overheard while inebriated to have spoken crudely about the President. Adams had been passing through Newark to the accompaniment of cannon when one tavern regular noted that the cannon had fired late, after the President had passed. "There goes the President and they are firing at his a--," the man remarked. That is when Baldwin was heard to say, according to the Newark *Centinel of Freedom*, "that he did not care if they fired thro' his a--." The seditious drinker was tried and convicted and committed to federal jail until his fine was paid. There seemed to be no safe place in political vocabulary between disloyal passion and abject tyranny.[55]

Federalists reemphasized their commitment to a liberty based upon security and established authority. Republicans clamored for a return to the Revolutionary confidence in public opinion and egalitarian presumptions, and were amazed that liberty could be defined in any other way. As much as Jeffersonians were infuriated by the administration's inquisition, arch-Federalist Fisher Ames admitted in 1799 that he was "terrified by the tendencies of democracy to anarchy," as he decried, in a comparable image of sorcery, the Republicans' "pestilent designs."[56]

Noah Webster was of an anxious frame of mind. He may have believed that England could not dictate American English, but he lacked Jefferson's fear that British influence put the durability of America's political independence in question. He also considered the French Revolution a disaster that ought to be irrelevant to the American scene, and yet, as he wrote to an exiled French aristocrat in 1796, it would be "a Herculean task, even in the United States, to keep the people from committing suicide." Webster had severed his bond with his close friend Republican Joel Barlow over their political differences. While Barlow, as robust in his liberalism as he was nationalistic in his writings, willfully mocked organized Christianity, the pious Federalist Webster consistently identified the goals of the American Revolution with the conservative social values of law, order, and deference. Long accused of arrogance, Webster now found Republican editors calling him names—a "self-exalted pedagogue," "quack," "self-dubbed patriot," and "incurable lunatic"—and the grammarian grew dazed and bewildered from the heaped-on abuse. In 1798 he left New York, where for several years he had edited the top-selling daily newspaper *American Minerva*. He returned to his native state, socially conservative Connecticut, and delivered the Fourth of July oration in friendly New Haven that year.[57]

Stating that anniversary festivals were necessary for "reviving public spirit" and "enkindling a flame of national ardor," Webster went beyond the rhetoric of fellow Connecticut Federalist Timothy Dwight and excoriated the "revolutionary frenzy" of the French Revolution, urging his countrymen to hold fast to those prudent principles which would deny French influence, so it could not "penetrate into this peaceful Republic." As to Jeffersonianism and the Republican party, unmentioned by name, he decried "ambition, under the specious cover of republicanism, and infidelity, under the deceptive title of reason." Were these forces to have their way, "dragging from the seats of justice, the wise and venerable, and replacing them with bullies and coxcombs; encouraging violence and robbery, under pretence of introducing a factitious equality . . . , dethroning God and trampling on man," only a "false philosophy" would remain. And here Webster found a phrase in vogue that year to suggest demonology in Republican alchemy: the Jeffersonians would bring "a greater scourge to society than a pestilence," as "unfit" government replaced the well-ordered state.[58]

Amid the political trials of the late 1790s, an early number of a Jeffersonian newspaper edited by Philip Freneau recorded "HAPPINESS: A DREAM." This column offered a critical, perhaps even cynical, readership the refrain: "HAPPINESS, after every thing that has been said of it, is in effect the *romance* of all men, the *history* of none. We taste of the pleasure, but never without an alloy; we seem to hold it fast within our grasp, and in an instant it slips, irrecoverably slips, out of our reach." Elusive happiness, or "felicity," shorn of its religious tones, was now an "idle whim," "fruitless desire." But "how delightful it is to *dream* of Happiness!" The writer admitted that he enjoyed the "chimera," this "phantom," and had unabashedly retained the "imaginary existence" of dream-borne incidents of pleasure, "with the sentiments they created." From the Revolutionary equation of happiness with the simple virtues of the American cause to this post-Revolutionary equation of happiness with the individual imagination, Republicans were discovering that as the politics of manners and propriety raged on, the power of illusion had grown.[59]

How different the approach of *The New-Hampshire Magazine*, with its "Observations on Man." Retrieving the conservative spirit of columns of the 1750s, this writer held that traditional Christian values never ceased to bring ease, indeed offered an earthly happiness: "Every soul of genuine sensibility is subject to unhappiness. The most pleasant corner of this world has, to the seeing heart, sources of disquietude." Yet the "seeing heart" could exert influence:

> If the mind is not serene, no earthly possession can produce happiness. Honour and popularity are flattering to every man's

feelings: But contentment is rarely united with them. Then be contented, O man, to be humbly good, and simply happy. Enjoy your own reflections and contemplations in retirement.— And let friendship and religion soothe the thorny road to your grave.[60]

These two contrasting perspectives symbolize the two directions in which happiness-seeking Americans were torn amid the caustic party disputes of the 1790s. National tranquillity was their common goal, experiment and imagination the watchwords of one, severe self-scrutiny and constant public decorum the prescription of the other. Democracy lay ahead, while a traditional concept of stately honor was unwilling to yield to it.

## THE WASHINGTON IMAGE

As the death of Franklin had opened the turbulent decade, so the death of Washington closed it. Of the approximately 2,200 titles to roll off American presses in 1800, some 400 focused in some way on the late President, who died on December 14, 1799. From the beginning of the Revolutionary War, the towering Virginian combined character with military prowess and a sense of duty and dignity as sturdy as the classical columns of the federal city that would shortly bear his name. If Franklin was harmony, Washington was stability. Just after Washington took command of the Continental forces in 1775, Rhode Island's "Fighting Quaker," General Nathanael Greene, wrote: "Joy was visible on every countenance and it seems as if the spirit of conquest breathed through the whole army." Abigail Adams to her husband shortly after: "The Gentleman and Soldier look agreeably blended in him. Modesty marks every line and feature of his face." She was moved to quote lines from the poet John Dryden: "Mark his Majestick fabrick! He's a temple / Sacred by birth, and built by hands divine." During the dark days of 1777, Henry Laurens wrote: "I speak plainly to you. General Washington's Life[,] his virtues are the only present props of our Cause. Should he drop Suddenly ... I cannot err in avering that we Should undergo most violent convulsions." Washington was designated the "father of his country" as early as 1778. According to its first valedictorian, Washington College, the first college chartered in Maryland (1780), was a "temple of virtue and knowledge," "dedicated to the illustrious name of WASHINGTON, rising into lasting importance for the benefit of future generations." Ezra Stiles in 1783 was perhaps the most effusive:

> O WASHINGTON! How do I love thy name! How have I often adored and blessed thy GOD, for creating and forming thee the greatest ornament of human kind! . . . The world and posterity will, with admiration, contemplate thy deliberate, cool, and stable judgment, thy virtues, thy valour and heroick atchievements. . . . The sound of thy fame shall go out into all the earth and extend to distant ages.[61]

No one else, not even Franklin, had inspired such confidence or stood as a comparable (possibly unattainable) model for patriotic thought and action.

In his *History of the American Revolution*, completed as Washington assumed the presidency, David Ramsay called the first U.S. President "the Man of the people" and described the mood of the day among federalists and antifederalists alike: "Though great diversity of opinions had prevailed about the new constitution, there was but one opinion about the person who should be appointed its supreme executive officer. . . . Unambitious of farther honors he had retired to his farm in Virginia . . . but his country called him by an unanimous vote." Typical of the unassuming posture he maintained, the patriotic Washington responded to Virginians bidding him farewell as he headed north to take office: "I do not feel myself under the necessity of making public declarations, in order to convince you, gentlemen, of my attachment to yourselves, and regard for your interests; the whole tenor of my life has been open to your inspection." In a world where sensibility stimulated the public morals, openness was meant to guide; Washington was to rule by character. Crossing the Delaware and heading toward Trenton, this time not to conduct war but to receive adulation from those who lined a road strewn with flowers, he heard a poem sung to him by "young misses": "Virgins fair, and matrons grave, / These thy conquering arm did save." Concern for tender hearts accompanied his stalwart virtue. His birthday, February 22, was celebrated annually while he was alive with banquets and other public demonstrations.[62]

Most Americans associated Washington's strength of character with the strength of the national family. This "most glorious son of liberty," the imposing chief executive, kept the nation from being torn to pieces through party conflict by hiding his frustrations and standing personally above the fray. Madison in 1790 had assured Jefferson that only one of Washington's character could have withstood the "satellites and sycophants" who surrounded him, without succumbing to a dangerous self-love. And Jefferson, as Secretary of State, recognized the need for Washington to accept a second term. The fragility of the union, already exhibiting a sectional split, caused him to address the President: "North and South will hang together, if they have you to hang on." Even after he resigned from the cabinet and later lost the President's confidence, even when, in the heat of party passion, he grumbled that Washington had become accustomed to "unlimited applause" from the electorate, Jefferson did not doubt Washington's integrity and remarked that the President's heart was republican.[63]

Described by Timothy Dwight as "a Man who, under God, has probably wrought for this country more blessings, than were ever wrought by any man for any country,"[64] he had come, then, to represent the unselfish solicitude of the patriot-father, the new nation's most esteemed benefactor and—as he had been for a quarter century—moral authority. When he died just two weeks shy of the new century, it surely seemed that more than a man's life had come to a close. Among the mourning portraits that were produced was one of the late President illuminated by divine light, lifted by a pair of angels, as the American Goddess of Liberty supported her downcast head with her hand. Another portrait featured Washington already heaven-bound, exuding rays of glory and leaving behind fifteen disconsolate, orphaned states positioned beside a mausoleum. A pageant at a New York theater, "full to overflowing," staged a pathetic display that was reported in that city's *Daily Advertiser*: the curtain rose to reveal a tomb "encircled by a wreath of oak leaves." Above it sat "the American eagle, weeping tears of blood." A scroll held in its beak was inscribed, "A Nation's Tears."[65]

Fisher Ames gave an oration in February 1800, expressing more than the nation's gratitude to Washington—there was a sense that the nation could scarcely come through its present political crisis without his watchful eye and "indispensable aid." The Massachusetts Federalist declared that he had personally observed upon the hero's death "the throes of grief that saddened every countenance. . . . Every man looked round for the consolation of other men's tears." The effect was a massive convulsion: "every heart shivered with despair for the future. The man who, and who alone, united all hearts, was dead—dead, at the moment when his power to do good was the greatest." His loss was "irreparable," for "two WASHINGTONS come not in one age." To Ames, this excellent man, "glowing with patriotic fires," was rare among men because he both thought and acted with "dignity and elevation." Washington's "inquisitive mind," he reflected, "always profited by the lights of others," yet "was unclouded by passions of its own." Washington had lived a heroic life, his soul "exercised to danger," "firm in adversity, cool in action, undaunted, self-possessed." From the beginning of his military service, Washington had been America's "most hopeful son." Fearless, yet cautious, he had gone on to conduct the Revolution "with order."[66]

Ames had a partisan purpose, and went on to link Washington's sobriety with the Federalist cause. There were but two kinds of liberty, the American and Revolutionary French. The former was the republican liberty Washington had fought for, "mild and cheering, like the morning sun of our summer, brightening the hills and making the vallies green." And further: "American liberty calms and restrains the licentious passions, like an angel that says to the winds and troubled seas, Be still." But that other liberty, Jacobin or fanatical Jeffersonian, meant violence, excess, immorality, "a monster"—or phantom?—"with eyes that flash wild-fire." The first President understood this, Ames insisted, he whose "pre-eminence is not so much to be seen in the display of any one virtue, as in the possession of them all." To the Federalists who claimed him, Washington was not just virtue but judgment. He knew better than to "pursue novelties," a typical jibe at Jefferson. And so, the speaker resolved, the historic age of Washington will be regarded like "the pole star in a clear sky . . . where so many virtues blend their rays."[67]

Washington's legacy may have served political purposes, but his most enduring value to the young republic was the simple fact that he became, almost instantly, the source of a great nostalgia. To quarrel passionately on the public stage was to disappoint and dishonor his memory. Washington defined the habits of the model citizen. It hardly mattered what the real Washington was like: a hungry land speculator, cold, austere, complaining, sensitive to criticism, impatient with the alleged indolence of certain of his slaves, angry enough to lead a massive army against the uncoordinated Whiskey rebels. Intellectually unoriginal, he served the nation best as a *symbolic* leader, whose constructed personality was what alone mattered. And so there developed a cult. It was he who had accorded the nation its honor, and in the early years, its unity. He had become untouchable. To discredit Washington was to belittle the nation.

## ENNOBLING EXPANSIONISM

Margaretta Faugeres, twenty-two-year-old teacher (and later playwright), published a poem about the Hudson River in 1793, likening the waterway's history to that of the ancient Nile and Tiber. New York's long river had witnessed heroic actions along its banks just as worthy of literary immortality as any classical adventure. The "majestic stream" endured "impious war" until Saratoga's victor, General Horatio Gates, "rescued Columbia from a cruel foe." America's "happy lot" was bound to its noble landscape.[68]

The poet unraveled the river's history by way of consecrating the land. Faugeres, writes literary scholar Nina Baym, "rises out of her everyday rounds into mystic communion with the sacred body of the nation." The female patriot's vision combined pride in the industrious American household (at this stage the site of most production) with literary taste; like the land, she combined usefulness with tranquillity. As teachers of a national morality, women of the republic could emerge from domestic life to celebrate the "family" feeling of the nation.[69]

As much as the rivers and farm acreage stretched the patriotic imagination, so other natural forms of life added an intangible spirit to the new republic. Revolutionary painter-propagandist Charles Willson Peale helped maintain the legend of the American bald eagle, featured on the Great Seal as the symbol of the nation's strength and resolve. Now the leading entrepreneur of the Jeffersonian circle, Peale kept a bald eagle in a tall cage in his Philadelphia natural history museum. A sign below the great bird read: "FEED ME DAILY FOR 100 YEARS." The eagle was meant to represent American empire and longevity for the new nation, Peale's hope that the Revolutionary consciousness would endure.[70]

Choruses projecting America's global mission continued to sing out. Pretending not to notice current partisan rancor, a poem in *The New-Hampshire Magazine* in 1793, titled "America," coupled "equal laws, reason and truth" with the value of "Unshackled commerce." To those beyond America's shores who came in contact with American ships and American values, the blessings of liberty and peace could not be far behind:

> O ye oppress'd! who groan in foreign lands,
> No more submit to tyrants' vile commands,
> While here a calm retreat from all your woes,
> Invites to freedom, joy, and blest repose.[71]

According to this outlook, the American man of commerce possessed habits soon to be universally applauded, as his activities became more widely known. Unlike others in his trade, the expansive republican was interested in the prosperity of the many rather than selfish gain. He would develop a seafaring standard that transcended national boundaries. The certificate of membership of the Union Society of Shipwrights and Caulkers (circa 1790) featured the Goddess Liberty standing before the American flag at the water's edge, in the company of the American eagle; the certificate of the Society of Master Sail Makers of the City of New York showed, under the motto "COMMERCE MOVES ALL," illustrations of craft workshops, industrious artisans, and sail makers coming to the aid of a grieving widow whose house had caught fire. This testified to American laborers' sympathetic disposition as well as their contributions to the national purpose. As Benjamin Rush, generally cool to commercialism and the rise of a merchant class, put it, commercial wealth did not have to be fatal to republican liberty, provided that commerce was "not in the souls of men."[72]

A 1797 poem about the maiden voyage of the *Empress of China*, which opened up the port of Canton to newly independent America in 1784, hailed the national identity. American trade was no longer to be forestalled by subjugation to the British sovereign:

> With clearance from Bellona [Roman goddess of war] won,
> She spreads her wings to meet the Sun,
> Those ancient regions to explore,
> Where GEORGE forbade to sail before.
>
> Thus grown to strength, the bird of Jove [the eagle]
> Impatient; quits his native grove,
> With eyes of fire and lightning's force
> Through the blue ether holds his course.
>
>           • • •
>
> Thus, commerce to our world conveys
> All that the varying taste can please:
> For us, the Indian looms are free,
> And JAVA strips her spicy tree.[73]

Undaunted Americans aspired to master the globe on their own terms, confident that as they carried the goods of prosperity, their happiness and liberty would carry humanity.

In his September 1796 Farewell Address, retiring President George Washington had prescribed a national foreign policy that would advance U.S. interests by steering clear of European rivalries. Drawing on the ideas of both Republican James Madison and Federalist Alexander Hamilton, Washington tried to avoid a partisan message. Indeed, his purpose in part was to heal the breach within America by condemning "faction" and putting nation above party interests. Peace for America, he proclaimed, was to be secured above all by avoiding "entanglements." America's goal lay "in extending our commercial relations with [foreign nations] to have with them as little *political* connection as possible." The American ideal Washington formulated and hoped would become political reality was to "controul the usual current of passions" at home, toward achieving universal effects.[74]

Equally revealing are the comments Washington appended to Madison's earlier draft when he asked Hamilton to edit the proposed valedictory in the spring of 1796. Here is how the President stressed the themes he wanted Hamilton to develop: (1) that "the allwise dispenser of human blessings has favored no Nation of the Earth with more abundant, and substantial means of happiness than United America"; (2) that "every citizen would take pride in the name of an American by considering that we ourselves are now a distinct Nation the dignity of which" would be reduced by allying with any other nation's cause; (3) that "we may always be prepared for War, but never unsheath our sword except in self defence," to encourage the new republic, with its rich resources, to build strength naturally. It was the land and its assets that augured empire, the land that provided the theater for a morally aggressive America to exhibit its potential to the world.[75]

In his 1797 Inaugural Address, John Adams praised Washington's example, calling the retired executive "a bulwark, against all open or secret enemies of his country's peace." Noah Webster, in his 1798 Fourth of July oration, echoed Adams's commendation and proclaimed that "America alone seems to be reserved by Heaven as the sequestered region, where religion, virtue and the arts may find a peaceful retirement from the tempests which agitate Europe." Typically for Webster, such panegyric begged to be extended: "If, in the old world, men are doomed to sleep away their existence in the torpor of slavery, or to live in endless hostility, perpetually shedding each other's blood, . . . we have the more reason to cling to the constitution, the laws, to the civil and religious institutions of our country, and to cherish the pacific policy which doubles the value of those blessings."[76]

Webster's was a cautionary tale in which America looked abroad

skeptically as it sought to secure peace at home. The French in particular, he felt, had impelled the Old World into "circumstances that are
more than usually hostile to morality." Americans should take heed,
because the "noblest efforts of wisdom and genius" were often defeated
by "blockheads," or the "licentious and unprincipled." In his strongest
lines, the Federalist spokesman sounded: "Never, my fellow citizens,
let us exchange our civil and religious institutions for the wild theories
of crazy projectors; or the sober, industrious moral habits of our country, for experiments in atheism and lawless democracy. *Experience* is a
safe pilot; but *experiment* is a dangerous ocean, full of rocks and shoals!"
Once again, the metaphorical sea was fraught with dangers, only navi-
gable if the inheritance of a lawful "liberty and empire" continued to
animate the American spirit.[77]

As American book publishing expanded during the 1790s, a greater
interest in the territories of America developed, no better reflected than
in *The American Gazetteer* by Jedidiah Morse. *The Gazetteer* was a comprehensive geographical index with drawn-out references to the origins
and contemporary character of towns and bodies of water across the
New World. Its pages reverberate with the anticipation of reaching a
readership that desired a fuller acquaintance with the enchanting new
empire waiting to be explored and settled. The distinctiveness of the
American view is even more potent when one compares it with the
Canadian experience—there "terror" before nature permeated the national literature. America's closest neighbor, so much longer Britain's
dependent, has been described as a "garrison culture confronting a hostile wilderness." Canada's writers consistently expressed alienation from
their overwhelming landscape; they composed images of homelessness
and fragmentation. This, of course, stood in stark contrast to the romantic and generally nurturing images of emboldened Americans, idealistic individualists in their encounters with a tamable, if not always
benevolent, landscape.[78]

Morse, like Filson in the prior decade, made the character of the
backcountry not simply inviting but an integral part of the nation's
march of progress. According to the *Gazetteer*, America was everywhere
healthy and safe. The "Georgia Western Territory" was featured,
with the injunction that its "excellency" of soil and climate "render

it . . . very important as a *frontier* in an exposed part of the United States . . . , of immense utility to the union and prosperity of the states." While concentrating on active improvements, the directory alluded to almost mystical natural endowments as well: Beyond the "luxuriant soil" and the wheat, rye, hemp, flax, and cotton that could be grown and profitably exported, timber along the Georgia frontier contained medicinal properties. Marveling at the simple beauty of transitional "Pittsborough" (Pittsburgh, population approximately 1,000), Morse noted: "The hills on the Monongahela side are very high, extend down the Ohio, and abound with coals. Before the revolution, one of these coal-hills, it is said, took fire and continued burning 8 years." Studying nature, civic-minded Americans had risen to the challenge of improving their environment. The manufacturing Van Rensselaer family had worked to make Albany, New York, a modern city with wharves, paved streets, and "a new and handsome style of building." Of commercially prospering Baltimore, "reckoned one of the finest harbors in America," Morse wrote: "The situation is low, and was formerly thought un-healthy, but, by its rapid increase, improvements have taken place, which have corrected the dampness of the air, and it is now judged to be tolerably healthy." Most of all, though, Americans were being sum-moned west. The Ohio River had a gentle current, "waters clear, and bosom smooth and unbroken by rocks and rapids." A vessel could float from Pittsburgh to New Orleans in twenty days. "If this be so," edi-torialized Morse, "what agreeable prospects are presented to our breth-ren and fellow-citizens in the western country!"[79]

Early emigration to Ohio was undertaken by a Boston-based joint-stock venture, the Ohio Company. Its organizers were veterans of the Revolution, officers all, who were displeased with the apparent decline in virtue among New Englanders and had an idyllic vision of consci-entious settlement of the West. The company associates deemed them-selves patriotic farmer-citizens after the model of General Washington, the modern Cincinnatus, able to set aside their weapons and return to a peaceful life. They envisioned systematic settlement of the frontier by cautious gentlemen developers, to be followed by industrious fami-lies responsive to the leaders' ideals. The investors, then, advocated restraint of individualism. If their guide was not the rugged frontiersman Daniel Boone but the distinguished patrician Washington, they were soon frustrated, for as immigration proceeded and Pennsylvanians, Virginians, and Carolinians joined New England Yankees in settling Ohio lands, different ideas about government and society produced tensions mirroring those on the national level, resulting in a Jeffersonian majority by 1800.[80]

As promises of liberty and happiness remained connected to mastery over the land, Americans of the 1790s were obliged to deal with the fate of liberty for Indians, in whose traditional territories they lived first as squatters, occupiers, and eventually (after federally sponsored treaties and/or wars) dispossessors. Just as independence and prosperity were enjoyed by white Southerners through the acquisition of slaves and use of their forced labor, so the spirit of independence came to western settlers in the possession of lands until recently inhabited by Indians. With the pacification of Kentucky, attacks and counterattacks kept the two cultures at each other's throats in contested lands in Ohio and Indiana, where independent bands of sword-brandishing white settlers were called "Big Knives." There they competed with the Indians for game and sometimes murdered unoffending Native hunters. The tribes complained to the federal authorities, to no avail, that the "Big Knives" were acting without restraint. Except for some Cherokees in western North Carolina and northwestern Georgia who imitated a white lifestyle and even owned black slaves, most Indians of the trans-Allegheny West subscribed to a worldview that dictated against the accumulation of private wealth and property. A rich spiritual life and relaxed social habits had produced strong, supportive communities.[81]

Traditional Indian concepts of liberty and happiness were beyond the consideration of an imperial-minded federal administration that valued exploitation of a rich land (as the white population grew and pushed west) over law and justice for the original Americans. Technologically unable to produce the goods they had come to rely on, the majority of Indians lost their earlier self-sufficiency. Bribery and co-optation prevailed in official U.S. thinking, a conscious design aimed at maneuvering Indians of the Old Northwest into selling lands that white immigrants desired. Ironically, the most notable prisoners of America's progress were materially deprived peoples who, until the effects of contact with Europeans became unavoidable, had enjoyed happiness and liberty in what approximated (in late-eighteenth-century terms) a simple democracy.[82]

For the restless many in the early republic, however, national growth was translated into a personal invitation. Thomas Jefferson did not let go of his earlier idealization of the American farmer during this decade, writing that the decent cultivator alone would prevent the virtuous character of the nation from being spirited away by covetous, effete speculators in stock paper. Farmers, he wrote in 1797, were "the true representatives of the great American interest, and are alone to be relied on for expressing the proper American sentiments."[83] A continuous stream of new settlers, without means, took the Wilderness Road to Kentucky in anticipation of finding paradise. They wanted to believe the splendid myth of the pastoral garden.[84]

Critical contemporaries recorded the expectations of these uncritical emigrants, noting their "delightful images of enjoyment" and visions of a wooded "luxuriance." Though it was in part land speculators whose "enchanting fables" attracted people west along the trail blazed by Daniel Boone, it was freedom, a vague but substantial stimulus, and not merely a desire for material wealth, that caused the population of Kentucky to grow from 73,000 in 1790 to 221,000 in 1800 to 400,000 in 1810. A Virginia traveler in the 1790s marveled at the industriousness of a corn producer he encountered along the Ohio River: "Well, I know one thing—you must have been G-- D--- poor or you would not have worked so hard." Short on labor to help them clear the land, frontier farmers with callused hands and sturdy axes readied several acres a year for planting, over time accepting itinerants who aided in chopping trees, splitting rails, and fencing acreage.[85]

The availability of land in the burgeoning region militated against social inequality (among white men, of course). As families grew in size, frontier tracts encouraged the growth of a society of near-equals who shared a belief in the healthful effects of economic independence. Desirable as this sounded, the Jeffersonian ideal of a nation of yeoman farmers was ever in danger. With a sense of foreboding, Congressman Jeremiah Crabb of Maryland explained the pattern of migration to his colleagues in 1796: "Lands had become so high in most of the old

States, that the hope of acquiring possession of the soil, and becoming independent, was lost; and the rents of lands had risen so high, that the tenants felt the oppression of their landlords, and their last hope of releasement from this oppression was by emigration to this new country which they looked on as common property." It was up to the federal government, he suggested, to allow ordinary people to fulfill their dreams. It was, in fact, he added, "essential for the survival of the re-public." Crabb's language was consistent; it was the Revolutionary vo-cabulary of "dependence," "oppression," and "tyrannical landlords" in asserting individual "independence" as a right in a land where all men were created equal.[86]

It is noteworthy that the egalitarian premise grew even while the facts indicate that land laws applicable to the settled frontier of the 1790s (western Pennsylvania and Kentucky) still favored the claims of a speculating few. The *Kentucky Gazette* was typical in poetically reas-suring its residents in 1797:

> Our soil so rich, our clime so pure,
> Sweet asylum for rich and poor—
> Poor, did I say!—recall the word,
> Here plenty spreads her gen'rous board;
> But poverty must stay behind,
> No asylum with us she'll find—
> Avaunt, fell fiend! we know thee not,
> Thy mem'ry must forever rot . . . [87]

Americans who wrote about their nation inevitably required powerful contrasts.

# CHAPTER SEVEN

# SOMETHING NEW UNDER THE SUN: 1801–15

IN *MODERN CHIVALRY*, his parody of American life, Hugh Henry Brackenridge examined the naiveté of this "new" people as he navigated in prose between two possible futures: the elitist and the egalitarian. Borrowing the technique of Sterne's *Tristram Shandy*, the author insinuated himself into the narrative during that section of the work published in 1805: "I use the term democracy as contradistinguished from the aristocracy; that is, a union of men of wealth, and influence." An American aristocracy had shown signs of reestablishing itself in the 1790s, he observed, until, committing errors in the administration of the government, it lost support and "the *democracy* prevailed." The author added: "I wish the *democracy* supported, which can be done only on the basis of *wisdom*, which contains in it truth, and justice." Brackenridge stressed that it was a democracy founded on responsible judgment more than pure egalitarian principles that he subscribed to; and yet he noted coyly for whom his picaresque tale was intended: "It is Tom, Dick, and Harry, in the woods, that I want to read my book."[1]

*Modern Chivalry* was produced in installments from 1792 to 1815. The story adapted to changes taking place in American society, but stuck to the adventures of its two main characters, Captain John Farrago and Teague O'Regan, the first a sturdy republican gentleman and the second his crass and dishonest companion. Together they ply the road that winds back and forth between republican prudence and democratic excess. Brackenridge himself was the son of a poor Scottish immigrant and a graduate of the College of New Jersey (Princeton), a frontier lawyer in Pittsburgh during the late 1780s, with a combative faith in his own ability to reason. He served one term in the Pennsylvania legislature before being turned out of office by a Teague-like opponent (an uneducated weaver). Convinced early that the Revolution's promise was being marred by the real voice of the American people—ambition—he was equally cynical about ill-informed popular opinion and the Federalists' pompous self-congratulation. In Pittsburgh, he maneuvered through the Whiskey Rebellion in 1794 by positioning himself as a moderating voice of reason. Sympathetic to their demands, he calmed the mob while pleading at the same time for government restraint toward the resisters. He was then obliged to protest his neutrality when suspected by federal expeditionary troops of inciting the rebels himself, and artfully apologized for any appearance of partisanship by making himself available to the government in subsequent trials. Brackenridge, in a word, wished to embody the highest ideals of republicanism—to possess a social conscience. He ended the decade of the 1790s in the Jeffersonian camp.[2]

Surely his immersion in the rowdiness of state politics inspired the novelist's testy prose. The reluctant democrat who authored *Modern Chivalry* was fearful of being called a democrat of the unruly kind and hopeful of removing the stain on the word. When Brackenridge returned in his text to muddy definitions, he associated *his* democracy with "love of virtue." Who, then, he asked, would be unwilling to be called a democrat? "Yet there have been revolutions in the public mind, with respect to the honorary, or disreputable nature of this application." He referred to the discredited democratic societies of the 1790s, the "intemperance" of some of which had "brought a cloud." It was thus that "Prudent men, and patriots, were willing to avoid a name which had incurred disreputation from the excesses of those attached to it." But, he finally pronounced,

> the term *democrat*, has ceased to be a stigma; and begins to be assumed by our public writers, and claimed by our patriots, as

characteristic of a good citizen. That of *republican*, which alone had been vented for some time, is now considered cold, and equivocal, and has given way, pretty generally, to that of democratic republican. In a short time, it will be simply, the *democracy*, and a *democrat*.

Brackenridge felt it safe to associate himself with a practical democracy like that of Periclean Athens, a democracy conscious of its own "errors" and "excellencies."[3]

His novel was meant to be taken as the text of that emerging democracy's self-examination. His concern for America's soul was expressed in humor. He joked about the nation's future and made incisive note of the tendency of the ambitious to overstate their talents. Self-interest routinely contested virtue—this was the national dilemma. It was in the "fermentation," or hearty agitation, between the "patrician class" and the "common people" that the "spirit of democracy" was "kept alive." Rather than seek to convince readers of a fixed political direction, Brackenridge railed good-naturedly at the end of the third volume: "I wish I could get this work to make a little more noise. Will nobody attack it and prove that it is insipid, libellous, treasonable, immoral, or irreligious?" He knew only too well the foibles of his countrymen and, long after his experience as the accused—both sides' antagonist—in the "treasonable" Whiskey Rebellion, he accepted the forces of social change the Revolution had unleashed.[4]

The flustered Joseph Dennie, editor of the anti-Jeffersonian weekly *Port Folio*, was one who did attack this new idea of a respectable democracy:

A democracy is scarcely tolerable in any period of national history. Its omens are always sinister, and its powers are unpropitious. With all the lights of experience, blazing before our eyes, it is impossible not to discern the futility of this form of government. It was weak and wicked in Athens. It was bad in Sparta, and worse in Rome. It has been tried in France, and has terminated in despotism. It was tried in England, and rejected with the utmost loathing and abhorrence. It is on trial here, and the issue will be civil war, desolation, and anarchy.[5]

Sniping at democratization in countless issues of his magazine, Dennie termed the common people "nearly the same" in every age and nation. "Their praise is often to be dreaded, and their censure is generally proof of the merit of the object." Public opinion, he insisted, ought instead to be "the clear and harmonious voice of the good and wise." Both sides were laboring under the conviction that language could be soothing in a well-ordered republic, or it could be a deadly disguise. Dennie again: "The abuse of language, or the substitution of names for realities, is one of the most successful instruments ever wielded in the demolition of governments."[6] All harked back to the start of the Revolution, when the *South-Carolina Gazette* charged a deceptively conciliatory-sounding British government after Lexington and Concord: "Arbitrary Power has always been introduced under the Sanction of respectable Words."[7]

Brackenridge's message, in any case, was less madcap than some of his more stirring vignettes hint at. The real Brackenridge was self-possessed, even Franklinesque in his moral commentary, as (couched in a father's advice) he celebrated the rare "felicity . . . in any age of the world" of being born in a democratic republic. "In order to be respectable," the aphorism went, "put not yourself above your strength. If you covet the honour of a public trust, think of qualifying yourself for it." So much for the edginess, the nerve, the anarchy, the insufferable challenge of Jeffersonian democracy.[8]

Brackenridge politicized literature as Jefferson applied a soothing literary style to the conduct of politics. Both hoped to persuade; both aspired to be the reasonable voice of a democratically inspired American culture independent of its British foundation. That independence was being realized in many ways: in the continued growth of a native book and newspaper publishing industry; in fashion, as men's powdered wigs, knee breeches, and silk stockings yielded to simpler pantaloons; in the democratization of art, wherein, for example, ordinary people sat for their portraits, a custom previously reserved for the upper class. Soon, American letters would feature lovable dialect speakers and a taste for literary creativity bound to catch up with that pride in the nation's political originality which was already apparent.

## CALL'D BY A NATION'S VOICE

In his more optimistic moments, Brackenridge perceived in the average citizen of America a palpable vigor and generative power that, with education added, might overcome the tenacity of human folly. And it was Thomas Jefferson, as incoming President, who sought to standardize that definition of healthful progress. In his Inaugural Address on March 4, 1801, four months to the day from the twenty-fifth anniversary of the Declaration of Independence, Jefferson spoke softly, but affectingly, and gave substance to the assumption of American exceptionalism, the idea that the United States has a unique history and superior destiny. Few Inaugural Addresses have aimed to mean as much to the course of American political life as this one, promising as it did to reactivate the principles of 1776.

The new President acknowledged that the election of 1800 had been a bitter and divisive contest, and he declared that its peaceful outcome— the successful transfer of power from a Federalist to a Republican—was a testament to the resiliency of representative democracy. For although "the animation of discussion and exertions" (Jefferson's rhetorical cushioning of what had bordered on libel) had tested the validity of the right of citizens to criticize their government, this was for the good. Americans were learning that, even at the expense of temporary harmony, the highest value ought to be placed on the intercourse of free minds: "Though the will of the majority is in all cases to prevail, that will, to be rightful, must be reasonable" and the minority accorded "their equal rights."[9]

He said he wanted to heal: "Let us, then, fellow citizens, unite with one heart and one mind. Let us restore to social intercourse that harmony and affection without which liberty and even life itself are but dreary things." This quintessential statement of the eighteenth-century man of elevated feeling and enlightened sentiment was punctuated next by the partisan politician's most heralded attempt to portray himself and his administration as a fully representative one: "But every difference of opinion is not a difference of principle. We have called by different names brethren of the same principle. We are all republicans—we are all federalists." For the "honest men" among his listeners and readers, Jefferson urged patience: they should not fear that his brand of republicanism would cause the experimental government to collapse, and they should not "abandon a government which has so far kept us free and firm." He called that government "the world's best hope."[10]

The third President had prepared careful drafts of his inaugural message, meaning to establish not just the tone of his administration but the tone of the progressive new century. In one handwritten version (very likely that which he read from his rostrum in the Senate chamber that day), he spaced key words and euphonic phrases in such a way as to suggest the desired cadence of delivery. He intended a pause at the end of each line.

> ... [all will] unite in common efforts for the common good
> all too w$^{ll}$ bear in mind th$^s$ sacr$^d$ princip$^l$ th$^t$ th$^o$ th$^e$ will of th$^e$
>     Major$^{ty}$ is in all cases to prevail
>     that will, to be rightful, must be reasonable
> that the Minor$^{ty}$ possess the equal rights w$^{ch}$ equal laws must
>     protect, & to violate would be oppression.
> Let us then, fellow citizens, unite with one heart & one mind;
>     let us restore to social intercourse that harmony and affection
>     without which Liberty, & even Life itself, are but dreary
>     things.
> and let us reflect ...

Then, memorably:

> we have called by different names brethren of the same principle.
> we are all republicans: we are all federalists.[11]

In the rhythm of his phrasing and the texture of his wording, Jefferson meant to project his conscience. He wanted his message to be emotionally uplifting, inclusive and inviting, intending a far different image of American political culture than that which the recently concluded presidential campaign had presented. The partisan President pretended to be more forgiving than he really was, trying to soothe his opposition as he rose to assert his optimistic viewpoint. If Republicans would narrow the gap between the governing and the governed, they would not do so in such a way as to segregate those who subscribed to Federalist beliefs. In essence Jefferson was promising to be a conscientious executive, a reasoning, respectful, and high-principled man, a thinker and harmonizer like the Franklin image, a pure, virtuous leader like the Washington image—to reflect his own fabulous conception of the constant American character.

If it was the circumspect philosopher, Jefferson as a generous and sentimental patriot, who stood behind these idealistic words, it was Jefferson the romantic student of natural science who wrote to Dr. Joseph Priestley three weeks later in language rich in natural metaphors: "As the storm is now subsiding, and the horizon becoming serene, it is pleasant to consider the phenomenon with attention. We can no longer say there is nothing new under the sun. For this whole chapter in the history of man is new. The great experiment of our Republic is new. Its sparse habitation is new. The mighty wave of public opinion which has rolled over it is new." There was a sense of motion and confidence in his style, an enchanted invocation of what Jefferson imagined to be destiny. America had weathered a time of great stress and strain, proving "a strength of character in our nation which augurs well for the duration of our Republic."[12]

The Alien and Sedition Acts would expire shortly, and citizens could expect to display their critical strength through a vigorous press—whether or not the President liked what he read.[13] The new Washington-based newspaper *National Intelligencer* was one that approved of the new President. It applauded his vision as it urged citizens—whom it conventionally designated as providentially blessed—to put God's commandments into practice: "America, though composed by the most heterogeneous materials . . . has prospered more than any nation hitherto, because these moral principles are most conformed to."[14]

While the Jeffersonian press heralded freedom of conscience, a surprising number of inaugural rituals wore a religious aspect, in contrast to what Federalists anticipated under a Jefferson regime. On the day of his inauguration, Jefferson was lauded in song at the German Reformed Church in Philadelphia. The ceremony began with a "SOLEMN INVOCATION," which read:

> Let our songs ascend to thee,
> God of life and LIBERTY:
> For grateful songs our tongues employ,
> The transports of a Nation's joy.

The service praised Jefferson as "THE PEOPLE'S FRIEND," declaring that "a Nation's ruin" had been averted as "th'auspicious morn" was unveiled that reawakened "a people's hopes." The new President was a man of the people known for devotion to country, for his pen's insistence on equality and rights; at the same time he was already fixed in the heavens, "a bright star of hope." Rescuing human rights from "sinking to an early grave," he had come forward, "employ'd by Heaven." He was in that sense more than a "friend"; he was an oracle, the medium connecting Heaven and the American people.

Awaiting insightful words from their oracle, the "CHORUS" next sounded:

> Rejoice, ye States, rejoice,
> And spread the patriot flame;
> Call'd by a Nation's voice,
> To save his country's fame,
> And dissipate increasing fears,
> Our favourite JEFFERSON appears.
>
> Let every heart unite,
> Th'eventful day to hail;
> When from the Freemen's Right,

The People's hopes prevail;—
That hence may horrid faction cease,
And honour be maintain'd with PEACE.[15]

As in 1776, the language of affection ("Let every heart unite") borrowed sensory metaphors ("patriot flame," "Nation's voice") to attest to American qualities that promised political justice ("Freemen's Right," "People's hopes"). But by 1800, with the apotheosis of Washington, Thomas Jefferson moved effortlessly from penman to receiver of the Nation's voice and, owing to his judicious wisdom, was raised to nearly divine status. The President, in this way, was a healer. To his supporters, he was not perceived to be an irreligious man.

At this early, fragile time in American nationhood, patriotic expression was not only devotional but so emotion-filled and revelatory in purpose that it regularly entailed rescuing the nation from the brink of chaos and disintegration. It was a dramatic moment of self-conscious national political transition. In the words of one public speaker: "A few momentary squalls and tempests have thickened over our heads; and for a time worn a threatening aspect. But the gloom has again been dispelled; and the prospect brightened before us." This hope, as ever, expressed bonds of affection: "Our governors and rulers are men of our own choosing—men after our own hearts."[16]

The new Republican majority identified the year 1800 as a watershed, when popular liberties were threatened. As in 1765–66 with the Stamp Act outrage, or the War for Independence itself, the "patriot flame" was kindled to preserve liberty. What William Pitt had been to the first crisis and Washington was during and after the second, Jefferson had ostensibly become to a new consensus as the nineteenth century got underway. Margaret Bayard Smith, wife of the publisher of the *National Intelligencer*, was enamored with Jefferson's personal style and wrote optimistically to her sister-in-law shortly after attending the President's inaugural in the packed Senate: "The changes of administration, which in every government and in every age have most generally been epochs of confusion, villainy and bloodshed, in this our happy country take place without any species of distraction, or disorder. This day, has one of the most amiable and worthy men taken that seat to which he was called by the voice of his country." Voices, even more than dreams, expressed the national apprehension of truth.[17]

Jefferson had attractively offered the olive branch that "we are all republicans: we are all federalists."[18] The Federalists, however, remained embittered. Their press organs ridiculed the architect of Monticello as an airy philosopher, a cranky tinkerer who occupied himself with unimportant mechanical contrivances instead of the public order, a man with an impractical and dangerous plan of government that would reduce rather than advance American honor. They saw the private Jefferson as an essentially naive and cowardly man, but at the core of his political being conniving and hypocritical for one who professed to be a harmonizer.[19]

Unlike George Washington, the first slave-owning Virginia President, Jefferson was identified by the Federalists as part of a tainted caste.[20] Sober New England voices increasingly condemned the Southern wing of the broadening Jeffersonian constituency for their lax demeanor and practical incompetence, as men unfit for public responsibilities. They felt that leading Southern white citizens, though well-to-do, were nurtured in a slave society and became dissipated by their constant exposure to the evil, groomed only to pass on lazy intellectual habits. Southern congressmen "rise like meteors out of the swamps and forests they inhabit," wrote a particularly disparaging Federalist, "and such is the force of their genius, trample on those who have been long accustomed to the meditations of statesmen." This opinion was echoed by a Southern Federalist who complained of the "low degraded situation of No. Carolina," a state "destitute of National character," that served as the "miserable appendage" of Jefferson's Virginia. How, asked Northern elites, could the ruling Southern planters be classed with forward-looking Americans, comprehending and contributing to *national* goals?[21]

Defining Jefferson's constituency as the "mob" and the "rabble," and the President's party faithful as "tyrants" who "conceal their designs of domination beneath the mask of liberty, and a *pretended* zeal for the rights of the people," "Christopher Caustic" lampooned:

And I'll unmask the Democrat,
Your sometimes this thing, sometimes that,
Whose life is one dishonest shuffle,
Lest he perchance the *mob* should ruffle.[22]

Those identified here as Democrats were mindless, owed allegiance to the mob, and lacked the backbone—and honor—to rise to any higher level of political sophistication.

And yet the Jeffersonians won the day. One year after it commenced publication, the *National Intelligencer* celebrated the new political scene. "There is something so interesting, and even sublime, in a Nation, now composed of millions and destined hereafter to be unrivaled in numbers, shaking off by Herculean efforts the chains of foreign despotism, and then with unexhausted vigor defending the rights of its citizens from internal invasion." To his allies, Jefferson was doing as he promised, moving the nation ahead without sacrificing individual rights to national power. This was "the basis of the only correct patriotism that can animate the human heart."[23]

As the ironic Brackenridge claimed, society's view of itself was changing. The *National Intelligencer* in 1802 explained that those "characters" who were "drunken and noisy at elections," the misnamed "sovereign people" whom Federalists derided as the weak spine of a Jeffersonian order, were "rather more harmless with their grog, than those legitimate sovereigns," like Rome's Nero, who had destroyed their societies. Democracy as the Federalists conceived it was illusory, because the lower orders whom the Federalists feared were in fact innocuous. *Representative* democracy meant ordered liberty, as the framers of the Constitution had envisioned.[24]

This was the way in which Jeffersonian optimism was expressed. The true "sovereign people" were not drunkards, but "the mass of virtue, wealth, talents and numbers, spread out from New-Hampshire to Georgia, and from the Ocean to the Mississippi," who declared through their "authorized agents" in Congress their "sovereign will." The average American was "more august and venerable, than the united kings and aristocrats collected from the rest of the globe." The knotted-up Federalist decade had caused citizens to become unproductively disputatious among themselves, but such political stagnation was safely past. Now, in a Jeffersonian order, republican ideals reflected Americans' maturation. The nation was being governed "happily," the antielitist principles of the Revolution alive and thriving: "History teaches us, that the throne is not more productive of virtue and talents, that [sic] the cottage; and our religion informs us, that a manger was selected as the birth-place of the divine missionary of God." To Jeffersonian enthusiasts there were only two subverters of self-rule: ignorance and predatory ambition.[25]

Though an intimate of the Adamses since the mid-1760s, by 1800 Mercy Otis Warren had come to prefer Jefferson's politics. Her three-volume history of the American Revolution, published in 1805, corroborated Jefferson's optimism about a national reconciliation. Her husband, James, even congratulated Jefferson on "the triumph of Virtue over the most malignant & virulent & slandering Party that perhaps ever existed." She marveled that only 150 years had elapsed between the time that "a few wandering strangers coasted about the unknown bay of Massachusetts" and the present, when "with courage and magnanimity scarcely paralleled by the progeny of nations," America had exchanged servile obedience for unity and independence. There was the word *magnanimity* again: disinterested patriotism, a native generosity linked to a calm, dignified spirit—the harmony-seeking Man of Feeling amplified. This notion remained at the heart of Americans' romance with themselves.[26]

Persistent identification of the new republic with a quality of public liberty previously unknown on earth led to a curious campaign to rename the nation. After Bostonian William Tudor in 1799 claimed that "America" was too general and might be replaced with "Columbia," others latched on to "Fredonia." Americans would become "Fredes" whose language would be known either as "Fredish" or "Fredonian." Noah Webster's long efforts toward a distinctive American language to challenge British linguistic dominion were bolstered by John Witherspoon, president of the College of New Jersey, who introduced the term *Americanism*.[27]

The Federalist magazine *Port Folio* was alarmed. In 1800 its editor, Joseph Dennie, under the pseudonym "Oliver Oldschool," defended British English against the supposed contaminants in American English. Though the spoken dialects were not nearly as far apart as they have since grown, political contention in America had somehow translated into a division over the propriety of introducing new elements and "nationalizing" the American language. The controversially titled *Columbian Dictionary of the English Language* (1800) was openly provocative with its promise of "many new words, peculiar to the United States." The *Port Folio* considered this work "a disgrace to letters," "absurd," "presumptuous," and boorish. The Federalist *Monthly Anthology* was so conservative that in 1809 it dismissed even the elitist idea of allowing linguistic innovation to be overseen by a self-selected national literary class, grumbling that American literature was "a kind of half cleared and half cultivated country." Nevertheless, like the Jeffersonian persuasion in politics, a more plain style of speech and writing was coming to replace the venerable British standard. The affectations of the British were censured anew in American Royall Tyler's *The Yankey in London* (1809), in which the mother tongue was said to exhibit a "grotesque air of pert vivacity." American speech was deemed more natural, distinctly superior to British polish.[28]

Moralistic New England Federalists may have resented the manners of the Southern leisure class and looked down upon the less educated Southern laborers, but proponents of the Jeffersonian synthesis attempted to deny political and sectional distinctions in their effort to promote national harmony. Shared identity, less real than imagined, emerged in commentary in the pro-administration press: "It is no easy thing to determine the sentiments of five millions of people scattered over a country so extensive as the United States," ran one article focusing on political appointments, yet "with a very few exceptions, there was scarcely a division of opinion among the most enlightened citizens. . . . This is a plain and clear manifestation of public opinion not confined to a single spot, but pervading the whole Union." A short time later, another article extended the Jeffersonians' putative faith: "The citizens of the United States are responsible for the greatest trust ever confided to a political society." Their native justice was bound to "ennoble the character of a nation."[29]

According to the Jeffersonian worldview, however, American republicanism still had to be wary of its opposite: antirepublicanism. Standing in the vanguard of the march to a world republican future, the experimental state needed constant self-strengthening to offset active antirepublican forces. There was no doubt in the minds of the ruling party that America had but one chance to succeed, that the present administration represented "the last and fairest experiment in favor of the rights of human nature," and that the "experiment" in virtuous government would be extinguished by the tyranny which succeeded it. In this respect the language of the decade 1765–75 had not softened. Great Britain remained the visible model of what might happen to America, the "confusion of free and despotic principles, modern refinements grafted on the relics of gothicism." As the new federal city, with insufficient housing and little polish, struggled to become a civilized capital, Americans were being warned to hold fast to the Revolution's principles: "Let it not be doubted, a high destiny is recorded in the volume of fate for the city of Washington! Our own levity, unsteadiness, or illiberality, can alone retard it."[30]

Republicans were on the lookout for deception all the while they spoke of their confidence in the future. Under such circumstances, the controversial character of the President became a measure of popular sentiment. "He cannot now be considered as the chief of a dominant faction," ran the all too clever Republican assessment, "but as the legitimate representative of public rights and opinions. Our own character as a people, and the individual character of every American participates in that of our chief magistrate." Jefferson as President was nationalized; once elected, a President no longer embodied his place of origin but belonged to all the people. The "enemies and defamers of Mr. Jefferson, who ascribe him a whole lifetime of vice and immorality," would "surrender the character of their own country" and paint Americans in the eyes of the world as "a base, ignorant and degenerate race." Those who admired the President thus protected his name for their own sake.[31]

Why this anxiety, the need to manifest the voice of the people in the chief magistrate? The founders had not thought partisanship healthy, and they could do nothing to temper it. Language was unfixed and differently understood. In spite of the populist sound of the words of the rights-affirming documents that had established the nation, the emerging democratic society was not the one the Revolutionaries had envisioned. Their plain republicanism had allowed for certain hierarchical norms to continue, for a mild deference in society to sustain the illusion of social calm.

"Our [state] governments are elective democracies," the *Boston Chronicle* proclaimed in 1803, "but we have the principles of those governments dressed up in so many horrible images, that some of us are induced to turn our backs on them with distrust and jealousy." People were urged to set aside their distrust and jealousy and assent to the level of political comfort (the "security," "happiness," and "dignity") they enjoyed at that moment. "Every man in America has the same right to gain wealth, obtain honors, and live securely. Our lives are as safe as the laws of a well regulated society can render them. . . . Are these not invaluable blessings? . . . And why is the name of a democrat, under these democratical constitutions, used as a term of reproach?" Such passages make clear that as selfhood and society were being redefined Americans were exhibiting a marked unease. Grandiose pronouncements masked a fundamental concern with the indeterminacy of the nation's destiny.[32]

## OPINIONS AS VARIOUS AS MEN'S FACES

As the nineteenth century step by step rendered more egalitarian expressions of democracy less dangerous and less unreliable, the aging vanguard of the Revolution was caught lagging and fell out of step. The popular imagination had a momentum all its own. The Revolution was being fulfilled in the minds of its inheritors, the second generation of leaders, who were being reared under a Jefferson presidency. Baptist Elias Smith did not require Brackenridge's literary license when he intoned at the end of Jefferson's second term: "The word DEMOCRACY is formed of two Greek words, one signifies *the people*, and the other the *government* which is in the people. . . . My Friends, let us never be ashamed of DEMOCRACY!" A redefinition of citizenship and authority animated public life.[33]

The so-called High Federalists became increasingly flustered as they became politically effete. Continuing to see themselves as the most prudent and credible public characters, they were unceasingly tormented by Jefferson's popularity and by the effective vocabulary of his political progeny. The Federalist *New-York Evening Post* complained of social-climbing writers who would impose "ridiculous and unjustifiable innovations upon our language." Unable to resist politicizing even a syntactical phenomenon, the paper offered an example of the proper use of the word *under* as a metaphorical element: "*Under* the specious name of *republican, patriot, friend of the people*, the credulous multitude are deceived by those who court their favor." They expected their readership to understand and approve.[34]

America appeared to be developing a civilization the old-style Federalists did not comprehend, one they expected would self-destruct but in fact did not. Out of touch, becoming obsolete, they were remnants of George Washington's administration, when different manners and a different set of cultural expectations prevailed. These well-bred eighteenth-century gentlemen had begun by self-confidently mocking President Jefferson's unpretentious dress and informal manner and ended as insignificant voices in an evolving sociopolitical dialogue, bowing *out* if not exactly bowing *to* the enlightened doctrine of popular consent to which, it turned out, they had only paid lip service. For a decade or so they would resort to name calling, bidding America return "with shame and contrition" to their idealized temper of well-bred virtue. In the process they would claim that their own calm sensibility (as the possessors of "generous feelings, delicate, noble and disinterested sentiments") was being overthrown by politicians with an outward temperament of softness who hid "hardened and degraded wretches" with "the fearful character of ruffians." The successful Jeffersonian was to be lampooned, as in the case of New York governor Daniel Thompkins in 1815, as "demure almost to saintship," whose "exterior simplicity borders on idiotism." His constituency was "the poor duped sucklings of democracy" who alone call him "lovely." Seeing past his zeal to identify with ordinary people, voters were supposed to unmask his "cunning and malice."[35]

By the election year of 1804, the President had already witnessed a good deal of success in remodeling the republic. The feared "democrat" did not dismantle government. With his Secretary of State and political alter ego James Madison, Jefferson had displayed the relatively conservative credentials of a Madisonian federalist of 1787. As early as 1802 Jefferson had confided his goal to fellow Republicans and forecast his achievement: "I shall take no other revenge than by a steady pursuit of economy and peace . . . to sink Federalism into an abyss from which there shall be no resurrection for it." He was convinced of this outcome because "candid federalists acknowledge that their party can never more raise its head." If the parties were "almost wholly melted into one," as Jefferson would claim after reelection, then only a few remaining pockets of resistance were yet to yield their "Anglomany" to—that newly coined word—"Americanism."[36]

In Shaftsbury, Vermont, on the Fourth of July 1804, after a reading of the Declaration of Independence to the accompaniment of patriotic pomp and song, a young lawyer named Orsamus Cook Merrill described "the cheerful face of things present" and envisioned "fields of futurity enamelled with the opening blossoms of greatness." Merrill was born in central Connecticut on the day following the Battle of Bunker Hill, in 1775. His death would come ninety years later, during the week when Lee surrendered to Grant and Lincoln fell a martyr. A Vermonter since age sixteen, he was to attain the rank of lieutenant colonel in the War of 1812 and then serve briefly in the U.S. Congress before becoming a state judge.[37]

With a future of national service ahead of him, Merrill pointed to both the native intelligence and historical mission of Americans. "Knowledge is the standing army of Republics," he said, reviving the symbol of Boston Massacre orations that had once coupled standing armies with political oppression. Jefferson's nation, he assured, had knowledge to convey both spatially and temporally. This people sought happiness not just for themselves, but were "transmitting it to posterity, and diffusing it through mankind generally." The patriot was recurring to a familiar formula: A healthy republic consisted of individual self-knowledge extended to national self-education, serenity and security within leading to confidence and status abroad. Recollection of the fragility of liberty, of past misfortunes and disharmonies (dependence on state power, social inequality, and the cult of influence), was an emotional safeguard against their resurgence.[38]

Joel Barlow was similarly forceful and quite specific in his 1806 prospectus in favor of a national university to be situated in Washington, D.C. Given the universal interest in preparing the "rising generation" to take American principles abroad, such an institution would effectively serve as a means of "bringing to perfection" the republican system of government, inviting "foreign observers who shall study our institutions," and establishing "a mode of preserving peace among the states." A national university would promote harmony, helping the states to bind themselves together within the federal government. That is, the states would recognize their common interests while maintaining their individuality, "without losing any sense of their dignity, but rather increasing it."[39]

Some thought the nation charmed, while others mourned its degeneration. In 1806, at age seventy, despondent ex-President Adams wrote to Benjamin Rush, a friend to both the second and third Presidents. America, Adams lamented bitterly, seemed bound to go the way of Europe: "Democracy is always so horribly bloody that it is always short-lived, and its atrocious cruelties are never checked but by extinguishing all popular elections to the great offices of state. I hope Americans will reflect on these things before it is too late." Two years later, to the same correspondent, Adams related in a similarly dark mood that he believed "avarice" to be "our national sin. . . . An aristocracy of wealth, without any check but a democracy of licentiousness, is our curse." Seemingly convinced that Revolutionary virtue and spirit had subsided, Rush signaled back: "I feel pain when I am reminded of my exertions in the cause of what we called liberty, and sometimes wish I could erase my name from the Declaration of Independence." Adams would come to see his younger countrymen as part of a confounding "masquerade." Politics, he thought, would transport the nation to hell; character had yielded to hypocrisy. Rush agreed at least that a covetous, selfish citizenry had become "bedollared." Where, the two aging Revolutionaries asked, had public virtue and national spirit fled?[40]

Despite such voices as Jefferson, Merrill, and Barlow proclaiming the ideal of national harmony as a harbinger of global republicanization, Americans on some level were faced with the "masquerade" Adams perceived, the rampant self-interest that accompanied the gradual democratization of society. Though he would not surrender his optimism, President Jefferson repeatedly used the word *schism* in his correspondence after 1804. Acknowledging division within his own party, Jefferson wrote, "For my part I determined from the first dawn of the first schism never to take part in any schism of republicans." He had expected "a spirit of intolerance" from malicious Federalists, but seeing like behavior within his party furnished "a poor presage of future tranquillity." Yet he did not admit surprise. To Virginia senator Wilson Cary Nicholas, he wrote, "The divisions among the republicans . . . are distressing, but they are not unexpected to me. From the moment I foresaw the entire prostration of federalism, I knew that at that epoch more distressing divisions would take its place. The opinions of men are as various as their faces." Jefferson insisted that these difficulties, like the "terrible passions" of Federalist reaction, were only temporary; his advice was to *"do what is right*, & generally we shall disentangle ourselves without almost perceiving how it happens." To trusted Secretary of the Treasury Albert Gallatin, Jefferson reasserted his deep commitment to private and public concord: "I have a sublime pleasure in believing [our administration] will be distinguished as much by having placed itself above the passions which could destroy its harmony, as by the great operations by which it will have advanced the well-being of the nation."[41]

The most telling set of occurrences attesting to national disharmony and possible disunion all involved Jefferson's first-term Vice President, Aaron Burr. Distrusted for having courted the Federalists when Republican electors miscalculated and inadvertently allowed the election of 1800 to end in a tie between the running mates, the ambitious

New Yorker in July 1804 had shot longtime nemesis Alexander Hamilton in a duel and fled first to Philadelphia and later to Georgia and Spanish-held Florida after New York and New Jersey issued indictments against him. He brazenly returned to Washington after Republicans eager to employ him in partisan combat had the indictments quashed. From November 1804 until his last day as Vice President in March 1805, Burr served at the head of the Senate, constitutionally presiding over the impeachment trial of Federalist Justice Samuel Chase, who was alleged to have slandered the administration from the bench. Amid these tumultuous stirrings, Burr maintained an orderly, dignified demeanor, causing grudging Federalists, if not to overlook the murder of their compatriot Hamilton, at least to note Burr's fairness. Chase was acquitted, and Burr, after bidding a tender farewell to the national legislature, proceeded west to instigate an armed assault on Spanish possessions and possibly to create a divided America.[42]

The Burr Conspiracy, as it became known, fell apart when a would-be conspirator alerted Jefferson to the plot. General James Wilkinson, Maryland-born governor of the Louisiana Territory, had been Burr's friend since they served together under Benedict Arnold in the unsuccessful American siege of Quebec in 1775. During 1806, the general forwarded evidence to the President that Colonel Burr intended everything from a military coup separating the western and the Atlantic states at the Allegheny Mountains to an attack on the nation's capital itself. Once betrayed by his friend, Burr was captured, thus beginning a series of trials, escapes, and brief imprisonments, at the end of which the resilient if outcast ex-Vice President averted conviction for treason. But the intense scrutiny of some citizens' aims and others' gullibility elicited new anxieties. In his Special Message to Congress in January 1807, Jefferson faced "depravity" head-on. He charged that Burr had looked to hire "ardent, restless, desperate, and disaffected persons" and had "seduced good and well-meaning citizens, some by assurances that he possessed the confidence of the government." To his old Philadelphia landlord, Thomas Leiper, the President readily acknowledged the damage Burr's "insurrectionary expedition" was doing to "harmony" in Congress and "tranquillity" in the nation at large, but he wrote confidently that the way such "schisms" were handled would ultimately stand as a testament to Americans' qualifications for self-government.[43]

On the other hand, around this time Federalist senator William Plumer of New Hampshire noted the alteration in the nation's political complexion that Jefferson was effecting when he wrote in his diary: "I live on friendly terms with all parties—I meet & converse freely with all—To a federalist I never repeat what the republicans say to me—or to a republican what the federalists communicate. They perceive this— it has given them confidence in me. My credit as a *party-man* with the federalists is gone." This did not make him comfortable with Thomas Jefferson, however. Plumer might have engaged in uninhibited conversations with the President on a number of occasions, yet a noticeable suspicion persisted between them. Commenting that the chief executive had expressed reticence about the brand of history Plumer was intending to publish, the senator criticized Jefferson's mutability, that "ambiguity of his style" and resort to obscure language which directed his "crooked [unpredictable] policy" and helped Jefferson "never to pursue a measure if it becomes unpopular." The senator, moreover, seemed pleased with a colleague who observed that all Presidents, including Washington, took "more pains to acquire popularity than to promote the interest of the United States."[44]

It was in the nature of Americans, after having warred against British caprice and corruption, to question the motives of those who held office and wielded power. In the 1790s Jeffersonians claimed that the Federalists were concealing a plan to subvert the constitutional balance, and in the early 1800s Federalists imagined both sly demagoguery and the despotism of the mob. Yet Plumer was demonstrably proud of his own sense of fairness; it was, he thought, the best possible exhibition of American character. In sharing lodgings with Kentucky's young Republican senator Henry Clay, newly arrived in Washington City, the New England Federalist remarked: "I dislike this practise of setting up such a partition wall ag[ains]t members of Congress, because one party are federalists & the other Republicans. The more we associate together the more favorable shall we think of each other." That may have been so, but no one wanted to admit that the Revolutionary ideal of a harmonizing union was mere wishful thinking.[45]

## REALM OF REVELATION

Plumer's housemate Henry Clay was a colorful transitional figure with a particular attachment to the land. He was born and bred in Virginia, and after studying under the same law tutor as Thomas Jefferson, migrated at the age of twenty, in 1797, to Kentucky along with those who had read Filson's Boone. As a young attorney, Clay settled in Lexington when it had a population of only 1,600. Unlike the self-consciously moderate Revolutionaries, who were for the most part careful not to appear ambitious or argumentative, Clay was suited not only for the American frontier but for the new Congress, once his countrymen reached the unavoidable conclusion that less modest and sometimes raucous voices were bound for the national political stage. The young Kentucky senator was brash, supremely self-confident, and had a flair for oratorical dramatics. When Plumer first encountered him at the end of 1806, he described the tall, slender politician: "intelligent, sensible & appears frank & candid." Two months later he adjusted his comments: "a man of pleasure—very fond of amusements—gambles much." Clay was famous for his high-stakes card playing. "He is a great favorite with the ladies— is in all parties of pleasure—out almost every night—gambles much here—reads but little. Indeed he said he meant this session [of Congress] should be a tour of pleasure." Despite such a reputation, Clay struck the harmonizing New Englander as "a man of honor & integrity." He was also a nationalist. He argued for America's right to grow.[46]

At this time, most anticipated that national growth would be realized in two ways: through maritime commerce and continental exploration. If the nation Jefferson described in his powerful First Inaugural Address was already deemed morally superior to Europe, it seemed inevitable to many, including the President, that it would become materially superior as well. America, Jefferson said, was "a rising nation, spread over a wide and fruitful land, traversing all the seas with the rich productions of their industry, engaged in commerce with nations who feel power and forget right, advancing to destinies beyond the reach of mortal eye." The President believed that a predominantly agricultural America, as it expanded, would be able to feed the world.[47]

For traditional Republicans, commerce represented several things. It was a symbol of America's rise, a necessary evil, a facet of everyday life to be looked upon suspiciously and checked periodically along moral grounds. To mark Jefferson's first Fourth of July as President, an orator in Maine affirmed the latter perspective: "This country produces all the necessities of life. We might live perfectly independent of any other country in the world. Commerce supplies us with little else but the gaudy superfluities of foreign climes. . . . As it makes us rich it increases pride and vanity; and makes us luxurious and indolent; and increases the miseries of the poor; and pampers the vices and follies of the more wealthy." He worried that "vigor and magnanimity, so necessary to the strength and permanence of government," would devolve to "degrading delicacy and effeminacy."[48] To Jeffersonians, that "manly firmness" the nation claimed in the Declaration of Independence demanded fortitude in resisting equally invasions of the land and intrusions upon moral contentment, both of which an enlarged intercourse with the wider world, though a necessary evil, implicitly threatened.

When not mired in rhetorical tirades against the aggressive pursuit of material gain, Jefferson's larger vision won broad support. Pennsylvania senator Dr. George Logan, onetime member of the Democratic Society of Pennsylvania, was a prominent farmer and Quaker. Addressing Congress at the end of 1805, he evoked the Republican commercial vision, noting that, without avarice, practical-minded America already was garnering wide respect for its produce:

> Most of the inhabited countries of the earth were visited by our navigators, and the striped flag of the union flattered the remotest harbors. Our countrymen have made material additions to the science of Geography. They have found markets unknown to commercial men before. They have deriv'd cargoes from the depths of the oceans, and laid the cod, the seal, the whale under contribution. They have exported the productions of their own country so fertile in the articles which sustain and cherish life, to all places where they were wanted, and brought home the crude materials or the manufactures of those regions

in return. By an energy and enterprise unexampled in the history of the human species, they have excited the jealousy of foreigners.[49]

Confidence building came first. Dr. Logan's ecstatic report was typical and unoriginal, adding little but breathless verbs—"flattered," "excited," and "cherished"—to earlier predictions for the "independent empire." The fantasy of other nations' jealousy was a transparent bolstering strategy underlying national policy.

Distinguished Quakers before George Logan had taken a profound interest in the natural gifts of the American earth. There was by this time already a long tradition of Quaker horticulture. The founder of Pennsylvania, William Penn, was an enthusiast, and a series of later scholar-adventurers, like the Bartram family, combined Quaker optimism and industry with a love of the national garden. William Bartram's life's work abounds in happy descriptions while evidencing scientific rigor; his 1803 *Elements of Botany* went through six editions by 1836. The long-lived Bartram inspired younger naturalists to appreciate the beauty and vulnerability of the "democratic" relationships among plant and animal species. Noting, for example, how fish in a clear Florida lake enjoyed equality, he added with an American's imaginative grasp of social fluidity: "The trout freely passes by the very nose of the alligator and laughs in his face, and the bream by the trout."[50]

Jefferson recorded his own encounters with the American sublime in his *Notes on Virginia* and had purchased Virginia's Natural Bridge from King George III in order to possess this wonder of nature, "cloven through its length by some great convulsion," and capable of causing extreme sensations in any human who stood atop it.[51] From Jefferson's and Bartram's minds to the nineteenth-century sublime is a very short step. Benjamin Smith Barton, botanist and guiding light of the American Philosophical Society, saw biblical truth in the scene at Niagara Falls in 1798; heaven spoke to him in the language of thundering waters. New Yorker William Cooper, father of the novelist James Fenimore Cooper, published his *Guide in the Wilderness* in 1810 and described his own experience at Niagara: "Sense dwells upon the image—thought wanders obscurely after something which it cannot grasp, and the beholder is lost in ecstasy as I am in description."[52]

The Louisiana Purchase opened a bright new chapter in America's chronicle of national self-discovery, ushered in through the painstaking accounts of President Jefferson's handpicked explorers Meriwether Lewis and William Clark. It is worth pointing to the self-conscious naming of Lewis and Clark's company of forty or so soldier-explorers: they were called the "Corps of Discovery." Since Columbus's voyages, all who tracked through America were impelled to uncover newness worthy of wide scrutiny, to marvel in discovery. It was this impulse to understand the continent which continued to bring enterprising Americans to imagine their home as a "realm of revelation," as Albert Furt-wangler has recently dubbed it.[53] Something divine and immortal stood before them wanting to be known. And for the discoverers, everything was meant to fit together, for the divine and immortal to be tamed and exploited and preserved—an apparent contradiction that did not appear to concern early Americans. Their purpose as a people was to work at realizing human aspirations, to perfect.

The Lewis and Clark expedition, conceived by Jefferson, was the culmination of a lifetime of commitment to the study of America's natural history and land improvement. Since his years in Europe, he had collected seeds from around the world and introduced new plants to America. He pursued interests in landscaping, soil fertility, gristmills, home manufacturing, and sheep breeding, and invented a moldboard plow of least resistance.[54] At nearly the same time as he was writing about the sublimity of nature in *Notes on Virginia*, the westward-looking Jefferson had submitted a proposal to the Confederation Congress for the organized settlement of the frontier and incorporation of new territories. As President in 1803, he was able to convince the U.S. Congress of the economic benefits of an expedition to follow the course of the Missouri River to the Pacific coast.

The way west was not convincingly mapped in anyone's mind. One Elie Williams wrote to an unnamed member of Congress in advance of the Lewis and Clark expedition of a certain logic that apparently required explication. "I presume that the object of the government [in expanding west] is not merely to facilitate the conveyance of the mail, but . . . as a cement in the union, inasmuch as it will encrease the attachment of the western people to the general government, and to the Atlantic shore: I mean the opening of one great and easy avenue through the mountains and rugged space which lays between the seat of the general government and the western country." At the beginning of 1806 "A CITIZEN" addressed the same national body in the newspaper forum: "When we take a view of the rising importance of the western country, encreasing in population beyond all former example, comprehending a tract of country as fertile, if not moreso, than any on earth . . . will it not be wisdom in the government to bind the whole together by the strongest ties?" Harmonious expectations were always voiced.[55]

On more than one level, then, from 1804 to 1806 the Lewis and Clark expedition guided Americans to an increased appreciation for the potential of their nation. In June 1805, Captain Lewis, a Virginian and until recently Jefferson's private secretary, described a "sublimely grand specticle" in his encounter with the Great Falls of the Missouri River, in present-day Montana. The discoverer was properly awed by the majestic unpredictability of nature, as he felt the abutment on which he stood "reverberate." He viewed the rocks below as the descending waters were pressed into "a perfect white foam which assumes a thousand forms in a moment sometimes flying up in jets of sparkling foam to the hight of fifteen or twenty feet." Returning the next day to find new words to describe the indescribable, Lewis reopened his log with "tremendous roaring" in his ears, as "the water descends in one even and uninterrupted sheet to the bottom wher dashing against the rocky bottom [it] rises into foaming billows of great hight and rappidly glides away, his[s]ing flashing and sparkling as it departs."[56]

Captain Lewis recorded that there were two great cataracts, one *"pleasingly beautiful,"* the other *"sublimely grand."* The pensive explorer, who liked to travel alone ahead of his party, next ascended a hill to view the adjacent country, and sighted immense herds of buffalo feeding on a distant plain. The Missouri there made a bend to the south, which he followed, "a smo[o]th and unruffled sheet of water of nearly a mile in width bearing on it's watry bosom vast flocks of geese." American nature provided wonders and sustenance and always challenge. Proceeding on, he shot a buffalo "through the lungs" and was left with an unloaded rifle as a white bear crept to "within 20 steps" before Lewis discovered it. He only fended off this "monster" after dashing for the river and posing waist deep in a bold "attitude of defence." Retracing his steps, he spotted a tigerlike animal and faced three more charging bulls before passing up the buffalo he had killed and heading back to camp. Reloading his rifle, the captain fantasized: "it seemed to me that all the beasts of the neighbourhood had made a league to distroy me." Rejoining his party sometime after dark, they having "formed a thousand conjectures, all of which equally foreboding my death," he sat and contemplated his "succession of adventures." In retrospect, as the explorer revisited that realm of revelation, he said it "wore the impression on my mind of inchantment; at sometimes for a moment I thought it might be a dream."[57]

This vignette from the pages of Captain Lewis's journal tells more than one story. Lewis as survivor was also Lewis as American commentator on the natural sublime—though his was an entirely derivative commentary. He was conforming to a vocabulary long since systematized by the likes of Edmund Burke and rhetorician Hugh Blair, and by Lewis's benefactor Thomas Jefferson. The European part of the formula was to describe the astonishing object with rapturous delight or sudden shock, and then, upon composure, provide a scientific account of its apparent physical nature. The American part of the formula was to add patriotic emotion: here a death-defying feat resulted in a remarkable recovery against strong odds. On America's landscape, where everything seemed to exist on a larger scale, fortitude led to the disclosure of sublime truth. Here what was real was merely *imagined* elsewhere. That is, in America the imagination was met by a powerful, inspiring *presence*.[58]

Lewis and Clark emphasized in their encounters with nature the need to extract nourishment from the land. Food procurement and preparation, subjects often featured in their combined journals, proved America's abundance; sustenance was possible as the rising generation conceived a westward-moving destiny. There were tremendous varieties of edible plants and animals, and trade and exchange among the settled Indians they met suggested advantages available to a socially responsible population, such that the settlement of hardy whites would contribute. There were lessons to be drawn both from those Indians who lived on the edge of starvation and from those who appeared to lead secure, routine lives. Forced to adapt as they traversed so many different climates, living in suspense and lacking all certainty, the discoverers whom President Jefferson had dispatched to "the westward" learned to hold together, to maintain strength—to prevail.[59]

The 1804 Fourth of July speaker in Shaftsbury, Vermont, personified this assertive ideology. How could anyone be anything but optimistic? "Plastic Nature has been lavish in her bounties, and has uniformly blended beauty and usefulness, variety and convenience. Our territory is extensive—the climate salubrious—the soil luxuriant and the productions various." The orator's refrain was by no means new, but it was now being used on behalf of the solidification of a union accustomed to partisan bickering. "The lofty mountains, and fruitful hills and vallies—the waving forests, and spreading lawns—the noble rivers, and commodious harbors, all essentially contribute to the delight and accommodation of the inhabitants, and hold out a mirror that reflects the true image of union, prosperity, and greatness." Harmony. Happiness.[60]

Not surprisingly, then, the following year in his Second Inaugural Address, Jefferson, too, associated happiness and liberty with the acquisition of new territory in the West: "The larger our association [the federal union] the less it will be shaken by local passions; and in any view, is it not better that the opposite bank of the Mississippi should be settled by our own brethren and children than by strangers of another family?" As to the Native Americans bound to be displaced by white American settlement and land development, the President had magnanimous words: "I have regarded [them] with the commiseration their history inspires. Endowed with the faculties and the rights of men, breathing an ardent love of liberty and independence, and occupying a country which left them no desire but to be undisturbed, the stream of overflowing population from other regions directed itself on these shores." Jefferson appeared to straddle a fence, with sympathy-inspiring Chief Logan on one side and enterprising white farmers, his prime constituency, on the other. Ultimately, the President contented himself in proclaiming that "liberally" furnishing Indians with the implements of "husbandry and household use" was going far enough toward teaching "agriculture and the domestic arts" and improving "mind and morals."[61]

Once again, who was there to mourn for Logan? Promoting the myth of benevolence shielded mainstream Americans from guilt and in fact showed the limits of sympathy. Religious mission, practiced already for many generations, justified subordination. Indian failure to convert fully was blamed on Indian shortcomings, on the persistence of "savage" behavior. There was no safe place in republican America for a society that was not actively inventing the future or responding as yeomen to circumscribed agriculture. Native American societies had to be assimilated or else confined to an inconsequential spot on the map. Despite its criticism of European vice, America was nevertheless blind to the corrosive effects of civilization on its own continent, in which the rhetoric of happiness and liberty masked the assertion of raw, expansive power and the neglect of noncitizens' natural rights and moral welfare.[62]

Revolutionary War physician and North Carolina politician Hugh Williamson's *Observations on the Climate in Different Parts of America* followed the same Jeffersonian formula, projecting harmony. "The soil of America," he explained, "which seems to produce animals of equal strength and firmness, but less ferocity of disposition, than are produced on the other continent, may probably give existence to a race of men, less prone to destroy one another, and more desirous to improve the understanding and cultivate the social virtues." The natural pigmentation of Native Americans, a tone between the pale European and dark African, was linked to the temperateness of the western continent. Declaring that it was the nature of that particular spot of earth to support benign purposes and friendly intercourse, Williamson deemphasized the history of hostilities between the so-called savages and their civilizing neighbors. He proposed that as more Indians became farmers in the Euro-American style, as the forests were cleared and the air discharged of the "gross putrescent fluid" of ponds and marshes, the physical health of the continent's inhabitants would immeasurably improve.

America was where the human species would overcome moral and biological stagnation alike.[63]

## THE REVOLUTION REVIVED

As they peered west in wonderment, Americans were still obliged to concentrate on Atlantic developments. In the spring of 1807, as the British were vigorously searching for deserters from the Royal Navy, they attacked the American frigate *Chesapeake* within sight of Norfolk Harbor. Tempers rose. Jefferson exclaimed that Britain had "touched a chord which vibrates in every heart."[64] He denied British ships access to U.S. ports and proposed to Congress an embargo affecting all belligerents—"peaceable coercion" to avoid all-out war. Citizens accordingly would be weaned of their dependence on foreign imports, as American farmers, Jefferson's presumed constituency, were obliged to forfeit their foreign markets.

Even before the President's initiative, Representative James Sloan of New Jersey calculated on a similar sense of America's growing importance on the map of the world. Americans wanted nothing to do with the Europeans, who seemed unable to avoid "butchering the human species." Recognizing the desirability of their products, Americans would "compel the haughty tyrant of the ocean to do that justice, which several of the most powerful nations in Europe have long strove in vain to effect." All were meant to understand that opposing England was not a sectional or partisan question but that, simply put, Europe needed America. To export, "we ask *favor* of no foreign power. We refuse *justice* to no foreign nation. We can and will, under Providence, maintain our right to be industrious and to exist."[65]

Jefferson's diplomatic ploy failed because it needed more time to succeed than Americans would forbear. American vessels decayed as they sat in their harbors. The massive embargo converted New England traders into smugglers and actually breathed new life into the Federalist party. Although sanctions were called off as James Madison succeeded his longtime friend to the presidency in 1809, intransigence and sus-

picion in both London and Washington led to increased military prep-
arations. A new Congress—more than one-third of the House of
Representatives were new members—asserted American honor and
pointed the nation to war.

In addition to Clay of Kentucky, John C. Calhoun of South Carolina and Daniel Webster of Massachusetts were stepping onto the public stage. In their first terms in the House of Representatives (Clay left
the stately Senate for the preferred "turbulence" of the House, where
he served, from 1811, as Speaker), these three embodied the boldness
of nineteenth-century patriotism: Webster the consummate orator,
whose solemnity and fluency as a practiced pleader and ability to convey
a historic sensibility mesmerized audiences; Clay and Calhoun, powerfully justifying war with England on the basis of a need to assert
freedom and independence for themselves, as their predecessors had
done. In a letter in which he also noted the unusual occurrence of
earthquakes, Calhoun put his premonition in succinct language: "This
is a period of the greatest moment in our history. . . . It is the commence[ment] of a new era in our politicks."[66]

Eager to avoid war, Representative John Randolph of Virginia (who
coined the term "War Hawks" to describe the likes of Clay and Calhoun) proclaimed his pride in the manner of the older-style Republican:
"Are we willing to bend the neck to England; to submit to her outrages?
No, sir. I answer, that it will be time enough to vindicate the violation
of our flag on the ocean." He admitted being afraid of the mighty
British navy, which accompanied its trading vessels to all ports, and
preferred to rely on the law of nations rather than plunge America into
a useless war. Randolph bade his colleagues remember that England
was "the first military Power of the earth." But this did not mean America should "crouch to the invader." "No! I will meet him at the water's
edge, and fight every inch of ground from thence to the mountains—
from the mountains to the Mississippi." But, Randolph finally determined, the republic George Washington had urged to stay out of European squabbles need not "bully and look big at an insult on your flag
three thousand miles off."[67]

The War Hawks, however, got their way. As he helped to build
war fever, Calhoun echoed the rich language of the Declaration of In-

dependence. War was "justifiable," he said on the floor of the House at the end of 1811, because of the "extent, duration, and character of the injuries received; the failure of those peaceful means heretofore resorted to for the redress of our wrongs. . . . The evil still grows, and in each succeeding year swells in extent and pretension beyond the preceding." In 1776 the Declaration had put it similarly: "a long train of abuses and usurpations, pursuing invariably the same object." And: "In every stage of these oppressions we have petitioned for redress in the most humble terms; our repeated petitions have been answered only by repeated injury." Injuries and redress collided once again. Calhoun proceeded: "It is not for the human tongue to instil the sense of independent honor. This is the work of nature; a generous nature that disdains tame submission to wrongs." The Declaration had pledged a nation's "sacred honor" to the cause of independence and invoked the entitlements of "the laws of nature and nature's God." Calhoun on impressment: America could not bear to abandon "our own commercial and maritime rights and the personal liberties of our citizens employed in exercising them." The Declaration: "He [George III] has plundered our seas, ravaged our coasts . . ." and "constrained our fellow-citizens, taken captive on the high seas, to bear arms against their country." In a speech during the fall of 1814, even as negotiations to end the war were in progress, Calhoun revisited the language of the Revolution. England remained to him "the most implacable and formidable" enemy, whose aggression came from "spite," whose demands for rights on American soil were "extraordinary." Making the comparison obvious, he added of the former mother country: "Her bosom is repossessed with the ambition and projects that inspired her in the year '76. It is the war of the Revolution revived—we are again struggling for our liberty and independence."[68]

Henry Clay, too, was ready for his generation to take over from the original Revolutionaries. During the first year of the war he wrote to Caesar Rodney of Delaware: "It is in vain to conceal the fact—at least I will not attempt to disguise with you—Mr. Madison is wholly unfit for the storms of War. Nature has cast him in too benevolent a mould. Admirably adapted to the tranquil scenes of peace—blending all the mild & amiable virtues, he is not fit for the rough and rude blasts which the conflicts of Nations generate." The resolution and talent to prosecute the war, Clay protested, lay with the young Congress: "You see & can appreciate the state of my feelings. I do not despair. The justness of our cause—the adequacy of our means to bring it to a successful issue—the spirit & patriotism of the Country . . . will at last I think bring us honorably out." Clay himself would participate in the negotiations at Ghent, Belgium, which brought an end to the war, though it was said by fellow negotiator John Quincy Adams that his approach to diplomacy was to pray for American victories while outbragging his British counterparts.[69]

After some early American successes, the War of 1812 yielded ample destruction but no real territorial advantage to either side. American morale steadily declined until, at the end of 1814, the indomitable Indian fighter General Andrew Jackson of Tennessee led his motley frontiersmen against a professional British force at the strategic port of New Orleans. For weeks, as news of the impending battle trickled in to the editors of unsympathetic newspapers, fears of "catastrophe" were set in type. But Jackson's men tore these tested British soldiers to shreds when the latter launched a morning assault on his earthen defenses across a fog-bound field. The steady aim of Jackson's riflemen on January 8, 1815, assured him national fame and accorded a despondent, war-ravaged America a much needed burst of national pride. Astonishingly, only seven Americans died on the battlefield, compared to seven hundred of the enemy.[70]

Unbeknownst to the combatants, the war had come to an end by the treaty signed shortly before the fighting in New Orleans. But the glorious end to the war—despite the inconsequential reversion to pre-war conditions stipulated in the treaty—augured a new era for a people keen on asserting their exceptional character and destiny. A Virginian wrote a "Song" on July 4, 1815, commemorating the action:

> See the sons of the west, like a dark cloud of night,
> With eagerness forth from their deep forests throng;
> Their death-tubes of terror prepar'd for the fight,
> Like their own Mississippi, impetuous and strong;
> Tis Jackson who leads

Them to glorious deeds,
Where the vaunting invader in agony bleeds;
Come, toast then our heroes, we swear this great day,
We will hand down in glory till time pass away.[71]

The antiadministration *New-York Evening Post* had to commend Jackson for his "unstudied simplicity and modesty" in performing the apparent miracle. It reprinted a poem written for the *New Orleans Gazette* called "The Retreat of the English":

A bloodless victory, on our side,
May well increase our general's pride;
For see—the field is only dyed
With *English* blood near Orleans.

· · ·

*Here's to the gallant GENERAL! Who*
Has saved our town and country too!
A braver man the world ne'er knew,
Than he who fought for Orleans.[72]

Alexander McLeod, a Scottish-born Presbyterian minister of New York, was among those who saw divine intervention in the war. In the same month as Jackson achieved his great victory, McLeod published *A Scriptural View of the Character, Causes, and Ends of the Present War*, in which he predicted increased piety, "moral order," and social cohesion resulting from this latest test of American virtue and enterprise. The book proclaimed: "A REPRESENTATIVE DEMOCRACY IS THE ORDINANCE OF GOD." It had been a war, McLeod insisted, for "strengthening the American democracy." Congressman George Troup of Georgia echoed McLeod's providential trust: "The God of Battles and Righteousness took part with the defenders of their country and the foe was scattered as chaff before the wind." A Methodist preacher similarly judged that the war had been thrust upon Americans to ensure their moral regeneration once prosperity had begun to appear too easy to attain; and now, because the country had turned again to God, "it appears evident that God has been on our side."[73]

The Baltimore-based *Niles' Weekly Register* expressed Americans' increased pride by updating Revolutionary era comparisons between England and America. Noting how the laboring poor suffered in the former nation, the editor boasted of the ease and surfeit of New World conditions: "It is by no means uncommon to see men whose only apparent means of livelihood is their daily labor, carrying home a turkey that will weigh from 10 to 15 lbs. . . . The fact is, that the sober laboring man, with a prudent and industrious family, barring accidents, can absolutely live as *full* as the man of ten thousand a year." The average American, Niles assured, lived better than the average Englishman. Those who were "the bone and sinew of a country" were like Crèvecoeur's simple farmers, sympathetic characters, moderate in their honest ambition.[74]

Affecting scientific method in an appendix to his tabulation of English and American qualities, Niles related the environment to America's "unparalleled" population growth: "The causes of it are obvious and imposing. The climate is healthy, land is plenty, the soil is bountiful, industry is rewarded and enterprise walks forth unrestrained—AND THE PEOPLE ARE FREE." Not quite finished justifying American values, Niles applied a witticism attributed to Benjamin Franklin, when the late patriot heard his country belittled by an Englishman who termed the climate unhealthy: " 'That is not yet fairly proved,' returned the sage, 'for all the children of the first settlers are not yet dead.' " Niles took pride in extending the Franklinian model: "The probability is . . . that at least one half of our wealthy men, over 45 years of age, were once common day laborers or journeymen, or otherwise very humble in their circumstances when they began the world." Americans, the editor averred, loved being reproached for their humble roots.[75]

In his comparison of the English and American ways of life, Niles had to address the fact of American slavery. He rationalized that "the condition of our slaves has been greatly ameliorated within the last 20 years; and that I really believe their present state is preferable to that of the laboring poor of *Great Britain*—except that the latter *think* they have freedom, and the others *know* that they have not." Like other

Americans who attempted to explain away the persistence of the "peculiar institution," Niles was placed on the defensive. Although the issue of slavery in the nineteenth century (as in the late eighteenth century) would be put second after the cause of union, increasing numbers of Americans understood that they could not endorse the institution when they prized liberty so vocally.

Antislavery was becoming a more powerful international force and would continue to attract attention. Humanitarian reform deriving from the Enlightenment was combining with a reformulation of Christian purposes. Philanthropy, such as the late Benjamin Franklin represented, and humility, such as a reemerging evangelical community purveyed, plus the sympathy and compassion professed by a society constructed on both natural rights and sensibility, all merged in a campaign to free humanity from guilt and self-deception.[76] William Hill Brown's sentimental novel of 1789, *The Power of Sympathy*, had addressed the issue of slavery after the author, a young Bostonian, distinguished between Southerners and Northerners. Accustomed to "a habit of domineering over their slaves," the former, he challenged, were "haughtier, more tenacious of honour, and indeed possess more of an aristocratick temperament." The latter were of more liberal minds: "all men are declared free and equal, and their tempers are open, generous and communicative." Prefiguring the Christian message of Harriet Beecher Stowe's *Uncle Tom's Cabin*, Brown affirmed, "Love softens and refines manners," "mends the heart, and makes us better men," and "gives the faint-hearted an extraordinary strength of soul."[77]

In the South prominent voices both protested and protected slavery. They dealt with the incongruous meanings of liberty by maintaining a pragmatic posture and emphasizing the distinct physical attributes of their landscape which indicated that change would take time. This was a rationale that, they would imagine, someone like William Hill Brown could not appreciate without having seen the South. The climate and soil determined the kinds of crops that were cultivated and conditioned the growth of plantations. The tedious summer work bred people, laborers and gentry alike, who tended to be slow and casual. These things seemed to be beyond human manipulation, so that Southern society should not be unthinkingly insulted. Before slavery was to become "moral" in the Southern vocabulary, it was "expedient"—a matter to be dealt with pragmatically and not urgently.

In the First Congress of the United States, slave-owning Virginians like Thomas Jefferson's college friend John Page had expressed sympathy with petitioners who wanted the national body to entertain antislavery resolves from Quakers and the Pennsylvania Society for the Abolition of Slavery. The "Voice of humanity," Page considered, deserved a hearing. But just as the Constitutional Convention had satisfied Georgia and the Carolinas in 1787 by enacting the three-fifths compromise, the U.S. Congress in 1790–91 allowed that slavery enabled the South to prosper. And so the desire to sustain union overcame ethical concerns.[78]

Jefferson was unusual for a Southerner in that he had wrestled with the question of slavery publicly from the time of the Revolution. He found African Americans' skin color unattractive and freed slaves unassimilable. While he thus viewed race mixing as "degradation," he still regarded himself as an informed, detached philosopher in an increasingly emotion-filled debate. He denied any passion or prejudice of his own as he reasoned through the imperative that blacks should be recolonized beyond America's limits. The apparent hypocrisy of Jefferson's position had been noted by a Federalist critic during the election of 1796. The unsuccessful candidate that year was accused of willingly sacrificing conscience to the acquisition of high office. Jefferson had dismissed blacks as inferior in reason and yet, in a letter made public, wrote free black mathematician Benjamin Banneker of Maryland that he believed slavery alone to be responsible for blacks' general lack of achievement. By 1814, Jefferson's ambivalence could be seen in the ineffective explanation he provided Edward Coles, a Virginian who had freed his slaves and sought Jefferson's aid in promoting a general emancipation. While protesting that Coles's generous sentiments had done honor to both his head and his heart, Jefferson said that he had long since assigned the issue to the heads and hearts of a later generation. He cautioned Coles that slaves were "as incapable as children of taking care of themselves," and that the younger man should "reconcile yourself to your country and its unfortunate condition." He recommended only that Coles speak out "softly but steadily" and await the day when a general consensus was built.[79]

Americans of this period were intent on building a society that preserved and consolidated a kind of liberty and happiness that only those people deemed competent for self-rule could enjoy. If privileged Federalists doubted the civic capacity of the unlettered whites whom the Republicans were supposed to be courting, certainly few placed unfree Southern blacks in the category of civic competence. Blacks were commonly assumed to be prone to emotional excesses and disruptive behavior if they did not receive direction. From here it became possible for white Southerners to rationalize their motives and confine their thoughts to practicing a benevolent paternalism, and for Northerners to ignore the details. The language of republicanism was refashioned to accommodate slavery.[80]

Since the acquisition of the Louisiana territory doubled America's expanse and held out tremendous new commercial prospects, Congress had been attentive to the effects the purchase would have on liberty in general and the institution of slavery in particular. An 1804 debate involving, among others, Senators John Smith of Ohio, James Hillhouse of Connecticut, and Samuel White of Delaware prefigured greater bouts with conscience yet to come. Georgia's James Jackson began arguing that Louisiana could not be cultivated without slaves. Kentucky's John Breckinridge (Clay's predecessor) replied cautiously, "I am against slavery," and then voiced his fear of massive slave revolts as the Caribbean had recently witnessed. Smith, who had spent "considerable time" in the Louisiana Territory, assured the others that white men would be able to prosper without slaves. He wished, for security reasons, that "our negroes were scattered more equally," and thanked God his home state of Ohio had banned slavery.[81]

The next day, debate continued, and Hillhouse remarked on the rapid increase in the black population of the South. Taking up the Ohioan's concern with "peace & security," he warned that introducing slavery into Louisiana would "add fuel to this tinder box." If Louisiana could not be cultivated without slaves, then the new territory would prove "a curse to this country" rather than "a paradise." Unconventionally, it would seem, John Quincy Adams cautiously reckoned that what was evil "in a moral sense" still had practical commercial uses. White of Delaware said, "I think it unfortunate that whenever this question is stirred, feelings should be excited that are calculated to lead us astray." He abhorred the "disgraceful traffick in *human* flesh" and urged that white men accustom themselves to labor in the torrid climate. It was Southern indolence, caused by slavery, and no other factor that was responsible for the people's relative poverty and dilapidation in housing; the North's free soil had nourished "strong, powerful & wealthy" people: "We boast of liberty & yet in the very bosom of our Country, establish slavery by law." In 1805 Pennsylvania's Isabella Oliver published an antislavery poem, applying the female conscience to this vexing issue:

> AMERICA! Wipe out this dire disgrace,
> Which stains the brightest glories of thy face . . .
> Oh, slavery! Thou hell engender'd crime!
> Why spoil the beauteous country in her prime.[82]

Striving for reason, America's empire builders inevitably resorted to warm language when they found themselves delimiting moral boundaries along with territorial ones. Conceptions of liberty and happiness and the ramifications of land and empire could turn ostensibly generous minds militaristic, while outside forces sometimes induced unexpected justifications. The nature of American slavery was ever volatile, and the arguments, as things turned out, rather malleable. In 1808 antislavery sentiment was given a boost when the slave trade was officially abolished—the first year it was legally possible to effect under the terms of the federal Constitution. Yet when Charles Jared Ingersoll, son of a Northern Federalist, published a nationalistic tract in 1810 to rebut European criticisms of the American character, among Ingersoll's arguments was the notion that slavery secured a sound social order.[83]

The younger Adams's tentative acceptance of commercial practicality, it seems then, was no anomaly. Without slavery, this logic went, it would be impossible for democratically inspired Americans to resist a complete leveling of the population. The proposition arose that slavery helped slave owners cherish their own liberty. Model Federalist

Timothy Dwight, clergyman and president of Yale, wrote in a nationalist mode: "The Southern Planter, who receives slaves from his parent by inheritance, certainly deserves no censure for holding them." The planter fulfilled his duty by treating his slaves "with humanity." Another clergyman and college president, Samuel Stanhope Smith of Princeton, repeated the rationale that both Africans and African Americans had long since conformed to slave society and were "accommodated to it from their infancy."[84]

Many in America, North and South alike, believed that a country divided into black and white was a "motley nation." Assimilation was not a popular view in any region, and recolonization of blacks to Africa became the policy preference of many who considered themselves humanitarians. Before abolitionism moved from incendiary language to mainstream thought during the middle decades of the century, the natural rights theory which dictated the Revolutionary creed that "all men are created equal" did not deter slavery advocates from proclaiming America a healthy republic. The Federalists' rationale is most curious. On the one hand, strong provincial bonds were apparent in the way they lashed out at the Jeffersonians when all that was left of their original strength was a small pocket of resistance in New England. On the other hand, the Revolutionary goal to achieve harmony among the nation's parts was nearly universal, allowing embattled Federalists to advance what should have stood out as an unattractive doctrine in their pursuit of larger principles. The common interest in solidifying a national identity somehow made it possible during the Virginia Republican dynasty of Jefferson-Madison-Monroe for Federalists to reflect Revolutionary era rhetoric. In this way, antislavery convictions yielded temporarily to an unresolved anxiety about being able to preserve free citizens' right to secure lives. For those who prized social order, abolition in a time of political imbalance and ambiguous foreign relations could be perceived as disruptive. Freed blacks, believed capable of wild emotionalism, might act to undermine the ordered society of their former masters, and lawless confusion might then spread.[85]

The general temper in America was protective, from the time a perceptible British challenge arose in Jefferson's second term through the War of 1812. Joel Barlow's Fourth of July oration in the nation's capital in 1809, just months after Jefferson retired and Madison succeeded him, serves as a monitor of the mood in this era of generational transition. Reiterating the Jeffersonian vision of an "empire for liberty," the Republican spokesman reminded his audience of the importance of judgment and conscience to nation building. "Minds of sensibility," he said, "accustomed to range over the field of contemplation that the birth of our empire spreads before them, must expand on this occasion to great ideas, and invigorate their patriotic sentiments." The continental expanse made America a "gigantic infant of a nation," able to "look forward to a state of adolescence, with confidence to a state of manhood. . . . Though as a nation we are yet in the morning of life, we have already attained an elevation which enables us to discern our course to its meridian splendor; to contemplate the height we have to climb, and the commanding station we must gain." The "gigantic infant" empire had nowhere to hide, as it constantly reminded itself of its novelty.[86]

As he continued to make his point with human growth and geographical metaphors, the Republican orator united sensibility and patriotic education: "Nations are educated like infants. They are what they are taught to be. . . . Our nation must, it can, its legislators ought to say it *shall* be taught to reason correctly, to act justly." Each citizen was "an integral member of the sovereignty; his is co-estate of the empire." To build that empire was an urgent issue, "which the heroes of our revolution, the sages of our early councils, the genius of civilization, the cause of suffering humanity have placed within our power and confided to our charge." In elevating the role of generous sentiment in nation building, this declared concern for "suffering humanity," Barlow was insisting that wisdom, benevolence and power had to combine—and this sufficed as a revelation of America's destiny.[87]

Barlow's epic poem *The Columbiad*, first composed as *The Vision of Columbus* (1787) and revised and published under the aforementioned title in 1807, had already spoken of the sympathetic dimension of America's foreordained rise. Once "from his old empire hurl'd," the American promised "peace and pardon" to the world. The universal message of the new nation arrived bathed in radiance:

Floods of unfolding light the skies adorn,
And more than midday glories grace the morn.

It was a "new-born day" that ushered in the nation's fame. Harbors "unfolded," welcoming free men to "cheerful toil," as the glory of America's outward-bound commitment was made known across the seas:

Links in the chain that binds all human kind,
The union'd banners rise at last unfurl'd,
And wave triumphant round the accordant world.

In Barlow's speeches and writings, the world was coming of age and advancing toward harmony because of America. *The Columbiad* fittingly concluded with its vision of "union o'er the world."[88]

Barlow was born in the 1750s and best represented the Revolutionary generation. To the succeeding generation of leaders, secure by 1815 in their political ascendancy, taking on the powerful British had been more than just a way of reasserting virtue in American life. General Andrew Jackson's remarkable victory over the best of the British army at the Battle of New Orleans proved that a proud, if historically young, nation could acquit itself well in confronting any European power with designs to arrest its continental destiny. Federalism disintegrated along with the triumph of this idea. The Federalist leadership was discredited for refusing to exhibit a sufficient level of patriotism during the late war and scorned for having believed England invincible. For a time, then, the two-party system rested. When it revived in the 1830s, the Whig party opposition to Jackson Democrats would fashion themselves from something called "National Republican."

And so, in the wake of the second war with Great Britain, the language of harmony had a wide resonance. *Niles' Weekly Register* led its "National Poetry" section with an account of the gentleman who had "watched the bomb-shells" burst around Baltimore's Fort McHenry "and at early dawn his eye was still greeted by the proudly waving flag of his country." It was Francis Scott Key's "Star-Spangled

Banner," of course, sung popularly (though it would not become the national anthem until 1931), that measured adolescent America's surging confidence. Madison's Secretary of the Treasury, Albert Gallatin, remarked of his countrymen: "They are more American; they feel and act more like a nation."[89]

# CHAPTER EIGHT

# WITH PINIONS HIGH POINTED: 1816-28

"A PATRIOTIC SONG" published in 1816 and signed by "The Western Bard," announced America's newfound poise as an aggressive
power. The Eagle "flies screaming, / With pinions high pointed, to
pounce on her prey." Once "rous'd," the "sons of Columbia . . . rise
and defend our fam'd Liberty tree." Language now ranged beyond
merely moral victories to masculine bravado: the nation's freemen
"swear by the sword and the altar, / To join the fierce Eagle, and make
a bold stand," "Determin'd to conquer, to die or live free."[1]

Having trounced Federalism along with the British army at New
Orleans, Republicans ironically came to accept an aggressive Hamiltonian economy, complete with national bank, federal sponsorship of
certain transportation projects, and a protective tariff in support of domestic manufactures. New York City artisans, who with martial spirit
had contributed their free labor to the war effort by erecting fortifica-
tions, celebrated peace and the promise of financial security. Their Mechanics Bank set up a large display featuring the mechanic insignia (a
hammer held firmly in hand) alongside an eagle, a cornucopia, and an
outward-bound vessel. Business and movement constituted American
resolve, as Europe quieted down after Napoleon's defeat and new emigrants—new farmers and laborers—landed on American shores.[2]

During the first three decades of the nineteenth century, Americans gradually came to fear less for the security of the republic. Ordered liberty prevailed. Democracy, no matter how defined, was seen no longer to threaten the foundations of government. In the words of historian Robert Wiebe: "Gentlemen of the 18th century sought to contain the society they led, their 19th century counterparts to release its energies. . . . Democracy's radical new principle was self-rule: people ruled themselves collectively, people ruled themselves individually."[3] Convinced that he now enjoyed "perfect" civil and religious freedom, Crèvecoeur's spirited farmer returned as the venturesome Jacksonian "common man."

A curious element in Jackson's rise was the inevitable comparison a nationalistic people made between the rough-hewn general and the first hero general of the republic, George Washington. Groomed since the decisive Battle of New Orleans as "the next Washington," skillful and Roman in his discipline and courage, patriotic in his motives, Jackson was colorful indeed, but also known to be capable of much ill will. He seemed to enjoy killing. In Americans' composite opinion, along with his admirable masculine sense of honor and fairness, he was temperamental and bellicose. To be ruled by one's passions and flawed in conduct was as great a divergence from the Washington image as was possible, for the first President's spotless virtue was ever growing in legend. Jackson had guts, but he was earthy, typical, a valiant incarnation of "one of us"—nothing about him was transcendent. There could arise no myth of perfection after Washington. The American had become too self-interested for any newfound hero to convince people of total disinterestedness. Because American women were beginning at this time to take on a prominent role in public projects to extend benevolence, American men were able to concentrate more on advancing themselves through their individual ambition. All the while, a *national* self-image of unselfishness persisted.[4]

The slavery issue was germinating, but it had not yet become as agonizingly painful in assessments of the national image as it would when abolitionist voices became more strident during Andrew Jackson's two terms as President (1829–37) and after Nat Turner's portentous 1830 slave revolt. Southern planters portrayed themselves as kind, generous, and moderate people, Christians worthy to be entrusted with the lives of those enslaved (in the same sense, one might argue, that the nation's elected representatives served as repository for the people's liberties). The Jeffersonian stalwart John Taylor of Caroline County, Virginia, expressed this view with relish. Though he subscribed to the belief that Southerners ought to transport freed slaves at public expense to a place where their virtues could be "reanimated," he was convinced that their erstwhile masters naturally wanted to look after their health and happiness, because the industry of slaves dictated how well the planter lived. Taylor saw as more detrimental to the republic than slavery the spiritlessness and corruptibility of those who rose to prominence through financial speculation, mere paper profits. A government of special banking interests, Northern industry propped up by high tariffs, tended not only to concentrate power among the few but to minimize the value of small-scale agriculturalists to the national economy. For Taylor, and increasingly for other Southerners reared on Revolutionary rhetoric, the broad masses were being caught in the web of a financial aristocracy; technically free whites in the North could be less secure and less happy than the technically enslaved.[5]

A proslavery Christian consensus fueled plantation power and the understanding that slavery illustrated the existence of God-given inequalities within the human race. The seductive idea that a natural inequality belonged in any "family" took on adherents. As white Americans felt freer, they became more intent on ridding themselves of "disorderly elements." The language they used deepened the meaning of skin color: blacks became "contaminated" in a quasi-medical sense; they were endowed with a too pronounced sexuality, and proved a "blight" and "foul stain" on the land. To rid America of what infected or suffocated it was meant to be an act of "cleansing." This self-serving view, palatable in parts of the North, was accepted by most but not all Southerners. Voluntary liberation of slaves continued to take place, and the interest in emancipation expressed by certain Virginia legislators in the state constitutional convention of 1829 was real.[6]

The American Colonization Society, founded in 1816, favored emancipation but regarded resettlement of unassimilable freed slaves to Africa as the only solution that would receive wide acceptance among whites. Slave owners James Madison, James Monroe, and Henry Clay were prominent supporters of this society, whose official organ recalled with great sympathy "the outward voyage, cruel seizure, and forcible abduction of the unfortunate African from his native home." In accepting Jefferson's distinction between voluntary amalgamation of Europeans in America and the brutally engineered captivity of the "exiled children of Africa" there, these white philanthropists emphasized the universal good feelings bound to result from their work. First, white Americans of "talent, integrity, and patriotism," acting in the interest of "national justice and moderation," would reap satisfaction in advancing America's reputation among the nations of the world. At the same time, they imagined the repatriated Africans would respond to this demonstration of "justice, conciliation, and humanity" by remaining in the orbit of a paternalistic, enterprising, Christian trading empire—America's newly homogenized sentimental democracy. Then "the philanthropist will exult at the wide prospect of happiness it presents."[7]

The false hope of the Colonization Society reflected the ambiguity of Revolutionary liberals' position that the race issue eventually could be resolved to the gratification of all. Hope crystallized in the imagined sensibility of an African-American community restored to dignity by returning to its original home: "Oh, unhappy Africa," lamented the unidentified writer of an 1825 story, "how long must thy soil be washed with the tears of those who weep for their nearest and dearest relatives, who have been torn away from them, and dragged into bondage."[8] The mirage of a healthy, harmonizing republic, lightened in color, only assured that more contentious public discussion of diverging ideologies—liberty with slavery versus liberty for all—was now unavoidable. The second generation of national leaders, whose political upbringing took place not during the unifying 1770s but during the divisive 1790s, was unable to resist the sectional pull that in due time would result in civil war.

The moral absolutism of Indian removal policy from the 1820s was similarly rationalized. Through a belief in time as a healer and racial separation as a prerequisite for positive cultural transitions, the philanthropic white liberal mind heralded the prospects for a more "civilized" Indian sensibility under the influence of continued but less direct contact with mainstream white America. From a safe distance, Americans of European origin marveled in the manner of the New Yorker of 1822 who had returned from a visit to New England: "I was gratified to find so many of the Indian names of rivers and mountains still retained, and that it was so easy to identify many of the places in whose history I had before taken much interest. Indeed I consider it quite necessary to the full enjoyment of the traveller . . . to recur occasionally to the ancient state of things." With momentary remorse, this visitor recognized himself "a usurper of the rights and an intruder on the native soil of heroes."[9]

Mirroring the paternalistic, covertly hostile program of the American Colonization Society, the philanthropic mind behind Indian removal was, in historian Bernard Sheehan's findings, "intrusive and compulsive in its determination to have its way. Though it praised the Indian male for his many abilities, it conceded native society nothing in the way of permanence. Philanthropy treated the tribes as objects of commiseration whose sole purpose after the arrival of the white man should have been the speedy adoption of civilization. It demanded a total transformation."[10] As America pushed back the frontier, its demand grew for a warm-blooded white man's democracy. New Americans saw legitimacy in the displacement of old Americans (Indians) for the greater good of a civilization at once free and orderly (if Indians were free and *dis*orderly). They believed they were acting to bring order out of chaos in taming their wilderness, and doing so for the betterment of humanity.[11]

## THE NEW FRANKLINS

The prescribers of sentimental democracy were a self-conscious people. They sometimes judged themselves to be virtuous, sometimes flawed, but always necessary actors on the international stage, convinced that if their collective goal was to be achieved, if the moral condition of the world was to improve, they had to hold to a distinctly American character—what they recalled of the ingenious, hardworking, and generous-spirited people originally excited (in their Revolutionary ardor) to meritorious display. This is why blacks and Indians were troublesome: Could these groups deemed inferior in merit ever "rise" to white America's ideal self-image? Alternately secure and anxious, sentimental democrats worked toward harmonious ends and optimistically professed their belief in the possibility of a national happiness.

In religious terms, they maintained the image of pristine America as a blessed refuge, a fruitful promised land. The new Jerusalem or new Eden was part of a symbolic language, more overt in earlier generations, when literal prophecy attracted more adherents. The nineteenth century's romance with America was not meant so much to revive the past—a nostalgic return to a walled city or a static biblical garden—as to reaffirm what has come to be understood by the term "American exceptionalism." If the original settlers had conjured an empty and inviting world, a self-contained world, and later colonists had set about to shape and achieve mastery over it, their descendants of the period after 1815 felt that they were indeed closer to that goal of total mastery, perfecting a system of benevolent exploitation.

Americans continued to assert that the language they spoke revealed their superior character and set America apart. For nearly three decades they had been suggesting that their regional idioms were less varied than dialects among different regions within England, indeed that English was *better spoken* in the New World than in the Old. Novelist James Fenimore Cooper addressed a British audience in his *Notions of the Americans* (1828): "We speak our language, as a nation, better than any other people speak their language." The age of linguistic deference to England was decidedly past. One American noted in that same year: "I never shall write what is now worshipped under the name of *classical* English. It is no natural language—it never was." When English visitors, including a young Charles Dickens, commented unfavorably on Americans' regional accents, or noticed drawls, nasality, and other supposedly unattractive elements, Americans became defensive and more insistent about the virtues of their language, inferring the virtue of the people. Some speculated that British English would in the future become unintelligible to Americans (and vice versa), while others celebrated the commonplace and all variations that coincided with the democratization of politics.[12]

This overall feeling, however, does not account for that remnant of uncomfortable Americans, prisoners of the past like Noah Webster, who were unwilling to face up to democracy. When Webster surrendered his anxious Federalist vision to evangelical Protestantism in 1808, a conversion that followed those of his wife and daughters, the disgruntled writer-editor replaced one dire cause with another. If democratization was inevitable in the enterprising republic of the everyman, then for an elitist who advocated a disciplining of the human passions, religious morality became the only conceivable means of bringing unity and peace to the country. Henceforth in his ruminations on the American Revolution, Webster conceived that the patriots' obedience to God had to have been of paramount importance to their victory. When in 1828 he completed his life's work, his *American Dictionary*, the nationalism that remained in its pages was indistinguishable from his Calvinist beliefs.

This troubled thinker had turned sharply from his *Dissertations on the English Language* of 1789. There were few Americanisms left in his dictionary. Indeed, the work was more favorably reviewed and proved more successful on the other side of the Atlantic; the first U.S. edition of 2,500 copies took fully thirteen years to sell through. Webster had surrendered to the principle that the language of England should not be allowed to degenerate, but that it should "bind the two nations together." He hoped that Americans would not forget "either the land or the language of their fathers." He gave definitions of *happy* (enjoying "a peace of mind in favor of God"), *duty, improve, laws, love,* and *author* ("God is the *author* of the universe") that attested to his revitalized religious faith. When he died in 1843, Noah Webster was long since disillusioned with America. The American language was accepting a new, even more radical philology, classifying popular speech and strengthening English with vigorous folk utterances. The commonplace was becoming a dignified form of the language.[13]

Relative to Europe, then, Americans were rough in their ways and challenging in their speech. But they never gave up wanting to be judged respectable. Manners changed with the "middling" effect of democracy, but morals were prized no less than in colonial times. The nation continued to advertise itself to the world as a model of progress, as a land where liberty and happiness were being maximized, where unblemished nature (the past), decent intentions (the present), and benevolent growth (the future) all harmonized.

In the years after 1815, the majority of Americans remained true to Jefferson's political principles but less connected to his ideas of political economy. Jefferson had promised progress without consolidation of the nation's wealth and without taxing farmers—progress, in effect, with nothing more than the people's honest labor and their President's rhetorical backing. America would prosper as a world unto itself, he thought, simple farmers peacefully spreading republican culture west across the wide and fertile continent. Magazine publisher Mathew Carey decisively countered the Jeffersonian idyll of "Arcadian cultivators." In an 1819 address subsequently published in his *Essays on Political Economy*, Carey exploded the myth of "the purity, the innocence, the healthiness, and the independence of agricultural employments" in favor of Hamilton's ambitious plan for a national manufacturing system. Industry did not have to debase morals, he said, just as farming did not automatically promote them.[14]

A new era of debt evolved, though not without fits and starts. The large-scale issuance of paper notes resulted in the Panic of 1819, ruining many overborrowed Americans when credit suddenly tightened and specie payment of outstanding loans was demanded by the recently rechartered Bank of the United States. After this, it was not just the sage of Monticello who cast a suspicious eye on the banking industry. But the new generation still preferred a different economy from the traditional Republican one. They wanted vigorous home markets and increased manufacturing, an integrated system with federal improvements such as Henry Clay proposed with his "American System." While he lived, the inflexible Jefferson (and later Jacksonian purists as well) feared that an overactive national government would corrupt the pastoral garden, though Clay in fact meant to fulfill Jefferson's vision, only by other means.[15]

Anxiety did not deter ambition. The new citizen was modeled after individuals as seemingly different as Benjamin Franklin and Andrew Jackson, men of persistent aspirations. Franklin, of course, was the prototype of the American rags-to-riches story, who loved books and gained recognition by writing and editing his way into influential social circles, then reasoning his way into state and national political circles— in short, success through individual enterprise and careful maneuvering. Though Franklin was often sly, he showed that ambition did not always lead to avarice and debased morals but could lead as easily to civic commitment and national respect.

Cast in the Franklin mold were Charles Thomson (one generation removed) and Mathew Carey (two generations removed), both Irish immigrants who arrived penniless in America—in 1739 and 1784 respectively—and whose love of learning and tireless industry turned them into distinguished students of science and philosophy with Franklinian notions of civic responsibility. Earning a good living as a Philadelphia merchant, Thomson revitalized Franklin's American Philosophical Society in the 1760s and saw his career peak as secretary of the Continental Congress. Carey, if less diversified, believed strongly in universal education and built up a reputation with his pen and publishing ventures.[16]

Then there is the life of New York craftsman Alexander Anderson, born in 1775, who taught himself engraving as a teenager by using pieces of copper and a pocketknife and furthered his knowledge of the trade by "peeping into the shop windows" of silversmiths as they did their lettering. Filial and industrious, Anderson paid his own way through Columbia College Medical School and alternated between work as a doctor and engraver until giving himself over to the latter profession full-time while still in his early twenties. Anderson went on to renown as the "father of American wood engraving," whose work appeared widely in books and newspapers. He survived nearly to his hundredth year. The long-lived Franklin was also proud of his artisanal origins—his tombstone identifies him as "Benjamin Franklin, Printer." At the opening of the Apprentices' Library in New York in 1820, master baker Thomas Mercein queried his audience: "Who can tell how many Franklins may be among you?"[17]

By varying their occupations and becoming worldly by first becoming shrewd, men of modest roots and intellectual promise were able to lift themselves above the more banal aspects of mass culture. In the new America, though, no one topped the symbolism of Andrew Jackson, the embodiment of American energy and passion. Born on the South Carolina frontier in 1767, Jackson was orphaned young. He read the law in North Carolina—if less compelled to scholarship, perhaps, than the Franklin model required—and subsequently migrated to Tennessee, where he became a land speculator. In the 1790s, long before distinguishing himself in battle during the War of 1812, he served as congressman, U.S. senator, and judge. Jackson lusted for wealth and power while professing to hate the rich and powerful. Risen from the masses, he achieved parity with the slave-owning aristocrats of the Old South. Yet the most important factor in his rise was not any political program so much as the faith he inspired. It was, as historian George Dangerfield wrote, "a faith in the individualist, of whom Jackson was the supreme example: as if the will power of self-made men, by a process of simple addition, made up the will power of the nation."[18]

National growing pains necessarily provoked new moral challenges. Not long after the War of 1812, Benjamin Oliver set out to combine a historically meaningful assessment of social progress with a prescription for religiously inspired benevolence. His *Hints for an Essay on the Pursuit of Happiness* warned that power led to complacency, not happiness. Happiness rather derived from tests of "the virtue of motives," without which there could be no moral or political equality. Attempting an investigation of present standards of conduct, Oliver reckoned that society had already come to terms with competition, rivalry, "continuous strife," and "cunning practices." Such behavior had grown "so common, that it is considered lawful, as being merely according to 'the course of trade.'" Inequality of happiness, he had to admit, was inevitable.

He bade his countrymen rediscover the godly way, knowing how much there was to overcome before achieving it. Unnamed "pleasures of the imagination" represented the "sources of all the corruption of the human heart. The best lead to weakness and effeminacy; the worst, to every enormity, crime, and abomination." As in the Revolutionary era, "weakness and effeminacy" implied a lack of industry and a deplorable disengagement from public responsibility. "Crime and abomination" meant the willful flight from a self-restraining morality. Useful study, useful labors, he said, helped one avoid imagination's excess.

Otherwise, citizens would be swayed by the "profligate," the "game-ster," the "sot," the "swearer," the "lounger," and the "fool," the last of whom "indulges romantic feelings." Oliver further urged, "As God's benevolence embraces the universe, so man's should be coextensive with the world in which we live." A cry for benevolence stimulated Oliver's vision of moral transformation, but he seemed at the same time to recognize that his ethereal and sweet-sounding language ignored what was really happening to the American people. And so the moralist was frequently forced to return to the contemporary scene: "In many cases," he allowed, "it is necessary for some men to perform offices, which require, that the heart should be hardened." Society had to be policed. Those whose professions obliged them to undertake the work of taming this errant people were performing a different kind of benevolence. "Let the rest of us thank God, that it is not necessary, that we should all lead the ox to the slaughter."[19]

Presiding over an increasingly competitive society at a time of rising nationalistic expression was James Monroe, the fourth Virginian elected to the nation's highest office. When his first administration got under-way in 1817, Monroe toured the Northeast, with the official purpose of inspecting coastal defenses, but as much to give substance to party reconciliation or combination. The Virginia Republican was every-where hailed. It was a Federalist-inspired Boston newspaper, the *Columbian Centinel*, that now coined the phrase "Era of Good Feelings" to describe the courteous, unimaginative Monroe's years as "caretaker" President. That summer a New England orator described patriotism as "the spontaneous devotion with which freemen regard the source of all their enjoyments."[20]

Good feelings, however, did not bring on a reduction of emotion in the language of Americans, whose concern for the national character did not lessen. Politics remained testy. Editor Hezekiah Niles, for in-stance, fervently defended General Jackson when the latter was branded by members of Congress for allegedly exceeding authority in taking his war against the Seminole Indians of Florida to Spanish-held territory in 1818. To some, Jackson was a would-be Caesar and, unlike Wash-ington, a general who crusaded without restraint, who took arbitrary steps without recognizing his subordination to the civilian authority—

who would abandon the Constitution. Congressional nationalists like Henry Clay retreated from their expansionist rhetoric to stop the imperious, charismatic Tennessee hero. Niles reprinted letters attesting to Jackson's "dignified and impressive," patriotic and republican, manner, while questioning the "passion and prejudice" of the general's detractors. Jackson himself wrote: "What I have done was for my country; had I erred in the discharge of my official duty, that error would have originated in the warmth of my devotion to her interest."[21]

The assertive language of this time combined a vocabulary of feeling with one of strength. Words expressed uncompromising sentiments. "An insidious dilapidation or violent dismemberment of the American union," wrote Niles on the delicate subject of states' rights, "is the darling hope that the enemies of liberty, at home and abroad, have hugged to their heart with demoniac fervor and constancy." Combative in his posture against a dynamic Supreme Court, the determined editor vented his spleen when it came time to represent "a redeeming spirit in the people," to whom public servants in a democracy remained accountable. Here was where Revolutionary rhetoric about bonds of affection joined outrage toward the insensitivity of the privileged and powerful: "And feeling as we do—as if the very stones would cry out if we did not speak on this subject!" Niles invoked the Revolution once again to anchor his attachment to "the collected wisdom of the nation," to "build up a NATIONAL CHARACTER, to inspire a *home feeling*, a proud and jealous regard of our rights as men."[22]

Nothing so aroused the sentiments of the nation's leaders in the questionably dubbed "Era of Good Feelings" as the controversy that surrounded the admission of Missouri as a state. The first territory acquired in the Louisiana Purchase to seek statehood, Missouri would have entered the union silently, according to constitutional law, and would have permitted slavery within its boundaries, had not a congressman from New York's Hudson Valley, James Tallmadge, introduced a bill that stipulated otherwise. Congress, he said, ought to ban further importation of slaves into Missouri and free all remaining slaves when they attained the age of twenty-five. There were not quite 3,000 slaves in 1810 and 10,000 by 1820, out of a population of 66,000.[23]

Tallmadge's Massachusetts colleague Timothy Fuller invoked the language of the Declaration of Independence in support of the Tallmadge resolution. Because they were born in "a *purely* republican government," slaves were entitled to "*liberty* and the pursuit of happiness." Those states holding slaves at the time of the nation's founding could continue the practice, Fuller argued, but there was no reason why the political existence of any new state would be in jeopardy if slavery, in accord with republican principles, was prohibited from establishing itself there. After Representative Thomas W. Cobb of Georgia next warned that the Northerners had "kindled a fire which all the waters of the ocean cannot put out, which seas of blood can only extinguish," Tallmadge tartly countered:

> Language of this sort has no effect on me; my purpose is fixed, it is interwoven with my existence; its durability is limited with my life; it is a great and glorious cause, setting bounds to a slavery, the most cruel and debasing the world has ever witnessed; it is the freedom of man. . . . If a dissolution of the union must take place, let it be so! If civil war, which gentlemen so much threaten, must come, I can only say, let it come![24]

The Missouri crisis not only allowed an impassioned common language to flourish but pointedly announced that the usual symbiotic relationship between the nation-promoting values of happiness-liberty and land-empire could break down, that these pairings could stand opposed as well as sentimentally allied. Issues of land threatened to suppress liberty, raising instead irreconcilable tensions. And if empire created division among the existing states, then it was not extending happiness.

Thus the various meanings of happiness and liberty in America wore a new and uncomfortable garb during the frenzied, prescient dispute over Missouri. An Ohio state legislator in 1820 took the occasion of a debate on the constitutionality of the banking establishment to proclaim that for the people of the western country, "patriotism is the ruling passion of their souls," and that nothing short of the removal of their liberties would provoke them to violence. State sovereignty was an admittedly volatile issue, he said, and needed to be handled cautiously, but he hoped no one would forget what it meant to be an American:

> The unexampled prosperity of our republic for forty years, has been upon the point of silencing for ever the enemies of liberty. In the last war America exhibited herself to the astounded potentates of Europe all the sublimity of national triumph. . . . A nation of freemen; revering their constitution; obedient to its laws; establishing by her example, the entire security of individual rights in a government founded on the basis of liberty and equality. Giving protection to the rich and the poor. Alike opposed to the tyrannical principle.[25]

Somehow, incongruously, at this uncertain moment liberty appeared more secure than union. Jealous of their rights, individuals and states held to principles in common with the national government but demonstrated an iron will that made rebellion conceivable. The American personality resisted regimentation. It stood up to any authority deemed invasive, even if that authority was duly constituted, and temporarily gone awry or perceived to be emotionally distant.

The Missouri debate weakened nationalist sentiment by questioning the morals of a particular segment of the union. Compromise was finally reached in a session dominated by Speaker of the House Henry Clay. Missouri entered as a slave state, Maine as a free state, and a line was demarcated to chart the entry of future slave and free states. Afterward, it became apparent that the nation as a whole was more concerned with financial recovery after the frightful Panic of 1819 than with the status of African Americans. Missourians themselves were less inclined to defend the South's socioeconomic structure than to enlarge their state's potential for commercial growth, with an eye toward the future of Spanish dominions in the Far West. The word *disunion*, as Clay remarked, was being hurled by members of Congress without any conception of what it might mean, and would mean, down the road.[26]

As the election of 1824 approached, the masses understood that a watershed was reached. Monroe was to be the last of the Revolutionary generation to serve as President. His potential successors were all of a different breed, billing themselves as inheritors of the Revolution, builders on its inspiring model of national virtue. A series of extended editorials in the *Cincinnati Gazette* in 1822, entitled "To the People" and presented under the pseudonym "BENJAMIN FRANKLIN," established a distinct mood and vision.

In the first installment, "Franklin" set the stage. He described himself as a typical American in character and intellect but an unsurpassed patriot about to announce the nation's "higher destiny." By now, liberty's foundation had been "firmly laid." America's "stability" promised a "happiness so unlimited" that other nations could easily imitate it. America had reached its first plateau as an established republic; it occupied a "proud eminence," and every (male) citizen, through his all-important exercise of the franchise, had "a right to be heard" in selecting the candidate with the greatest "patriotism" and "talent" to set the course for the future.[27]

In the next installment "Franklin" examined sectional politics. A President from the North might help pull the nation together after Missouri, he proposed tentatively, though on second thought "public feeling" acknowledged no sectional identity among America's Presidents: "all feel a pride in our national character." The "wisdom" of Jefferson, Madison, and Monroe, their "talents and virtues," were decidedly "national property." Sectional jealousies carried into presidential contests would not result in better leadership, and therefore citizens should resolve to honor "the bands of union," to go beyond identification with "the neighborhood in which we live." American freemen were bound to exercise "charity" to other parts of the union in the interest of the general liberty.[28]

From this point in the series, "Franklin" focused on Monroe's prospective successors. John Quincy Adams was a man of "sincerity," "classical prudence," and "transcendant ability." His Federalist background was not to be viewed as a detriment now that political party distinctions had blurred. He could be a unifier. "United at home, we cannot fail to be respected abroad," the columnist reminded his readers. "A union of sentiment and of interest, will command prosperity"—joining patriotic sentiment to a national economic imperative.[29]

Unlike "Franklin's" characterization of a profound and intellectually resilient Adams, whose experience would further national prosperity, the portrait of Henry Clay centered upon a discussion of appearances:

> He never fails to interest those whom he addresses. On those subjects which admit of a high degree of pathos, he excels most. Here the enthusiasm of the speaker, becomes excited to the utmost; all the powers of his soul are roused into action. His whole system becomes agitated. He thinks of nothing but his subject. His hearers, ere they are aware, sympathize in his feelings, and partake of his enthusiasm.

This Clay was the Man of Feeling in an evangelical mode, stripped of his quiet and simple benevolence. While patriotism and generous sympathy (American sensibility) united in the ideal national leader, in Clay's case the mesmerizing effect of the orator's words suggested something else: the imposition of a deceptive art. He aimed to persuade by conveying that he was sincere, and yet he might not be:

> Sometimes the grandeur of his conceptions appear[s] to be unlimited. They add fire to his genius . . . The storm of passion is at its height. His auditors yield themselves to its guidance, because they have not resolution or power to resist it. . . . After a release from so powerful an influence, the mind may gradually recover itself, by recurring to the facts of the case, and the principles which should govern. In this way, the fallacy of the argument may be detected, and its errors exposed.

The complex Kentucky legislator possessed a weighty intellect, yet "no man excels him in wielding the passions." The politically canny Clay could draw forth feeling: "he feels himself, and that causes others to feel." Clay's "great secret" was that "his own feelings possess the highest degree of susceptibility," once the trademark of the worthy Man of Feeling, now a quality made suspect because Clay seductively applied feeling in order to modify the truth. There was great ambiguity here:

Once the aggressive, captivating, hard-drinking, poker-playing, and woman-fancying Clay was identified as a Man of Feeling, the relevance of Mackenzie's model was lost.[30]

It required seven installments of "To the People" before the columnist's choice was finally revealed. John C. Calhoun of South Carolina was visible and active, serving as Monroe's Secretary of War from 1817 to 1825 (at thirty-five the youngest cabinet appointee). He was said to possess the ideal balance of qualities: the "susceptibility of feeling" that the experienced Adams did not quite exhibit and "the fire of genius" and "unequaled powers of understanding" that Clay's smoke screen obscured for an electorate perhaps equally responsive to intellectual persuasion and the culture of sympathy and feeling. Calhoun's strength "is not the effect of passion," yet "the blaze of light which he emits, is constant and increasing." He did not ignore sentiment by any means, though. His "feelings and principles" alike were "genuine," and "his feelings admit of no disguise; he is always just what he appears to be." Calhoun's "persevering industry," "cheerfulness," "firmness and republican virtue" combined to signify the new idealized American self-image. *This* Man of Feeling was less given to softness but nonetheless pure: a trustworthy, effective, and forward-looking nationalist.[31]

Disappointingly for "Franklin," Calhoun dropped out of the presidential campaign of 1824 before it heated up. In one of the most interesting elections in American history, John Quincy Adams, the incumbent Monroe's choice, won a close race (decided in the House of Representatives) after Clay persuaded his supporters to endorse the stout New Englander over Andrew Jackson, who, though he entered late, won a plurality of both the popular and electoral vote. Then, after the election was decided, Adams appointed Clay Secretary of State, eliciting cries of a "Corrupt Bargain" from Jackson supporters.[32]

## WHEN THE FOUNDERS DIE

The moral identity of Americans—the mass of free people and their elected leaders alike—continued to be the stuff of much public conversation. In their final years, patriarchs Thomas Jefferson and John

Adams mended their old political rupture and enjoyed an affectionate but still provocative correspondence. Expressing a lack of identification with the rising generation's less restrained style of life, Adams inquired of the restless Virginian in 1819: "Will you tell me how to prevent riches from becoming the effects of temperance and industry? Will you tell me how to prevent riches from producing luxury? Will you tell me how to prevent luxury from producing effeminacy intoxication extravagance Vice and folly?" The ongoing Missouri debate had caused Adams to ruminate about the strength of the union forged in 1787: "I know it is high treason to express a doubt of the perpetual duration of our vast American empire, and our free Institution[s]," but in disquieting reveries he saw the nation cut in two, or chopped up into the dominions of self-styled satraps, "as many Nations in North America as there are in Europe." Hoping that the Missouri question would finally "follow the other Waves under the Ship and do no harm," he went on to describe that test of national harmony uncertainly as an "intricate knot." Jefferson, in turn, warned that the congressional power to "regulate the conditions of the inhabitants of the states," and to liberate the slave population within a given state, might only serve to unleash a catastrophic race war: "Are our slaves to be presented with freedom and a dagger?" he posed. Adams allowed that while the prospect of race war was terrifying, slavery had been "a black cloud" hanging over America for his entire political life; he owned that he himself could not do what was needed, nor do as the genius Franklin had done literally—"invent a rod to draw from the cloud its Thunder and lightning."[33]

Both Revolutionary sages concurred that this dangerous issue was beyond the horizon of their late years' prognostications. Finally Jefferson, never long abandoning his optimism, and invoking the long-understood metaphor of liberty as transportable, transmissible light and heat, reflected upon the larger national image he and Adams had helped to construct: "I will not believe our labors are lost. I shall not die without a hope that light and liberty are on a steady advance. . . . In short, the flames kindled on the 4th of July 1776 have spread over too much of the globe to be extinguished by the feeble engines of despotism." He hoped for a more peaceful society than the one they had watched develop: "how much happier for man the Quaker policy is, and that the life of the feeder is better than that of the fighter." Both men reasoned alike in the fatalistic sense, Adams at eighty-seven, Jefferson at seventy-nine, that, in the latter's words, "when the friends of our youth are all gone, and a generation is risen around us whom we know not, is death an evil?"[34]

Americans' faith in the impending triumph of knowledge over prejudice in their country was a legacy of the founders that the next generation took up. The intelligence or "national information" that Adams had honored in his Inaugural Address animated these younger leaders. Supreme Court Justice Joseph Story, a former Federalist appointed to the Court by President Jefferson, typified the new inclusiveness when in 1826 he hailed the "universal love and power of reading" as a feature of a healthy, spirited, enlightened republic. In a competitive society, individual achievement had to be linked to literacy, to free inquiry, and to civic pride. Impressive figures like Justice Story and his friend the charismatic orator Daniel Webster—who invested his Revolutionary heroes with a national consciousness and declared the present "the age of improvement"—could rise to occasions because the public was better informed than ever before. Being well informed had become fashionable: the lyceum movement begun in the late 1820s brought sociable, practical-minded speakers on scientific, philosophical, literary, and historical subjects to wide audiences bent on intellectual enrichment and moral growth.[35]

In an age when newspaper reading was expanding rapidly, when election campaigns were spreading excitement, and Baptist and Methodist exhorters elicited outpourings of religious enthusiasm, a colorful language possessing emotional force expressed America's future promise. Increasingly since 1800, emphatic typography—exclamation points, question marks, italics, and boldface—fortified the slogans which carried political rhetoric to an ever-widening electorate. The use of spoken idiom in public writings magnified a democratic mythology, as politicians acquired popular nicknames like "Old Hickory" for Jackson, "Harry of the West" for Clay, and "Black Dan" (referring to his dark complexion and penetrating eyes) for Webster.[36]

If he was not at all representative of the rising "common man," still the powerful, outspoken Webster recorded some of history's most informative statements concerning Americans' preoccupation with the transition from the legendary feats of the Revolutionary age to new nineteenth-century expectations. After the simultaneous deaths of John Adams and Thomas Jefferson occurred on July 4, 1826, the fiftieth anniversary of the Declaration of Independence, the Massachusetts congressman (and soon to be U.S. senator) read a joint eulogy that took an eerie coincidence and rendered it sublime.

The orator saluted the past: "The tears which flow, and the honors that are paid, when the founders of the republic die, give hope that the republic itself may be immortal." How much more poignant when on "the great day of national jubilee, in the very hour of public rejoicing . . . they took their flight together to the world of spirits." The deaths of the two distinguished ex-Presidents was, Webster decreed, the happy conclusion to a great epic: "Poetry itself has hardly terminated illustrious lives, and finished the career of earthly renown, by such a consummation."[37]

The statesman's forward vision took over. The link connecting America to "former times" was now officially severed. The future had begun to overtake the past. Recurring to sea metaphors, which had long been employed by the American literati to illuminate the passage of time and the uncertainty of life, Webster enjoined: "Like the mariner, whom the currents of the ocean and the winds carry along, till he sees the stars which have directed his course and lighted his pathless way descend, one by one beneath the rising horizon, we should have felt that the stream of time had borne us onward till another great luminary, whose light had cheered us and whose guidance we had followed, had sunk away from our sight." Jefferson's yet unknown deathbed adieu addressed to his surviving daughter similarly proclaimed the end of life's voyage: "I go to my fathers; I welcome the shore." The future indeed beckoned, and yet the Revolution lived because America's principal spokesmen found in its lessons an anchor. The founders had bequeathed resolution and fortitude to the next generation.[38]

For Webster, neither was America adrift nor the winds and ocean currents random. God continued to guide the nation's destiny while orchestrating the departure of its constitutive founders in a most affecting way. The perfectly timed deaths of Adams and Jefferson offered evidence "that our country and its benefactors are objects of His care." From eternal time and purpose, the orator next moved metaphorically to the light of intelligence that animated the sages. The memory of their lives, he said, of their universally recognized greatness, was not a "temporary flame" but "a spark of fervent heat, as well as radiant light, with power to enkindle the common mass of human kind." Their enduring intellect "leaves the world all light, all on fire." Another familiar metaphor came into play, the founders' work on earth as a tree nurtured from seedling: "The tree which they assisted to plant will flourish, although they water it and protect it no longer; for it has struck its roots deep ... [its branches] stretch their protecting arms broader and broader, and its top is destined to reach the heavens. We are not deceived. There is no delusion here. No age will come in which the American Revolution will appear less than it is, one of the greatest events in human history."[39]

As much as Jonathan Mayhew had posited the requirements of American happiness and liberty in 1750, Webster now, in his conclusion, affirmed America's romantic self-image at the end of the period of national conception: "This lovely land, this glorious liberty, these benign institutions, the dear purchase of our fathers, are ours; ours to enjoy, ours to preserve, ours to transmit. Generations past and generations to come hold us responsible for this sacred trust. . . . The world turns hither its solicitous eyes." His final oratorical swell reestablished the idea of America's greatness as self-evident truth: "It cannot be denied, but by those who dispute the sun, that with America, and in America, a new era commences in human affairs. . . . If we cherish the virtues and the principles of our fathers, Heaven will assist us to carry on the work of human liberty and human happiness."[40]

To commemorate the fiftieth Fourth, New Yorkers gathered as artillery salutes were fired, the Declaration of Independence was read, and roasted oxen served, first to the military and then to ordinary citizens. A full-length likeness of Jefferson was put on display. There were evening fireworks from atop City Hall to cap off the day's festivities. It was a week later that the city learned of the well-timed deaths of the second and third Presidents. Then, to honor this "singular and unex-

pected" coincidence, another gathering took place, and this time muffled drums sounded as a state regiment marched. Solemn music wailed
from an organ inside the Middle Dutch Church. Bells tolled nonstop
during the morning hours from eight to nine o'clock and in the evening
from six to seven, as businesses were closed.[41]

It is striking, too, that the Declaration of Independence acquired
its modern sanctity in the 1820s, when Federalist insistence that Congress as a whole had fashioned the document faded, and Jefferson was
enshrined as the author, and not mere draftsman, of America's birth
certificate. The aura of the Revolution brightened and enlarged. Henry
Laurens Pinckney, whose name evoked two of the most noted Revolutionary families of the South, stated in 1818: "The heart-melting period
is fast approaching, when the surviving patriots of the revolution will
meet the eye & hear the voice of their departed friends. . . . Oh! Who
could behold their venerable forms, and not feel his spirit kindle at the
sight?" Books circulated that celebrated the national conception. In
1819, Joseph Sanderson announced a project which became the nine-
volume *Biography of the Signers of the Declaration of Independence*, published
between 1823 and 1827. In 1822 Hezekiah Niles came out with *Principles
and Acts of the Revolution in America*. In the 1830s the new Whig party,
though reconstituted from Federalist fabric, would claim Jefferson as
their own, no longer a partisan but the symbol of a pure and noble era.[42]

In the 1820s Americans nostalgic for the Revolution were centering
their attention on replicating the spirit of the founding generation, conceiving, creating, building, associating, and sustaining—in that order.
In sacred moments, private ambition yielded to thoughts of national
prosperity, the common destiny soothing sectional grievances. As the
old Revolutionaries died off and the romance with their deeds deepened, the collective memory took on new life.[43] Employing a strategy
not unlike Webster's in the eulogy, a poem about the jubilee celebration
of the Fourth of July compared the passing of the Revolutionary generation to a "glorious light" moving into the distance:

> Here, mingling, see a various group—
> Gray veterans lift their kindling eyes—

> And sanguine youth, a shouting troop,
> Hail the pure light of freedom's skies.
>
> . . .
>
> And a still anthem seems to swell
> Up in the pure and fragrant air,
> Bidding that glorious light farewell,
> So calm, beneficent, and fair.

The old men in this fading pageant "talked of the former years, / With voices broken with their tears." The funereal pause in an inspired march to the future expressed Americans' heightened sense of sympathy as a component of their patriotism.[44]

Congress evidenced this trend by enacting legislation to award pensions to aged militiamen, recording their testimonies and revisiting the stories of their youthful trials in joining the fight for independence. The courage of Nathan Hale, an obscure detail of the war rarely mentioned in the last decades of the eighteenth century, was newly celebrated from the 1820s on. The martyred captain, Washington's articulate spy summarily executed in the fall of 1776, was lauded by his sergeant, Stephen Hempstead, in a newspaper article in the *Missouri Republican* in 1827 that was reprinted in the *Long Island Star* and the Hartford *Courant* that same year. In the 1830s, Hale's contemporaries made appeals for recognition of the captain's sacrifice. Septuagenarian Yale alumnus and Revolutionary War surgeon Eneas Munson, Jr., wrote a letter, printed in the new *American Historical Magazine and Literary Review*, that asked: "Cannot you rouse the dormant energies of an ungrateful republic, in the case of Capt. Hale, to mark the spot where so much virtue and patriotism moulder with his native dust?" Subsequent memoirs would extend the tale of the Revolutionary paragon until Hale became in the late nineteenth and early twentieth centuries the stuff of biography and patriotic ballads.[45]

America of the 1820s adopted an assertive, forward-looking pose, illustrated by the language used in a poem published in the *New-York Advertiser* not long before the nation elected rugged individualist Andrew Jackson from the western frontier to its highest office:

> Theirs is a pure republic, wild yet strong,
> A "fierce democracie," where all are true
> To what themselves have voted—right or wrong—
>
> · · ·
>
> They love their land, because it is their own,
> And scorn to give aught other reason why.[46]

The "fierce democracie," as pure in its energies as it had claimed to be as an "infant empire" a half century earlier, was feeling "scorn" for those who could not or chose not to understand it.

## NATURE'S NATION

The opening description of the central New York landscape in James Fenimore Cooper's 1823 novel, *The Pioneers*, nostalgically seeks to recapture a familiar sentiment. It is shortly after the Revolution, at the new settlement of Otsego. Peaceful communities glisten in the daylight, a friendly addition to nature's harmony; the romantic sublime and serenely picturesque happily combine:

> It is among these hills that the Delaware takes its rise; and flowing from the limpid lakes and thousand springs of this region, the numerous sources of the Susquehanna meander through the valleys, until, uniting their streams, they form one of the proudest rivers of the United States. . . . The vales are narrow, rich and cultivated; with a stream uniformly winding through each. Beautiful and thriving villages are found interspersed along the margins of the small lakes . . . [47]

The unblemished landscape predominates in thought, while civilization stops short of marring God's creation.

Cooper finishes his characterization by suggesting the course of improvement: "Roads diverge in every direction, from the even and graceful bottoms of the valleys, to the most rugged and intricate passes of the hills. Academies, and minor edifices of learning, meet the eye of the stranger, at every few miles, as he winds his way through this uneven territory." Exhilaration is the overall sensation in this buoyant presentation of all that is possible for a "moral and reflecting people" under that government "which flows from unfettered liberty of conscience," where "every man feels a direct interest in the prosperity of a commonwealth." As a recent analyst of Cooper's writing has argued, the description of the unpeopled land is both intentionally general and ideologically distinct. The author's words are consistent with the visions of Franklin, Crèvecoeur, and Jefferson, painting a picture of progressive agrarian comfort, invariably glorifying America.[48]

Cooper's visual strategies distinguish him from those who preceded him in describing the land. Moral and dramatic elements in his narratives are routinely enhanced by topographical symbols. He finds landmarks in nature and embellishes actual scenes he knows in the Hudson Valley and that part of upper New York traditionally inhabited by the Six Nations of the Iroquois. Setting actions from prospects more than the lower altitudes, he has the eye of the landscape painter, offering variety and contrast. At the same time, his gaze is a wide-angle lens that sweeps across the land before pinpointing the site where some action will take place or something new will become significant: the "little plain," "a solitary silent spring," "the margin of a lake," "an open space, that surrounded a low green hillock," rock ledges, waterfalls, a precipice, a beaver pond, "undulating" country, "wide fields of frozen snow," "dark foliage of the hemlock," shadows cast from "high and broken summits" onto "ground ragged with rocks, and intersected with ravines." The land is always significant, not just described but *in motion*, so that the author's wilderness hero must be, in one critic's words, "scrupulous in managing his spacial coordinates."[49]

Cooper furthered in America a romantic conception of the land that coincided with what English romantic poets Samuel Taylor Coleridge and William Wordsworth were writing about: a fresh, pulsating feeling arising from rejection of eighteenth-century scientific skepticism, a religiosity founded in the power of nature that added soulfully to individual freedom. Romanticism in the nineteenth century brought the unfettered heart back to the study of nature and restored humanity to a place of mystery and uncertainty. Narrative became more forceful, offering bright new characterizations of the sensory world. The search for the Homeric epic of America's creation (the true inheritance of classical culture), as Philip Freneau, Joel Barlow, and others had ambitiously attempted, gave way to a literature of individualism.[50]

Born the year Washington assumed the presidency, Cooper, like Brackenridge before him, honored the American spirit as he criticized the morals of American society. He was witness to self-interested people engaging in profit taking, manipulation, and deceptive politics, a republic often insensitive to its slow subversion of Revolutionary purposes. For this reason, Cooper introduced in *The Pioneers* his wilderness hero Leatherstocking, or Nathaniel (Natty) Bumppo, a loose imitation of Daniel Boone. Leatherstocking reappears in *The Last of the Mohicans* (1826) and *The Prairie* (1827), in which the hero dies; and again in *The Pathfinder* (1840) and *The Deerslayer* (1841) which resurrect him. Natty possesses the Revolutionary virtues: he is compassionate as he invites compassion, temperate yet resolute, a magnanimous friend, a free spirit—a modest republican.

In *The Pioneers* he is older and perhaps less idealistic than he becomes in the subsequent novels, but he demonstrates the character of the natural frontiersman, tolerant and honor-bound. The untutored humanist is most proficient at conducting life beyond the walls of civilized settlement. In the story, Natty's quest for liberty and privacy runs up against the law—the cold, assertive, selfish, and unfeeling posture of state authority. Society treads on the self-sufficient, warmhearted independent whom it sees as a subversive. Natty reigns in the forest, but he feels truly alone under the public eye. His simple integrity is only protected when he is removed from modern and sophisticated rules and regulations. Organized religion interferes with his hunting (just as he observes it slowly destroying the purity of the Indians). Defiant to the end, Leatherstocking and his Indian counterparts seem best suited for that life which is timeless, the pastoral idyll where mind and spirit thrive amid a natural serenity. This is not so much to deny reality as to shun the kind of material progress which works to subvert human vitality.[51]

The real Daniel Boone, meanwhile, survived until 1820. A variety of tales, poetry, and painting continued to celebrate the aging pathfinder. In an 1823 account a relative of Colonel Boone declared that the wilderness seeker, feeling Kentucky too cluttered with settlers, had withdrawn to frontier Missouri "to live as remote as possible from every white inhabitant, except those of his own family." Artist Thomas Cole produced a painting in 1826 showing Boone content in his isolation, scowling at the civilized world. Alternately portrayed as innocent and uncorrupt or assertively misanthropic, Boone in his last years was romantically construed to be living the life of a benign patriarch of the forest, ignorant of political strife.[52]

The way conventionality was criticized in Cooper's Leatherstocking novels, along with the vigor and productivity the natural landscape evoked, showed that American history, both for romantic export and for patriotic reminiscence, could be used differently than before. Visions of the American present became fresh fodder for thinking about human nature. As Webster contended in his eulogy of Adams and Jefferson, nature could not be divorced from America's personality, even as material progress was transforming the wilderness. According to this tradition, civilization's distortions—ignoring or forgetting primitive ideals—led to banality and mediocrity as well as corrupt morals. But in the 1820s, the untamed wilderness of America was more: whether desolate or uplifting it operated on a grand scale and was somehow part of the national promise. American nature varied from fruitful (both in its virgin state and as cultivated) to the stormy sublime, and for the first time afforded diversion, recreation, for significant numbers of civilized people.[53]

"Romantic piety," as historian Perry Miller put it, "did not always require institutions." Without any government direction, a quasi-religious veneration of the pristine surroundings was permanently shaping Americans' refashioning of the idea of America, mirroring the popular enthusiasm for evangelical action that was in the air at the same time. The remaining forests ensured that the nation would not lose its desirable simplicity. American romantics took to reconciling Cooper's portrait of a nature gradually receiving civilization with earlier expressions of American sublimity. This was how Americans would find the means to preserve their integrity as a people of the land. Civilization could herald prosperity just so long as it did not give up its direct appreciation for the incomparable mountains, lakes, and forests that had inspired the people's association of the precious land with love of liberty. In the American mind, open space and yielding earth both actuated human decency and promoted cultural independence. Again, in Miller's words, "it is Nature's nation, possessing a heart that watches and receives."[54]

Throughout the period 1750–1828, Americans demonstrated how scrupulous and insistent they could be in designing the way they would fit nature and its cultivation into their expanding (and unfailingly romantic) idea of America. As early as Robert Beverley's 1705 *History and Present State of Virginia*, the Indians at home in America's blissful, blessed garden landscape were praised for their generosity and faithfulness, qualities which grew from their liberated existence and their attachment to pristine nature. If, in improving the garden, the Virginians, according to this scenario, "corrupted" the happy innocents, then they in turn lapsed into indolence from time to time because of that irresistible power exerted by the natural wilderness over the good intentions of the civilizing conscience.[55] This yin and yang of nature and civilization continually occupied eighteenth- and nineteenth-century minds. Primitivism was idealized, poeticized, but ultimately seen to be counterproductive to "improvement." Americans' vigorous attachment to their variegated landscape elevated the role of the "retreat" without proposing that it remain "wild." Only human dominion over nature would lead to perfection. Typical of the post–War of 1812 sentiment in this regard was Henry Laurens Pinckney's 1818 Fourth of July address in Charleston: "Streams, long inaccessible to commerce, now pour their treasures at [America's] feet, and emigration has added to our own, the skill and industry of every other clime. Refinement inhabits where barbarism reigned." America was a "lavish land" where a thankful people were preparing to "rival, if not surpass all others."[56]

The sublime could be best admired when seen as an inspirational encounter, not a permanent address; when allied to happy, prospering villages; when intellectualized and attempted on the canvas or the printed page. The beautiful was meant to be tended, shaped, and developed—copying the Creator's art in order to enrich the human spirit. As much as it was an actual or imaginable place, the pastoral garden was a tool in the minds of nationalists who were calling for a better world modeled on America. The pastoral garden provided health to the national culture. No one was more at home in the garden than the Indian hunter-warrior, who was in the process of being dispossessed of his ancestral territory. That "noble savage" was now used in a literary sense, as much as the white pioneer, to symbolize the survival of Eden. As yet the inherent contradiction was not recognized.

Thomas Jefferson had known discord over a long public career and concluded that, despite it all, America's extent represented America's greatest hope. He wrote in retirement to a former French diplomat that, contrary to the principle of Montesquieu, who could not imagine republican government succeeding except in a small territory, "the larger the extent of the country, the more firm its republican structure, if founded, not on conquest, but in principles of compact and equality." The nostalgic Jefferson still thought the character of his countrymen plain enough to replicate virtuous small-scale republican government as expansion west proceeded. As an old man he stood atop Monticello and took in essentially the same vista he had been reared on in the middle of the previous century. When a British army officer visited him and the two gazed into the distance together, Jefferson pointed to a cone-shaped mountain some forty miles away. It had a cleft that changed shape at different hours of the day from season to season. Jefferson found the illusion mesmerizing, likening it to the phenomenon of "looming" that sailors sometimes reported in their sightings on the ocean. He went on to tell the British lieutenant that the freedom and happiness of Americans arose from "local circumstances." He described an ingenious people with leisure time to cultivate their minds after cultivation of the land was complete. Jefferson enjoyed his illusions and allowed a distilled image of rustic citizens reading mathematics "and other useful works" define for him the real fruit of American independence.[57]

Another strain in American thinking after the War of 1812 was the need to proclaim the successful blending of agriculture and commerce, and state with confidence that fears of Americans' corruption amid industrial society were past. In his 1817 Fourth of July oration at Brown University, young Benjamin Franklin Allen, a senior, restated the Franklin-Crèvecoeur-Jefferson pastoral romance, but added that it was the healthy balance between agriculture and commerce that now fore-told a world at peace. America, said Allen, had secured itself from the "avarice" that threatened republics "by maintaining a just medium be-tween the commercial and agricultural interests." Until this moment in history, he declared, the love of wealth and material comfort had con-sumed "every noble sentiment of the human heart." But with "that hardy independence, which is the offspring of the agricultural spirit, and that liberality of sentiment, and refinement of manners, which is the offspring of commerce," America had grown "respectable."[58]

This combination of heart, hardiness, and worldly knowledge her-alded a shift in the language of national self-definition. Secure in its institutions, America could now safely expand its trade and other con-tacts with foreign countries, engaging, Allen said, in such enterprise as "enlarges the understanding, ameliorates the heart." The result of America's outward push would be to eradicate those "national preju-dices and national antipathies, which, from age to age, have deluged the world in blood." In other words, the maturing republic, uniform in sentiment and cleansed of weakness and vulnerability to corruption by exposure to effete European ideas and practices, wore a kind of protec-tion. Going abroad in search of enlightened communion would finally vindicate the cause of the national heart.[59]

All this was possible because the rhetoric that argued a moral su-periority over Europe was again sharpening in America. Henry Laurens Pinckney's 1818 oration was vindictive in tone as it addressed an old subject: "Where now is the impious hand which pointed to the sub-mission and dissolution of our empire?" The threatening aspect of foreign designs on America had been "chastened into reverence," and "domestic disaffection"—New England's resistance to the late war—had "subsided into peace." He restated: "The progress of our country has overthrown the theories, and ridiculed the ignorance of Europe." Americans could now "look with pity upon the proudest portion of the globe."[60] The Cincinnati newspaper carrier's ritual New Year's address to readers in 1820 versified this same feeling. Notwithstanding the dev-astating Panic of 1819, America remained a land of growth, Europe a place of derangement, brutal militancy, and thorough despair:

Europe's mad powers with all their art essayed
To beat the reeking sword to share and spade,
And gather harvests where their soldiers bled:—
'Twas hammering helmets into beef and bread,
A task beyond their wits; and now starvation
Drives out their hungry swarms from every nation.
   Not thus Ohio:—Surfeit is our bane,
Fields over rich, and barns o'erfilled with grain;
We curse the times, rag banks, and dearth of money,
Yet drown and suffocate in milk and honey.[61]

Despite their concerns over a lack of hard currency, Ohioans' romance with their rivers and streams, groves and woodlands, was potent. Natural abundance could not but alleviate any problems created by "rag banks." The people boasted of their prospering communities as they wrote odes to nature.

Transcendent Niagara Falls increased in stature as America's symbol of pride in its natural wonders, while the Erie Canal, completed in 1825, linked Ohio farmlands to the Atlantic and made Niagara more accessible to travelers. The impressive canal counterposed against ungoverned nature a humanly engineered marvel that demonstrated American ingenuity and a positive commercial spirit. There was something seductive about this tableau, at once proving the natural landscape primordial and supreme, chaotic and pure, and western New York State amenable to progress. Niagara expressed America's fascination with danger, a willingness to accept challenges of all kinds, to test wills and energies. The climactic fight in Cooper's first successful novel, *The Spy* (1821), takes place at Niagara, where the patriotic hero, having survived the action of the Revolution, dies during the War of 1812 and is buried. In 1825 Daniel Webster journeyed directly from his commemoration address on the fiftieth anniversary of the Battle of Bunker Hill to the "grand spectacle" at Niagara, writing, like Meriwether Lewis at Montana's Great Falls, a long, descriptive letter in which he attested to the "deep feeling" of the scene: "Water, vapor, foam, & the atmosphere, are all mixed up together in sublime confusion." It was in the 1820s that European visitors as well were able to come to Niagara, to take stairways, paths, and footbridges and stare out from a stone tower at the American panorama. It was presumed that they would follow the reasoning of Americans and recognize that this was a uniquely blessed land set apart from "ordinary" beauty.[62]

Like Boone's Kentucky in the 1780s and 1790s, Ohio after statehood in 1803 mixed political democracy, a promising economy, and consciousness of "improving" nature. Indeed, Ohio proved to be an even greater success story. Virginia Republicans purchased land in the northwest frontier and gradually contested the power of those New England Federalists who comprised the original Ohio Company. These newcomers were as ambitious as their elite predecessors in finding a steady market for their surplus production of meat, flour, grain, furs, hides, and whiskey. After the War of 1812, manufacturing expanded, turnpikes were constructed, and stagecoach and flatboat service announced the end of frontier living. Busy roads, like spokes of a wheel, led to the centrally situated capital of Columbus. Twenty state-chartered banks were established between 1815 and 1819. That year, newly elected Governor Ethan Allen Brown proclaimed: "Roads and canals are the veins and arteries to the body politic." By 1825 Ohio was the fourth most populous state in the union, primed by the Erie Canal to link its interior sections with the eastern seaboard through a series of its own state-commissioned canals. Attracting New York and English investment, the Ohio canal publicists put thousands of Irish immigrants to work for cash wages, alongside local farmers. On July 4, 1827, the Ohio and Erie Canal opened, dramatically linking the East to the Old Northwest. As the canal era blossomed, Ohioans felt they were winning a race and, if initially localist in their anxious ambition, became sanguine about the democratic implications of public transportation projects, confident that every place within the state could potentially be an integral participant in the nation's growth. Ohio could boast of having achieved "civilization" in a few short decades, living up to the imagined future that Crèvecoeur, Jefferson, and others had projected for the nation's outlying regions, progress assured by the enterprising "genius" of the people.[63]

Illinois, which gained statehood in 1818, had a significant number of Kentuckians and Tennesseans, as well as others from the original thirteen states. At the age of twenty-one, robust Kentucky-born Abraham Lincoln came here in 1830 to seek his livelihood. The prairie's rugged early settlers, sociable folk, improvers of land, were destined to repeat the pattern of promotion, supplying material for the construction of a Western image steeped in American virtues: individual generosity and hearty enterprise within a vital political democracy. James Hall, a veteran of the Niagara campaign during the War of 1812, was an early literary voice for the state. He arrived in Illinois in 1820, trained as a lawyer, and established the *Illinois Gazette*. Hall's *Letters from the West*, a travelogue written in the same vein as Crèvecoeur's work, was first published in 1828, while its author was serving as the state's treasurer.

Keenly aware of the tradition in which he was writing, Hall praised the late Daniel Boone as a man of "dauntless courage and eccentric habits," recognized as the progenitor of all American pioneers. Boone's life presented "a glowing picture of the sufferings of those who subdued the western forests." Hall maintained that there were few traces of British origins left in the Americans of his day. English writers and speculators who journeyed in the new West erred because they misunderstood American energy, and did little to allay the animosity still harbored by this mildly unforgiving veteran of the last war: "If the English have found bad treatment at our taverns, it has been produced by their own offensive manners. There is no country in the world in which a well bred traveller will experience more courteous civility, or enjoy more wholesome or neater entertainment, than in ours." Hall's nationalism was undisguised.[64]

Throughout his travels, Hall observed an "American spirit," "the same American character," despite the obvious sectional distinctions. "The soul of the hero" had been evidenced in the War of 1812, where there were no Northerners or Southerners, only patriots. Americans, he insisted, owned the "most strongly marked" national character in the world. His Letter XV, titled "National Character," made certain distinctions: the New England Yankee exhibited a "sense of duty" that went along with a sometimes shrewd, even tricky, but hardy and independent manner; and the Virginian was *profusely hospitable*," exhibiting a lively generosity made possible by the leisure time his exploitation of unpaid labor afforded. Still, said the agreeable Illinoisan, "the people in both [sections] are high minded, spirited lovers of liberty, tenacious of their honour, and quick in their resentments; they equally loathe every thing in the shape of oppression, encroachment, or dictation. . . . They both have those generous feelings, which must always form a part of that character of a free, brave, and enlightened people." Able to overlook the deleterious effect of "quick . . . resentments," he concluded that all Americans shared "the same daring soul and inventive genius; and that aptitude or capacity to take advantage of every change, and subsist and flourish in every soil and situation."[65]

Hall called the West "the land of promise," just as, for decades, many on both sides of the Atlantic had been calling America as a whole. The West had become the engine of future American enterprise. People there were being tested every day: "They looked back with a kind of shuddering triumph at what they had accomplished; they looked forward with a trembling hope at what was to come. I thought I could see in their faces regret, hope, fear, resignation—but they spoke cheerfully, and expressed no dissatisfaction." Like Crèvecoeur's country folk of the Revolutionary era, these western Americans, once settled, were charitable to destitute foreigners arrived at their doors; "for an American is never seen to turn a houseless wanderer from his door, or to refuse a morsel to the hungry." One cannot escape the spirit of the Man of Feeling in such words, or fail to observe that eighteenth-century sensibility persisted in this time of mass enterprise. People in the expanding union were, if Hall was correct, open in their embrace of a spirited diversity. Emigrants from the East, collecting at Pittsburgh for their trip down the Ohio River, were a "motley" cross section, yet a gloriously humble model, of the growing nation: "Some arrive with furniture, farming utensils, and servants, and push forward, confident in their ability to overcome every obstacle; some come burthened with large families, and but little worldly gear; and others, happy at such a time in their 'single blessedness,' come alone, errant knights, leaving all their cares behind them." Hall's hodgepodge, "all sorts of folks crowding to the west," feared and dreamt alike.[66]

This same pioneering spirit was assigned to the popular character in the congressional session of 1820–21, as Senator Thomas Hart Benton of Missouri spoke on the proposed settlement of Oregon Territory. Eager to compete with Great Britain for the Asiatic trade, he fully intended that individual American trailblazers would be "laying the foundation of a future empire." American occupation of the Pacific Northwest "could not fail to produce great and wonderful benefits. Science, liberal principles in government, and the true religion, might cast their lights across the intervening sea." The language was reminiscent of the commercial-religious enthusiasm of the 1780s and 1790s, when the maiden voyage to Canton of the American vessel *Empress of China* roused poetic celebrants. Benton was envisioning that "the valley of the Columbia might become the granary of China and Japan, and an outlet to their imprisoned and exuberant population." Thus the inhabitants of the "most despotic" and "freest" governments would become neighbors and friends, just as a more confident America, with nothing left to fear from Great Britain, was sounding out the possibility of forgiving the failed parent for past depredations.[67]

The inspired senator acknowledged that his suggestion, founded in the spirit of philanthropy, was "nothing but the fruit of the seed planted in my mind by the philosophic hand of Mr. Jefferson." With corresponding drama, Harvard professor Edward Everett, about to embark on a long and distinguished political career, stated in 1824 that America's move west was symbolic of universal progress, "the human family, led out by Providence to possess its broad patrimony." How could there be a mere sectional interest in "the delight of beholding civilized nations rising up in the desert." It was a moment of great sentiment for the nationalist: "Whithersoever the sons of the thirteen states shall wander . . . they will send back their hearts to the rocky shores, the battlefields, the infant settlements of the Atlantic coast. These are placed beyond the reach of vicissitude. They have already become matter of history, of poetry, of eloquence." In this time of movement, the living seeds of a prosperous present and a richly imaginable future were sufficient to build upon whatever attachment one bore to the hallowed ground of his or her earlier ancestry. The romantic temperament cherished the past—the American essence—and invested equally deep emotion in the anticipated fruit of new settlement.[68]

Again it is the oratory of Daniel Webster, principal motivator of the rising nation, that symbolizes the identification of America's land and imperial destiny with its liberty and happiness. Speaking in Boston in 1825, he saw fit to dispute the saying that "prosperity sometimes hardens the heart." He understood the Americans of his day to be uniquely generous because of the favorable conditions in which their liberty had grown: "We may all rejoice in the general prosperity, in the peace and security which we enjoy, and in the brilliant success which has thus far attended our republican institutions. These are the circumstances which may well excite in us a noble pride." Americans' aggressiveness, moreover, was channeled toward the betterment of their fellow creatures, who responded enthusiastically to the American example. Others were professing the desire to belong, in spirit if not territorially, to the union of sentiment: "In whatever part of the globe men are found contending for political liberty, they look to the United States with a feeling of brotherhood, and put forth a claim of kindred."[69]

The independent peoples of South America most immediately and most demonstrably gave evidence of Webster's assertion. Europe's hold on the globe was declining as America's rose: "When these states," he said of the Southern Hemisphere, "thus newly disenthralled and emancipated, assume the tone and bear the port of independence, what language and what ideas do we find associated with their newly acquired liberty? They speak, Sir, of constitutions, of declarations of rights, of the liberty of the press, of a congress, and of representative government. Where, Sir," he posed rhetorically, "did they learn these?" Webster was infused with unabashed pride, as he answered his own question: "with power that seems to wake the dead, on the plains of Mexico, and along the sides of the Andes," it was "the Spirit of Continental Independence, the Genius of American Liberty," once confined to the hills of New England, that had already altered the history of the world. America was the active element in a global regeneration: "In the wonderful spirit of improvement and enterprise which animates the country," in the opening of roads and navigation of rivers, "a new era has arisen. . . . We tread on a broader theatre." Webster visualized the resolve of a national community, the perseverance of a people who seemed quite assured that in very little time their combined strength of mind would add convincing power to their already tenacious judgment.[70]

President James Monroe's last annual message to Congress echoed these confident assertions that America's prosperity was already real and secure and would acquire martial features: "It is manifest," he stated in 1824, "that the situation of the United States is in the highest degree prosperous and happy. There is no object which as a people we can desire which we do not possess or which is not within our reach." Like Webster, Monroe broadcast an imperial welcome: American interests extended "to every part of the inhabited globe and to every sea which our citizens are carried by their industry and enterprise, to which they are invited by the wants of others, and have a right to go." To protect those interests he would render the Atlantic coastline "impregnable." By "augmenting our navy," and by performing necessary "duties" to ensure the happiness of, in particular, the Latin American republics, the United States would develop a military presence of unprecedented range and activity. In pursuing hemispheric leadership, America was to rely on both national strength and "a generous spirit." This was the formula of the sentimental democracy to come, happily and deliberately uniting its philanthropic urges with an aggressive foreign policy.[71]

The destiny of America was manifest well before the phrase was coined in 1845. It was manifest in Monroe's address, in the epic poetry of Joel Barlow, and in the resounding voice of Daniel Webster. To a significant bloc of Americans, there seemed something "natural" and inevitable as well as righteous in their confident pursuit of empire. First the millennium had been fixed in modern geography; then British liberty, once admirable, had yielded to a greater and more enthusiastic manifestation of itself. The secular end of the divine spirit was entrenched in the land mass which could in a very short time bridge Europe and Asia. America was poised to fulfill what had been the dream of explorers and mercantilists for centuries.

# CHAPTER NINE

SENTIMENT AND SYMPATHY:
TRANSITIONS

THERE IS ONE underlying theme in this book that speaks most plainly to the idea of an American pursuit of happiness: Without a language of feeling, the American Revolution would have existed only in the minds of the most narrowly philosophical. Sensibility was a critical device in the promotion of patriotic sentiment and in the idealized conception of republican politics. Rough-minded men, or Stoics untempered by any softer virtue, were deemed ill equipped to participate fully in republican discourse.[1] Contemplative statesmen needed the aid of the sympathetic imagination and an appreciation for human affection to advance the republic beyond its mere mechanical structure. The "heart" of the United Colonies, which had proved itself in winning the Revolution against an army judged to be superior,[2] was amplified in the years following 1783 to provide a rhetoric (admittedly a rhetoric that was only partially successful) whereby contesting views and a resurfacing of self-interest and opportunism could be diffused as the nation's moral purpose enlarged.

The contribution of masculine sensibility to the national character has been distinctly drawn in the foregoing chapters, as a people no longer British projected an empire of generous humanity across a fruitful land. The present chapter will deepen those images while assessing the qualitative changes that occurred from the Revolution to the election of Andrew Jackson, demonstrating how sentiment and power, long seen as mutually exclusive categories of thought and action, merged into the alluring, if paradoxical, ideology of benevolent aggressiveness essential to sentimental democracy.

Let us start, then, by recovering the Man of Feeling as an American patriot. The entire vocabulary of sensibility was engaged in Royall Tyler's successful comedy of manners, *The Contrast*, written in 1787 and performed in New York, Philadelphia, and elsewhere. Near the outset of the play, the character Maria, a young woman whose purity of heart was augmented by reading the works of Samuel Richardson and Laurence Sterne, pronounces the "facts" of her female faculties:

> Who is it that considers the helpless situation of our sex, that does not see we each moment stand in need of a protector, and that a brave one too. Formed of the more delicate materials of nature, endowed only with the softer passions, incapable, from our ignorance of the world, to guard against the wiles of mankind, our security for happiness often depends upon their generosity and courage. . . . Ten thousand temptations allure us, ten thousand passions betray us; yet the smallest deviation from the path of rectitude is followed by the contempt and insult of man, and the more remorseless pity of woman.[3]

Her father, Van Rough, is interested in monetary gain to the exclusion of moral sentiment, and criticizes Maria for acquiring too high ideals in the pursuit of happiness through a love match. He blames her reading of sentimental literature, which he terms "trumpery." The shortsighted, fortune-hunting Van Rough desires instead that she marry a man named Dimple (who is clearly a libertine) simply because of his apparent wealth. The obedient daughter is set to honor her father's wishes over the dictates of her own heart.

Enter Colonel Henry Manly, the embodiment of masculine sentiment and American patriotism. Accepting that "female conversation softens our manners," and having discovered pleasure in Sternean empathy, he is, to his sprightly sister Charlotte, grave, sober, and solid, a contrast to her own acknowledged gaiety, airiness, and coquetry. His generous sensibility has been made acute through service in the Revolutionary War; even his sword is a gift of the Marquis de Lafayette, and a symbol of enlightened brotherhood. Manly is animated by nostalgic regard for his wartime .comrades, and he is sustained by an uncomplicated love of political liberty. He had come to "solicit the honourable Congress" for pension money for "my brave old soldiers." When told by Dimple of the "brilliant exhibitions of Europe" that render America an inferior society, he responds that "untravelled" Americans who love their native country are "laudable," that their simple patriotism "adds to their own happiness." Europe offered him no example of virtue or achievement superior to that of the United States.

Inattentive to his betrothed Maria, Dimple deceives Charlotte and her friend Letitia with seductive conversation learned abroad. Meanwhile, Manly and Maria meet by chance. Despite the purity of their love, the two honest characters vow to sacrifice their happiness in order to uphold social propriety: Maria will comply with her father's wishes and Manly will desist from "invading the rights of another." The corruptions of Dimple, who openly disdains the mere "amusements" of America, finally come to light. The unsentimental Van Rough, seeing perhaps better material gain with the promising Manly, stands no longer in the path of destiny. Dimple, who has duped others for the last time, offers only one defense of his behavior: he has become "refined" through his tour of Europe. Before exiting in shame, he obliquely challenges Manly, who affirms that only two causes would bring him to withdraw his sword: defense of his country or defense of a lady's honor. But Dimple's death at his hands would be "a glory you do not merit." The audience and readers are meant, of course, to conclude that Dimple's vaunted Old World "polish" is tarnish, that American simplicity is virtue. Colonel Manly, the masculine ideal of his time, is modest in his bearing, a vision of American integrity. He does not maintain the aggressive air of a grizzled veteran but calmly wears the mark of poise, of sentiment under control. As a result, the man of worth earns the life of peace and contentment he desires.[4]

In 1792, the Philadelphia *General Advertiser* printed the epitaph of a soldier, slain in battle, whose qualities reiterated the importance of masculine sensibility:

Congenial with his *nature* were the *habits* of
   *military* life—
The virtues of GENEROSITY and VALOUR
   he possessed in an eminent degree—

Like the fictional Colonel Manly, Captain Patrick Phelon deserved "HAPPINESS ETERNAL" because he was both an affectionate friend and "a friend to ALL MANKIND," a Man of Feeling of who sacrificed his personal interest to promote the happiness of others. And as with Manly, nothing could "abate his patriotic ardour":

in the cause of *Liberty* and *America,*
His friendship was heightened into enthusiasm

He sacrificed personal fortune,

Found himself destitute of every thing,
Save his HONOUR and INTEGRITY;

As a republican who exhibited masculine sensibility,

To a *native openness of heart*
   he added
An *honest plainness* of SENTIMENT[5]

This was an important moment in American mythmaking. It was Crèvecoeur's "farmer of feelings" who first marveled that from a "promiscuous breed" of Europeans grew a people of sensibility. Americans possessed a "decency of their manners." They made the most of what nature had provided them. In Jefferson's America, too, "there is not a country on earth where there is greater tranquillity . . . where strangers are better received, more hospitably treated, and with a more sacred respect." And the European recipient of his letter, Maria Cosway, would find this to be true because she was "sensible."[6]

The foregoing chapters make it abundantly clear that the impetus for a feeling of unity or consensus among mutually jealous states came in response to the widely perceived and easily identifiable threat from England. Americans were defining themselves collectively as a people in the midst of a battle for survival. As they worked to fortify the idea of America in opposition to their political mother, they drew upon the culture of sensibility and ethic of sentiment for a language of commitment and contingent understanding. The patriotism they pronounced was a visceral response to the Revolutionary environment, more emotional than rational, and made to seem perfectly natural.

Inspired to publicize the American love of liberty and the resolve of a people who would not tremble before a shameful "Inhumanity," a fired-up John Adams wrote for a London newspaper before the end of the Revolutionary War: "Men are governed by Words. Their passions are inflamed by Words." Henry Laurens rhetorically sought to sway a South Carolina loyalist with no other "bribe" than "the Love of Mankind the Love of Liberty & the esteem of present & future generations." Americans had suffered "grievances," endured a "laudable strife" with "unexampled patience & forbearance." Implicitly, as they spoke out with honorable indignation against injustice and cruelty, they deserved a sympathetic response.[7]

Americans believed they were justified in advertising their character as a model for other peoples. As Paine declared in the second part of his *Rights of Man* (1792), the new nation had "made a stand, not for herself only, but for the world."[8] So had Joel Barlow identified the relationship between America's sentimental identity and the growing sense of mission when he spoke on July 4, 1787, in Hartford, Connecticut: The American mind was "dilated with the great idea," therefore bound to "realize a liberality of feeling which leads to a rectitude of conduct." In due course, American character would "excite emulation throughout the kingdoms of the earth, and meliorate the condition of the human race." After first constituting themselves as a nation, the People of Feeling bore the moral responsibility to legislate for humanity, to contribute to "the general happiness of mankind."[9]

In the Whig tradition of political thought, civic humanism was promoted by manners. The Whig conversational ideal, supporting its political tastes, expressed an internal discipline leading to enlightened communion. With the establishment of the American republic, the moral ideology that Richardson had introduced in his sentimental fiction, and that Sterne, Mackenzie, and others had enlarged upon, was fully internalized. Americanized, sensibility conceived liberty as a moral condition; to love liberty was to live with humanitarian purposes. To be a true American was to apply one's sincere, self-monitored sympathy to the cause of civilization. Affective literature, from pointing out the fragility of nerves and human susceptibility, had found its way to stimulating an idealized national sense of mission.

In the unwritten lexicon of Revolutionary America, the republican, like Colonel Manly, was an individual of sensibility, the antirepublican aristocrat unpleasant and vulgar. The republican conducted himself or herself with expressions of an "elevated feeling," refinement of taste, principled modesty. The antirepublican was vain, had an appetite for coarse pleasure, and was ambitious for office. It was to this extent that the Scottish philosophes had left their imprint, men like Adam Smith, or the Earl of Shaftesbury, who saw no greater good than "social affections and human sympathy," who wanted men to be "all serene, soft, and harmonious." Shaftesbury urged his readers to cultivate "a mind subordinate to reason, a temper humanised and fitted to all natural affections, . . . a thorough candour, benignity and good nature." This was enlightened sentiment, and in America it was reflected in a leadership whose primal impulse was understood to be unpretentious and republican, who recognized in the educable masses every prospect for moral, intellectual, and (ultimately) businesslike progress.[10]

From the Revolutionary crisis onward, if not before, American public discourse was about establishing feeling. In his 1810 lectures on rhetoric at Harvard, John Quincy Adams, scion of the hard-nosed but passionate Federalist President, remarked that the American style consisted in "the art of mingling moral sentiment with oratorical splendor," an eloquence he suggested might be equal to that of the ancients.[11] When treated as unruly inferiors by the monarchy to which they had for so long committed themselves, the injured Revolutionaries had been moved to answer contempt with the crowning (or, rather, uncrowning) eloquence of the strong new language that defined their moral nationhood.

Sentiment stood alongside a concept of public virtue at the core of

American Revolutionary doctrine. George Washington declaimed in 1783: "The researches of the human mind after social happiness have been carried to a great extent. . . . [T]he free cultivation of letters, the unbounded extension of commerce, the progressive refinement of manners, the growing liberality of sentiment . . . have had a meliorating influence on mankind and encreased the blessings of society."[12] Sensibility—here the elevated exertions of the heart in creating sociable man—was integrally bound with political progress. The patriotic *Columbian Magazine* further expressed the same conviction: "The real happiness of society consists of actions whereby men benefit one another. . . . Virtue is the only means to produce social harmony." Morality had "its root in the heart, and its fruit in actions." Superimposed on these notions, as the inaugural edition of Brackenridge's *United States Magazine* projected in 1779, was an understanding that principles of government were "derived from feeling, whereas the form of a government was derived in accord with reason."[13] Sensibility was a sign of sincerity, and sincerity was integral to any discussion of the justness of political acts. To future patriots as well, America's genius would never be treated separate from the decent impulses of its founders, who are credited with having joined sentiment to reason.

The American character had to be forged, then reshaped over time, in a process of individual, regional, and national self-scrutiny. In doing so, early America's leaders examined the world around them with intense interest. They had to encounter real conditions, describe and mold them, in order to move forward in the realization of their unifying vision of progress. They had to account for and then overcome regional differences, especially because, according to eighteenth-century thinking, climate as well as human physiology conditioned the sensibility of a people. Physician David Ramsay recorded in his 1789 *History of the American Revolution* that those accustomed to the latitude of New England could contain their passions more readily "under the command of reason and interest" than Southerners, who were of "warm spirits," living "where a warmer sun excites a greater degree of irascibility." Jefferson described in similar terms the differing character of Northerners and Southerners, so predictable that "without the aid of a quadrant [one] may always know his latitude." And Crèvecoeur generalized the positive effects of the nurturing soil of America: "We are nothing but what we derive from the air we breathe, the climate we inhabit, the government we obey." Physical and moral attributes were connected. "Good conduct and temperance," the French American held, emerged from a "smiling country."[14]

Over a period of more than six years, the Revolution enhanced the operation of Americans' sensory receptors. It was not only their resolve as an independent people but the persistence of their sensible values that was being tested in war. Ramsay wrote that the stationing of British troops in Boston from 1768 had produced an "irritable state" (again, the physiological nature of sensibility) in which "every incident, however trifling, made a sensible impression."[15] Sensible citizens apprehended danger. Martial genius could be hailed and bloody victories celebrated, but regardless of the necessity of killing the enemy, the people of the various states should restrain excesses of passion and uphold the code of the Man of Feeling. Shortly after the decisive Battle of Yorktown, for example, "An American Soldier" wrote in the *Pennsylvania Gazette* of Lord Cornwallis's moral failings: A general ought to possess "that dignity of soul which exalts the conqueror above the insolence of the triumph, and elevates the vanquished above meanness and despondence." But Cornwallis had been "callous to the tender emotions of compassion, and steeled against the miseries of your fellow creatures."[16] In other words, he was all that undermined the progressive instinct of sensibility.

With a Revolutionary consciousness, Mercy Otis Warren directly employed the language of sentiment to further cultural cohesion. In a prefatory address to her 1805 multivolume *History*, she announced her intention to paint "sudden convulsions, crowded scenes, and rapid changes" attending the trials of a people yearning to recover the blessings of "peace, liberty, simplicity, and virtue." The first volume opens with a discussion of the human character and the nobility of purpose ever stimulating human activities. Truth, she stated, could only be revealed "when the feelings of the heart can be expressed" without the disguise of prejudice. Her task—America's task as she saw it—was to recover a convincing and affecting sense of the passion and fortitude which had spawned the Revolution.[17]

National self-definition and moral and political progress, or "improvement," are indistinguishable in Warren's text. Throughout, she records the morals and emotions of the dramatis personae of the Revolution, their "ardour," "avidity," "grateful feelings," "high-spirit," and "obligations of politeness," or "want of humanity." There are breathless phrases of heartrending prose: "With the sword uplifted, pushing their execrable purpose to exterminate the last vestige of freedom"; "the barbarous abuse of the hapless females who fell sacrifices to their wanton and riotous appetites"; "A dead and dreary silence reigns over an extent of five or six hundred miles of these once full peopled plains."[18] Sorrow and sympathy abound, and moral rectitude and righteous indignation serve as her protagonists.

Warren profoundly illustrates the shock to Americans' emotional system produced by feelings of betrayal and abandonment. Their suffering was the direct result of the tenacity of their moral principles. As of 1776,

> the severities of the British government towards the American colonies, had not yet taught them to express themselves in any other modes of language, but what indicated firm attachment to the mother country; nor had they erased the habitual ideas, even of tenderness, conveyed in their usual modes of expression; when they formed a design to visit England, it had always been announced, "I am going home." Home, the seat of happiness, the retreat of all the felicities of the human mind, is too intimately associated with the best feelings of the heart, to renounce without pain, whether applied to the natural or the political parent.[19]

In *The Man of Feeling*, when the aggrieved father of a hapless prostitute reencounters his daughter in the company of the compassionate Harley, his most moving words are these: "We can never, never recover the happiness we have lost! But time may teach us to remember our misfortunes with patience."[20] Events that shattered domestic peace, quiet pride, and self-possession were dramatically affecting. Holding on to the idea of "home," and the anxiety inherent in any attempt to reconstitute it in the wake of moral collapse, involved feelings of the greatest moral weight.

The transformation of sensibility into patriotism, into the romantic self-image that republicans had devised for their new nation, is no better exemplified than in the correspondence of Benjamin Rush over the course of twenty-five years. In 1775, the Philadelphia physician and Revolutionary wrote a sentimental letter to his wife, Julia Stockton Rush, that featured an extended invocation of Sterne. It began: "A man who interests his heart or head in every thing (Stern[e] says) may find entertainment or instruction in *any* thing. I have always been of our author's opinion, and have never walked across a field so barren as not to yield a small share of one or both of them." Rush next regaled his wife with the tale of his encounter with an aged farmer, reproducing their dialogue in the Sternean mode. The farmer, at first opaque and uncommunicative, was moved to reveal his private history only after Rush had demonstrated the power of his own sensibility. And then: "This was the question that touched the key of his heart." It was similar to the experience of Sterne's Yorick in *A Sentimental Journey*, who enters a farmhouse presided over by "an old grey-headed man." Sharing a meal and conveying his heartfelt emotions in a look of sensibility, Yorick sits beside the old farmer, listens to the singing and watches the dancing of children and grandchildren, as the farmer tells his visitor that such simple amusement "yielded a chearful and contented mind." In Rush's patriotic account, the song and dance are missing but heartfelt amusement is understood, as the farmer presents the physician with a picture of the superior virtues of the simple American agriculturalist, who prefers for his children's upbringing pastoral pleasure and home-grown virtue over the pillars of the academy.[21]

In a 1790 letter to then Congressman James Madison, Rush, thinking about republican education, urged that funds earmarked by the Secretary of War for universal military training be given over to schools instead. In his postscript, the physician-educator commented idealistically that "teaching our young people industry and morality" would end war. The prospect of doing good for oppressed humanity always animated Rush; dispensing "disinterested benevolence" was, to his mind, Congress's duty, even if no one in that body would live to see his good works bear fruit. "Truths resemble trees," he told Madison, "some ripen in a short time, while others require half a century or more to bring them to perfection. . . . To plant a forest tree, says Dr. [Samuel] Johnson, is the most *disinterested* act of benevolence a man can perform, for it is impossible for him to live long enough afterwards to enjoy any benefit of his labor." Rush's sensibility allowed him to appreciate the poignancy of performing good deeds with no prospect of reward. He thought that the mark of a true republican statesman was to engage with the heart in conceiving social policy.[22]

Perfectibility of human behavior was a possibility only within a society where enlightened sensibility was steadfastly aimed at. In this same mode, Rush addressed the problem of putting an end to African-American slavery throughout the republic. Believing in the efficacy of acts of charity, he congratulated John Nicholson in 1793 on that gentleman's offer to contribute £100 to a black church, informing him that the "poor Africans" were "affectionate and grateful." The happy outcome of such deeds, the "increasing prosperity of blacks," led him to propose additional programs for their betterment. Selling farmland on moderate terms, he believed, would set the precedent of successfully colonizing self-supporting Africans within the limits of the United States rather than looking abroad. He wished that the number of men of sentiment and goodwill would ever increase, that the republic could be based on humane interactions and future-directed benevolence.[23]

Though in his correspondence with John Adams during the last decade of his life Rush berated his countrymen for their fall from grace, he could still write Jefferson in 1800: "I will not admit that we have been deceived in our early and long affection for republican forms of government." In this nostalgic letter, while mourning the persistence of "human follies," Rush claimed that he still retained his old faith in the curative properties of "republican temper . . . spirit and exertions." Love of country was rooted in a sentimental optimism. "No good effort is lost," he wrote the candidate assuredly. And when the following spring a victorious Jefferson issued his First Inaugural Address, Rush became downright buoyant. He saw sensibility in action on the streets of Philadelphia as men of differing politics "shook hands with each other immediately after reading" the "solemn and affecting" address.

In this letter Rush distinctly coupled the "virtues" of "national *stability* of opinion and conduct" with "national *integrity* and *humanity*." Here was the core value sustaining American humanism as Rush had perceived it over a quarter century. He reckoned the new President's sublime sentiment to be of equal value to "your fellow citizens, to the nations of Europe, to all the inhabitants of the globe, and to posterity to the latest generations." America's enlightened moral posture, its spirit of generosity, stood as a beacon, ready to rescue the human race from every form of oppression that existed.[24]

It should come as no surprise, then, that Rush was also among the most vocal of American men who believed that American women did not have to remain ignorant of politics but could be taught to argue the principles of republican government without inviting social disorder: "The opinions and conduct of men are often regulated by the women in the most arduous enterprises of life; and their approbation is frequently the principal reward of the hero's dangers, and the patriot's toils." As in an ancient Greek epic, America's "fair" inspired masculine rectitude. While Rush did not transcend his generation and propose full equality of public participation, he did prominently advocate women's education, "that they should think justly upon the great subjects of liberty and government." This was unusual enough. But his logic was simple: Men and women shared an interest in applying the lessons of sensibility to active citizenship.[25] Virginian William Wirt wrote to his wife in 1809–10 about the difficult balance he sought their daughter to achieve, in what amounts to Rush's prescription: "I want her to be something better than common, not a bold unblushing lady of fashion, nor a loquacious & disgusting pedant: but an happy union of female gentleness and delicacy, with masculine learning & genius— simple yet elegant—soft and timid, yet dignified & commanding."[26]

In embracing a nostalgic patriotism, lawyer Orsamus Cook Merrill of Vermont, in his 1804 Fourth of July address, evoked the Americanized culture of sensibility to the letter. "We travel on in the light of Independence," he crowed, "elated with a train of pleasing emotion and sublime conceptions, all corresponding and associating with the correct opinions, and ennobling principles, that glowed in the generous bosoms of those consistently daring sages, now pavilioned in the silence of the tomb, whose deeds it is our pride to applaud, whose virtues we revere, and should emulate, and for whose memory we drop the warm tears of sensibility." To this one orator, at least, the lighted path brought thorough emotion, sublime happiness, and a proper appreciation for the value of historical lessons.[27]

With current political dissension in mind, Merrill's harmonizing voice went on to proclaim that it was "a proud trait in the American character" that made possible a union of the states in 1776. That union represented "the sober and dignified triumph of sentiment and of peaceful action—and that *sentiment* and that *action* were *American*." In other words, sentiment and an unselfish regard for others prevented sectional grievances or party battles from heating up. Dialogue in a republican setting had to be contained within sensible terms; sentiment under control (here, tempered with humility) produced altruism and empathy, the pursuit of a common happiness. Merrill nevertheless recognized the difficulties associated with these expectations: "When men act from *feeling a grievance*, there is a boundary to their passions; when they act from disappointment, and a zeal for certain opinions, the influence of imagination gives unbounded license to their passions." Imagination was a part of compassion and benevolence (the source of justice), but an imagination that was excessive and unproductive did not belong in a harmony-seeking union. Only when this moral object was attained and imagination properly directed could America truly fulfill its destiny to bring the light of liberty to others around the world.[28]

In the end, it was a combination of factors that produced the culture of sentiment and sympathy: the eighteenth century's long and grievous experience with seemingly unavoidable tragedy (wars, shipwrecks, mortal diseases, complications attending childbirth), the European Enlightenment that encouraged both humanism and science, and a growing ideal of refinement that asked men and women to behave respectfully and generously. Eighteenth-century Americans helped one another cope with their common distresses. As the republic's first leaders embraced the philosophy of good government, and as rational Christianity dissuaded many from a resort to miraculous cures or mere resignation to God's will, a new emotional system took hold. Heartache was still inevitable, but there was hope for progress from the scientific mind, a mastery over nature.

To recognize a common humanity amid this striving for political and social happiness was to work to achieve peace and plenty. The popular Sterne synthesized such a productive spirit in *A Sentimental Journey*, and Mackenzie did similarly in *The Man of Feeling*. But for such writers, reveries and pleasures were easily shattered by the experience of a sentimental affliction, by a commitment to others' sufferings. Indeed, it often seemed that, in this morally demanding culture, empathy, more than anything else, let individuals know their lives had value. In the 1820s that culture of sympathy was still alive, evidenced in James Hall's *Letters from the West*, in which struggling pioneers persuade the author: "Those who are driven by misfortune from their homes, go like exiles from the land to which fond recollection attaches a thousand charms, to a wilderness which fancy clothes with a thousand terrors. Every sympathy is awakened, and every tender feeling thrilled with anguish." American intrepidity and aspiration evoked American sympathy.[29]

SENSIBILITY, HOWEVER, was not universally embraced. To the extent that the shift from the classical politics of virtue to the rise of capitalism—liberal modernity—involved a struggle between the subordination of self-interest and the celebration of self-willed acquisitiveness, the very public disagreement over policy which engaged Thomas Jefferson and Alexander Hamilton in the 1790s can be viewed on one level as a conflict over sensibility.

Within the theoretical framework of sensibility, philanthropy, though rooted in the desire to bring happiness, was impotent without the mind's action (reason) to counteract spontaneous (physiological) expressions of human weakness. In Sterne's illustrative *Tristram Shandy* and *A Sentimental Journey*, benevolence is based on the interaction of reason and emotion, aided by imagination and sexual feeling.[30] This was Jefferson's essentially balanced perspective, a dreamy optimism tempered by a reverence for science and the science of government; but it was far from Hamilton's principles. To the New Yorker, government benevolence reflected the prudent exercise of power, undiluted reason; sentiment could only weaken national resolve. Hamilton claimed that Jefferson and Madison had "a womanish attachment to France and a womanish resentment against Great Britain." They permitted a weak, overindulged passion to defeat sound judgment.[31] But to Jefferson, the self-styled man of sentiment, his own sensibility was an expression of masculine, not feminine, virtue, with a stoical strength lodged within. This form of sensibility was indistinguishable from the republican sensitivity to popular opinion which he felt ensured the dignity of republican government.

Hamilton was the voice of risk taking, of mobilizing capital. His was a modern, internationalist economic policy in an era when conservatives like Jefferson were trying to hold on to an idealized vision of quiet expansion for an autonomous American agriculture.[32] The nostalgic Jefferson feared any disturbance in the pattern and character of American settlement. The ambitious Hamilton sought to jolt the economy into a higher level of performance and aimed to demonstrate his leadership by changing the face of America. Jefferson's ideal was of a subtle and self-restrained government, preserving at once local and regional harmony and national frugality, simplicity, civility, and traditional humanism. Hamilton could not realize *his* ideal without aggressive action. The two were temperamental as well as political opposites.

Intensifying the discord between George Washington's two ideologically imposing cabinet officers, Jefferson's political and personal allies contented themselves by speculating on the ramifications of Hamilton's messy extramarital affair with Maria Reynolds, probing a possible link between his personal morals and the use of public funds. In 1791, according to Hamilton's apologia published as a pamphlet in 1797, Maria Reynolds had called on him at home, in "a seeming air of affliction." She explained that her cruel husband had left her, and she appealed to Hamilton's "humanity." He, then, out of "convenience" (in Hamilton's words), asked her address and later paid a visit to deliver a sum of money. Helping a woman in distress was very much an act of sensibility. However, in Hamilton's case, the protagonist-narrator transgresses, acknowledging the single "crime" of having given himself over to "the ardour of passion." To critical contemporaries responsive to the culture of sensibility, this was no less than an admission of a serious moral flaw; the ardent Hamilton was as deceitful and unrestrained as the character Montraville in Susanna Rowson's *Charlotte Temple* (first published in America in 1794). In this novel, the most popular work of American fiction before *Uncle Tom's Cabin*, an army officer of feigned sensibility seduces a virtuous, filial young woman and causes her ruin while unconvincingly protesting his reliance on conscience and rationalizing his selfish actions.[33]

Portraying himself as a man seeking only "honest fame" in the face of "odious insinuations" and "defamation," the defensive Hamilton, himself a man who rose to prominence as a soldier, proceeds in his apologia with a complex tale of extortion. James Reynolds, the "profligate" and "weak" husband, enters as a willful conspirator, the ostensibly aggrieved husband covetous of pecuniary favors which the vulnerable public figure Hamilton might extend. "As to Mrs. Reynolds," writes Hamilton, "if she was not an accomplice, as it is too probable she was, her situation would naturally subject her to the will of her husband." Unaccountably, though, even after becoming suspicious, Hamilton had continued to see Mrs. Reynolds. He remained in a state of "irresolution" owing to her persistent supplications and could not "disentangle" himself, as "all the appearances of violent attachment . . . were played off with a most imposing art." Feminine wiles were befuddling, and he sought to disengage gradually.[34]

Wishing to divert criticism by euphemistically calling the affair an "enigma," Hamilton at the same time claimed that the dictates of sensibility obscured truth and rendered communication deceptive. With open disdain for unmanly conduct, he shifted the emphasis in his pamphlet from the emotionally unstable, politically irrelevant wife to the cagey, vindictive husband, by far the greater object of his recrimination. It was James Reynolds whose pretended "delicacy," whose "sensibility" (Hamilton uses both words directly) hid a dark design to dissuade the Treasury Secretary from honorably ending the affair and maintaining the appropriate separation between public and private life. Reynolds's affectation of injury, then, his display of sensibility, was a rude trick to magnify Hamilton's need for atonement.[35]

To the unrepentant Hamilton, calling vulnerability a virtue was to encourage flattery and other forms of manipulative behavior. Sentiment obscured rationality and could lead to false steps. Sympathy could backfire. Importantly, it was masculine and not feminine sensibility that Hamilton most distrusted, and it was a lack of sensible regard, a lack of self-restraint, that the Jeffersonians conveniently fixed upon in their condemnation of the wily adulterer. If Hamilton resembled Rowson's Montraville, then Jefferson reflected both Charlotte Temple's caring and sympathetic father (epitomized in his declaration that "the truly brave soul is tremblingly alive to the feelings of humanity") and the very tone of the narrator of the novel. As a Man of Feeling, Jefferson can be seen as one who is protective of feminine virtue through sensitivity to the American people's experiences of subjection (to undemocratic tyranny) and seduction (by the charismatic appeal of a false kind of protection manufactured by Hamiltonians in boasting of superior honor and claiming to deserve to represent the people's interests).[36] The Hamilton-Jefferson conflict was emotion-filled and intensely personal. In the sense that Henry Adams later intended when he wrote of the political Jefferson as one whose elevated character centered on his "delicacy," who "felt a nervous horror" for "contentiousness," Hamilton sought to combat what he disparaged as a feminine weakness. Jefferson, on the other hand, saw his adversary as one who, in lacking sensibility, could also be said to lack respect for the people. This was unpatriotic.[37]

The earliest source of the Jefferson-Hamilton controversy, Jefferson's 1792 letter to President Washington, speaks volumes. As Secretary of State, Jefferson asked the mediating President to judge which of his two cabinet members had exhibited "purity" and "conscientious adherence" to his office. He countered Hamilton's charges against him as a deceiver by accusing Hamilton of being the real intriguer, "spelling my name & character at full length to the public [in newspaper columns] while he conceals his own." The unsigned attack was, to Jefferson, a villainous act. Hamilton had trampled on "the dignity, & even decency of government." He had charged Jefferson with crimes he should have charged himself with, who had wasted the government's revenue and had been the "prostitutor" of government to "the purposes of corruption." Jefferson self-righteously proclaimed that Hamilton's words were "the slanders of a man whose history, from the moment at which history can stoop to notice him, is a tissue of machinations against the liberty of the country which has not only received and given him bread [he was born and raised on Nevis, in the West Indies] but heaped it's honors on his head." This was criticism of Hamilton's character as much as his politics, his antirepublican lack of sensibility relating to a lack of patriotism.[38]

For Hamilton, though, Jefferson's grievance was a smoke screen meant to shield his own frailty, even cowardice. Honor was above all a matter of a man's soldierly courage and political vigor and candor and much less meaningfully a display of such softness and gentility as Jefferson personified, shaped by qualities with which sensible females might as easily identify. As a young wartime aide to General Washington and himself a gritty hero of Yorktown, Hamilton saw value in affairs of honor. This explains, at least in part, why he disparaged any weakness in political temper or actions. His morals fixed on the judgment of his peers, on maintaining the integrity of his political thought and not compromising his public principles. He was an ambitious, confrontational being who continually asserted that he was candid, consistent—a man of his word. Charming and confident, he promoted himself as someone around whom men of like-minded principles could rally; his robustness, his stamina would sustain Federalism. He held to an uncompromising code of masculine honor in 1804 when he gave his life in a duel with political foe Aaron Burr. In that fatal exchange, Hamilton followed the rules of engagement and maintained his gentleman's courage. Dueling was a means of answering a serious charge that, to Hamilton, was a legitimate feature of an honorable political world and accorded with the laws of nature. If Jefferson, who considered dueling barbaric, conformed to the culture of sensibility, Hamilton conformed to a masculine culture incompatible with the less demonstrably aggressive Virginian's.[39]

The questionable nature of sensibility was hinted at even earlier, if less aggressively, in John Adams's reaction to Thomas Paine's *Common Sense* when that momentous pamphlet first appeared in 1776. Abigail Adams wrote her husband that she was "charmed with the Sentiments" in Paine's work, wondering how any "honest Heart, one who wishes the welfare of their country and the happiness of posterity can hesitate a moment at adopting them." John Adams allowed that Paine's "Sentiments" were "generally approved," but that even with its concise style, *Common Sense* was replete with "Whims, some Sophisms, some artfull Addresses to superstitious Notions, some keen attempts upon the Passions." These things did not impress him, but rather caused him to grow suspect. Paine's sensibility, in other words, could be affectation, an untrustworthy pose, an emotion conjured for the purpose of seducing the public. To Adams, probing beneath the surface, Paine's writing was not original nor his blueprint for union well developed. When in later writings, as Adams knew Paine's methods better, the pamphleteer continued to appeal to the power of sentiment and sympathy, the New Englander became even more cold and cynical toward him.[40]

In Mason Weems's popular early biography of George Washington (1800), the hero took on some of the sentimental qualities the author imagined a Washington ought to possess and to which his readership would respond (as in any prescriptive eighteenth-century novel) with heightened moral sentiment. In Weems's account, after young George admits cutting down the cherry tree with his hatchet, the happy father delights in his son's heroic act of virtue. The author offers: "It was in this way by interesting both his *heart* and *head*, that Mr. Washington conducted George with great ease and pleasure along the happy paths of virtue."[41]

Parson Weems's unlikely explanation aside, in the age of sentiment George Washington was ice. His value to his country did not lie in his softness (of which he apparently possessed little), but in his sturdiness, his tenacity. He had imposed an iron discipline on his army, conveying vigilance, courage, command. His gravity inspired respect, but it did not allow for intimacy.[42] He represented the side of virtue that only one man could appropriate: he, and he alone, stood *above* sentiment. He was the object of adoration not because of a sentimental or sympathetic nature but because of the general belief that he possessed an ability to oversee the union with godlike judgment. For this unique designation Washington had to "sacrifice" his presumed desire for amiability (and the presumed desire to enjoy sentimental reveries) in order to serve the public, in order to remain an uncorruptible being above interest and beyond feeling and fallibility.

While he lived he was republican disinterestedness incarnate. After his death, Washington became a superhuman symbol. He was the boy who could not tell a lie, the President who had sacrificed all pleasure to undertake his ultimate national service. He was a calming voice to bring order amid times of frenzied fear, conspiracy theories, and the real threat of structural breakdown. Ordered liberty appeared most realizable under his solemn, watchful gaze, his stately presence. Washington did not crusade—that was for scrappy politicians armed with fresh vocabularies of liberty and happiness and with plans to extend and enhance the *sensations* of liberty and happiness. If Washington was to represent judgment, he could not indulge in the world of sensations by assuming the same quality of vulnerability as ordinary men. To use a military metaphor, he promoted the idea that America was a fortress of freedom; to use a physiological metaphor, he guarded the body of the nation from invasions and the nation's heart from mutinous assaults from within. He was in either case the personification of an ideal of solidarity, sobriety, harmony, unity, unanimity. He was the one President who faced no political opposition, who did not subscribe to any faction. Magnified into a polar star, the distant father, the emotionally protected benevolent ruler, though not a king, presided alone.

THE LANGUAGE OF sentiment, the culture of sensibility, may have served evolving patriotism, but it coexisted with a countervailing language and policy of power and growth, perhaps best associated in the period before the War of 1812 with Alexander Hamilton. Jefferson's traditional humanism would lead to self-assured, even sanctimonious statements about the extraordinary civility and nobility which directed the American conscience. Hamilton's proud, straightforward, and equally effective language—rooted in his profound concern with matters of honor while negating or redirecting the tumult of his private passions—was fostering a different kind of national self-assurance and determination, centered on a stable national revenue, exploitation of industrial potential—pride through demonstrable strength.[43] These two facets of cultural identity, born of separate interpretations of masculine honor and civility, were unyielding and irreconcilable in the first years of the federal republic, but they would eventually merge, because both expressed equally the resiliency of the American imagination. In an ironic twist, while Alexander Hamilton was noted for having challenged sensibility, after he died a martyr's death the Federalist *New-York Evening Post* printed a poetic eulogy that named "Ye Children of Columbia" the "Offspring of feeling" who "Heave the swoln sight, and drop the tear" over his coffin.[44]

To understand how the two strains converged, it is necessary to explain why the Man of Feeling became passé in the 1820s. For one, he was a man of privilege in a society that was democratizing. He was easily lampooned. An anonymously written book titled *Fragment of a Journal of a Sentimental Philosopher* was published in New York in 1809, written, according to its introductory "Advertisement" to unmask "pretenders to philanthropy and benevolence." In quasi-diary form, imitating the stream-of-consciousness narrative of Sterne's *Tristram Shandy*, the "sentimental philosopher" details his reputedly successful effort to distinguish himself among the society of sensible humanity by promoting perverse attitudes. He intrigues people by dressing in a slovenly way and in doing the opposite of what is respectable: "talked of the soul of sympathy—sweet cords of sentiment—unsophisticated sensibility—even made an attempt to dance—was awkward—so much the better—good dancing quite common here—my bear-like movements more interesting—imputed to genius and uncontrollable sensibility—the girls all enraptured with me."[45]

Sensibility had become so conventional that it bored people. In *Fragment of a Journal* it was of use as a casual ploy to win the hand of a young woman who looked for such bearing in a suitor. On one of the philosopher's outings, he "even shed tears—passed for exquisite sensibility and benevolence—some notion of making one of these girls my wife." (Such deception recalls the character of Dimple in *The Contrast*, whose sensibility is falsely cultivated and productive of a foppish adroitness exquisitely exposed.) With whimsical self-satisfaction, the author proposes that feints toward the rakish seduction of women are needed to bring new life to a tired society. "I do not despair," the ludicrous philosopher records, "of producing a complete revolution in domestic society—a total change in the principles, sentiments, feelings, tastes, and conduct of women. . . . I shall be the founder of a new school of philosophy in this country, distinguished by an *ism* to my name." That "school" promoted "the philosophy of motion—the pure sentiment of gesture," a pseudoscientific approach to public speaking and public display in which empty gesture was meant to appear significant. In this construct, the trivial becomes essential for social success: "The power of gesticulation collects, fixes, and embodies the sublimest flights of genius. . . . It infuses a soul into the inert mass of words—gives life to language." It was the Scots who had produced this vacuum, decried in this satire for "not blending *sentiment* enough with their reasoning." The perverse philosopher claims, in a lucid moment, that the eighteenth century's pursuit of the "perfectibility of man" is no longer credible. Society was complex, multilayered; true, unforced eloquence demanded greater substance than that which the culture of sensibility offered.[46]

Washington Irving's Rip Van Winkle, from the story published in 1820, is a Man of Feeling, whose sensibility facilitated his comic portrayal. The familiar character in American lore falls asleep in the Catskill forest one day while America is a happy colony and awakes a generation later, having slept through the entire Revolution. The old-fashioned Rip is generous but weak, too vulnerable for his own good. Though he "would never refuse to assist a neighbor, even in the roughest toil," he was "ready to attend to anybody's business but his own." The unambitious hero's pre-Revolutionary happiness is in fact foolishness: "If left to himself he would have whistled away his life in perfect contentment." Irving's Man of Feeling is hounded by "the daring tongue" of a persecuting wife, and only his dog Wolf remains, in terms of the compassionate heart, a like companion. A despairing Rip escapes "the labor of the farm and clamor of his wife" and strolls into the woods with Wolf, "with whom he sympathized as a fellow-sufferer in persecution." That the author emotionally equates the idle Rip Van Winkle with his poor but "honorable" dog is a revealing transposition of the language of sensibility: "Wolf would wag his tail, look wistfully in his master's face, and if dogs can feel pity, I verily believe he reciprocated the sentiment with all his heart."[47]

William Godwin tried to salvage the Man of Feeling by giving him greater dimension and a sexual identity. In *Fleetwood: Or, The New Man of Feeling* (1805), the main character is a dreamy youth, an only son without a mother, who is easily charmed by the beauties of nature and, like Sterne's "Sentimental Traveller," "fond of penetrating into the cottages of the poor." One day Fleetwood rescues a drowning peasant and returns him to his sweetheart, and like Mackenzie's Harley, cares so much for this "honest family" that he becomes their patron and prevails upon his father "to bestow a farm upon the lovers." Fleetwood owns that "I experienced a disinterested joy in human relief and human happiness" and "exulted in my own benevolence." From here, however, he veers from Harley's straight and narrow path to virtue, discovering carnal desire in Paris and the Swiss Alps before returning to England with a young woman whose entire family has recently perished in a shipwreck. But Mary is of inconstant mental health, and Fleetwood begins to suspect her of infidelity. He banishes her from his house and it is not until much later that he realizes her innocence. The man he has suspected of stealing his wife's affections in fact rescues Fleetwood's sinking fortunes, reuniting the New Man of Feeling with his deserving wife. The critic of the highly regarded *Edinburgh Review* disliked the novel intensely, writing that a man prone to "the furious impulses of passion . . . is not a man of sentiment but a madman; and far from sympathising with his feelings, we are only surprised at his having the liberty of indulging them beyond the precincts of Bedlam." This "determined egoist" surely lacked "the amiable virtues of a Harley." Sensibility without purity was no longer sensibility.[48]

Nineteenth-century Americans were coming to recognize the limitations, even the sterility, of the ethic of sensibility on an individual level. It could not subsist in a competitive environment—the circumstances occasioned by urban growth, by a significant rise in the free labor force working outside the home, by increasingly specialized business districts, and the coming of a universal white male franchise (the removal of property qualifications for the vote). Sensibility came to appear class-bound. An aggressive economic climate combined with the agency of the family in rearing more self-assertive children. The rough-and-tumble world of politics and the educational processes of patriotism and party allegiance had a considerable impact on the socialization of the rising generation. And the doctrine of competition, directed toward men, did not have to rely significantly on affectionate ties.[49]

The reframing of sensible virtues into a strictly female category can be gleaned from prescriptive literature as well. *The Juvenile Port-Folio and Literary Miscellany* ran a series of vignettes for its youthful readers in 1814–15, emphasizing the problems inherent in an excessive display of sensibility. The traditional construction was unchanged: there was in the female "more gentleness, more softened amiableness than men possess, . . . more sensibility, more influence upon the heart." She "invigorates his hopes, and impels him to laudable enterprizes," and finds in return "a protector, and one who will for her encounter the roughness and jarrings of the world from which her nature would shrink." And yet, "sentiment and feeling" had to be distinguished from tearful self-indulgence. To grow "so tender" as to "be ready to weep for a fly" was improper, for "though warm affections; and tender feelings, are beyond measure, amiable and charming when perfectly natural, and kept under the due control of reason and principle; yet nothing is so truly disgusting, as the affectation of these or even the unblinded indulgence of such as are real. Compassion was not impressed on the human heart, only to adorn the fair face with tears." Masculinity, too, newly emphasized "ardent valor." The intrepid war veteran, generically portrayed, was now inherently wise as well as brave: "His mind, active and vigorous—burning with the thirst of honour—flew to posts of danger with a rapidity which gave tenfold value to his military exertions. . . . Fortune, too, seemed enamoured of his valour, for she preserved his life" while depriving him, in this instance, of one hand. Vignettes designed to instruct still associated Beauty and Pity but added interdiction of maudlin excess.[50]

These images were reduplicated in the *New-York Mirror, and Ladies' Literary Gazette* for 1825. The eighteenth-century style of self-sacrificing, "making little concessions, or pardoning little errors," was directed at this time merely to women: "The happiness of this life consists much in the interchange of kind affections, and of tender sympathies and mutual condescensions. We must live for each other." A story titled "Delicate Sensibility" told of a deserving young female married to an upstart man of commerce and rude exhibitionist. She was unsuccessful in her efforts to tame his undignified public vanity, and still adopted the model response: "It is because I feel myself bound by duty, and by a deep sense of his goodness . . . that I would do or suffer anything to shade his foibles." After her premature death, the unreformed husband became even more "dissipated and contemptible," while the woman of sensibility lived on through the model of "feminine delicacy, gratitude, and prudence" she had consistently exemplified. A subsequent piece titled "Woman" was authored by a man (unidentified by name) who warned against "excess of feeling," while upholding the admirable "female tenderness and sensibility" that properly self-governed males understood. Depicting the existing tension between sensibility and masculine assertiveness, he meant to assure women that there were still men like himself who not only could be "melted by some fond sigh, or captivated by some fascinating tear-drop," but also could be moved to "champion" and "vindicate" woman. And he claimed that he was offering these assurances as "the genuine feelings of my heart."[51]

From the time Sir Walter Scott's popular first novel, *Waverley*, was published in 1814, the literature American males read moved beyond the convention of seduction and reformation, beyond the epistolary form, to a more active view of history and manners. *Waverley* tells the story of an insurrection in the Scottish Highlands in 1745, with a main character who is brave, imaginative, and intuitive. Scott did not probe the hearts of his female characters, and wrote of his first hero: "So far was Edward Waverley from expecting general sympathy with his own feelings . . . that he dreaded nothing more than the detection of such sentiments as were dictated by his musings." The courtship plot, central to eighteenth-century sentimental literature, was placed on the periphery of narrative interest. These principles distinguished Scott from the authors of what were called "common novels," and from—as one of the author's correspondents wrote him—the "prim sententiousness" of female novelists. *Waverley*, and Scott's many novels which succeeded it, possessed a new air of authority, with clear gender boundaries. Vigorous masculinity combined with a cheerful sympathy; the individual pursued self-interest for the general good. And yet, it is well worth noting that Scott dedicated his first novel to Henry Mackenzie.[52]

Prior to Scott's rise, novel reading was criticized widely, because with the exception of Richardson, Mackenzie, and their ilk, novels were primarily written by women for women and were thought to over-stimulate, to produce unreal expectations of romantic excitement in a generation which prescribed self-restraint for both men and women, but especially for women, entrusted as they were to set the example for otherwise unruly men. The culture of sensibility, then, was always used as a social weapon by those who feared that tendencies toward gender equality would undermine patriarchal power in the republic. A representative piece from Noah Webster's *American Minerva* warned of the "disagreeable effect produced by a free and indiscriminate perusal of novels. They imperceptibly create a false and artificial sensibility" which "tickles the nerves and floats in the fancy, without leaving any impressions on the heart, or influence on the conduct." A woman taken with romance, a "discolored view of the affairs of the world," sacrificed "tranquility and welfare" to mere gratification. No novel, Webster proposed, should be put before "young persons and, peculiarly so for young females," until it had been judged by "persons of speculative curiosity" qualified to offer moral direction.[53] With Scott, however, sentiment was shown to be dull by itself. Sentimental description was invoked often enough, but the author's singular masculine characters, worldly and brave, dominated the narrative. American male authors, beginning with James Fenimore Cooper in the early 1820s, were to adopt a similar strategy.

History writing differed from fiction writing. Mercy Warren, known as the author of poetry and dramatic satire in the 1770s and 1780s, could go on to write a prominent history of the American Revolution not simply because she was a direct witness and knew intimately some of the major participants. As a female endowed with a "sensible" gift and not unsatisfied with the male regime, she was warmly acknowledged to possess an observant eye as to the male character. The struggle for independence was considered to be as much about the triumph of an ideal character as a series of military events; therefore a literary figure like Warren (and like the British historian Catharine Macaulay who preceded her) was deemed qualified to compose a multivolume history. In an age of sentimentalism, Warren did not transgress upon male authority but spoke to a transcendent patriotism. The less distinguished women of her generation who wrote emotion-laden novels, however, were thought capable of dismantling a carefully constructed paternalistic system, had males not presumed to judge and restrict the content of their writings.[54]

In any event, as education—including female education—expanded, reading became less restricted for all. Texts continued to reflect a tradition of moral didacticism, but female characters in novels, through self-teaching and self-discipline, grew more resistant to seduction. At the same time, sentimental literature by women, written exclusively for women, deepened in melodrama. Along with the obligatory tears, it contained images of a happy domesticity, or as one leading literary scholar typified these romantic canvases: "broad barns bursting with yellow grain, its wide chimneys suggesting friendly hearthstones." Whether depicting sunny scenes or long winter evenings, the old homestead included a "venerable patriarch conducting family worship or presiding at family dinner." In these novels, sentimental bachelors wished for just such a quiet state of affairs, swayed by right-thinking young women rather than tempting saloons.[55]

As the nineteenth century progressed, female characters became ever more resourceful in response to the untrustworthiness of morally derelict males. This did not, however, release women from subordinate roles. They were meant (or "designed" by God) to fulfill a duty to society as agents of gentility, producing a moral climate in which pure patriotism could thrive. Beyond fiction, women were asked, as before, to allow men to protect them (representing their opinions by proxy), to remain insulated from the public (except as consumers), and to accept passivity before the law. Meanwhile, the restless, romantic male self, sincerely ambitious, determinedly professional, was preparing, like America itself, to surge ahead. The nineteenth century was transforming the way men modeled their thoughts and actions, and drawing a further line of separation between delicate (if less naive) women and themselves. To the extent that novel writing became a male preserve, it was no longer quite so elegant, instructive, or even realistic—but noticeably more adventurous.[56]

The election of 1828 brought masculinity to the public in a new way, as the Jackson campaign combined political sense with masculine redefinition. The honest and active "People," in the language of a comprehensive Jackson pamphlet, contested the effeminate *"champions of Aristocracy."* If during James Monroe's two terms a "happy union of sentiment" prevailed, his successor, the inactive John Quincy Adams, had countenanced "duplicity and cunning." This sedentary President was charged with having borrowed his wisdom from books, naturally lacking "adequate strength and felicity of expression." His writing (and by inference his person) was incomplete in the "manly beauties." Jackson, on the other hand, was "warmly and powerfully supported by an enlightened, virtuous, and patriotic people." It was unique to the Jackson campaign that warmth and power combined with enlightened virtue. Moreover, Jackson's were "stern virtues," not soft virtues, because aggressive action was needed to check the "wanton growth" of the "noxious weed" of aristocratic privilege in America.[57]

The Tennessean had fought for his country's freedom with "valor and matchless skill," the literature trumpeted, again putting forward decidedly heroic masculine traits. It was owing to his "practical wisdom, sound, discriminating judgment, tried integrity, and ardent patriotism" that Jackson had "subdued the merciless savages." The "ardent" general was individualistic in his pursuit of patriotic ends; he led by strategic example. He was a man of well-defined purposes rather than abstract identifications, unlike Colonel Manly of *The Contrast*, who may have fought nobly in the Revolutionary War but whose masculinity was defined in terms of an unflappable moral posture and a transcendent, less earthy brand of integrity. Jackson was equipped, then, to oppose and defeat the "unhallowed and deadly touch"—mere effeminate "touch"—of aristocracy. Though admittedly without literary talent, he possessed something more valuable and more desirable: an "energetic mind," a military man's ability to "estimate the talents of others." Jefferson was quoted as having spoken of Jackson as "a clear-headed, strong-minded man." Washington himself was no more a scholar than Jackson, if the absence of that qualification should alarm members of the voting public. As to the general's experience as a duelist and supposed lack of a placid temperament, it could be pointed out that the man identified as Adams's protégé, Henry Clay, had fought a duel as a more mature man than Jackson, who, younger in years and young in spirit, had taken a forgivable if "impetuous" turn. (Clay had challenged Virginia senator John Randolph in 1826; each duelist fired twice, but neither was injured.) Dueling was conventionally decried, yet at the same time held up as a mark of manliness; it was Jackson, true, but (tempering the charge) Clay as well who by his act "invited all the high-minded and brave, the youthful and inconsiderate" to "resort to the pistol." These were the facts, simple facts. Not only Jackson but Americans at large possessed "an inextinguishable spark of valor." In a nation where "every citizen is armed . . . any attempt to encroach on the rights of such a people, by the application of force, would be worse than madness. Even the women of America," as a last resort, "would arm against the tyrant."[58]

Jackson, like the virtuous Jefferson before him, had been "calumniated" at the time he stood for the highest office. "Those who formerly traduced [Jefferson]," wrote the Jackson campaign publicist, "are now his eulogists." The sturdy Jackson, "the Nation's Hero," could withstand all "slanders." Those who did not know any better were being seduced and deceived by sly, designing aristocrats, whose efforts to retain power under President Adams were "spasmodic." ("Spasms" signified vulnerability in the vocabulary of sensibility.) Jackson, in final contrast, was indefatigable, a "more than Spartan hero." The physicality expressed in this representative campaign tract established moral self-discipline in a way that diverged plainly from sensibility of old. If America's women, in a Jacksonian framework, did not resort to arms, they could at least, like Spartan women steeled in sending sons to war, honor the masculine code of honor and active patriotism.[59]

Many patriotic women, as well as hero-worshipping men, must have identified with Andrew Jackson's defiant act of passionate, patriotic manhood in protecting the honor of his wife when they were accused of bigamy during the rancorous campaign of 1828. Rachel Jackson was branded an immoral woman for having abandoned her first husband, Lewis Robards, in 1791, after becoming caught up in a passionate romance with the brash man-on-the-make, Andrew Jackson. Their subsequent union was technically adulterous, the Jacksons having innocently misinterpreted a tentative document as a legal divorce decree. Uncomfortably, after thirty-seven years of marriage, candidate Jackson was obliged to defend his wife's virtue and his own character.[60]

Anti-Jacksonians charged that Jackson was a seducer, morally culpable for robbing another man of his wife. He was unmistakably without "honorable sensibility" and therefore even the longevity of his marriage could not make a case for the "indulgence" of "sympathy." The "youthful hero" of this adventure in seduction, "in the first stages of manhood," had committed an "outrage" not only against Lewis Robards but against society. Such a man as Jackson, who defied social norms and behaved recklessly (as witnessed anew in the 1818 Seminole war), was said to be undeserving of the public trust. Airing the dusty details of this controversial marriage was legitimized, one newspaper explained, because "the National character, the National interest, and the National morals, were all deeply involved." And Rachel Jackson, though suffering from a fatal heart condition, could not avoid being held accountable either. Her immodesty allegedly matched her husband's profligacy: she did not possess the moral qualities demanded of a President's wife.[61]

Reacting to the torrent of charges, Jacksonians lashed back at their opponents, offering testaments to Jackson's loyalty as a friend, as a patriot, as a morally upright man who conformed to traditional American values. "His strong manly sense," ran one such tract, "his integrity and warmth of heart," had earned the admiration of "the blunt yeomanry." He "imbibed their frank and generous spirit." Pointedly, they charged, Rachel Jackson's first husband had been a cruel and jealous man who once threatened an innocent Jackson with a whipping, eliciting Jackson's appropriately measured reply that he would give that man "gentlemanly satisfaction." Though this duel never took place, Jackson had stood his ground as a true American, a morally secure American, should.[62]

Conflating an office seeker's private and public morals was nothing new, of course. When he published his long, circuitous apology in the Reynolds matter, Hamilton had had to acknowledge that he understood the dictates of the prevailing sensibility—masculine gentility and generosity—even while rejecting the deceptive tool which the evocation of sensibility had represented for the blackmailing Reynolds. During the election of 1800, Jefferson's reputed atheism was translated into an invitation to licentiousness in a Jefferson presidency, a moral offense with both a private and a public dimension. And while in office, two politically inspired incidents of alleged sexual misconduct were publicized: the titillating idea of the President's having taken a slave mistress and his admission of having once propositioned his neighbor's wife thirty-odd years before. Jefferson's allegiance to the culture of sensibility prescribed a sturdy silence on the first, more crudely detailed issue, and a private communication with the offended husband in the second instance (it appeared, in any case, that Jefferson's neighbor was resurrecting the old memory for purely partisan reasons). The Man of Feeling could not be identified with unrestrained passion, only the passion to perform humanitarian deeds.[63]

By 1828, however, in such high-profile controversies, sensibility had been overthrown. Jackson's defense was not that he possessed sensibility but that he consistently had exhibited masculine competence, that he would not shy from the field of honor to defend his wife's virtue or his own consistency of moral character, or, for that matter, his country's right. He resorted to the exercise of power to advance justice, as he would to pronounce the cause of liberty. The moral use of power was prized. Unlike the power-oriented Hamilton thirty years earlier, Jackson did not have to show softness in his composition to assert his moral nature, though to do so would not necessarily have been unappealing.[64] Committed to harmonious purposes, Jefferson was ill at ease with the employment of raw power; nor did he, in his last years, support the political ambition of the untutored, apparently belligerent Tennessee general, despite the suggestion in the aforementioned campaign literature. By 1828, though still obsessed with both individual and national moral self-definition, Americans did not define righteousness or recognize strength in terms of eighteenth-century masculine sentiment. The independent man of action had defended female honor on the unruly frontier—this was an embodiment of American honor.[65]

In December 1828, Rachel Jackson, "the solace of his retirement and the partaker of his reproach," was, in the words of an early Jackson biographer, "taken by a short but severe sickness." An attending physician described the scene: "Then it was that all the feelings of the devoted husband burst forth. His breast heaved, and his soul seemed to struggle with a load too oppressive for frail humanity." To a physician still responding to the literature of natural sympathies, strength did not require coldness, but welcomed internal upheaval. This was evolved eighteenth-century sensibility. The biographer went on to eulogize Rachel Jackson in solemn verse:

> She loved the manly heart that made her blest,
> She loved the patriot flame that warmed his breast. . . .

The "vile assailants" who had dared to paint the "patriot wife" a bigamist were infamous:

> Oh shame to manhood! That our times have seen
> Monsters possessed of man's uplifted mein [*sic*, for *mien*],
> Whose hearts the base, unfeeling tale could frame,
> That tried to blast so pure a being's fame![66]

Jackson's universal manhood rose, strong and assertive yet refusing to ignore "frail humanity," while shameful men monstrously capable of insulting a devoted and virtuous wife slinked back into the shadows.

Margaret Bayard Smith, a mainstay of Washington society and Jeffersonian in her temperament, nervously anticipated Andrew Jackson's accession to the presidency. Writing to her sister of "the irresistible allurements of ambition," she observed after learning of Rachel Jackson's death that only this woman of "universal charity and benevolence," "possessed of goodness tho' destitute of talents," could control "the violence of his temper." Smith was echoing the common belief that women soothed male roughness—and that in this case "not only the domestic circle but the public will suffer," as Jackson, the unpolished Indian fighter, lost the one "restraining and benign influence" in his life.[67]

———

IN 1840, THREE YEARS after Jackson retired from the presidency, the Ohio Whig convention was held in Columbus on Washington's birthday, establishing a new tone for patriotic sensibility as it established the presidential candidacy of William Henry Harrison. John G. Miller's pamphlet, reproducing the speeches made at that forum, was designed to bring out the "temper and character," "the spirit, the pathos, the sentiment that moved upon the hearts of the multitude of patriot men" in assembly. Whigs had come to national prominence by branding Jackson a tyrant, the familiar epithet a People of Feeling had been giving, conventionally, since 1776, to the leader of that party or entity which was the object of their recrimination. In this case, the party of Jackson was "incompetent and unfaithful," an organ of "corruption and despotism." The Whigs asserted, too, that Jackson's successor, Martin Van Buren, had proven to be a man "whose history addresses itself to no generous sympathy—whose character commands no feelings of veneration and tenders no quality to attract the kindness of our common nature." In other words, sensibility was wasted on the party of Jackson.[68]

A Whig columnist described the advance of the Whig faithful to the 1840 convention grounds in a parade held the day before the proceedings commenced: The "dense and uninterrupted stream of the REAL DEMOCRACY pouring onwards. . . . All the grand gala of patriotism swept by us like the magic transitions of a drama. Onward poured the stream." The parade was a sentimental deliverance, bringing "honest Republicans" and "the friends of liberty" together under a new banner. From Harrison's West, where "men in their humble dwellings have hard hands and strong arms and stout hearts to defend their rights," a venerable candidate with "a patriot's nerve" had rallied young and old to express "the deep, the stern, the earnest emotion of men who had discovered danger and fortified themselves to meet it." It was an "intercommunication of mind and mind, and heart and heart, and hand and hand" that "disclosed to every mind the unity of purpose, the concord of feeling, the identity of sentiment" destined "to concentrate the energies and efforts of so many thousand freemen upon a single object—THE RESTORATION OF THEIR GOVERNMENT." In these sentences, the recent marriage of the language of sentiment and power is evident: men with "strong arms and stout hearts" are also united in "the concord of feeling." Like their eighteenth-century predecessors, the Whigs had set themselves up not simply as the party of opposition but as the possessors of genuine and justifiable popular sentiment. They had revived the quintessential American symbol, lost to those in power who continued deceptively to claim to represent the people faithfully. Appropriating masculine sentiment and adding "a patriot's nerve," the Whig party could now alone claim to embody American democracy, sentimental democracy.[69]

Until this period, when he was resurrected as a composite, as a mainstream American, the Man of Feeling was in every incarnation a member of the elite class. He invariably possessed sentiments which bound him to the common man, causing delicate women to respond as well to his outstanding virtue and altruism. But he was not really at one with the objects of his sympathy. As the common man rose to take his place in the active democracy, he did not require the guiding moral authority of the Man of Feeling, except, perhaps, as a symbol of his own heart. If the culture of sensibility was to influence his behavior, it was by way of that feminine sensibility which retained its purpose (in accord with a patriarchal authority that resisted women's public presence) by conditioning male ardor. As the nineteenth century progressed, that ardor found a positive place in men's public ambitions, in an increasingly independent public life.

Recalling Samuel Johnson's *heart*-prefixed words of a half century earlier, by the time of the first edition of Noah Webster's *American Dictionary* (1828), a more extensive range of such words had come to be accepted into American English. *Heart-expanding* was defined as "enlarging the heart; opening the feelings." Add *heart-alluring* ("suited to allure the affections"), *heart-appalling* ("dismaying the heart"), *heart-bred, heart-buried* ("deeply immersed"), *heart-hardened* ("unfeeling"), and *heart-quelling* ("conquering the affection") to complete a picture of profound sensations. Compare Dr. Johnson's *heart-burned* (an inflammation) to Webster's more thorough *heart-consuming*, the old *heart-whole* (connoting imperviousness) to the new *heart-robbing* ("depriving of thought; ecstatic"). The images now presented described a more intrusive action upon the heart, while the underlying acceptance of human vulnerability before an external power remained comparable. In this way, the sentiment which came to underlie an ever-growing democratic spirit partook of the age of sensibility. Sensibility bespoke a certain charm. It was present in religious hope and determination, in the pathos and tenderness of an emerging literature.[70]

If moral philosophers like the Earl of Shaftesbury and Adam Smith and the philosophically inclined Rush and Jefferson had had an appreciable effect, sensibility would have been applied through the sincere efforts of political men to govern the United States with mildness and compassion. The proponents of sensibility thought that feeling could be productive, and in this they were not wrong. What Rush and Jefferson learned, however, was that the heart awakened not only virtue but ambition as well. The Man of Feeling's expectations, then, were at once noble and absurd. It may be fair to conclude that rejection of the Man of Feeling is what effectively marked America's cultural independence, as European manners yielded to American pluck and opportunism.

Even Henry Mackenzie recognized that sensibility in public men was not always practical. This did not make such sentiment useless or undesirable, only pathetic. In Mackenzie's novel, as the Man of Feeling is dying, he considers himself "blessed with a few friends who redeem my opinion of mankind." But as the woman he has loved from a distance draws near his room for their final, cathartic encounter, Harley sighs to his companion, "There are some feelings which perhaps are too tender to be suffered by the world. The world is in general selfish, interested, and unthinking." What is called "weakness" on earth, he surmises, will be better appreciated in the world to come. In the meantime, sensibility remains too good for most mortal men; only a sensible woman can hope to offer man the proper inspiration to conduct himself virtuously.[71]

The eighteenth century sought to move the hearts of humanity through affecting eloquence, sympathetic acts of kindness and philanthropy, and small acts of sacrifice, all to prove that uncommon behavior could overcome common prejudice. The masculine sentiment which animated public figures during and after the Revolution urged identification with female or lower-class vulnerability. It is this which sparked individual acts of generosity.

Seemingly favored by nature and destined to become the site for human perfectibility, independent America recast the culture of sensibility into an ideal image of its national self.[72] From the crucible of the Revolution emerged the idiom of America's moral self-regard, the beginnings of a patriotic language. This highly self-conscious people, even with their vices exposed in prominent letters and publications after 1783, exerted themselves to keep the faith of Paine's refrain in *Common Sense*: "The cause of America is in a great measure the cause of all mankind." America's victory vindicated the cause of the heart and justified further belief in a union predicated on sentiment and sympathy.[73]

In the nineteenth century—the divisions are not meant to be chronologically precise—rhetorical strategies shifted as national purposes were defined through mobility and expansion and quantifiable growth. Americans did not become unfeeling, but they turned away from the risks of extreme sensibility. They preserved by other means the eighteenth century's emphasis on compassionate appreciation of merit and distinction. Feeling now coexisted with plain profit seeking, once too readily associated with dishonesty and social disharmony. This, then, was sentimental democracy, the conjunction of "natural" (generous) feeling and steady, deserved material progress—an automatic expression of moral superiority. Sentiment continued to mark the country's achievement, as much as canals and railroads and steamboats and western settlement did. It was just that sentimental democrats, more outwardly aggressive men than sentimental Revolutionaries, identified less with others' vulnerability and allowed benevolence to be transferred to society, to the church, and to female-directed associations, where such activity tapped female "nature" as it was then understood.

Public happiness and ordered liberty remained the terms of American self-definition, and Americans still saw themselves as of old, aiming to exhibit personal virtues and the consistency of character which informed their political union. Benjamin Franklin Allen of Brown University's senior class restated for a new generation on July 4, 1817: "Union in a *republic* must not consist in cold, external, lifeless form. It must consist of that unison of sentiment and feelings, which connects every heart."[74] Even so, the nation's moral mission to remake the world became less decorous, less subtle. Increasingly self-absorbed, Americans applied the vocabulary of feeling to an acceptable exercise of power. Whereas eighteenth-century men of sentiment, a select group professing gentle and gracious manners, negotiated from interested idealism, nineteenth-century men of movement, who had dissolved delicacy and dismantled the Federalists' world of deference, designed practical new conditions of possibility. For them, an active, autonomous empire required more than ever a permanent presence and a convincing military establishment.

With these developments, nineteenth-century America became estranged from its predecessor except for a nostalgia inspired by symbols such as George Washington in marble and James Fenimore Cooper's moral pioneer (and moral Indian) in print. Meanwhile, whether it was courteous to upstart America or stubbornly disdained it, the outside world came to ruffle the active people less and less; America was the source of all feeling that mattered. Since that time, embracing liberal urges, sentimental democracy has flowered, increasingly accepting internal variation, without ceasing to believe in the possibility of fashioning a harmonious whole.

# CHAPTER TEN

# LEGACIES OF NATIONAL CHARACTER

LATE COLONIAL AMERICANS regularly—almost obsessively—voiced their concern with moral character, and this naturally translated after independence into a concern with the national character. Congressman James Bayard in 1806: "We must learn to insist upon our national rights, or by and by none will belong to us. We must learn to defend our honor as a people, or soon we shall be without national character."[1] This usage of the word *character* was not neutral in tone; it meant national virtue or self-esteem, a recognized and deserved honor. A Jackson supporter in 1828 reflected on the boost to American pride occasioned by the 1815 Battle of New Orleans: "Our national character was elevated and our citizens secured, perhaps for ages, from injury and insult, by the respect and awe, excited principally by one unparalleled achievement." Here the national character was even more plainly defined both as unity of parts and global reputation.[2]

Debates over language routinely assessed the status of the American nation. The *North American Review* in 1815 wondered about the future of an American literature, given the fact that American English derived from a nation "totally unlike our own." The journal put it crisply: "How tame will his language sound, who would describe Niagara in language fitted for the falls at London bridge, or attempt the majesty of the Mississippi in that which was made for the Thames?" But even if attempts could be made to standardize it, language, as Noah Webster had found, was a malleable thing and most subjective.[3]

William Cullen Bryant, an American writer of the post-Revolutionary generation who wrought a genteel poetry, soberly assessed the state of American verse for the same journal in 1818. He was not blindly patriotic, but temperate and critical. Revolutionary era poets like Freneau, Barlow, and Trumbull had embellished greatly, he wrote. They had tried a "national poetry" but fell short of the "genius" and "taste" of the European model. The poetry of the young nation, Bryant explained, reflected promise but at the same time an understandable lack of sophistication. "Literary ambition" took time to awaken; the American effort so far was credible and should not be judged too harshly. With less objectivity he added that the "pervading spirit of nationality and patriotism" was a phenomenon: "[N]ational gratitude, national pride—every high and generous feeling that attaches us to the land of our birth, or that exalts our characters as individuals" would direct Americans toward "perfection" in the poetic art.[4] In the meantime, the creative use of American English was as nervous and ungoverned in seeking to establish a national literary personality as it was obscure and volatile in the interpretation of domestic political affairs.

Washington Irving, a writer as cosmopolitan as the poet and essayist Bryant, was an important figure in the evolution of the American literary imagination who grew up in post-Revolutionary New York but spent the years 1815 to 1832 in Europe. In his well-received *Sketch Book*, first published in 1819, Irving included a piece called "English Writers on America." In it he observed "with feelings of deep regret" that America was disparaged by English travelers owing to "an illiberal spirit" pervading their generally "prejudiced" accounts. Writers who called Americans boorish and backward were confused, he insisted, because they could not yet understand what was brewing in the republic: "The national character is yet in a state of fermentation: it may have its frothings and sediment, but its ingredients are sound and wholesome; it has already given proofs of powerful and generous qualities, and the whole promises to settle down into something substantially excellent." These vocal commentators from across the Atlantic whom Irving felt impelled to critique had apparently come to America expecting private gain. But America, Irving pursued, was not "an El Dorado, where gold and silver abounded, and the natives were lacking in sagacity." Wealth was being accrued as a result of "industry and talent," by contending with "the common difficulties of nature." Americans were "an intelligent and enterprizing people."[5]

Implicit in Irving's explanation of the national character was the notion that America was honest about itself and improving at every stage. As time went by, its character as a nation would inevitably come to be appraised fairly and accurately by foreign observers. English prejudice aside, "the world at large is the arbiter of a nation's fame; with its thousand eyes it witnesses a nation's deeds, and from their collective testimony is national glory or national disgrace established." Americans, Irving noted further, unlike those tainted with Old World "national prejudices," had "sprung into national existence in an enlightened and philosophic age . . . and we forego the advantages of our birth, if we do not shake off the national prejudices, as we would the local superstitions, of the old world." Only such an open, even-tempered people as the Americans could find the beneficence to state fearlessly that there was "no country more worthy of our study than England"; in manners, in intellectual activity, in "moral feeling," English habits remained "congenial to the American character." England was "a volume of reference, wherein are recorded sound deductions from ages of experience," still valuable for America to enlist "to strengthen and to embellish our national character."[6]

Irving began his professional life in Federalist circles during Jefferson's first term. His earliest literary efforts showed an irreverence for the state of republican society and a longing for what he conceived to be a solid tradition and the greater sense of order that prevailed earlier. He parodied provinciality; he saw his countrymen as they were—a sporting people, an aggressive people, consistently on the make. They were prone to excess, to faction, to an ignoble, even degenerate behavior, and to a merely tongue-wagging patriotism, which demonstrated a weakness of character. This evaluation is clearest in Irving's 1809 *History of New York*, an impulsive (it would seem) burlesque.[7]

Beginning in the 1820s, Irving reviewed the past somewhat differently, relying on intuition more. As he grew less irritated with the society in flux that was the early American republic, he joined those narrative historians of the romantic period whose style was to privilege "sense" over evidence and precision. In comparing the sensibilities of Irving and Sir Walter Scott, William L. Hedges has written of what history meant to the romantics: "that a large part of the present is the impression the past makes on its consciousness."[8] And so Irving himself went on to become a mythmaker for an America increasingly responsive to the emotional power of historic memory.

Irving could not simply embrace Americanism as the Revolutionary poets had, with blind approbation. The nation that was undertaking experiments in popular politics needed to recover a gentility (something from the British past) in order to achieve coherence, to prevent the acceleration of social decay. Yet, as in the work of Scott and Cooper, the physical setting of each historical re-creation—transcendental attributes of nature—contributed to revelations of the national character (here meaning, more generally, the distinctive traits of an amalgamated people). Americans studied the topography as part of the conscious fashioning of an outgoing independent spirit that could be widely shared and praised, an effort to find a common denominator to bind the many. Human knowledge tapped nature to produce vague if perceptible affinities, powerful myths; through this technique alone, the potential of America was increased.[9]

Harmony was, everywhere and always, elusive, but Americans to this point in their history had refrained from suggesting too strongly that harmony was an impossible dream. Republican sensibility was coming to coexist with democratic acquisitiveness and expansion. Visionary architects of commercial empire reckoned that westward exploration would lead to a cost-effective means for Europe to ship its goods to China by an overland route across America, a notion that would persist through the 1840s and the railroad age. Even when quixotic plans failed, however, Americans seemed to have a knack for regrouping, adjusting to new situations and conjuring new strategies for exploitation, profit, and, with it, a justification for their idealism. It was while such assumptions were early taking hold that Lewis and Clark had set out, destined to further the romantic American notion that something providential, fortuitous, or serendipitous could be seen in occurrences: the American hero saved, literally, in the nick of time, from the physical point of no return, or the nation, figuratively speaking, saved from the disintegration of its noble dream. The evasion of death by the Corps of Discovery during their long journey from 1804 to 1806 illustrated this American "truth."

Irving's romantic pose was that of a man of candor propelled like America into a large, mysterious, fantastic realm. He was, like his own invented character in "The Voyage," cut loose and "sent adrift upon a doubtful world," "driven by the uncertain currents of existence," "given to day dreaming and fond of losing himself in reveries," immersed in "a delicious sensation of mingled security and awe." He questioned as he drifted imaginatively between the present and the past, much like his most enduring creation, Rip Van Winkle. It was for others, not for Irving, to rhapsodize a more deterministic American destiny—to connect and secure the people of nature's nation.[10]

Nature, empire, and the American character merged in the mind of painter Thomas Cole. In his 1836 series of five canvases, *The Course of Empire*, the images were timeless but the meaning to America was undisguised. The rise and fall of the empire was divided into stages: a haunting, primitive, but vigorous state of nature; summery pastoral tranquillity; "Consummation," a triumphant civilization, oblivious to nature; stormy "Destruction," sending citizens crashing into the turbulent sea (clearly a man-made horror); and the final "Desolation," wherein nature had recovered its hold on the world, and climbing vines covered the ruined pillars of a crumbled marble temple under skies once again placid and primordial. American viewers were meant, of course, to receive a moral lesson. The fate of the nation hung on the people's capacity to retain a consciousness of and dedication to the early idyll. At the same time, the panoramic Hudson Valley vistas of Cole and others suggested that there was a new freedom taking hold in the artist's imagination. America's landscape conveyed a resplendence, breadth, and sublime majesty. The nation's moral objectives were visible, in a way, in the romantic painters' near-mythic depictions. Through the romantic sublime, the artist, like the novelist, was able to invent a story that stood as a metaphor for national self-discovery. This was the romantic self-image most literally.[11]

In the same year that Cole produced *The Course of Empire*, illustrating the spiritual dangers of material progress when unaccompanied by an authentic appreciation of the natural landscape, the republic's most noted banker, Nicholas Biddle, gave an address on the American farmer in Philadelphia. Agriculture represented "one of the purest enjoyments of this life," he said, "and the best preparation for the future." It was a "healthy occupation" offering "calmness of mind" and demanding a "high spirit of manliness and independence." Like Jefferson and "Sylvanus Americanus" before him, Biddle emphasized that the attractions of the farmer's ways "must have deep roots in the human heart, since they have in all times fascinated at once the imagination, and won the judgment of men."[12]

If one takes the banker's words to heart, the American way continued to draw upon the farmer's widely approved decency and uncorruptibility, enabling national character to profit from the "highest dreams of those high spirits." America's citizens possessed the "loftiest feelings of personal independence," something so obvious to Biddle that it need not be proved. "The American farmer," he maintained, "is the exclusive, absolute, uncontrolled proprietor of the soil. His tenure is not from government. The government derives its power from him. There is nothing above him but God and the laws; no hereditary authority usurping the distinctions of personal genius; no established church spreading its dark shadow between him and heaven. . . . His character assumes a loftier interest by its influence over the public liberty." The by now institutionalized happiness and liberty of America depended upon "these men, powerful like their own forests . . . to heal, to defend, and to save." Publisher Mathew Carey's strictures about the equal, or perhaps greater, morals of the manufacturer, did not disturb Biddle's reverie. He meant to do as Crèvecoeur had done earlier, to take the nurturing farmer as a metaphor for what *could be* in America. The ideal citizen thrived on potential, on the strength of belief, on the myth of perfect justice, on the rhythmic superlatives that comprise the vocabulary of American liberty.[13]

Statistics meant less than memory and parable to the patriotic imagination. Aside from the cautionary tone implicit in the writings of Bryant and Irving, the idea of a national destiny predicated on the
Revolutionary moral consciousness was winning over the mass of citizens in nineteenth-century America. The sentimental aspect of America's sweeping democracy had much to do with the assumption that, as
a liberty-loving people with energy as boundless as their continent, they
ought to wield a benevolent power (enlarging as their hold over the
land tightened), before long to invigorate such tired civilizations as Europe and China. As the century went forward, the missionary impulse
first directed toward Native Americans was to be focused on the Chinese, seen in American eyes to be equally indolent, equally redeemable
as their aboriginal North American counterparts. The civilizing democracy was an indisputable good, most persuasive, they imagined,
when it was conveyed in the spirit of philanthropy, with sentiment and
sympathy underlying it.[14]

The 1840s, the decade in which the term "manifest destiny" was
coined, saw the acquisition of an even more vast western territory than
previously secured. James K. Polk's one-term presidency (1845–49) extended U.S. administration to nearly the present-day continental
boundaries. Missouri editor and Oregon traveler William Gilpin typified the new nationalism when, transported, he wrote in 1846:

The *untransacted* destiny of the American people is to subdue
the continent—to rush over this vast field to the Pacific
Ocean—to animate the many hundreds of millions of its people, and to cheer them upward . . . to agitate these herculean
masses—to establish a new order in human affairs . . . to
regenerate superannuated nations . . . to stir up the sleep of a
hundred centuries—to teach old nations a new civilization—to
confirm the destiny of the human race . . . to emblazon history
with the conquest of peace . . . to unite the world in one social
family—to dissolve the spell of tyranny and exalt charity—to
absolve the curse that weighs down humanity, and to shed
blessings round the world.[15]

Energetic conduct was meant to produce supranational harmony. America was called upon to "regenerate" effete civilizations, to "transact" its destiny of conquering peacefully and uniting the world. Sentimental democracy reached new heights as American "charity . . . shed blessings."

Walt Whitman, son of a Long Island carpenter-farmer and himself a newspaper contributor and editor before becoming known as a poet, was a nationalist-expansionist as well. History, for Whitman, was a journey, and Americans were indomitable travelers. Sentiment and sensuality abound in his collected works, and imagination typically outruns practical prescription. In the poem "Pioneers! O Pioneers!" he celebrates the outward-bound nation:

> All the past we leave behind,
> We debouch upon a newer mightier world, varied world,
> Fresh and strong the world we seize, world of labor and the march,
>    Pioneers! O pioneers!
>
> We detachments steady throwing,
> Down the edges, through the passes, up the mountains steep,
> Conquering, holding, daring, venturing as we go the unknown ways,
>    Pioneers! O pioneers!

Progress became ever more uncompromising for what was, in the poet's phrase, the "resistless restless race" of nineteenth-century white America.[16]

Patriotic ideals may not always comport with reality, but Americans, buoyed by the productivity of the land and the people, were always striving to be originals. The Civil War had tested the nation's endurance, of course, and brutally exposed the agony that feeling made possible, but, as Henry Adams subsequently put it, "chaos often breeds life, when order breeds habit. The Civil War had bred life."[17] After Appomattox, as immigrant laborers from Europe were being urged to achieve "100 percent Americanism," a cultural reconciliation gradually occurred between North and South. Union and generosity were seen to go together: In an 1887 magazine article, one nationalistic veteran recalled movingly the moment when General Ulysses S. Grant decreed at the surrender that Confederate officers would not have to give up their shining swords or private horses. The writer, present at the ceremony, had noticed a change in General Robert E. Lee's demeanor at that instant. In a modern chronicler's words, the combined heroism of the two armies melded into a "celebration of martial grandeur and the glorification of the imperial nation-state." The fraternity of North and South expanded, fighting side by side in the Plains wars against pockets of resistant Indians and in the glorious Spanish-American War.[18] It is not surprising that in the imperial age there emerged the competitive intensity of patriot Theodore Roosevelt, scornful of inferior peoples and committed to superintending acts of moral progress.

Henry Adams observed this turn of events as well when in 1868 he perceived his countrymen as "new." Having just returned from seven years in London as the son of and aide to a diplomat, he regarded himself as an outsider. Of Americans' unstoppable energy, he wrote: "The American mind exasperated the European as a buzz saw might exasperate a pine forest." Europeans of this period found Americans practical, vigorous, "acute," but at the same time conventionally common and so predictably action-oriented that they were unwilling to listen to others. The "bluff, brutal" British in particular saw them as ignorant and machinelike. These "new" Americans Adams was encountering, or reencountering, in the postbellum years seemed, as much to him as to the British, self-absorbed and self-sufficient. What was most remarkable about them? he posed. As Adams noted, they

> must, whether they were fit or unfit, create a world of their own, a science, a society, a philosophy, a universe, where they had not yet created a road or even learned to dig their own iron. They had no time for thought; they saw and could see, nothing beyond their day's work. . . . Above all, they naturally and intensely disliked to be told what to do, and how to do it, by men who took their ideas and their methods from the ab-

stract theories of history, philosophy, or theology. They knew enough to know that their world was one of energies quite new.[19]

This Adams, the grandson and great-grandson of independent-thinking Presidents, understood that component of the sentimental democracy which displayed its energy through a kind of innovation that could be rebellious at times and accompanied by a lack of deference toward learned traditions. Shooting from the hip, as it were, Americans preserved of the past only what was useful to the present. In his memoir, Adams repeatedly called himself an eighteenth-century man, one who was looking to find his place in an unfamiliar setting. Though he thought his values precious, they did not fit America's mood as the nineteenth century proceeded. The national self-image and nation-building ambition had become ever more self-centered, ever more morally secure, with minimal conscious regard for any larger Western intellectual tradition. Clearly the nation governed by "virtue and talent" that John Adams had once believed in had long since evolved into a hardier, more broadly competitive society of the dollar-worshipping. But had the *idea* of America changed that much?

Benedict Anderson has given modern analysts a compelling perspective on nationhood: an imagined political community, too large for members to know one another, yet "in the minds of each lives the image of their communion."[20] His definition seems apt for this study. The image of communion, the romantic self-image, sustained an ideology that proclaimed a goal of harmony without reasonably confronting the prejudices now most hurtful and enduring in the historical imagination: the exclusion of dark-skinned people, aboriginals, "undesirable" immigrant groups, and women from equal participation and equal enjoyment of happiness and liberty.

The nation, itself an eighteenth-century Enlightenment construction, meant more as it became something that ordinary people would give up their lives to defend. Nationalists would go on to erect tombs to unknown soldiers to prove that the modern age was, in Anderson's words, "saturated with ghostly *national* imaginings."[21] The American community became sacred. It developed a canon of resonant stories and texts—the Boston Massacre, Paul Revere's Ride, the Declaration of Independence, Nathan Hale, Daniel Boone, the works of Washington Irving and James Fenimore Cooper, etc.—that made sacrifice sublime and national history sparkle with a possessive folk culture of unending novelty. As Ernest Gellner has remarked, it is in the name of the folk culture that nationalism conquers emotionally, its symbolism drawn from the health and vigor of these "typical" people.[22]

Eighteenth-century America could only dreamily and abstractly utter its message of universal liberation. The nineteenth century was somewhat more profound in its application of power for purportedly philanthropic ends. The twentieth century, torn by national, regional, and global struggles to protect human rights and concomitant struggles to reduce racist brutality and other forms of bigotry, advanced alongside changing sensibilities deemed appropriate for the ethnic reconstitution of societies. At the end of the twentieth century, as a larger place in history has been given sympathetically to those to whom it was long denied—the unlettered, the politically oppressed—what has not changed is that Americans still desire to pass on a moral identity to their posterity. These days, the question of whether such a thing as national identity really exists is sharply debated. Recent books have offered different scenarios for a redefinition of America's parts in order to "restore" America's whole. The issue remains unsettled.[23]

The ultimate source of all American optimism remains the Revolution. No matter how willing to expose their societal flaws Americans have been, an association with the founding generation has continued to assure that the country's construction of political liberty presents the hope of human enlightenment. The Revolutionary generation set in motion an enduring conceit, that the humane purposes construed at the time of America's inception could be sustained in thought and activity and had only to be made apparent for others to want to follow America's lead.

The nation's claim became greater as its confidence swelled in the age of expansion, leading to sentimental imperialism in the Far East by the end of the nineteenth century and assumption of the role of world's policeman in the atomic age. A hearty embrace of naval and later air power directed American actions abroad, while a rhetorical sentiment and sympathy for the plight of colonial peoples grew alongside it. Ultimately this modern formulation expressed itself through American-led international bodies such as the United Nations and the World Bank. From World War II on, giving aid to promote "peace" and "social harmony" was another way of rewarding pro-U.S. governments that might otherwise be swayed by the communist model of economic order. Perhaps distorting the importance of the Third World in achieving America's new goal of preponderant power over modern tyranny, Washington sought to co-opt regional nationalist movements and create a binding system that contained communism. As historian Melvyn Leffler has put it: "Preponderance did not mean domination. It meant creating a world environment hospitable to U.S. interests and values." In that sense, the moral stance undergirding America's view of its global mission had not changed, even with a naked acceptance of the politics of power.[24]

Establishing national character as a positive good through the dissemination of propaganda and economic and cultural aid was one thing. But, even more profoundly, in waging the Cold War against Moscow, America needed to see proof of its eternal attraction to the oppressed seeking justice; it was no less so than when Revolutionary era patriots construed a moral imperative to undertake aggressive actions against their own unfeeling parent and invited to western shores able-bodied refugees from arbitrary rule. Asserting its power, the United States responded to communist tyranny with an old impulse. It proclaimed to the world its moral leadership and conveyed its moral architecture, this time perhaps unselfconsciously, as an ultimatum: allies and client states were obliged to promote an image of themselves compatible with America's self-image.

If America placed itself at the hub of the twentieth century's democratic Enlightenment, as the guiding light for a holistic system of peaceful progress, other nations had to be willing to join in making an enemy of communism or any other ambiguous hegemony. They have been asked to struggle alongside America to defeat drug lords and anarchic terror, conforming to the "global" moral vision that is Pax Americana. The search for order in a disorderly world has always been made less anxious for Americans through the belief that their ethic is universally applicable.

Belief in a regenerative America was widely questioned at home, of course, during the era of Vietnam and Watergate and the Iranian hostage taking—low points in American self-esteem. But the patriotic impulse to identify America's virtues recovered and persisted through the 1980s. Coinciding with Ronald Reagan's assumption of the presidency in 1981, the magazines operated by Time, Inc., undertook a "Special Project" called "American Renewal," aimed at discovering a cohesive national purpose by abandoning extreme and divisive positions and relying instead on rational thought. (The American Revolution and Jefferson's "Revolution of 1800" professed the same goal of humanistic transformation through individual and collective moderation.)

"The belief in an ever better tomorrow," *Time*'s extended coverage began, "that the U.S. has a strong and beneficial role to play in the world—these constitute the American secular religion." The nation's democracy having been shaken by a sagging global reputation, and by a perceived "lack of will, failure of nerve, moral decay, selfishness and sloth, the shattering of community feeling," only a "disciplined effort" and the "rare virtue" of patience promised to yield the acceptable outcome: a deserved national pride. "The need for renewal," the opening article, written by *Time*'s editor in chief, proclaimed, "ranges well beyond economics, politics, and defense; it encompasses ethics, morale, social and spiritual values." Another headline in the same issue read: "Needed: individual awareness of a new sense of nationhood." The special issue went on to invoke such potent words and phrases as "national mood," "awakening," "immense resources—physical, intellectual, spiritual," "success and virtue," "civic morale," "vast creativity," "can-do faith," "pledge," "moral responsibility," "moral harmony," "aggressively wholesome," and "the American spirit." The obvious resemblance to the values and language of national identity publicized between 1750 and 1828 suggests what little effect material change can sometimes have.[25]

*Time*'s prognosis and prescription emphasized America's role as a moral force in the world. It reflected assumptions about popular government nurtured during "America's century." Popular government was typically meant to resolve problems without a resort to extreme violence. (This is merely an ideal, of course, an ideal Americans invented.) When the sentimental democracy cannot stop war, it must show that a compassionless power compels the ultimate action, that popular will demands it, too—a popular will that extends beyond America's shores to the people of the world, for whose humanity America now expresses sympathy. The interest of "the people" justifies policy, no matter how coercive.

The Reagan years, thought by many to have had the effect of souring sympathy and respect for a larger humanity for the sake of "American renewal," were succeeded by the opposing dogma of multiculturalism, pursuring national harmony by embracing the cause of America's parts. Of this, historian David Hollinger writes: "The once-popular notion that there might be an American character or even culture was widely discredited as a nationalist equivalent of a universalism understood to deny diversity." Rights of individuals, he suggests, have been replaced with rights accorded to groups in the interest of a too careful, perhaps even too respectful multicultural principle of harmonious living. "Distinctive communities" have become, in modern parlance, "nationlike, each one a unique product of distinctive historical forces and circumstances."[26]

One naturally wonders whether the primal commitment of citizens to the American nation has remained strong in the age of multiculturalism. On the eve of the twenty-first century, the link between virtue and performance may be felt with less assurance than it was at the time of the Revolution, but few Americans would go so far as to say that the *idea* of America is dead, not still fundamentally a constructive vision expressing the enterprising humanism of a creative people. Sentimental democracy still combines independence with invention and productivity, a touch of healthy rebelliousness, and an appreciation for human dignity. It is sure of itself and still amenable to change from within. It is equally expressive of unconstrained action and quiet duty. It is meant, in all things and at all times, to support the common good. It declares that one person's success does not inhibit another's but serves as a model worthy of emulation. It thrives on testing new methods and testing one's humanity. Americans continue to idealize themselves as a self-made people, any one of whom could rise from obscurity, as Benjamin Franklin and Abraham Lincoln and Frederick Douglass did.

Amid the many changes of the twentieth century, America's romantic self-image was captured by Hollywood and then fed by Hollywood back to mainstream America and around an envious world. From the 1920s, Hollywood became the outstanding purveyor of sentimental democracy, convincing people that everyone wanted to live the idealized American life. The sugary Frank Capra film *It's a Wonderful Life* resolves tensions inherent in modern society by declaring that Americans must have faith in one another; democracy, like Man of Feeling George Bailey's Building and Loan, is people power sustained by sentiment. Happy endings are, as one film critic notes, "not only a recompense for the life lived well but also a pat on the back for the society that makes it possible to live life well."[27] Whether the "other" in action films is the Nazis, Soviet communism, unshaven terrorists, the Blob, or an asteroid, they are entities beyond the bounds of sympathy; civilization is protected by the benevolent aggression of the sympathetic American hero—colorful, inventive, unselfish, reasoning (when others panic), the community-conscious rugged individualist, product of a land of liberty.

This is a lesson Americans of necessity promote. As Rupert Wilkinson has pointed out, they still fear being owned, enslaved, psychologically broken by those who would manipulate their long-constructed social identity.[28] Film heroes, albeit with an often banal pretense of conviction, defend the romantic self-image, just as astronaut hero turned senator John Glenn of Ohio did on a visit with the leaders of China in 1996. Pointing out deficiencies in that government's human rights record, the senator lost his patience when China's Deputy Foreign Minister suggested a moratorium on negative comments: "I told him," Glenn explained later, "we're not that kind of country. China has a few top leaders who decide what the country is going to do and it happens. In our country, every individual is a king."[29]

Transcendent George Washington, that unswerving, virtuous marching man, no longer leads his flock forward. He has long since become as wooden as his much maligned set of teeth. Who has come to embody that "genuine" American spirit? Independent frontiersman Daniel Boone was succeeded in the popular imagination by whimsical western figures like Davy Crockett and Buffalo Bill, a bull of a President named Theodore Roosevelt, and film personalities like Gary Cooper, John Wayne, and Clint Eastwood. The odd but lovable American combined a kind of simplicity and eccentricity with an honorable distinction that rendered power less invidious than it would be in the hands of non-Americans. The morals of the American hero have had to appear beyond reproach. And yet, despite moon shots and gold medals, many Americans wonder whether the nation has lost its resiliency. Technological progress has produced in Hollywood as many dystopian fantasies as ennobling possibilities.

Nevertheless, the combination of sympathy and power in American enterprise has been durable, and no better illustrated than with the carefully timed release of the movie *Independence Day* on July 4, 1996. As the late-twentieth-century equivalent of the western hero (combining raw nerve with masculine sentiment), the independent President–fighter pilot hero leaves the bedside of his dying wife to redeem humanity after an alien invasion. Notably, to salvage the spirited American-led order, a squadron from the Islamic community joins Israel in an airborne display of global harmony—all nations lined up behind the compassion and boldness of America's resolve.

There can be no doubt that the American legacy has contributed passionate poetry to the ideal of a human community. In his State of the Union Address on February 4, 1997, President William Jefferson Clinton took his place among two centuries of sentimental democrats when he pronounced an old confidence: "America," he intoned, "is far more than a place. It is an idea." Both ominous and inviting, sentimental democracy wafts over a land that continues to entertain rebellious pilgrims and welcome new visions, attempting self-discipline while convincing others of its virtues.

# NOTES

## INTRODUCTION

1. *The Speech of Logan, By T. Jefferson; The Shrubbery, By Potter; Old Edwards, By Mackenzie* (New York, 1803?). Owned by the American Antiquarian Society. The printer William Elliot subsequently brought out novels by female writers offering moral instruction to young people. For statistical information on novels printed in late-eighteenth-century America, and the relative popularity of *The Man of Feeling*, see Robert B. Winans, "Bibliography and the Cultural Historian-Notes on the Eighteenth-Century Novel," in William L. Joyce et al., eds., *Printing and Society in Early America* (Worcester, Mass., 1983), esp. 178–81.

2. *Notes on Virginia* was the only book Jefferson published in his lifetime. The 1787 London edition of 1,000 copies was printed by John Stockdale. An American edition was printed in Philadelphia in 1788. For details, see William Peden, ed., *Notes on the State of Virginia* (Chapel Hill, N.C., 1955). Jefferson recorded the "Speech of Logan" in his Memorandum Book in 1775 after hearing of it at the Governor's Palace in Williamsburg; a variant appeared in the *Virginia Gazette* on Feb. 4, 1775. See James A. Bear, Jr., and Lucia A. Stanton, eds., *Jefferson's Memorandum Books: Accounts, with Legal Records and Miscellany, 1767–1826* (Princeton, N.J., 1997), 385.

3. Published in Philadelphia by Samuel H. Smith.

4. An emotional history studies attributes and the process of self-fashioning in individuals, communities of discourse (in this case print culture), and nations in such a way as to recapture the "life" of the past, emotional standards, and how history felt as it was being shaped. A new study on this subject is Peter N. Stearns and Jan Lewis, eds., *An Emotional History of the United States* (New York, 1998).

5. Bernard Bailyn, *The Ideological Origins of the American Revolution* (Cambridge, Mass., 1967); Ernest Lee Tuveson, *Redeemer Nation: The Idea of America's Millennial Role* (Chicago, 1968); Henry F. May, *The Enlightenment in America* (Oxford, 1976); Sacvan Bercovitch, *The American Jeremiad* (Madison, Wis., 1978), quote at 176.

6. Jay Fliegelman, *Prodigals and Pilgrims: The American Revolution Against Patriarchal Authority, 1750–1800* (Cambridge, 1982); Melvin Yazawa, *From Colonies to Commonwealth: Familial Ideology and the Beginnings of the American Republic* (Baltimore, 1985); Gordon S. Wood, *The Radicalism of the American Revolution* (New York, 1992).

7. G. J. Barker-Benfield, *The Culture of Sensibility: Sex and Society in Eighteenth-Century Britain* (Chicago, 1992); Anne C. Vila, *Enlightenment and Pathology: Sensibility in the Literature and Medicine of Eighteenth-Century France* (Baltimore, 1998).

8. David Waldstreicher, *In the Midst of Perpetual Fetes: The Making of American Nationalism, 1776–1820* (Chapel Hill, N.C., 1997), 1–13. For a good discussion of the history of the concept of American exceptionalism and its cultural importance, see Michael Kammen, "The Problem of American Exceptionalism: A Reconsideration," *American Quarterly* 45 (March 1993), 1–43, also Seymour Martin Lipset, "American Exceptionalism Reaffirmed," in Byron E. Shafer, ed., *Is America Different?: A New Look at American Exceptionalism* (Cambridge, 1991), 1–45.

9. Scholars who have examined literary and artistic conventions in early American development include Nathan O. Hatch, *The Sacred Cause of Liberty: Republican Thought and the Millennium in Revolutionary New England* (New Haven, Conn., 1977), on sermonic conventions; Simon Schama, *Dead Certainties* (New York, 1991), on the canonization of Joseph Warren by artist Benjamin West; Cathy Davidson, *Revolution and the Word: The Rise of the Novel in America* (New York, 1986), chap. 8, on the gothic mood; Fliegelman, *Prodigals and Pilgrims*, chap. 7, and Barry Schwartz, *George Washington: The Making of an American Symbol* (New York, 1987), on nostalgia for George Washington.

## 1. SENTIMENT AND SYMPATHY: BEGINNINGS

1. Merrill D. Peterson, ed., *The Portable Thomas Jefferson* (New York, 1975), 290–92.

2. On loyalists' emotional distinction from the patriots, see Janice Potter, *The Liberty We Seek: Loyalist Ideology in Colonial New York and Massachusetts* (Cambridge, Mass., 1983), chap. 3.

3. From Jefferson's draft, in Peterson, ed., *The Portable Thomas Jefferson*, 235–41.

4. Jay Fliegelman, *Declaring Independence: Jefferson, Natural Language, and the Culture of Performance* (Stanford, Calif., 1993), 26, 187–89, on the spoken voice and citing Wilkes. There is nothing new, of course, in choosing the Declaration as an instrument for retelling the narrative of America's self-creation: Carl L. Becker emphasized a Lockean stimulus in assessing eighteenth-century human relations, law, and the moral justification for government. See *The Declaration of Independence: A Study in the History of Political Ideas* (New York, 1922). This argument has now been updated and the political culture further dissected by Pauline Maier, *American Scripture: Making the Declaration of Independence* (New York, 1997). Devaluing the political Locke, Garry Wills was the first to term the Declaration "A Sentimental Paper," though in linking Jefferson's moral worldview to a cultural perspective that is similar to that which this book details, Wills did not choose to elaborate on subsequent nation-building energies. See Wills, *Inventing America: Jefferson's Declaration of Independence* (New York, 1978). Henry F. May loosely fit the Declaration into a discussion of intellectual emancipation, "harmonizing sentiments" amid providential murmurings, while Sacvan Bercovitch found meaning in the Declaration as a quasi-religious ritual. See May, *The Enlightenment in America*, esp. 155–64, and Bercovitch, *American Jeremiad*. Finally, Thomas Gustafson has observed that an exuberant people overturned the King's English; as "an intensive language-learning lesson," the Declaration represented to him "the art of crafting an honest sentence." See Gustafson, *Representative Words: Politics, Literature, and the American Language, 1776–1865* (Cambridge, 1992), 253–57.

5. Ezekiel Whitman, *An Oration Commemorative of the Declaration of Independence of the United States of America* (Portland, Me., 1801), 11; R. Douglas Hurt, *The Ohio Frontier: Crucible of the Old Northwest, 1720–1830* (Bloomington, Ind., 1996), 237.

6. See especially Davidson, *Revolution and the Word*.

7. Peter Gay, *The Enlightenment: An Interpretation* (New York, 1966 & 1969), 2:29.

8. Late-eighteenth-century Americans' anxiety about threats to their liberties owing to

self-interest, opportunism, or simply tyranny from above has been widely characterized. For some classic commentary on this subject, see Wood, *The Radicalism of the American Revolution*, 169ff; idem, *The Creation of the American Republic, 1776–1787* (Chapel Hill, N.C., 1969), 606–15; Lance Banning, *The Jeffersonian Persuasion: Evolution of a Party Ideology* (Ithaca, N.Y., 1978), 119–21, 150–54, 248–49, 268–70; Bailyn, *The Ideological Origins of the American Revolution*, 144–57.

9. Frank Baasner, "The Changing Meaning of 'Sensibilité': 1654 till 1704," *Studies in Eighteenth-Century Culture* 15 (1986): 77–96.

10. Gay, *The Enlightenment*, 2:12–23, 30.

11. In his important 1739 *Treatise*, David Hume also elaborated on "impressions," under which he classified "all our sensations, passions and emotions, as they first make their appearance on the soul." See Hume, *A Treatise of Human Nature*, ed. L. A. Selby-Bigge (Oxford, 1978), 1.

12. Robert A. Erickson writes that in the eighteenth century the heart was the source of courage, integrity, inner religious conviction, and "above all—by the mid-eighteenth century—sympathy, compassion, and 'consciousness,'" the "essential core of humanity." Consciousness as conscience indicated the individual's profound awareness, even internalization, of the distresses of another. See Erickson, *The Language of the Heart, 1600–1750* (Philadelphia, 1997), 198. See also Catherine Glyn Davies, *Conscience as Consciousness: The Idea of Self-Awareness in French Philosophical Writings from Descartes to Diderot* (Oxford, 1990); Richard E. Aquila, "The Cartesian and a Certain 'Poetic' Notion of Consciousness," *Journal of the History of Ideas* 49 (1988): 543–62.

13. On Richardson and Cheyne, see Barker-Benfield, *The Culture of Sensibility*, 7–9; quote is from G. S. Rousseau, "Nerves, Spirits, and Fibres: Towards Defining the Origins of Sensibility," in R. F. Brissenden and J. C. Eade, eds., *Studies in the Eighteenth Century III* (Canberra, 1976), 154–55. This perspective is quite pronounced in *Medical Extracts of the Nature of Health, With Practical Observations: and the Laws of the Nervous and Fibrous Systems* (London, 1796).

14. Barker-Benfield, *The Culture of Sensibility*, 25. The particular danger thought to be inherent in a "passion for learning" is explored in Vila, *Enlightenment and Pathology*, chap. 3.

15. John Mullan, *Sentiment and Sociability: The Language of Feeling in the Eighteenth Century* (Oxford, 1988), chap. 5, "Hypochondria and Hysteria: Sensibility and the Physicians"; Ralph Ketcham, *James Madison: A Biography* (Charlottesville, Va., 1971), 51–52.

16. Entry of Jan. 16, 1807, in Plumer, *William Plumer's Memorandum of the United States Senate, 1803–1807*, ed. Everett S. Brown (New York, 1969), 575–76.

17. Andrew Burstein, *The Inner Jefferson: Portrait of a Grieving Optimist* (Charlottesville, Va., 1995), 80; Barker-Benfield, *The Culture of Sensibility*, 17.

18. James Rodgers, "Sensibility, Sympathy, Benevolence: Physiology and Moral Philosophy in *Tristram Shandy*," in L. J. Jordanova, ed., *Languages of Nature* (New Brunswick, N.J., 1986), 122; for extensive treatment of the impact of von Haller's work, see Vila, *Enlightenment and Pathology*, esp. chap. 1.

19. Benjamin Rush, *Lectures on the Mind*, ed. Eric T. Carlson et al. (Philadelphia, 1981), 238ff. Compiled from Rush's lecture pamphlets written and revised between 1791 and 1811; Arthur May, *An Inaugural Dissertation on Sympathy* (Philadelphia, 1799).

20. "Of the Passions, As They Display Themselves in the Look and Gesture," *The Universal Asylum, and Columbian Magazine* (Jan. 1791); Susanna Rowson, *Charlotte Temple*, ed. Cathy N. Davidson (New York, 1986), 62; *The New-Hampshire Magazine* (Jan. 1793); William Hill Brown, *The Power of Sympathy* (New York, 1937), 1:10. The fictional recipient of these words regards this communication of newfound love as "a tumult—such an ebullition of the brain in these paroxysms of passion." The supposedly love-struck then defends his "new system." Ibid., 12–15; J. C. Lavater, *Essays on Physiognomy; for the Promotion of the Knowledge and the Love of Mankind* (Boston, 1794), quote at 31. When the 1817 New York edition of *The Pocket Lavater* was issued, many new and updated illustrations were added, with the assertion, "Physiognomy is the very soul of wisdom" (p. 5). On gentility, conversation, and

socialization in the eighteenth century, see Richard Bushman, *The Refinement of America* (New York, 1992), chaps. 2 & 3; for the European antecedents, see Norbert Elias, *The Civilizing Process* (New York, 1978 [1939]).

21. See Fliegelman, *Declaring Independence*, 31, 36–37, 40–42, quote at 115.

22. Note that Edmund Burke's *A Philosophical Enquiry into the Origin of Our Ideas of the Sublime and Beautiful* had appeared two years before Smith's work, linking psychology and aesthetics, and touching on similar ideas of imaginative empathy with the distresses of others. Hume preceded both in writing on the impulse and natural effects of compassion, in *A Treatise of Human Nature*, 368–71.

23. Adam Smith, *The Theory of Moral Sentiments*, ed. D. D. Raphael and A. L. Macfie (London, 1976), 122, 137.

24. In *Inventing America*, Garry Wills emphasizes the Scottish Enlightenment in the elite education of numerous signers of the Declaration of Independence. See esp. chap. 11. See also May, *The Enlightenment in America*, 343–44, in which the Scottish school is described as a body of thought "united by tone and origin rather than by doctrine."

25. Barker-Benfield, *The Culture of Sensibility*, 105–8; Douglas Anderson, *The Radical Enlightenments of Benjamin Franklin* (Baltimore, 1997), 28–44, 68. In 1768 Laurence Sterne contributed this injunction: "Ye whose clay-cold heads and luke-warm hearts can argue down or mask your passions, tell me, what trespass is it that man should have them? Or how his spirit stands answerable to the father of spirits, but for his conduct under them?" See Laurence Sterne, *A Sentimental Journey Through France and Italy*, ed. Graham Petrie (New York, 1967), 118.

26. Joseph F. Kett and Patricia A. McClung, "Book Culture in Post-Revolutionary Virginia," *Proceedings of the American Antiquarian Society* 94 (1984): 97–147; Kenneth Cmiel, *Democratic Eloquence: The Fight over Popular Speech in Nineteenth-Century America* (Berkeley, Calif., 1990), 32–33.

27. Hugh Blair, *Lectures on Rhetoric and Belles Lettres* (Philadelphia, 1833), lecture 2, 17–20.

28. Ibid., 24–29.

29. Montesquieu, *The Spirit of the Laws*, trans. and ed. Anne M. Cohler et al. (Cambridge, 1989), Book 19, chaps. 5 & 27, 310, 327–28.

30. Hume, *A Treatise on Human Nature*, 602–5; Albert O. Hirschman, *The Passions and the Interests: Political Arguments for Capitalism Before Its Triumph* (Princeton, N.J., 1977), 24–25.

31. Sentimental types described in Harold William Thompson, *A Scottish Man of Feeling: Some Account of Henry Mackenzie, Esq., of Edinburgh* (London, 1931), 102–4.

32. Herbert Brown, "Charles Brockden Brown's 'The Story of Julius': Rousseau and Richardson 'Improved,'" in James Woodress, ed., *Essays Mostly on Periodical Publishing in America* (Durham, N. C., 1973), 35–53. Brown's letter was to Joseph Bringhurst, Jr., May 20, 1792.

33. Sterne, *A Sentimental Journey*, 108. In an analysis of Sterne, Max Byrd takes note of the mid-eighteenth-century view that sensibility in men was in fact desire refined into sympathy. He cites a line from Richardson's *Clarissa*: "Sentimental affection . . . is but lust in disguise." See Byrd, *Tristram Shandy* (London, 1985), 52. Thus, ambiguity was pronounced in even the most substantial account of moral conviction, nobility, and integrity, as Richardson meant to expose in his portrayal of Clarissa, who struggles not to love her seducer. The irrational does not have to triumph to suggest the recurrent anxiety among flawed humanity. See, for example, Morris Golden, "Richardson and the Bold Young Men," in John Carroll, ed., *Samuel Richardson: A Collection of Critical Essays* (Englewood Cliffs, N.J., 1969), 161–80.

34. R. F. Brissenden, *Virtue in Distress: Studies in the Novel of Sentiment from Richardson to Sade* (New York, 1974), 53–55, 117; Barker-Benfield, *Culture of Sensibility*, chaps. 5 & 6; Smith, *Theory of Moral Sentiments*, 152. There were always, however, limits to the desirability of masculine softness. Noting his young grandson's tenderness, Connecticut minister Joseph Fish wrote his daughter and son-in-law in 1766 that he witnessed "such Ardent Love for you [all],

especially his Mamma, that we are a little concerned [lest?] his Affection should overcome his Manhood." See Joy Day Buel and Richard Buel, Jr., *The Way of Duty: A Woman and Her Family in Revolutionary America* (New York, 1984), 48. Jonathan Boucher, tutor to George Washington's stepson, John Parke Custis, expressed a similar anxiety in attempting to balance sensibility with prudent manhood: "Yr Son came to me teeming wth all the softer Virtues: but then I thought, possess'd as He was of all the Harmlessness of the Dove, He still wanted some of the Wisdom of the Serpent. . . . But how will You forgive Me if I suffer Him to lose in Gentleness, Simplicity, & Inoffensiveness, as much as He gains in Address, Prudence, & Resolu[tio]n?" (Boucher to Washington, Aug. 2, 1768, *Papers of George Washington*, Colonial Series, 8:123.)

35. Herbert R. Brown, "Elements of Sensibility in *The Massachusetts Magazine*," *American Literature* 1 (1929–30): 286–96; Ernst Cassirer, *The Philosophy of the Enlightenment* (Princeton, N.J., 1952), 302–6; David Marshall, *The Surprising Effects of Sympathy: Marivaux, Diderot, Rousseau, and Mary Shelley* (Chicago, 1988), chap. 1, quotes at 18, 21; for an analysis of Marivaux's sentimental novel *La Vie de Marianne*, in which the heroine's physiognomy mirrors her *"noblesse de coeur,"* see Vila, *Enlightenment and Pathology*, 128–40; Sterne, *A Sentimental Journey*, 137; Mackenzie to Betty Rose (his cousin), July 8, 1769, in Thompson, *A Scottish Man of Feeling*, 107. The main character's father (and model of masculine sensibility) in Susanna Rowson's *Charlotte Temple* declares that "the truly brave soul is tremblingly alive to the feelings of humanity." See Rowson, *Charlotte Temple*, ed. Davidson, 17.

36. Hector St. Jean de Crèvecoeur, *Letters from an American Farmer* (Garden City, N.Y., 1964), 23, 33.

37. Henry Mackenzie, *The Man of Feeling* (New York, 1821), 111; Mackenzie, *The Man of the World* (Philadelphia, 1799), 143. This novel involves the darker side of sensibility, and features a character named Sir Thomas Sindall, who twists the code of manners, acts without restraint, and is finally brought down. To this "counterfeit," "generosity and courage are the virtues he boasts of possessing; but his generosity is a fool, and his courage is a murderer." (Ibid., 33–34.)

38. Jefferson to Cosway, Oct. 12, 1786, *The Papers of Thomas Jefferson*, ed. Julian P. Boyd et al. (Princeton, N.J., 1950– ), 10:446–47, 449. Sterne was perhaps the most poetic in his use of this device: "With what a moral delight will it crown my journey, in sharing in the sickening incidents of a tale of misery told to me by such a sufferer? To see her weep! and though I cannot dry up the fountain of her tears, what an exquisite sensation is there still left, in wiping them away from off the cheeks of the first and fairest of women, as I'm sitting with my handkerchief in my hand in silence the whole night besides her." Sterne, *A Sentimental Journey*, 66.

39. Samuel Johnson, *Dictionary* (London, 1783), n.p.

40. Sterne, *A Sentimental Journey*, 33, 44–45. The date of Sterne's first recorded use of the adjective *sentimental* is 1740, when he was twenty-seven, in a letter to a young woman. He was referring to the "sentimental repasts" they had shared, the recollection of which brought tears to his eyes. Polite English society popularized the word later in that decade, prompting one female correspondent of Samuel Richardson to query that author on its full meaning in 1749. See Thompson, *A Scottish Man of Feeling*, 92–93.

41. Jefferson to John Stockdale, Jan. 28, 1787, *Papers of Thomas Jefferson*, 11:85; Abigail Adams to James Lovell, Feb. 13, 1780, *Adams Family Correspondence*, ed. L. H. Butterfield (Cambridge, Mass., 1963), 3:273; Eustace-Sterne correspondence cited in Griffith J. McRee, *Life and Correspondence of James Iredell*, vol. 1 (New York, 1857), 27–28. For a more detailed analysis of Sterne's "Sentimental Traveller," see Brissenden, *Virtue in Distress*, chap. 2; Mullan, *Sentiment and Sociability*, chap. 4; and Burstein, *The Inner Jefferson*, chaps. 2 & 3, containing also an American perspective on *Tristram Shandy*.

42. Mackenzie, *The Man of Feeling*, 136–57, 197–98.

43. A Mackenzie biographer has noted: "Harley's sensibility is characterized by his impulsiveness, a nervous kind of excitability that makes him respond almost instantly to an emotional experience." See Gerard A. Barker, *Henry Mackenzie* (Boston, 1975), 29–30.

44. *The Speech of Logan, By T. Jefferson; The Shrubbery, By Potter . . .* , 27–52, quotes at 43,

45. John Potter, a minor English writer, did not publish widely in America. In one volume, however, a guide to moral conduct for young people, he wrote of the passions: "They are an inseparable appendage of our humanity; we cannot divest ourselves of them without ceasing to be men." He recommended, predictably, that the passions be placed "under the regulation of reason, and subservient to our happiness: When we can conduct them properly, they become the instrument of the most eminent virtues." See Potter, *The Words of the Wise* (Philadelphia, 1790), chap. 10.

45. *Encyclopédie*, vol. 5 (1765), cited in Brissenden, *Virtue in Distress*, 47.

46. Steven C. Bullock, *Revolutionary Brotherhood: Freemasonry and the Transformation of the American Social Order, 1730–1840* (Chapel Hill, N.C., 1996), quotes at 139, 140.

47. Judith Sargent Murray, *The Gleaner: A Miscellaneous Production in Three Volumes* (Boston, 1798), 3:217–24, as reprinted in Sheila L. Skemp, *Judith Sargent Murray: A Brief Biography with Documents* (New York, 1998), esp. 149.

48. Building on the work of Linda K. Kerber, especially *Women of the Republic: Intellect and Ideology in Revolutionary America* (Chapel Hill, N.C., 1980), Rosemarie Zagarri relates the Scottish Enlightenment to female intellectual development. While women were prohibited from a direct participation in political debate (because men had decreed public outspokenness to be a willful abandonment of feminine qualities), morals taught by mothers and political sentiments and patriotism expressed by wives in the appropriate context had wide and enduring influence. As "faithful friends and agreeable companions," wives of the Revolutionary generation were mixing more with political men and becoming a significant force in shaping public manners and morals. See Zagarri, "Morals, Manners, and the Republican Mother," *American Quarterly* 44 (June 1992): 192–215. Jan Lewis also discusses how an evolving language of feeling and mood elevated women's social stature, in *The Pursuit of Happiness: Family and Values in Jefferson's Virginia* (Cambridge, 1983), esp. chap. 6; see also Lewis, "The Republican Wife: Virtue and Seduction in the Early Republic," *The William and Mary Quarterly* 44 (Oct. 1987): 689–721, and Ruth Bloch, "The Gendered Meanings of Virtue in Revolutionary America," *Signs* 13 (1987): 37–58. A new and compelling interpretation of the place of men and women in civil discourse is David S. Shields, *Civil Tongues & Polite Letters in British America* (Chapel Hill, N.C., 1997). For a somewhat satirical statement on sensibility and the reformation of male manners in post-Revolutionary America, see "On the Happy Influence of the Female Sex in Society," *The Universal Asylum, and Columbian Magazine* (Mar. 1791).

## 2. SCHEMES OF FUTURE HAPPINESS: 1750–64

1. Bernard Bailyn, ed., *Pamphlets of the American Revolution, 1750–1776* (Cambridge, Mass., 1965), 210.

2. On Mayhew's rhetorical devices, see Thomas Gustafson, *Representative Words: Politics, Literature, and the American Language, 1776–1865* (Cambridge, 1992), 201–2.

3. John Adams to Hezekiah Niles, Feb. 13, 1818, *The Works of John Adams*, ed. Charles Francis Adams (Boston, 1856), 10:288.

4. For a thorough discussion of threatening images of the sea in early America, see Haskell Springer, ed., *America and the Sea: A Literary History* (Athens, Ga., 1995).

5. Mayhew, *Discourse*, in Bailyn, ed., *Pamphlets of the American Revolution*, 213–14.

6. Ibid., 237, 237n.

7. Ibid., 247. This assessment of the range of meanings for *liberty* reflects a discourse alive since the late seventeenth century when John Locke noted that liberty was perpetually "tumbling" between tyranny and anarchy. Those espousing moderate social reform tended to rediscover Lockean thinking whenever they debated religion and conscience, power and right, fixed standards and changing opinions. For this discussion in the context of the instability of language, see Gustafson, *Representative Words*, 158–64.

8. Mayhew, *Discourse*, 247.

9. Mayhew, *Two Discourses* . . . (Boston, 1759), 60–61, cited in Bailyn, ed., *Pamphlets of the American Revolution*, 210.

10. On fatalistic elements in the search for happiness, see generally Rhys Isaac, *The Transformation of Virginia, 1740–1790* (Chapel Hill, 1982); Hatch, *The Sacred Cause of Liberty*; Ruth Bloch, *Visionary Republic: Millennial Themes in American Thought, 1756–1800* (Cambridge, 1985); Bercovitch, *American Jeremiad.*

11. *The New American Magazine*, Mar. 1758; *Oxford English Dictionary*, Second Edition (Oxford, 1989), 2:607. The OED gives the 1635 example from Quarles: "What's lighter than the wind? A thought. Than thought? This bubble world." I thank Lesleigh Brisson for calling my attention to "Alexander's Feast."

12. *The New American Magazine*, June & Dec. 1758. The eighteenth century generally has been characterized as a time when the West was obsessed with definitions of happiness. Pope's *Essay on Man*, Jean-Jacques Rousseau's *Emile*, Samuel Johnson's *Rasselas*, the Marquis de Chastellux's *De la Félicité Publique*, Voltaire's *Philosophical Dictionary* and *Candide*, and a variety of other prominent works are cited in discussions of the philosophical nature of the human species in search of happiness. The evolving concept of primitive simplicity or, in American terms, the "noble savage," added to the eighteenth century's fascination with the subject. Europe's representations of America as alternately backward and uncorrupted, and the combination of innocence and wisdom attributed to Benjamin Franklin, relate as well to this trend. See Henry Steele Commager, "The Pursuit of Happiness," in Commager, *Jefferson, Nationalism and the Enlightenment* (New York, 1975), 93–121.

13. Robert DeMaria, Jr., *Johnson's* Dictionary *and the Language of Learning* (Chapel Hill, N.C., 1986), 25, 78–79. Robert A. Ferguson writes that American intellectuals of the Revolutionary era used the metaphor of light to suggest "the transference from conflict to saving knowledge." In America more than in Europe, Ferguson adds, the metaphor of light was conveyed with "confidence and authority." At the same time, American writers of the "formative era" were "obsessed with the half formed, the partially visible," and inserted "light" into their prose as a means of bringing "unknown space under the control of experience." See Ferguson, *The American Enlightenment, 1750–1820* (Cambridge, Mass., 1997), 28–29.

14. *Pennsylvania Gazette*, Sept. 5, 1754.

15. *Virginia Gazette*, Nov. 21, 1751.

16. See, for instance, *Virginia Gazette*, Jan. 24, Jan. 30, & Sept. 15, 1752; *The Journal of Esther Edwards Burr, 1754–1757*, eds. Carol F. Karlsen and Laurie Crumpacker (New Haven, Conn., 1984), 198–99.

17. *The New England Magazine of Knowledge and Pleasure*, No. 3 (1759).

18. *Pennsylvania Gazette*, June 6, 1754.

19. Edmund Burke, *A Philosophical Enquiry into the Origin of Our Ideas of the Sublime and Beautiful*, ed. James T. Boulton (London, 1958), 34.

20. *Pennsylvania Gazette*, June 6, 1754. Another early joining of "liberty" and "happiness" with a religious idiom occurs in the Sept. 5 issue of that year, referring to the threatening French and Indian alliance on the Pennsylvania frontier: "The temporal and spiritual *Liberty* and *Happiness* of our Children, are a sacred Trust, which the Supreme Ruler of the Universe hath committed to our Charge."

21. *Pennsylvania Gazette*, July 11, 1754.

22. Cited in Hatch, *The Sacred Cause of Liberty*, 46.

23. Wood, *The Radicalism of the American Revolution*, 13–15.

24. This balance is best described in Bailyn, *The Ideological Origins of the American Revolution*, chap. 3. For a probing view of the philosophy of nature at this time, see Ernst Cassirer, *The Philosophy of the Enlightenment* (Princeton, N.J., 1951), esp. chap. 2.

25. Bailyn, *Ideological Origins of the American Revolution*, 233; Winthrop D. Jordan, *White*

*Over Black: American Attitudes Toward the Negro, 1550–1812* (Chapel Hill, N.C., 1968), 269–80; James Brewer Stewart, *Holy Warriors: The Abolitionists and American Slavery* (New York, 1976), 5–23; Thomas E. Drake, *Quakers and Slavery in America* (New Haven, Conn., 1950); Jean R. Soderlund, *Quakers and Slavery: A Divided Spirit* (Princeton, N.J., 1985). In the age of Enlightenment, this age of intellectual inquiry in which laws of nature and universal standards came to be applied, moral teachings influenced some, while economics ultimately occupied more. Individual manumissions occurred on a voluntary basis. But when slaveholding North Americans were in need of a favorable comparison, the deplorable state of slavery in the West Indies always seemed to make them less culpable.

26. Howard Temperley, "The Ideology of Antislavery," in David Elitis and James Walwin, eds., *The Abolition of the Atlantic Slave Trade: Origins and Effects in Europe, Africa, and the Americas* (Madison, Wis., 1981); David Brion Davis, *The Problem of Slavery in Western Culture* (Ithaca, N.Y., 1966), chaps. 10 & 14. Davis states that it was Smith's *Theory of Moral Sentiments* that "provided a moral basis for condemning slavery." (See ibid., 433.)

27. In the early years of Southern settlement, strong, small communities formed and slaves learned to cope with white domination. Cultural borrowing among black, white, and red in effect created a hybrid civilization. But as eighteenth-century patterns evolved, a greater percentage of slaves (in the Carolinas especially, but in Virginia as well) came directly from Africa, making slave communities less united and less "American." It was not until the eve of the Revolution that indigenous slave births outnumbered importations. See Lorenzo Johnston Greene, *The Negro in Colonial New England* (New York, 1942), chap. 9; Ira Berlin, "Time, Space, and the Evolution of Afro-American Society on British Mainland North America," *American Historical Review* 85 (Feb. 1980): 44–78; John B. Boles, *Black Southerners, 1619–1869* (Lexington, Ky., 1983), chap. 2; idem, *The South Through Time*, vol. 1 (Englewood Cliffs, N.J., 1995), 66–73; Allan Kulikoff, *Tobacco and Slaves: The Development of Southern Cultures in the Chesapeake, 1680–1800* (Chapel Hill, N.C., 1986); Joyce E. Chaplin, *An Anxious Pursuit: Agricultural Innovation and Modernity in the Lower South, 1730–1815* (Chapel Hill, N.C., 1993), 53–59; Edmund S. Morgan, *American Slavery, American Freedom: The Ordeal of Colonial Virginia* (New York, 1975).

28. Deborah Gray White has suggested that slave owners in fact kept slave families together as much to manipulate and control them, for there was always the implicit threat of breakup as punishment for any apparent lack of cooperation. See White, *Ar'n't I a Woman? Female Slaves in the Plantation South* (New York, 1985).

29. Larry E. Tise, *Proslavery: A History of the Defense of Slavery in America, 1701–1840* (Athens, Ga., 1987), chap. 5.

30. *Reminiscences of an American Loyalist, 1738–1789*, ed. Jonathan Bouchier [sic] (Boston, 1925), 96–97.

31. James Otis, *The Rights of the British Colonies Asserted and Proved*, in Bailyn, ed., *Pamphlets of the American Revolution*, 339–40, 344. (The reference in Montesquieu's *Spirit of the Laws* can be found in Part 3, chap. 5, a cynical defense of the enslavement of Negroes.)

32. *Papers of Benjamin Franklin*, 4:247, 7:84–85. Benjamin Mecom's *New England Magazine* for Aug. 1758 also included "On the Use, Abuse, and Liberty of the Press," insisting, "Such a Liberty can never be dangerous." See also May, *The Enlightenment in America*, chap. 2.

33. Bland, *The Colonel Dismounted*, in Bailyn, ed., *Pamphlets of the American Revolution*, 319–21.

34. Ibid. Through their writings in the late 1750s and early 1760s, prominent Americans in addition to Bland expressed a primary identification with the long-term interests of England. They understood themselves to be important participants in the unfolding glory of the British Empire. Conscious of having risen above the wilderness which had first greeted them, they pursued what Jack Greene has called "zealous imitation" of England "to achieve metropolitan recognition that they were still in fact Englishmen." So when the proud voices of metropolitan England discounted the distant Americans' contributions or pointedly expressed their conviction that the colonists were culturally inferior to them, anxious Americans looked for opportunities to assert their moral strengths along with their moderate behavior, industry, and loyalty to England. It was in this context that they began to require verification from

London when they claimed English civil liberty. They sought to convince the mother country to accord them a more palpable respect. As the 1760s proceeded, colonial writers, so long drawn to English models, began to reshape the American identity in such a way as to highlight the qualities they possessed that their transatlantic brethren had overlooked. See Jack P. Greene, "Search for Identity: An Interpretation of the Meaning of Selected Patterns of Social Response in Eighteenth-Century America," *Journal of Social History* 3 (1970): 189–220. Greene's *Peripheries and Center: Constitutional Development in the Extended Polities of the British Empire and the United States, 1607–1788* (Athens, Ga., 1986) traces Anglo-American relations in more detail, emphasizing Britain's lack of coercive resources. See also T. H. Breen, "Ideology and Nationalism on the Eve of the American Revolution: Revisions Once More in Need of Revising," *The Journal of American History* 84 (June 1997): 13–39. On the British self-conception and the center-periphery dynamic, see Linda Colley, *Britons: Forging the Nation, 1707–1837* (New Haven, Conn., 1992). This trend, the intensification of the language of American pride, was aided by the proliferation of newspapers, reaching larger and larger numbers of ordinary people, read and reread to groups who gathered round to listen. In the early 1760s, postriders improved tenuous links between major population centers, and common purposes began to emerge. See Philip Davidson, *Propaganda and the American Revolution, 1763–1783* (New York, 1973); also Wm. David Sloan and Julie Hedgepeth Williams, *The Early American Press, 1690–1783* (Westport, Conn., 1994), and David A. Copeland, *Colonial American Newspapers: Character and Content* (Newark, Del., 1997).

35. *Papers of Benjamin Franklin*, 4:225–34.

36. Ibid.; Anderson, *The Radical Enlightenments of Benjamin Franklin*, chap. 5. These ideas were wholly consistent with Franklin's well-known community boosterism, having conceived and matured voluntary associations in Philadelphia since the 1720s. He had been urging his fellow subjects all along to be deferential to London, while his voluntary associations—the precocious young men's club called the Junto, the Philadelphia Library Company, the Union Fire Company, the American Philosophical Society—remained expressly independent of the state. Such models of community reform and improvement, furthering principles of social order and economic growth, were conducive to ambitious individualism and would be replicated widely during the democratization of American life in the nineteenth century. See Sally F. Griffith, " 'Order, Discipline, and a Few Cannon': Benjamin Franklin, the Association, and the Rhetoric and Practice of Boosterism," *The Pennsylvania Magazine of History and Biography* 116 (Apr. 1992): 131–55.

37. See the 1760 travelogue fashioned by Norman Risjord in his Introduction to *Jefferson's America, 1760–1815* (Madison, Wis., 1991), 1–26.

38. Jack P. Greene, "Travails of an Infant Colony: The Search for Viability, Coherence, and Identity in Colonial Georgia," in Greene, *Imperatives, Behaviors, and Identities: Essays in Early American Cultural History* (Charlottesville, Va., 1992), 113–42. A similar mood prevailed among Connecticut farmers. After the establishment of the Susquehannah land development company in 1753, ordinary, self-respecting American men, wanting simply to provide for their families, bought stock and moved to northern Pennsylvania, while others took advantage of land sales in Vermont and New Hampshire. Owning land offered freedom and placed them beyond the control of those who would rather have seen them remain in Connecticut as tenant farmers. While the old order mocked these "romantic expeditions"—there was, as a cautionary writer for the *Connecticut Courant* put it, no reason to believe "that we live too thick"—the movement onto wilderness lands proceeded apace, a testament to Americans' willingness to take chances as they readily challenged the social authority. See Richard Bushman, *From Puritan to Yankee: Character and the Social Order in Connecticut, 1690–1765* (Cambridge, Mass., 1967), 256–59.

39. "The Occasional Writer, No. 3," *The New American Magazine*, Mar. 1758.

40. "The Country Farmer, No. 1," *The New American Magazine*, Jan. 1758.

41. "The Itinerarium of Dr. Alexander Hamilton," in Wendy Martin, ed., *Colonial American Travel Narratives* (New York, 1994), 187.

42. *Boston Gazette*, Feb. 11, 1760.

43. "On Happiness," *The New England Magazine of Knowledge and Pleasure*, No. 3, 1759.

44. *The New American Magazine*, Oct. 1759.

45. *Boston Gazette*, Dec. 25, 1758.

46. "The Itinerarium of Dr. Alexander Hamilton," in Martin, ed., *Colonial American Travel Narratives*, 189.

47. *The New American Magazine*, June 1758.

48. See Howard H. Peckham, *The Colonial Wars, 1689–1762* (Chicago, 1964), and Fred Anderson, *A People's Army: Massachusetts Soldiers and Society in the Seven Years' War* (Chapel Hill, N.C., 1984).

49. Samuel Davies, *Religion and Patriotism the Constituents of a Good Soldier* (Philadelphia, 1755), 3–5, 9.

50. Sermon of May 29, 1754, excerpted in *Pennsylvania Gazette*, Aug. 29, 1754.

51. Franklin to Richard Jackson, Oct. 7, 1755, *Papers of Benjamin Franklin*, 6:217.

52. Bartram to Franklin, July 29, 1757, *Papers of Benjamin Franklin*, 7:246. British regulars stationed in frontier forts seemed lax in repelling Indian attacks whether near themselves or near settled communities.

53. Anderson, *A People's Army*, chap. 1.

54. Washington to Robert Dinwiddie, Mar. 10, 1757, *The Papers of George Washington*, Colonial Series, ed. W. W. Abbot and Dorothy Twohig (Charlottesville, 1983–    ), 4:112–114.

55. "Letter from General Forbes' Army," in *Boston Gazette*, Dec. 25, 1758.

56. *Boston Gazette*, Feb. 11, 1760.

57. Byles, *A Sermon Delivered March 6, 1760 . . .* , cited in Hatch, *The Sacred Cause of Liberty*, 43, 49. Sacvan Bercovitch has written that the French and Indian War "proved to be a triumph equally for English foreign policy, for the colonies' burgeoning free-enterprise institution, and for the rhetoric of the American jeremiad. . . . Clothing imperialism as holy war—the clergy summoned the colonists to an Anglo-Protestant errand into the Catholic wilderness." See Bercovitch, *American Jeremiad*, 115. For another powerful treatment of the Catholic threat related in millennial images, see Bloch, *Visionary Republic*, 42–59.

58. Franklin to Lord Kames, Jan. 3, 1760, *Papers of Benjamin Franklin*, 9:7.

59. Governor Dinwiddie to Gist, Sept. 11, 1750, in *George Mercer Papers Relating to the Ohio Company of Virginia*, ed. Lois Mulkearn (Pittsburgh, 1954), 7.

60. Woody Holton, "The Ohio Indians and the Coming of the American Revolution in Virginia," *The Journal of Southern History* 60 (Aug. 1994): 453–78.

61. "A Plan for Settling Two Western Colonies," *Papers of Benjamin Franklin*, 5:456–63.

62. Hurt, *The Ohio Frontier*, 4–5, 41–45, 57.

63. Washington to James Wood, Mar. 30, 1773, and Feb. 20, 1774, *Papers of George Washington*, Colonial Series, 9:205–6, 490. Washington's claim to the land was based on a royal proclamation of 1763 relating to service in the French and Indian War.

64. Richard Slotkin, *Regeneration Through Violence: The Mythology of the American Frontier, 1600–1860* (Middletown, Conn., 1973), 191. William Smith's 1765 *Historical Account of the Expedition Against the Ohio Indians* identified the Indians' love of liberty through the words of soldier Thomas Hutchins: "The love of liberty is innate in the savage, and seems the ruling passion in the state of nature." With only more book learning and "sentiment," or "common feelings of humanity," the Indian could adapt to republican ways, for their attachment to spiritual and earthly harmony was real. (See ibid., 233.)

## 3. A People of Enthusiasm and Self-Control: 1765-75

1. Adams to Hezekiah Niles, Feb. 13, 1818, *Works of John Adams*, 10:288. While believing that the Revolution had long been brewing, Adams expressed astonishment one month after the signing of the Declaration of Independence at the coalescence of a real revolutionary resolve: "Would any Man, two years ago, have believed it possible, to accomplish such an Alteration in the Prejudices, Passions, Sentiments, and Principles of these thirteen little States as to make every one of them completely republican, and to make them own it? Idolatry to Monarchs, and servility to Aristocratical Pride, was never so totally eradicated, from so many Minds in so short a Time." (Adams to Richard Cranch, Aug. 2, 1776, *Adams Family Correspondence*, 2:74.)

2. Hamilton quote in Martin, ed., *Colonial American Travel Narratives*, 192; Laurel Thatcher Ulrich, *Good Wives: Image and Reality in the Lives of Women in Northern New England, 1650-1750* (New York, 1982), 215-19; Stephanie Coontz, *The Social Origin of Private Life: A History of American Families, 1600-1900* (New York, 1988), chaps. 3 & 4. On frontier settlement patterns, land use, and class conflict, see Alan Taylor's *Liberty Men and Great Proprietors: The Revolutionary Settlement on the Maine Frontier, 1760-1820* (Chapel Hill, N.C., 1990), and Richard Beeman, *The Evolution of the Southern Backcountry: A Case Study of Lunenburg County, Virginia, 1746-1832* (Philadelphia, 1984), which gives attention to religious and ethnic issues, as a "hybrid culture" forms in which gentry values meet frontier conditions.

3. Jack P. Greene, *Pursuits of Happiness: The Social Development of Early Modern British Colonies and the Formation of American Culture* (Chapel Hill, N.C., 1988), 170-75, 196-99; Van Doren, *Benjamin Franklin*, 220-23; Charles M. Andrews, *The Colonial Period of American History* (New Haven, Conn., 1938), 4:414-15.

4. The disposition to tax the colonies, wrote South Carolina historian David Ramsay in 1789, was "strengthened by exaggerated accounts" of Americans' wealth. See Ramsay, *The History of the American Revolution*, ed. Lester H. Cohen (Indianapolis, 1990 [1789]), 1:51; also see Edmund S. Morgan and Helen M. Morgan, *The Stamp Act Crisis: Prologue to Revolution* (Chapel Hill, N.C., 1953).

5. P. D. G. Thomas, *British Politics and the Stamp Act Crisis: The First Phase of the American Revolution, 1763-1767* (Oxford, 1975), quote at 91; for a general discussion of the language of American self-definition in this period, see Christopher K. Brooks, "Controlling the Metaphor: Language and Self-Definition in Revolutionary America," *Clio* 25 (Spring 1996): 233-54.

6. Pauline Maier, *From Resistance to Revolution: Colonial Radicals and the Development of American Opposition to Britain, 1765-1776* (New York, 1972), chap. 4; Christopher Ward, *The War of the Revolution* (New York, 1952), 75-76.

7. *Boston Gazette*, Oct. 7, 1765. Similarly, in the *Pennsylvania Gazette*, Nov. 14, 1765, a letter from New York to "A Gentleman in London" referred to the "shocking Act" which "filled all British America, from one End to the other, with Astonishment and Grief. . . . We saw that we, and our posterity, were sold for Slaves."

8. Bailyn, *Ideological Origins of the American Revolution*, 234.

9. *Pennsylvania Gazette*, Feb. 20, 1766.

10. A recent study of the concept of liberty in early America distinguishes the eighteenth-century understanding of "liberty" and "slavery" from modern constructions. Political scientist Barry Alan Shain stresses that within "liberty" was an understood self-regulation and self-restriction in opposition to licentiousness or "an indifference to the true moral order." Liberty, he argues, was rationally limited and incorporated with a sense of obedience to God. The individual enjoyed liberty in the service of God or the public good—not autonomously, as the concept of "liberty" has since come to mean. The meaning of "slavery" as well had to do with an ordering of the soul as much as the lack of a political voice. License was slavery

to one's passions; a thief, a drunkard, a lusting sinner were all deemed slaves in the lexicon of New England ministers, if not more broadly. Any action bringing moral confusion was servility. Liberty therefore implied moral self-assertion. See Shain, *The Myth of American Individualism: The Protestant Origins of American Political Thought* (Princeton, N.J., 1994), 161–66, 301–9.

11. Uncited Virginia column, in *Pennsylvania Gazette*, Apr. 21, 1768.

12. Joseph Warren to Edmund Dana, Mar. 19, 1766, in Richard Frothingham, *Life and Times of Joseph Warren* (New York, 1971 [Boston, 1865]), 20–22.

13. *Boston Gazette*, Oct. 7, 1765.

14. *Boston Gazette*, Oct. 7, 1765.

15. That "disaffection" was expressed officially, too. The Massachusetts Assembly appealed directly to the royal governor: "If His Majesty's American subjects are not to be governed, according to the known stated rules of the constitution, as those in Britain are, it is greatly to be feared that their minds may in time become disaffected." Reported in the *Pennsylvania Gazette*, Nov. 14, 1765.

16. *Pennsylvania Gazette*, Jan. 2, 1766, reporting events of October and November of the previous year.

17. *Boston Gazette*, Nov. 11, 1765.

18. *Pennsylvania Gazette*, Nov. 14, 1765.

19. Friends of America in England noted in the same metaphorical context that trying to stop passage of the Stamp Act was, for them, like attempting to alter nature: "We might as well have hindered the sun's setting. But since it is down, My Friend, and it might be long ere it rises again, let us make as good a night of it as we can. We may still light candles." The American response indicated: "The Sun of Liberty is fast setting, if not down already in the American colonies: But I much fear, instead of the candles you mention being lighted, you will hear the works of darkness." (Letters to the printer of July 11 and Sept. 24, 1765, reprinted in the *Pennsylvania Gazette*, Mar. 6, 1766.)

20. *Pennsylvania Gazette*, Apr. 24, 1766. In fact, while Grenville disputed Pitt and others on Parliament's right to tax the colonies and prepared resolutions to "censure" the American "mobs," the king sought a modified bill, "grieved," in his own words, "at the accounts of America. Where this spirit will end is not to be said . . . it requires more deliberation, candour, and temper than I fear it will meet with." See Thomas, *British Politics and the Stamp Act Crisis*, 164–65.

21. *Boston Gazette*, Jan. 13, 1766.

22. See David Waldstreicher, "Rites of Rebellion, Rites of Assent: Celebrations, Print Culture, and the Origins of American Nationalism," *The Journal of American History* (June 1995), 37–61; regarding the theatricality of American protests, see Peter Shaw, *American Patriots and the Rituals of Revolution* (Cambridge, Mass., 1981).

23. Christopher Gadsden to Capt. Burden, Feb. 20, 1766, in Maier, *From Resistance to Revolution*, 106–7.

24. *Pennsylvania Gazette*, June 5, 1766.

25. Jonathan Mayhew, *The Snare Broken* (Boston, 1766), iv, 7.

26. Ibid., 16–17. The black population of New England (slave and free) in 1775 was approximately 16,000 out of a total population of 660,000, or 2.4 percent. As slaves they worked in the active maritime industry as sailors, elsewhere as common laborers, ditch diggers, and messengers, on farms as cooks, coachmen, and personal attendants, and in artisanal positions as carpenters, blacksmiths, ropemakers, spinners, weavers, and printers. Many were multitalented "handy" men. Some free blacks in late colonial New England agitated for racial equality, such as Lucy Terry Prince, a poet who attempted to persuade the trustees of Williams College to admit her son, and the racially mixed Prince Hall, who sought admission to the all-white Freemasons and eventually set up the first African-American lodge. See Greene, *The Negro in Colonial New England*, 290–334.

27. Mayhew, *The Snare Broken*, 20–21.

28. Ibid., 21–25.

29. Ibid., 32–35.

30. Townshend cited in Ramsay, *The History of the American Revolution*, 1:54; "Sketch of a Declaration . . . against Breaking the Non-Importation Agreement," in the *Pennsylvania Gazette*, June 28, 1770; Washington to George Mason, Apr. 5, 1769, *Papers of George Washington*, Colonial Series, 8:178.

31. *Boston Gazette*, Dec. 19, 1757. See also discussion of the tension between the colonial militia tradition and British military professionalism in Daniel Boorstin, *The Americans: The Colonial Experience* (New York, 1958), 352–72, and Charles Royster, *A Revolutionary People at War: The Continental Army and American Character* (Chapel Hill, N.C., 1979), 35.

32. *Boston Gazette*, Feb. 6, 1769; *South-Carolina Gazette*, Apr. 13, 1769; address presented by Boston selectmen to Governor Francis Bernard on Feb. 27, 1769, in *Pennsylvania Gazette*, Mar. 16, 1769; *Autobiography of Benjamin Rush*, ed. George W. Corner (Princeton, N.J., 1948), 139.

33. *Boston Gazette*, Mar. 12, 1770.

34. Hatch, *The Sacred Cause of Liberty*, 91–93, 106; Edmund S. Morgan, *The Challenge of the American Revolution* (New York, 1976), chap. 4.

35. *Boston Gazette*, Mar. 12, 1770.

36. *Boston Gazette*, Mar. 12, 1770.

37. Special supplement to the *Boston Gazette*, June 25, 1770.

38. *Boston Gazette*, July 9, 1770.

39. Samuel Adams to Franklin, July 13, 1770, *Papers of Benjamin Franklin*, 17:186–93.

40. "The Rise and Present State of Our Misunderstanding," in *The London Chronicle*, Nov. 6–8, 1770, *Papers of Benjamin Franklin* 17:268–73. On the Anglo-American language of affection, reciprocal duties, and the body metaphor, see Yazawa, *From Colonies to Commonwealth*, esp. chaps. 1 & 5. Gordon Wood's examination combines the familial metaphor with contractual imagery; both personalized the relationship between England and her colonies, while the contract allowed colonists to justify their resistance on the basis of an essential equality. See Wood, *The Radicalism of the American Revolution*, 162–67.

41. *Boston Gazette*, Feb. 18, 1771; Letter to Clerk of Council, June 21, 1770, in *Documents of the American Revolution, 1770–1783*, vol. 2, ed. K. G. Davies (Shannon, Ireland, 1972), 110–17.

42. *Orations Delivered at the Request of the Inhabitants of the Town of Boston to Commemorate the Evening of the Fifth of March, 1770* (Boston, 1785), 7–16.

43. Ibid., 17–24.

44. Ibid., 24–28.

45. *Boston Gazette*, Mar. 9, 1772. On Massachusetts lanterns, or lanthorns, see David Hackett Fischer, *Paul Revere's Ride* (New York, 1994), 99.

46. *Pennsylvania Gazette*, May 24, 1770.

47. *Pennsylvania Gazette*, Apr. 19, 1770.

48. *Pennsylvania Gazette*, June 14, 1770.

49. "The Rise and Present State of Our Misunderstanding," Nov. 6–8, 1770, *Papers of Benjamin Franklin*, 17:273.

50. *Boston Gazette*, May 20, 1771.

51. Franklin to Massachusetts House of Representatives, July 7, 1773, *Papers of Benjamin Franklin*, 20:282–83. This turn in Franklin's posture was noted in later years by the first major chronicler of the Revolution, South Carolinian David Ramsay (1749–1815), who wrote that

Franklin "loved peace, and the extension of human happiness." Endeavoring to secure "the unity of the empire" while reserving for the colonies the right of internal self-government, he labored long, Ramsay explained, to prevent war, though the intransigent and misdirected British "abused" the diplomat. See Ramsay, *History of the American Revolution*, 1:160, 168.

52. This is not to minimize the effect of the change in status that the Revolution brought to mechanics. Once viewed uniformly as a lower order of society, they came to be regarded as the vanguard of resistance, men sacrificing for the public good—also "shock troops" employed by the elite. See Howard B. Rock, " 'All Her Sons Join as One Social Band': New York City's Artisanal Societies in the Early Republic," in Howard B. Rock, Paul A. Gilje, and Robert Asher, eds., *American Artisans: Crafting Social Identity, 1750–1850* (Baltimore, 1995), xii–xiv. On mechanics' values and political goals more generally, see Gary B. Nash, "Artisans and Politics in Eighteenth-Century Philadelphia," in Nash, *Race, Class, and Politics: Essays on American Colonial and Revolutionary Society* (Urbana, Ill., 1986), 243–67.

53. Benjamin Woods Labaree, *The Boston Tea Party* (New York, 1964); Wesley S. Griswold, *The Night the Revolution Began* (Brattleboro, Vt., 1972), 96; Davidson, *Propaganda and the American Revolution*, 65–82.

54. *Diary and Autobiography of John Adams*, ed. L. H. Butterfield (Cambridge, Mass., 1961), 2:85–86.

55. *Autobiography of Benjamin Rush*, 89.

56. The *Boston Gazette* on Mar. 2, 1772, boasted: "Liberty has taken deep root in America, and cannot be eradicated by all the Tories in the universe. . . . The union of the provinces is the great hinge on which our liberties turn, and the ease with which these united provinces can at any time be formed into an invincible commonwealth, is now well understood."

57. Richard D. Brown, *Revolutionary Politics in Massachusetts: The Boston Committee of Correspondence and the Towns, 1772–1774* (Cambridge, Mass., 1970), esp. chaps. 3, 6, & 7. Letter from Boston Committee of Correspondence to Salem, May 12, 1774, illustration opposite p. 95. The Committee was in contact with comparable groups as distant as Charleston, South Carolina. (Ibid., 180–81.)

58. Jefferson later claimed that the Virginia Committee of Correspondence predated that of Massachusetts, although it was Samuel Adams's correspondent Richard Henry Lee who appeared most active in its formation. See Dumas Malone, *Jefferson the Virginian* (Boston, 1948), 170–71.

59. Samuel Sherwood, *A Sermon Containing Scriptural Instructions to Civil Rulers . . .* (New Haven, Conn., 1774), 79.

60. June 11, 1774, in *The Papers of William Livingston*, ed. Carl E. Prince (Trenton, N.J., 1979), 1:16–19.

61. *South-Carolina Gazette*, Dec. 19, 1774.

62. Nov. 21, 1774, in Frothingham, *Life and Times of Joseph Warren*, 394.

63. Ward to Dickinson, Dec. 14, 1774; Dickinson to Lee, Oct. 27, 1774, in *Letters of Delegates to the Continental Congress*, ed. Paul Smith (Washington, D.C., 1976–  ), 1:269, 250.

64. *Diary and Autobiography of John Adams*, Sept. 3, 1774.

65. William Wirt Henry, *Patrick Henry: Life, Correspondence and Speeches* (New York, 1891), 1:257–68.

66. Ibid.; Henry S. Randall, *Life of Thomas Jefferson* (New York, 1858), 1:101–2.

67. Richard Sill to Nathan Hale, Mar. 5, 1775, in George Dudley Seymour, *Documentary Life of Nathan Hale* (New Haven, Conn., 1941), 31; Fischer, *Paul Revere's Ride*, 51–52.

68. Fischer, *Paul Revere's Ride*, 69–70, 75.

69. Ibid., 97; Frothingham, *Life and Times of Joseph Warren*, 427–40, 457, 461.

70. Richard D. Brown, *Knowledge Is Power: The Diffusion of Information in Early America, 1700–1865* (New York, 1989), 248–50.

71. Fischer, *Paul Revere's Ride*, 274; *Pennsylvania Gazette*, Apr. 27, 1775.

72. Washington to George William Fairfax, May 31, 1775, *Papers of George Washington, Colonial Series*, 10:367–68.

73. Ward, *The War of the Revolution*, chap. 8.

74. Frothingham, *Life and Times of Joseph Warren*, 513–17, 521–22; John C. Dann, ed., *The Revolution Remembered: Eyewitness Accounts of the War for Independence* (Chicago, 1980), 4; John F. Berens, *Providence and Patriotism in Early America, 1640–1815* (Charlottesville, Va., 1978), 65.

75. *Orations Delivered at the Request of the Inhabitants of the Town of Boston*, 187, 190–92. Another Revolutionary doctor and patriot, David Ramsay, wrote in his 1789 *History of the American Revolution* that Warren "fell a noble sacrifice to a cause which he had espoused from the purest principles." He was "universally beloved and universally regretted," and his "undaunted bravery" on Bunker Hill was in part responsible for subsequent British "respect for Americans intrenched behind works." Ramsay, *History of the American Revolution*, 1:190–91.

76. "Address of Lieut. Geo. Gilmer to the First Independent Company of Albemarle County," June 2, 1775, in *Papers of George Gilmer of Pen Park, 1775–1778, Miscellaneous Papers, 1762–1865, of the Virginia Historical Society* (Richmond, Va., 1887), 72–73, 77–82.

77. Timothy Hancock is of no known relation to the more celebrated patriot John Hancock. His hand-sewn 124-page diary lay undiscovered since the nineteenth century, and remains unpublished and in a private collection. I wish to thank the owner, who graciously loaned it.

78. *South-Carolina Gazette*, Sept. 7, 1775.

79. *Pennsylvania Gazette*, Sept. 20, 1775.

80. *Boston Gazette*, Oct. 7, 1765.

81. *Pennsylvania Gazette*, June 14, 1770.

82. "A Virginia Planter," in *South-Carolina Gazette*, Nov. 14, 1766.

83. William Bartram, *Travels in Georgia and Florida, 1773–1774*, annotated by Francis Harper (Philadelphia, 1943), 141, 160; Helen Gere Cruickshank, ed., *John and William Bartram's America* (New York, 1957), 193; Mercer to Washington, Dec. 18, 1770, *Papers of George Washington*, Colonial Series, 8:419.

84. Ernest Lee Tuveson, *Redeemer Nation: The Idea of America's Millennial Role* (Chicago, 1968), 103–6. Another scholar who has argued persuasively that individual and national salvation were linked in the emergence of America's "civil religion" is Nathan Hatch. See in particular "The Origins of Civil Millennialism in America: New England Clergymen, War with France, and the Revolution," *The William and Mary Quarterly* 31 (1974), 407–30.

85. *Boston Gazette*, Oct. 7, 1765.

86. *Boston Gazette*, Feb. 18, 1771.

87. *Pennsylvania Gazette*, Mar. 29, 1770; *Boston Gazette*, Jan. 8, 1770.

88. *Pennsylvania Gazette*, Dec. 20, 1770.

89. *Orations Delivered at the Request of the Inhabitants of the Town of Boston . . .*, 25.

90. Joseph J. Ellis, *After the Revolution: Profiles of Early American Culture* (New York, 1979), 79–80. "Rising Glory" was the first in what would become a string of epic American verse over the next several decades. Because America possessed continental stature, it seemed to demand a national epic to transmit its glory to posterity. References abound to Homer and Virgil of the ancient world, to Milton of a rising British civilization. To these, America was bound to add brave heroes defending liberty and the ties of family and friendship, a river of achievement coursing through a territory with sublime possibilities. See John P. McWilliams, Jr., *The American Epic: Transforming a Genre, 1770–1860* (Cambridge, 1989).

91. *Boston Gazette*, Nov. 25, 1771.

92. "The Farmer Refuted . . . ," Feb. 1775, *Papers of Alexander Hamilton*, ed. Harold C. Syrett (New York, 1961–87), 1:93–94.

93. Ibid., 152–58.

94. *Essex Gazette* cited in *Pennsylvania Gazette*, Nov. 29, 1775; *Pennsylvania Gazette*, Aug. 9, 1775.

95. See Bernard Bailyn's characterization of Americans' moral example to the European world, in Bailyn, *Ideological Origins*, 160–61.

## 4. THE AMERICAN DREAM: 1776

1. On determinism in nature versus determinism in politics, see Charles A. Miller, *Jefferson and Nature: An Interpretation* (Baltimore, 1988), chap. 5.

2. As Linda Kerber explains, women were expected to regard politics, and certainly the politics of war, as "unsavory." On the political identity of women during the Revolution, see Kerber, *Women of the Republic*, esp. chap. 3.

3. Article identified as Paine's in Daniel Edwin Wheeler, ed., *Life and Writings of Thomas Paine* (New York, 1908), 110–21.

4. On generational aspects of the Revolution, see especially Michael Kammen, *A Season of Youth: The American Revolution and the Historical Imagination* (New York, 1978); Peter Charles Hoffer, *Revolution and Regeneration: Life Cycle and the Historical Vision of the Generation of 1776* (Athens, Ga., 1983); Shaw, *American Patriots and the Rituals of Revolution*.

5. Though not identified as such in the magazine, Irus was an antagonistic beggar in Homer's *Odyssey*, named after a messenger of the gods.

6. This view of nature in Enlightenment thinking is discussed in Miller, *Jefferson and Nature*, chap. 4 and 244–48; Cassirer, *Philosophy of the Enlightenment*, 65–69, 93–96; Gay, *The Enlightenment*, 2:455–61.

7. Jefferson to John Randolph, Aug. 25, 1775, *Papers of Thomas Jefferson*, 1:241–42. Randolph's reply was generous: "Tho we *may politically* differ in Sentiments, yet I see no Reason why *privately* we may not cherish the same Esteem for each other which formerly I believe Subsisted between us." Randolph to Jefferson, Aug. 31, 1775, in ibid., 244.

8. Richard Sennett has written in this vein that, in the Enlightenment understanding, public behavior was meant to exist in equilibrium with private emotions. "While man *made* himself in public, he *realized* his nature in the private realm. . . . Together, public and private created what would today be called a 'universe' of social relations." (Sennett, *The Fall of Public Man: On the Social Psychology of Capitalism* [New York, 1977], 18–19.) In the language of sentiment and sympathy, this means that one's self-realization entailed embracing sensibility on an individual level and then extending personal feelings of benevolence to add to the social good. It also means that one's natural self was obliged to take on a social or artificial identity. Jefferson's consciousness—his presumed intimacy with Randolph cast as a public appeal— should be viewed in this context. See also Thomas Schlereth, *The Cosmopolitan Ideal in Enlightenment Thought* (Notre Dame, Ind., 1977).

9. Gay, *The Enlightenment*, 1:123–24.

10. Sigmund Freud, *On Dreams*, trans. James Strachey (New York, 1952 [1901]), 89–104.

11. See definition of *humanitas* given in Gay, *The Enlightenment*, 1:107–8.

12. James H. Kettner, *The Development of American Citizenship, 1608–1870* (Chapel Hill, N.C., 1978), 173–84.

13. See especially Royster, *A Revolutionary People at War*, chaps. 1 & 2.

14. Seymour, *Documentary Life of Nathan Hale*, xxv–xxxii, 307–14, 324–25.

15. *The Pennsylvania Magazine*, March 1776. There seems here to be influence from John Locke's rational understanding of dreams as the "loose and incoherent manner of thinking" within a mind of sensation and reflection that cannot invent ideas beyond what exists in the waking person's mind. See Locke, *An Essay Concerning Human Understanding*, Book 2, chaps. 1 & 19. Curiously, two hundred years after Locke, Freud would write: "One day I discovered to my great astonishment that the view of dreams which came nearest to the truth was not the medical but the popular one, half involved though it still was in superstition." See Freud, *On Dreams*, 15.

16. *The Pennsylvania Magazine*, Mar. 1776.

17. Oct. 3, 1778, *Papers of Henry Laurens*, ed. Philip M. Hamer (Columbia, S.C., 1968– ), 14:379–81.

18. *Autobiography of Benjamin Rush*, 85–86.

19. *The United States Magazine*, Mar. 1779.

20. *Common Sense*, in *Thomas Paine: Collected Writings* (New York, 1995), 27.

21. Ibid., 5–6, 20–24, 32.

22. Josiah Quincy, Sr., to Franklin, Mar. 25, 1775, *Papers of Benjamin Franklin*, 22:6. On the younger Quincy's relationship with Franklin in London, see Carl Van Doren, *Benjamin Franklin* (New York, 1938), chap. 18.

23. *Common Sense*, 28–29, 42. Returning to the metaphor of maturation in "The American Crisis III," Paine would pose rhetorically on the second anniversary of Lexington and Concord: "Is it the interest of a man to be a boy all his life?" (Apr. 19, 1777, in *Thomas Paine: Collected Writings*, 122.)

24. *Common Sense*, 19, 23, 50–53.

25. E. Stanly Godbold, Jr., and Robert H. Woody, *Christopher Gadsden and the American Revolution* (Knoxville, Tenn., 1982), 149–51.

26. Ibid., 61, 95, 112–14.

27. Entries of Mar. 1 & 4, 1776, *Diary and Autobiography of John Adams*, 2:235–36.

28. Hodgkins to wife, Sept. 30, 1776; Clinton to Peter Tappen, Sept. 21, 1776, in Henry P. Johnston, *The Battle of Harlem Heights* (New York, 1897; rept. 1970), 144–45, 172–74; Hancock diary, entry of July 21, 1776.

29. *The Pennsylvania Magazine*, Apr. 1776.

30. Ibid.; Bartlett to John Langdon (Portsmouth, N.H., merchant), July 1, 1776, *The Papers of Josiah Bartlett*, ed. Frank C. Mevers (Hanover, N.H., 1979), 83–84.

31. Page to Jefferson, Apr. 6, 1776, *Papers of Thomas Jefferson*, 1:287.

32. *Autobiography of Benjamin Rush*, 148.

33. Malone, *Jefferson the Virginian*, 219.

34. *Papers of Benjamin Franklin*, 22:480–81.

35. Apr. 29, 1776, *Papers of Henry Laurens*, 11:207–8.

36. Maier, *American Scripture*, 157, 159.

37. In *American Scripture*, Pauline Maier updates Carl L. Becker's 1922 classic, *The Declaration of Independence*, arguing that the Declaration neither expressed a political philosophy unique to Jefferson (he can best be described as its draftsman) nor sprang forth suddenly: state and local declarations of independence or instructions to delegates to embrace independence were being produced before Jefferson lifted his quill pen. Jefferson's striking cadences gave the document force, but the language was the language of the day. It reflected the tradition of the English Declaration of Rights, dating to the seventeenth century (which provided a context for ending an old regime), and it incorporated meanings much in vogue

among the patriot elite in 1776. Maier's analysis only errs in diminishing Jefferson's contributions relative to the Congress, which served as his editor.

38. May, *The Enlightenment in America*, 7–9, 38; Becker, *The Declaration of Independence*, 53–58.

39. John Locke, *An Essay Concerning Human Understanding* (London, 1735), 1:215–19. I thank Richard D. Brown for providing photocopies of the 1735 edition.

40. Extracted from sections of Aristotle's *Rhetoric* and *Nicomachean Ethics*, in V. J. McGill, *The Idea of Happiness* (New York, 1967), 13–35. Aristotle can be interpreted as "Lockean" and "Jeffersonian" insofar as he adds to his definition of happiness the politically resonant "secure enjoyment of the maximum of pleasure; or as a good condition of property and body." His ideal government privileged aristocratic over democratic virtue only until the time when citizens became wise and virtuous enough to warrant self-rule. His "pleasure" was not tinged with any hedonist potential (as the notion of pleasure would be in the eighteenth century) but merely associated sensations with the perfectibility of an activity or human faculty.

41. Locke, *Essay Concerning Human Understanding*, 217–19.

42. Laurence Sterne, *The Sermons of Mr. Yorick* (Oxford, 1927), 1:3. Jefferson apparently owned several editions of Sterne's *Sermons* over the course of his life, separately and as a part of Sterne's complete works. For those volumes listed in Jefferson's 1815 library catalogue, see E. Millicent Sowerby, *Catalogue of the Library of Thomas Jefferson* (Washington, D.C., 1952–59), 2:138, 4:445–46. George Washington as well owned an early edition of Sterne's *Sermons* (London, 1761); see *Papers of George Washington*, Colonial Series, 7:346; Jefferson to Peter Carr, Aug. 10, 1787, *Papers of Thomas Jefferson*, 12:15; Burstein, *The Inner Jefferson*, 54–55. Note, too, that Henry Mackenzie composed a long poem published in 1771, titled "The Pursuits of Happiness," which dealt with individual morality. One portion reads:

> If to be happy, mortals must be good,
> We blindly err, the term's misunderstood.
> To be happy, man must court content,
> And bless the gracious lot by fortune sent.

This definition of happiness as placid contentment is not profound, and there is no reason to think that Jefferson or the American Revolutionary generation gave particular attention to Mackenzie's curiously titled poem (it may not even have been published in America before the Revolution), though his Man of Feeling was well known. See Henry Mackenzie, *The Pursuits of Happiness* (New York, 1801).

43. *The Papers of George Mason*, ed. Robert A. Rutland (Chapel Hill, N.C., 1970), 1:287. Jefferson had access to Mason's document—if it had not been placed in his hand, he would have seen either an early version in the *Pennsylvania Evening Post* on June 6 or, more likely, its publication in the *Pennsylvania Gazette* on June 12, the day after the Committee of Five was directed by Congress to compose the Declaration. See Maier, *American Scripture*, 268 n59.

44. This view is also espoused in Adrienne Koch, *Power, Morals, and the Founding Fathers: Essays in the Interpretation of the American Enlightenment* (Ithaca, N.Y., 1961), chap. 3.

45. *Virginia Gazette*, Oct. 18, 1776.

46. Print deposited at the Massachusetts Historical Society, and as an illustration in *Papers of John Adams*, ed. Robert J. Taylor et al. (Cambridge, Mass., 1977–    ), 4:346.

47. John Adams to Abigail Adams, July 3, 1776, *Adams Family Correspondence*, ed. L. H. Butterfield (Cambridge, Mass., 1963), 2:30–31.

48. Howard Mumford Jones, *The Pursuit of Happiness* (Cambridge, Mass., 1953), 23–25.

49. *Common Sense*, in *Thomas Paine: Collected Writings*, 28–29, 36–37.

50. On feminine symbolism and the land, see Annette Kolodny, *The Lay of the Land: Metaphor as Experience and History in American Life and Letters* (Chapel Hill, N.C., 1975).

51. Hancock diary, entry of Oct. 20, 1776.

52. Buel and Buel, *The Way of Duty*, 132, 134, 147.

53. John Trumbull, *M'Fingal*, in Edwin T. Bowden, ed., *The Satiric Poems of John Trumbull* (Austin, Tex., 1962), 105.

54. Maier, *American Scripture*, 78, 83–84; *Virginia Gazette*, Aug. 24, 1776.

55. For an unsympathetic view of Jefferson's motives relative to slavery at the time of the Declaration and through the Revolution, see Paul Finkelman, *Slavery and the Founders: Race and Liberty in the Age of Jefferson* (Armonk, N.Y., 1996), chap. 5.

## 5. ACTUATED BY A VIGILANT AND MANLY SPIRIT: 1777–88

1. Ebenezer Fletcher, *The Narrative of Ebenezer Fletcher, A Soldier of the Revolution* (Freeport, N.Y., 1970 [1866]). The captivity narrative was a familiar genre in early America, dating to the seventeenth century, and was generally meant to strengthen the moral resolve of individuals and uphold the values of Anglo-American civilization.

2. Ibid. For portrayals of loyalist arrogance, see Robert M. Calhoun, "The Reintegration of Loyalists and the Disaffected," in Jack P. Greene, ed., *The American Revolution: Its Character and Limits* (New York, 1987), 51–74.

3. Michael A. Bellesilles, *Revolutionary Outlaws: Ethan Allen and the Struggle for Independence on the Early American Frontier* (Charlottesville, Va., 1993), 195.

4. Ibid., 129, 150–55.

5. Ibid. Ethan Allen's rugged sense of independence and devotion to his fellows was tested in other ways as well during the war. He negotiated with a tentative Continental Congress, tying Vermont's support for the war to its lawful separation from the state of New York. Amid these negotiations he slyly left the door open to a reconciliation with his sworn enemy, entertaining (one cannot be sure how seriously) the prospect of securing Vermont's independence from New York as a British protectorate. (See ibid., 195–98.) Even before Allen highlighted his own heroism and spread propaganda for the war effort, his exploits were used by others. John Leacock of the Philadelphia Sons of Liberty published a play in May 1776 entitled *The Fall of British Tyranny*, featuring the death of Joseph Warren and the separate, virtuous efforts of Washington and Allen. Other American characters in the play were given the desirable names "Dick Rifle," "Peter Buckstail," and "Mr. Freeman," while the British villains were "Lord Kidnapper" (Lord Dunmore, who dissolved the Virginia House of Burgesses in 1773, removed gunpowder from storehouses, and incited slaves to desert plantations), "Admiral Elbow Room" (General Howe), and "Mr. Caper" (General Burgoyne). See Kenneth Silverman, *A Cultural History of the American Revolution* (New York, 1987), 310–12.

6. Henry to R. H. Lee, June 18, 1778, cited in Royster, *A Revolutionary People at War*, 158.

7. *The United States Magazine*, Jan. 1779.

8. *Pennsylvania Gazette*, June 20 & Feb. 14, 1781.

9. *Virginia Gazette*, Jan. 17, 1777. Recall almost identical remarks early in the French and Indian War by the Reverend Samuel Davies, who had urged volunteers to practice religion and to avoid "the Fury of enflamed Passions, broke loose from the Government of Reason," and maintain "calm, deliberate, rational Courage; a steady, judicious, thoughtful Fortitude, the Courage of a Man, and not a Tyger." See Davies, *Religion and Patriotism the Constituents of a Good Soldier*, 3–5.

10. *Virginia Gazette*, Jan. 17, 1777; Mackenzie, *The Man of Feeling*, 86–101.

11. Royster, *A Revolutionary People at War*, 235.

12. Ibid., 227–28, 235–37.

13. Ibid., 143.

14. Rush, *Autobiography*, 151.

15. Royster, *A Revolutionary People at War*, 289–94.

16. Ramsay, *History of the American Revolution*, 2:642–43.

17. Washington to Governor Benjamin Harrison, June 12, 1783, text in *Virginia Gazette*, July 5, 1783; also in *The Writings of George Washington*, ed. Worthington Chauncey Ford (New York, 1891), 10:254–65. A similar commentary on the age is given by Connecticut's Timothy Dwight in *A Valedictory Address* (New Haven, Conn., 1776), that "every species of knowledge, natural and moral, is arrived at a state of perfection, which the world never before saw." (Cited in Melvin Yazawa, "Creating a Republican Citizenry," in Greene, ed., *The American Revolution: Its Character and Limits*, 291–92.)

18. Silverman, *A Cultural History of the American Revolution*, 425; characterization of Peale made by Gouverneur Morris to Alexander Hamilton (see *The Selected Papers of Charles Willson Peale and His Family*, ed. Lillian B. Miller [New Haven, Conn., 1983–    ], 1:397–98); Ellis, *After the Revolution*, 43–44, 65, describing how the columned arch caught fire and disintegrated before the day of celebration.

19. Lillian B. Miller, "Charles Willson Peale as History Painter," in Lillian B. Miller and David C. Ward, eds., *New Perspectives on Charles Willson Peale* (Pittsburgh, 1991); John E. Ferling, *The First of Men: A Life of George Washington* (Knoxville, Tenn., 1988), 82–83; John Adams to Abigail Adams, Aug. 21, 1776, *Adams Family Correspondence*, 2:103–4.

20. *Pennsylvania Gazette*, July 16, 1783. This is what Terence Martin refers to when he describes "the power and purity of genesis" in establishing that America was conscious of its own conception and birth. As John Quincy Adams would later pronounce, the United States had *spoken* itself into existence as a nation. See Martin, *Parables of Possibility: The American Need for Beginnings* (New York, 1995), 36–37, 43.

21. *Pennsylvania Gazette*, July 16, 1783.

22. "The Trifler, No. V," *Columbian Magazine*, Sept. 1787. One scholar has contended that the "spread-eagle" patriotism of the *Columbian Magazine*, a strident vehicle of post-Revolutionary literary nationalism, actually reflected more self-doubt than certitude in so loudly insisting on America's moral superiority and rising glory. See Lawrence J. Friedman, *Inventors of the Promised Land* (New York, 1975), chap. 1. For a balanced view of this question, see Waldstreicher, *In the Midst of Perpetual Fetes*, chap. 2.

23. Robert A. Gross, *The Minutemen and Their World* (New York, 1976), 137–38, 167–68.

24. *Pennsylvania Gazette*, July 23, 1783.

25. Ezra Stiles, *The UNITED STATES Elevated to GLORY and HONOUR* (Worcester, Mass., 1785 [1783]), 9, 59.

26. Ibid., 60–61.

27. Ibid., 65–68, 96.

28. Rush to Charles Nisbet, Dec. 5, 1783, *Letters of Benjamin Rush*, ed. L. H. Butterfield (Princeton, N.J., 1951), 1:315–16.

29. John Adams to Abigail Adams, Aug. 14, 1776, *Adams Family Correspondence*, 96–97. For the reverse of the seal, Jefferson proposed adding to his biblical scene the two Saxon leaders "from whom We claim the Honour of being descended and whose Political Principles and Form of Government We have assumed." To Jefferson, the Saxons had introduced a particularly relevant notion of popular liberty. In his bold pamphlet of 1774, *A Summary View of the Rights of British America*, he claimed that this early Germanic people had migrated to England without forfeiting their natural right to choose the form of government which best suited them.

30. *Columbian Magazine*, Sept. & Oct. 1786. The 1766 watercolor by Thomas Davies, *Niagara Falls from Above*, features a perched and a soaring bald eagle, offering the combined symbols of promise and triumph. See Elizabeth McKinsey, *Niagara Falls: Icon of the American Sublime* (Cambridge, 1985), 89–90 and Figure 7.

31. *Columbian Magazine*, Oct. 1786.

32. *Pennsylvania Gazette*, Sept. 20, 1775.

33. The eagle would come to be attached to America's peace-extending, nation-building "flight" across the Mississippi with the Lewis and Clark expedition of 1804–6. The governor of Kentucky proclaimed as the expedition was underway that the westward movement of America represented the extension of freedom. He observed that "as the eagle in fable was the bird of Jove, so our eagle of American freedom, is the bird of the living God." He implored God to provide "guardian care" for its "newly extended flight." (Address of Nov. 6, 1804, printed in the Washington, D.C., newspaper *National Intelligencer*, Dec. 3, 1804.)

34. Bercovitch, *American Jeremiad*, 124. Bercovitch adds the 1794 comment of David Austin, disciple of the evangelical Jonathan Edwards, who found a more apt reference in Revelation 12:14: "If any should be disposed to ask what has become of the eagle, on whose wings the persecuted woman was borne into the American wilderness, may it not be answered, that she hath taken her station upon the Civil Seal of the United States?"

35. Here, for example, is Samuel Osgood, a member of the Confederation Congress from Massachusetts, to a fellow congressman: "I apprehend we have a much fairer Opportunity now, to obtain a Just Decision of the Extent of our Country [meaning Massachusetts], than it was possible for us to have, whilst under the irresistable Controul of a Power that could say, thus far shall ye extend & no farther." See Osgood to John Lowell, Nov. 14, 1782, *Letters of Delegates to Congress*, 19:383–84.

36. Merrill Jensen, *The Articles of Confederation: An Interpretation of the Social-Constitutional History of the American Revolution, 1774–1781* (Madison, Wis., 1940), chap. 4; Peter S. Onuf, *The Origins of the Federal Republic* (Philadelphia, 1983), quote at 178–79; David P. Szatmary, *Shays' Rebellion: The Making of an Agrarian Insurrection* (Amherst, Mass., 1980). The local context of the rebellion is explored in Robert A. Gross, ed., *In Debt to Shays: The Bicentennial of an Agrarian Rebellion* (Charlottesville, Va., 1993).

37. Rachel N. Klein, *Unification of a Slave State: The Rise of the Planter Class in the South Carolina Backcountry, 1760–1808* (Chapel Hill, N.C., 1990), 104–7.

38. Ibid., 109–30.

39. Jeremy Belknap to Ebenezer Hazard, March 3, 1784, *Belknap Papers*, 5th Series (Boston: Massachusetts Historical Society, 1877), 308–15.

40. Ibid. Recall the allusion to John Adams's later reflection on the Revolution in his 1818 letter to Hezekiah Niles: "Thirteen clocks were made to strike together—a perfection of mechanism, which no artist had ever before effected."

41. Ibid. Northerners, Thomas Jefferson observed at this time, were "sober," industrious, but "chicaning," his fellow Southerners "candid," yet also "fiery" and "indolent." Americans of this period routinely made a study of themselves, cataloguing similarities and differences among their parts. When distracted from the call to justify their moral superiority over Europe, they were prone to dissecting their collective conscience and questioning whether they possessed republican virtue. European writers may have expressed dismay with Americans' hypocrisy in propounding a concept of liberty to the world while retaining slaves at home, but few regarded the institution as a dominant characteristic of the American republic. See Jefferson to the Marquis de Chastellux, Sept. 2, 1785, *Papers of Thomas Jefferson*, 8:468, and Jack P. Greene, *The Intellectual Construction of America: Exceptionalism and Identity from 1492 to 1800* (Chapel Hill, N.C., 1993), 154–57.

42. Belknap to Hazard, March 9, 1786, *Belknap Papers*, 5th Series, 431.

43. Washington to Benjamin Harrison, Jan. 18, 1784, *Writings of Washington*, ed. John C. Fitzpatrick (Washington, D.C., 1931–41), 27:305–6.

44. *Pennsylvania Gazette*, Jan. 25, 1786.

45. *Pennsylvania Gazette*, Jan. 18, 1786.

46. See Peter S. Onuf, *Statehood and Union: A History of the Northwest Ordinance* (Bloomington, Ind., 1987).

47. Elizur Goodrich, *The Principles of CIVIL UNION and HAPPINESS considered and recommended* (Hartford, Conn., 1787), 5–7, 19–22.

48. Gaillard Hunt and James Brown Scott, eds., *The Debates in the Federal Convention of 1787 Which Framed the Constitution of the United States of America* (New York, 1920), 325–26, 419. Based on James Madison's note taking.

49. Ibid., xci, 130–31.

50. Ibid., 107–8, 351–54.

51. Federalist #57, in *The Federalist Papers*, ed. Clinton Rossiter (New York, 1961), 351, 353. In line with these observations, the eminently practical Madison hoped to persuade the distrustful with a "candid review." He bade them to reason as he did, that an evenly composed, equalizing federal government could control excess. He employed stabilizing phrases like *happy combination* and *aggregate interests*, and morally sensitive terms like *justice, consciousness, communication, rights*, and, most particularly, *enlightened views and virtuous sentiments*—as well as *zeal*—to make his points. See Federalist #10, in ibid., 81–84.

52. Rush to Belknap, Feb. 28, 1788, *Belknap Papers*, 398; see also Wood, *Creation of the American Republic*, 426.

53. Ibid., 524.

54. Montesquieu, *The Spirit of the Laws*, 22, 35–36.

55. James Otis, "The Rights of the British Colonies Asserted and Proved," in Bailyn, ed., *Pamphlets of the American Revolution*, 424; Gage to Viscount Barrington, Aug. 5, 1772, cited in Fischer, *Paul Revere's Ride*, 39; Potter, *The Liberty We Seek*, chap. 2.

56. Willi Paul Adams, *The First American Constitutions: Republican Ideology and the Making of the State Constitutions in the Revolutionary Era* (Chapel Hill, N.C., 1980), 107.

57. John Adams, "Letters from a Distinguished American," Letter #5, published Sept. 11, 1782, and Letter #12, undated but written the same year, for *Parker's General Advertiser and Morning Intelligencer*, in James H. Hutson, ed., *Letters from a Distinguished American: Twelve Essays by John Adams on American Foreign Policy, 1780* (Washington, D.C.: Library of Congress, 1978), 19–20, 48.

58. George Mason to George Mason, Jr., June 1, 1787, *The Papers of George Mason*, 3:892.

59. Herbert J. Storing, ed., *The Complete Anti-Federalist* (Chicago, 1981), 2:214–53.

60. Ibid., 234, 254–68. For a fuller exposition of the character of antifederalism, see Saul Cornell, *The Other Founders: Anti-Federalism and the Dissenting Tradition in America, 1788–1828* (Chapel Hill, N.C., 1999), esp. chaps. 3 & 4. I thank Professor Cornell for bringing to my attention elements of sentiment and sympathy in the antifederalists' language.

61. See Terence Ball's discussion of "Brutus" in "A Republic—If You Can Keep It," in Terence Ball and J. G. A. Pocock, eds., *Conceptual Change and the Constitution* (Lawrence, Kans., 1988), 137–64.

62. Russell L. Hanson, " 'Commons' and 'Commonwealth' at the American Founding: Democratic Republicanism as the New American Hybrid," in ibid., 165–93. On the enduring changes in public life understandable through the expanding meanings of words like *democracy, industry, class, art*, and *culture*, see Raymond Williams, *Culture and Society, 1780–1950* (New York, 1958).

63. "A Short Enquiry, how far the Democratic Governments of America have sprung from an affection for Democracy," *Columbian Magazine*, Sept. 1787.

64. Federalist #10, in Rossiter, ed., *The Federalist Papers*, 81–84.

65. Rush to David Ramsay, Mar. or Apr. 1788; to John Adams, Jan. 22, 1789, *Letters of Benjamin Rush*, 2:453–55, 498–99.

66. Banning, *The Jeffersonian Persuasion*, chap. 2. Gordon Wood has proposed that under the pressure of debate during those four months in convention, "scattered strands of Whig

thought, used disconnectedly for years but never comprehended as a whole, were picked up and brought together by the Federalists and woven into a new intellectual fabric, a new explanation of politics, of . . . beauty and symmetry." See Wood, *Creation of the American Republic*, 14–41, 65–81, quote at 524.

67. Finkelman, *Slavery and the Founders*, chap. 1.

68. The old virtuoso Benjamin Franklin had closed the Constitutional Convention by commenting on the chair in which George Washington, nominal president of the convention, was sitting. A sun was painted on the back of the chair, and Franklin said that he had been gazing at the motif for months "amid the vicissitudes of my hopes and fears" before concluding that it was a rising and not a setting sun. See Hunt and Scott, eds., *Debates in the Federal Convention*, 583.

69. George Everett Hastings, *The Life and Works of Francis Hopkinson* (Chicago, 1926), 406–8; Silverman, *A Cultural History of the American Revolution*, 582–85.

70. Rush to Elias Boudinot, *Letters of Benjamin Rush*, 1:471.

71. Silverman, *A Cultural History of the American Revolution*, 581–82, 585–87. On the relevance of federalist and antifederalist language to the patriotic celebrations of the 1780s, see Waldstreicher, *In the Midst of Perpetual Fetes*, 85–107.

72. Dennis E. Brown, *Grammar and Good Taste: Reforming the American Language* (New Haven, Conn., 1983), 7–18. The French official of 1789 was unknowingly concurring with a proposal which then-diplomat John Adams had addressed to the Continental Congress in 1780. (Ibid., 17.)

73. Jefferson to Martha Jefferson, March 28, 1787, *The Family Letters of Thomas Jefferson*, ed. Edwin Morris Betts and James Adam Bear, Jr. (Columbia, Mo., 1966), 35.

74. Noah Webster, "On the Education of Youth in America" [1790 text], in Frederick Rudolph, ed., *Essays on Education in the Early Republic* (Cambridge, Mass., 1965), 41–77.

75. *M'Fingal*, in Bowden, ed., *The Satiric Poems of John Trumbull*, 108–10.

76. Ibid., 183–88.

77. Ibid., 201–10.

78. Mar. 6, 1780, and Mar. 5, 1783, *Orations Delivered at the Request of the Inhabitants of the Town of Boston*, 142, 177–82. It was at the Boston town meeting on the day of Welsh's oration that the Fourth of July format was agreed to, evidently because the end of the war signified the triumph of the reason- and passion-filled Declaration; this then enabled the outrage associated with the bloody Fifth of March to recede into a dimmer light on the stage of providential history. See James Spear Loring, *The Hundred Boston Orators* (Boston, 1856), 156.

79. *Orations Delivered at the Request of the Inhabitants of the Town of Boston*, 177–82.

80. Stiles, *The UNITED STATES Elevated to GLORY and HONOUR*, 12–13.

81. Ibid., 44, 50–53, 57–58, 68.

82. Crèvecoeur, *Letters from an American Farmer*, 21–25.

83. Ibid., 40–41.

84. Ibid., 42–43.

85. Ibid., 25–35.

86. Ibid., 40–48.

87. Ibid., 46–47, 184.

88. Ibid., 5–6.

89. Leo Marx, *The Machine in the Garden: Technology and the Pastoral Ideal in America* (New York, 1964), 117.

90. *Notes on Virginia*, 64–65. Although many erudite Americans, like Crèvecoeur, ad-

mired Raynal's work, recognizing the author as a staunch lover of liberty and critic of the enslavement of Africans, Raynal irritated Jefferson for his unsubstantiated assertion that the human species had degenerated physically in the New World. This is made plain in the *Notes*.

91. Ibid., 84–85.

92. Ibid., 58–60, 87, 138–43. Jefferson's distinction between blacks' and Indians' potential for assimilation partook of the historical association of skin pigmentation and prejudice and was influenced as well by the relative populations of the two groups. During the eighteenth century, color became a factor in describing Native Americans, as their dwindling numbers reduced their power to fend off settlement. Previously regarded almost entirely in terms of their condition of life, as redeemable "savages," they became darker in colonial writers' depictions (and their apparent designs on civilized society darker, too) as their "tawny" or "copper" complexion removed them from the mainstream. The New England missionary and founder of Dartmouth College, Eleazar Wheelock, referred to his Indian students as "black." Nevertheless, in the vocabulary of the time, their potential for darkness did not make it impossible for them to "whiten," nor did it make them so unattractive as to cause reconsideration of the colonists' goal of assimilating the natives by educating them, "improving" the character of their society and, while acknowledging that they enjoyed a kind of primitive liberty, preparing them over time to enjoy a more advanced form of political happiness. See Alden T. Vaughan, "From White Man to Redskin: Changing Anglo-American Perceptions of the American Indian," in Vaughan, *Roots of American Racism: Essays on the Colonial Experience* (New York, 1995); James Axtell, *After Columbus: Essays on the Ethno-History of Colonial North America* (New York, 1988); Bernard W. Sheehan, *Seeds of Extinction: Jeffersonian Philanthropy and the American Indian* (Chapel Hill, N.C., 1973). For an excellent analysis of Jefferson's scientific racism in the context of the compromises needed for ratification of the U.S. Constitution, see Alexander O. Boulton, "The American Paradox: Jeffersonian Equality and Racial Science," *American Quarterly* 47 (Sept. 1995): 467–92. Few who were intimately acquainted with slavery went as far as Jefferson in attempting to deal with the historically potent emotions associated with the institution. Quite typical was the reserved humanity of Henry Laurens, who sympathized with the plight of his and his countrymen's slaves but was resigned to the perpetuation of slavery. He comforted himself by making note of his own expressions of benevolence, because he could not imagine the South awakening to a completely free society. Laurens remained convinced that blacks' inferiority made their state of subordination "insurmountable." See Gregory D. Massey, "The Limits of Antislavery Thought in the Revolutionary Lower South: John Laurens and Henry Laurens," *The Journal of Southern History* 63 (Aug. 1997): 495–530.

93. Peter S. Onuf, " 'To Declare Them a Free and Independent People': Race, Slavery, and National Identity in Jefferson's Thought," Presidential Address, Society for Historians of the Early American Republic, College Park, Pa., July 19, 1997.

94. *Notes on Virginia*, 164–65. "While we have land to labour then," Jefferson wrote further, "let us never wish to see our citizens occupied at a work-bench." Cities, he felt, with their crowded factories, reflected moral principles that were un-American, that sapped the nation's healthful energy. "It is the manners and spirit of a people," he concluded, "which preserve a republic in vigour." On the vices of European political economy relative to America's agrarian promise, see Drew R. McCoy, *The Elusive Republic: Political Economy in Jeffersonian America* (Chapel Hill, N.C., 1980). Benjamin Rush also claimed: "Farmers and tradesmen are the pillars of national happiness and prosperity." See Rush to Elias Boudinot, July 9, 1788, *Letters of Benjamin Rush*, 1:472. In her valuable study, Annette Kolodny explores the different relationship American women had to the land, and the impact on female character formation, in *The Land Before Her: Fantasy and Experience of the American Frontiers, 1630–1860* (Chapel Hill, N.C., 1984), esp. chap. 2.

95. John Mack Faragher, *Daniel Boone: The Life and Legend of an American Pioneer* (New York, 1992), 227–33 and chap. 7, quote at 230. In Boone's later years, Judge John Coburn of Louisiana Territory would point out that, after selflessly organizing the defense of the remote frontier and establishing settlements "at his own risque," the beloved frontiersman had not succeeded financially as either land speculator, surveyor, tavernkeeper, or trader.

96. John Filson, *The Discovery of Kentucke and the Adventures of Daniel Boon* (New York, 1978), 7–9, 50–82. Facsimile reprint of the 1784 first edition.

97. Samuel Henderson (of Guilford County, North Carolina) to John Gray Blount, Aug. 12, 1782, *The John Gray Blount Papers*, ed. Alice Barnwell Keith. 2 vols. (Raleigh, N.C., 1952), 1:28–29.

98. John Marshall to Arthur Lee, Apr. 17, 1784, *Papers of John Marshall*, ed. Herbert A. Johnson et al. (Chapel Hill, N.C., 1979– ), 1:119–20.

99. Filson, *The Discovery of Kentucke and the Adventures of Daniel Boon*, 12–14, 21, 28–29, 49, 54–55.

100. Blair, *Lectures on Rhetoric and Belles Lettres*, 32–33; Jeremy Belknap, *The History of New-Hampshire*, vol. 1 (Philadelphia, 1784), 23.

101. Peter S. Onuf, "Liberty, Development, and Union: Visions of the West in the 1780s," *The William and Mary Quarterly* 43 (Apr. 1986): 179–213, quote at 203.

102. Washington to the President of Congress, June 17, 1783, and to Henry Knox, Dec. 5, 1784, in *Writings of Washington*, 27:17–18, 28:4.

103. Joel Barlow, *An Oration*, facsimile reprint in *The Works of Joel Barlow* (Gainesville, Fla., 1970), 12.

104. Ibid., 20.

105. Jefferson to Church, Feb. 17, 1788, *Papers of Thomas Jefferson*, 12:601.

## 6. TORMENTED BY PHANTOMS: 1789–1800

1. Noah Webster, *Dissertations on the English Language* (Boston, 1789), facsimile reprint (Gainesville, Fla., 1951), vi, ix, 23–24.

2. Kenneth Cmiel, " 'A Broad Fluid Language of Democracy': Discovering the American Idiom," *The Journal of American History* (Dec. 1992), 917. Webster, it should be noted, was more concerned that American English should be an orthographically and grammatically correct language than that it should issue from a peculiarly American character. He wished, that is, to manipulate the language and was too impatient to await naturally developing forces of cultural identity. On this perspective, see Michael P. Kramer, *Imagining Language in America: From the Revolution to the Civil War* (Princeton, N.J., 1992), 54–56.

3. Cynthia M. Koch, "Teaching Patriotism: Private Virtue for the Public Good in the Early Republic," in John Bodnar, ed., *Bonds of Affection: Americans Define Their Patriotism* (Princeton, N.J., 1996), 28–31, 51–52. The theme of 1776 was expressed by others in 1793, as in a report on the Fourth of July fireworks display in Philadelphia: "Such festivals renew feelings, which ought not to be suffered to decay under the cold touch of TIME." See *General Advertiser (Aurora)*, July 3, 1793.

4. Caleb Bingham, *The Columbian Orator* (Boston, 1817), 234–39, 300. After graduating Dartmouth in 1782, Bingham maintained a school for young women before opening a popular bookstore and publishing business in Boston.

5. Davidson, *Revolution and the Word*, chap. 2; Richard R. John, *Spreading the News: The American Postal System from Franklin to Morse* (Cambridge, Mass., 1995), 30–36; Szatmary, *Shays's Rebellion*, 63.

6. *American Minerva*, Dec. 9, 1793. Webster's "Address to the Public" was repeated on the front page of Dec. 10; Jefferson's conversation with President Washington, the "Plan for Expediting Postal Service" (Mar. 1 & 4, 1792) and letter to Timothy Pickering of Mar. 28, 1792, are in *Papers of Thomas Jefferson* 23:184, 192, 347–48. Jefferson carefully recorded the movements of all postriders.

7. Davidson, *Revolution and the Word*, chap. 2.

8. Rush to Smith, Aug. 10, 1802, *Letters of Benjamin Rush*, 2:851–53. Smith, ironically, had belittled Franklin's scientific achievements more than thirty years earlier. See Van Doren, *Benjamin Franklin*, 284–85.

9. William Smith, *Eulogium on Benjamin Franklin* (Philadelphia, 1792), 1–2.

10. Ibid., 2–7.

11. Ibid., 10–19.

12. Ibid., 36–40.

13. *The New-Hampshire Magazine*, June 1793.

14. *The Time Piece; and Literary Companion*, Aug. 16, 1798, reprinting poem dated Nov. 7, 1792.

15. Hamilton to Adams, Aug. 16, 1792, *Papers of Alexander Hamilton*, 12:209; Burstein, *The Inner Jefferson*, 210–19, 240–41; Banning, *The Jeffersonian Persuasion*, chap. 5; Dumas Malone, *Jefferson and the Rights of Man* (Boston, 1951), 286–306, 420–77; Stanley Elkins and Eric McKitrick, *The Age of Federalism: The Early American Republic, 1788–1800* (New York, 1993), 92–131. To Jefferson's way of thinking, his old friend, now Vice President, John Adams had made a mistaken political choice—this was a case of a onetime republican no longer finding the aristocratic elements in the British political system untenable.

16. *State Gazette of South-Carolina*, various issues during 1793, cited in Klein, *Unification of a Slave State*, 207.

17. Malone, *Jefferson and the Rights of Man*, 354–70.

18. "Catullus No. III," in *Gazette of the United States*, Sept. 29, 1792, *Papers of Alexander Hamilton*, 12:498–506.

19. "An American," "Catullus No. IV," and "Metellus," in *Gazette of the United States*, Aug. 4, Oct. 17, & Oct. 24, 1792, *Papers of Alexander Hamilton*, 12:157–64, 582–83, 613–17.

20. Jefferson to Washington, Sept. 9, 1792, *Papers of Thomas Jefferson*, 24:351–59; on Jefferson's debt to Franklin and Monroe's defense of Jefferson, see Burstein, *The Inner Jefferson*, 170–72, 211–12.

21. *General Advertiser* (*Aurora*), July 6, 1793. Franklin's grandson Benjamin Bache edited this pro-French newspaper, whose columns traced the progress of French republicanism with "rapturous admiration," explaining the Revolution's excesses as "regrettable." *Aurora*'s readers saw "an universal revolution, and a glorious aera of liberty" in progress, aimed at destroying despotism in the world. See various issues; above citations are from issues of Jan. 18 & 21, 1793.

22. See Bloch, *Visionary Republic*, chap. 7, "Francophilic Millennialism and Partisan Republican Ideology." There was a significant element of traditional anti-Catholicism within this perspective. A writer published in the *State Gazette of South-Carolina* in 1793, for example, saw Britain's alliance with the pope against Revolutionary France to mark the fulfillment of biblical revelation: "either tyranny must be on the eve of being destroyed in Europe or that Europe itself is on the eve of being once more sunk into the abyss of Gothic ignorance, barbarity, and bondage." The French Revolutionaries, though seen as deists at best, were credited with assailing the papal Antichrist, and that in time they would come to adopt Protestant Christianity. (Ibid., 171–73.)

23. July 4, 1793, cited in Claude M. Newlin, *The Life and Writings of Hugh Henry Brackenridge* (New York, 1937), 133. Similar language is conveyed that same year in the address of the controversial French Revolutionary minister to the United States, Edmond Genêt, meeting with sympathetic Philadelphians. Overcome with the "affectionate joy" on supportive Americans' faces, the minister asked whether he could offer some "spontaneous effusions of the heart," and when done, was said to have "touched the feelings of every auditor," according to a column in the *General Advertiser*. See Waldstreicher, *In the Midst of Perpetual Fetes*, 134–35.

24. Philip S. Foner, ed., *The Democratic-Republican Societies, 1790–1800: A Documentary Sourcebook of Constitutions, Declarations, Addresses, Resolutions, and Toasts* (Westport, Conn., 1976), Introduction, 64–65.

25. Ibid., 66–67.

26. Ibid., 282–89.

27. *The Herald*, July 14, 1794, in ibid., 290–93.

28. Ibid., 315–17, 439–41; Storing, ed., *The Complete Anti-Federalist*, 2:253–54, 267.

29. Foner, ed., *The Democratic-Republican Societies*, 32; Ketchum, *James Madison*, 354–55.

30. Thomas P. Slaughter, *The Whiskey Rebellion: Frontier Epilogue to the American Revolution* (New York, 1986); also Slaughter, "The Friends of Liberty, the Friends of Order, and the Whiskey Rebellion: A Historiographical Essay," and James Roger Sharp, "The Whiskey Rebellion and the Question of Representation," both in Stephen R. Boyd, ed., *The Whiskey Rebellion: Past and Present Perspectives* (Westport, Conn., 1985); Foner, ed., *The Democratic-Republican Societies*, 29–30.

31. *American Minerva*, Mar. 30, 1795.

32. *The Time Piece; and Literary Companion*, June 29, 1798; Jefferson to Elbridge Gerry, May 13, 1797; to Arthur Campbell, Sept. 1, 1797; to Aaron Burr, June 17, 1797, *The Writings of Thomas Jefferson*, ed. Andrew A. Lipscomb and Albert Ellery Bergh (Washington, D.C., 1905), 8:285, 337, 312.

33. Rowson, *Charlotte Temple*, ed. Davidson, 35. A new and appealing study of *Charlotte Temple* and the works of Charles Brockden Brown, analyzing sympathy and dramatic self-presentation, sentiment, and will in the 1790s, is Julia A. Stern, *The Plight of Feeling: Sympathy and Dissent in the Early American Novel* (Chicago, 1997).

34. Noah Webster, *A Grammatical Institute of the English Language* (Hartford, Conn., 1783), 114–18.

35. Timothy Dwight, *The True Means of Establishing Public Happiness* (New Haven, Conn., 1795), 12–15, 20; Gregory Clark, "The Oratorical Poetic of Timothy Dwight," in Gregory Clark and S. Michael Halloran, eds., *Oratorical Culture in Nineteenth-Century America: Transformations in the Theory and Practice of Rhetoric* (Carbondale, Ill., 1993), 57–77.

36. Dwight, *The True Means of Establishing Public Happiness*, 16, 20, 38.

37. Ibid., 6., 12–13, 27, 38.

38. Julia Stern describes a hierarchical phenomenon, "gothic bedrock masked by a sentimental topsoil," in comparing the idealized community of compassion in the 1790s with an underlying disappointment she identifies over the incompleteness of the American founding. The widespread "outpouring of feeling," she states, masked the real repercussions of violence and injustice of the age, a "post-Revolutionary morbidity." The relationship she points out between the culture of sympathy and gothicism explains Charles Brockden Brown's movement from "The Story of Julius" to *Wieland*. See Stern, *The Plight of Feeling*, chap. 1, esp. 8–9.

39. Charles Brockden Brown, *Wieland, Or the Transformation: An American Tale* (Garden City, N.Y., 1973), 30, 102–3, 110, 114, 181, 214, 229, 239.

40. Introduction by Eugene R. Sheridan to *Jefferson's Extracts from the Gospels: "The Philosophy of Jesus" and "The Life and Morals of Jesus,"* ed. Dickinson W. Adams (Princeton, N.J., 1983), 10–42; Jenny Graham, *Revolutionary in Exile: The Emigration of Joseph Priestley to America, 1794–1804* (Philadelphia, 1995); Burstein, *Inner Jefferson*, 258–61.

41. *Notes on the State of Virginia*, ed. Peden, 160; Edwin S. Gaustad, *Sworn on the Altar of God: A Religious Biography of Thomas Jefferson* (Grand Rapids, Mich., 1996), 91, 112–18, 215–16; Jefferson to Rush, Sept. 23, 1800, *Writings of Thomas Jefferson*, ed. Lipscomb and Bergh, 10:175.

42. Peter Thacher, *The Nature and Effects of Christian Sympathy* (Boston, 1794), 7–11, 20.

43. Harry Ammon, *James Monroe: The Quest for National Identity* (New York, 1971), chap. 7; Elkins and McKitrick, *The Age of Federalism*, 406ff.

44. *General Advertiser (Aurora)*, March 20, 25, & July 4, 1795.

45. *General Advertiser (Aurora)*, Sept. 26, 1796.

46. Jeffrey L. Pasley, " 'A Journeyman, Either in Law or Politics': John Beckley and the Social Origins of Political Campaigning," *Journal of the Early Republic* 16 (Winter 1996), 531–69.

47. On the disjunction between Adams's Revolutionary and presidential character, see Peter Shaw, *The Character of John Adams* (Chapel Hill, N.C., 1976), and Joseph J. Ellis, *Passionate Sage: The Character and Legacy of John Adams* (New York, 1993).

48. A similar connotation for the word *innocence*, virtuous behavior, is suggested in a poem printed in the *Virginia Gazette* on Aug. 3, 1776:

> He needs no arms for his defence,
> That's fortify'd with innocence.
> Virtue's fortress impregnable
> No fortune can molest.

Inaugural Address of Mar. 4, 1797, in *Speeches of the American Presidents*, ed. Janet Podell and Steven Anzovin (New York, 1988), 27.

49. On the interference of Hamilton in Adams's decision making, see Elkins and McKitrick, *The Age of Federalism*, chap. 13.

50. Godbold and Woody, *Christopher Gadsden and the American Revolution*, 250.

51. *The Federal Songster: Being a Collection of the Most CELEBRATED Patriotic SONGS, Hitherto Published* (New London, Conn., 1800).

52. There were actually two Alien Acts, "An Act concerning Aliens" and "An Act respecting Alien Enemies." The Alien Act only provided a longer waiting period for naturalization of the foreign-born; the Alien Enemies Act defined hostility against the government and prescribed penalties. The Sedition Act was technically termed "An act for the punishment of certain crimes against the United States." All three were approved within a three-week period during June and July 1798. See James Morton Smith, *Freedom's Fetters: The Alien and Sedition Laws and American Civil Liberties* (Ithaca, N.Y., 1956), 435–42.

53. Jefferson to Taylor, June 1, 1798, in Peterson, ed., *The Portable Thomas Jefferson*, 476.

54. Smith, *Freedom's Fetters*, 116–30, 180–81.

55. Ibid., 270–73.

56. Cited in ibid., 264.

57. Ellis, *After the Revolution*, 195–202; Richard M. Rollins, *The Long Journey of Noah Webster* (Philadelphia, 1980), 84–87. *American Minerva* changed its name several times after 1796 but continued under Webster's direction. See ibid., 159n. Joel Barlow, meanwhile, had been in Europe associating with Revolutionary sympathizers like Priestley and Paine.

58. Noah Webster, *An Oration Pronounced Before the Citizens of New-Haven on the Anniversary of the Independence of the United States* (New Haven, Conn., 1798), 11–13.

59. *The Time Piece; and Literary Companion*, Apr. 24, 1797. Freneau's *National Gazette*, published in Philadelphia, had shut down in late 1793. *The Time Piece* was published thrice weekly in New York.

60. *The New-Hampshire Magazine*, June 1793.

61. Friedman, *Inventors of the Promised Land*, 46; Nathanael Greene to Samuel Ward, Sr., July 14, 1775, *The Papers of Nathanael Greene*, ed. Richard K. Showman (Chapel Hill, N.C., 1976), 1:99; Abigail Adams to John Adams, July 16, 1775, *Adams Family Correspondence*, 1: 246; Henry Laurens to John Lewis Gervais, Sept. 5, 1777, *Papers of Henry Laurens*, 11:498; Fliegelman, *Prodigals and Pilgrims*, 200 (the seventh chapter, "George Washington and the Reconstituted Family," provides analysis of the first President's value to a people who had successfully thrown off a tyrant father and found a "new paternity," a virtuous replacement in their affections); *Pennsylvania Gazette*, July 16, 1783; Stiles, *The UNITED STATES Elevated to GLORY and HONOUR*, 70–71.

62. Ramsay, *History of the American Revolution*, 656–60; *Pennsylvania Gazette*, Mar. 6, 1796, in Schwartz, *George Washington: The Making of an American Symbol*, 77–79, 83–84.

63. Jefferson to Madison, June 9, 1793, *Papers of Thomas Jefferson*, 26: 241 (this is Jefferson's recollection of words Madison had spoken to him three years earlier); Jefferson to Washington, May 23, 1792, ibid., 23:539; Jefferson to Archibald Stuart, Jan. 4, 1797; to Dr. Walter Jones, Jan. 2, 1814, *Writings of Thomas Jefferson*, ed. Lipscomb and Bergh, 8: 265, 14: 46–52. On Washington's own efforts to guard his reputation as a moral hero, see Wood, *The Radicalism of the American Revolution*, 206–7.

64. Dwight, *The True Means of Establishing Public Happiness*, 40.

65. Schwartz, *George Washington*, 101–2, with illustrations.

66. Fisher Ames, *An Oration on the Sublime Virtues of General George Washington* (Boston, 1800).

67. Ibid.

68. Nina Baym, *American Women Writers and the Work of History, 1790–1860* (New Brunswick, N.J., 1995), 72–73.

69. Ibid. On republican motherhood and the inculcation of patriotic values, see Kerber, *Women of the Republic*, chaps. 7 & 9.

70. In a 1792 broadside, Peale promised that "the wilds of America will furnish a very considerable variety." He was instrumental in developing American species as a source of national pride: "The sight, alone, of our large animals, collected together in good preservation, surely would be pleasing if not instructive: the elk, the moose deer, the buffaloe, the white bear, the sea-cow, the tygers, and many others perhaps unknown (at present) to us." Promoting his museum in 1795, Peale published a piece about the eagle in the Philadelphia *Aurora*: "The American Eagle, commonly called the Bald Eagle, belonging to the Museum, is now in the tenth year of his age." Describing the state of its plumage and the lightening color of its bill and eyes, he added, "To ascertain the longevity of this kind of Eagle is a matter of curiosity, and may gratify lovers of natural history in a future period." The onetime itinerant portrait painter asked that the symbolic eagle be maintained "after my decease." See Charles Coleman Sellers, *Mr. Peale's Museum: Charles Willson Peale and the First Popular Museum of Natural Sciences and Art* (New York, 1980), 89–90. Broadside in *The Selected Papers of Charles Willson Peale and His Family*, 2:15. In 1806, Capitol architect Benjamin Henry Latrobe wrote Peale for advice on modeling an American eagle, fourteen feet from wing to wing, for a frieze in the House of Representatives. He was concerned that the Italian sculptor who was assisting him might produce a Roman or Greek eagle, and "the glaring impropriety of character" present in such a rendering would be detected by discerning Americans. See Latrobe to Peale, Apr. 18, 1806; Peale to Latrobe, Apr. 22, 1806, ibid., 958–60.

71. *The New-Hampshire Magazine*, June 1793.

72. Rock, " 'All Her Sons Join as One Social Band,' " in Rock et al., eds., *American Artisans*, 163–66; Ralph Lerner, "Commerce and Character: The Anglo-American as New-Model Man," *The William and Mary Quarterly* 36 (1979), 13–36, Rush quote at 23.

73. *The Time Piece; and Literary Companion*, Apr. 17, 1797.

74. Felix Gilbert, *To the Farewell Address: Ideas of Early American Foreign Policy* (Princeton, N.J., 1961), esp. 137–39. See also the interpretation of Washington's personal bitterness at the time of his writing the address, in Elkins and McKitrick, *The Age of Federalism*, 492–97.

75. Gilbert, *To the Farewell Address*, 144–47.

76. Adams, Inaugural Address, Mar. 4, 1797, in *Speeches of the American Presidents*, 27; Webster, *An Oration Pronounced Before the Citizens of New-Haven*, 9–15.

77. Ibid.

78. Myra Fehlen, *American Incarnation: The Individual, the Nation, and the Continent* (Cambridge, Mass., 1986), 34–39. Fehlen makes reference to Morse's text as evidence that "the myth of America has been *both* ideal and material." (Ibid., 9–10.)

79. Jedidiah Morse, *The American Gazetteer* (Boston, 1797), n.p. A foldout map in center of the *Gazetteer* offers such place identifications as: "Very large Meadows" for the otherwise uncharted land of southern Illinois, "Fine Prairies" just to the west of Fort Knox, Kentucky, and "Barren Land" above the Tennessee River. Over much of the map, Indian names predominate.

80. See Andrew R. L. Cayton, *The Frontier Republic: Ideology and Politics in the Ohio Country, 1780–1825* (Kent, Ohio, 1986), chap. 2; Hurt, *The Ohio Frontier*, chap. 6.

81. Ibid., chaps. 4 & 5; Anthony F. C. Wallace, *The Death and Rebirth of the Seneca* (New York, 1969); idem, *The Long Bitter Trail: Andrew Jackson and the Indians* (New York, 1993); Colin G. Calloway, *The American Revolution in Indian Country: Crisis and Diversity in Native American Communities* (Cambridge, 1995); John Ehle, *Trail of Tears: The Rise and Fall of the Cherokee Nation* (New York, 1988).

82. R. David Edmunds, *Tecumseh and the Quest for Indian Leadership* (New York, 1984), esp. chap. 3; Calloway, *The American Revolution in Indian Country*; Sheehan, *Seeds of Extinction*.

83. Jefferson to Arthur Campbell. Sept., 1, 1797, *Writings of Thomas Jefferson*, ed. Lipscomb and Bergh, 8:337–38.

84. Of the stages of history, as understood in the late eighteenth century, the pastoral phase (which succeeded the savage or hunter phase and preceded the advanced agricultural and commercial phases) was remarkable for a simplicity and virtue unsullied by excessive material expectations.

85. Arthur K. Moore, *The Frontier Mind: A Cultural Analysis of the Kentucky Frontiersman* (Lexington, Ky., 1957), 26–30, 41–42; Hurt, *The Ohio Frontier*, 234, 241.

86. Congressman Crabb's address, Apr. 5, 1796, cited in Alan Taylor, "Land and Liberty in the Post-Revolutionary Frontier," in David Thomas Konig, ed., *Devising Liberty: Preserving and Creating Freedom in the New American Republic* (Stanford, Calif., 1995), 82–83. The number of landless men in western Pennsylvania hovered around 40 percent of the total adult male population, while the top 10 percent of propertied men owned 35 percent of the land. In Kentucky in 1800, 45 percent of adult white males were landless. Ohio then became a more attractive place for ordinary people with independent aspirations to settle. (Ibid., 87.) For a discussion of the general desire of frontiersmen in the 1790s for an active federal defense of settlements, and for a particular discussion of authority and regional identity (and seeds of political competition) north and south of the Ohio River, see Andrew R. L. Cayton, " 'Separate Interests' and the Nation-State: The Washington Administration and the Origins of Regionalism in the Trans-Appalachian West," *The Journal of American History* 79 (June 1992): 39–67. In 1804, Congress passed a land act which reduced the down payment ordinary settlers had to disburse to acquire public lands in the West, making small-scale farming more appealing. Meanwhile, private speculators in Ohio began selling off lands on a barter basis, accepting flour, whiskey, pork, beef, and iron nails in lieu of cash payment. See Hurt, *The Ohio Frontier*, 173–74.

87. *Kentucky Gazette*, Apr. 1, 1797, cited in Henry Nash Smith, *Virgin Land: The American West as Symbol and Myth* (Cambridge, Mass., 1950), 132.

## 7. SOMETHING NEW UNDER THE SUN: 1801–15

1. Hugh Henry Brackenridge, *Modern Chivalry*, ed. Claude M. Newlin (New York, 1937), 471–72.

2. See characterizations of Brackenridge and his fictional personae in Ellis, *After the Revolution*, chap. 4, and Wood, *Creation of the American Republic*, 480–82.

3. *Modern Chivalry*, 530–31. For an engaging discussion of Brackenridge's purposeful manipulation of American English in highlighting politicized conversation, see Christopher Looby, *Voicing America: Language, Literary Form, and the Origins of the United States* (Chicago, 1996), chap. 4.

4. *Modern Chivalry*, 7–8, 19, 250.

5. *Port Folio*, Apr. 23, 1803. A regular column in the *Port Folio* called "The Lay Preacher" used biblical allegory to denounce promiscuous democratic assemblies. The Midian well to which Moses once repaired was likened to "fashionable watering places" in the present age. Where once the women drawing water were subject to "attacks of brutality" by the "clamorous boors" who haunted the watering site, now "Midiantish *Democrats*, influenced by the wonted churlishness, impudence, boorishness, and ferocity of the *republican* character," did ill. Moses, who had helped "insulted maidens" in "a pleasing instance of primoeval politeness," had become a Federalist, who alone knew the delicacy of conduct expected of good breeding. (*Port Folio*, July 6, 1805.)

6. *Port Folio*, Jan. 11, Feb. 16, July 20, & Sept. 28, 1805.

7. *South-Carolina Gazette*, Sept. 26, 1775.

8. Brackenridge, *Modern Chivalry*, 297.

9. First Inaugural Address, in Peterson, ed., *The Portable Thomas Jefferson*, 291.

10. Ibid., 291–92.

11. Handwritten drafts of Jefferson's First Inaugural Address, in *Jefferson Papers*, Library of Congress. See Fliegelman, *Declaring Independence*, 4–28, on Jefferson's pauses. Compare also Kenneth Silverman's comments on Jefferson's rhythmic composition of the Declaration of Independence, in Silverman, *A Cultural History of the American Revolution*, 318–19.

12. Jefferson to Priestley, Mar. 21, 1801, *The Writings of Thomas Jefferson*, ed. Paul Leicester Ford (New York, 1905), 8:22.

13. In fact, Jefferson would routinely express consternation with what he called libels and "the caricatures of disaffected minds" in antiadministration newspapers. In the wake of Republican clamor over the Sedition Act he did not, however, wish to involve the federal government in prosecutions for newspaper slander. See Dumas Malone, *Jefferson the President: First Term, 1801–1805* (Boston, 1970), chap. 13.

14. *National Intelligencer*, Dec. 10, 1800.

15. Mar. 4, 1801, *Jefferson Papers*, Library of Congress.

16. Whitman, *An Oration Commemorative of the Declaration of Independence . . .* , 13–14.

17. Margaret Bayard Smith, *The First Forty Years of Washington Society* (New York, 1906), 25.

18. In the pamphlet version of Jefferson's Inaugural Address published in New York by William Durell, the speech was presented straightforwardly in pages-long paragraphs. There were but two words italicized in the text: *republicans* and *federalists*. See *Speech of Thomas Jefferson, President of the United States; Delivered in the Senate Chamber of the Capitol, the 4th of March at 12 o'Clock* (New York, 1801).

19. The letters newly appointed Chief Justice John Marshall sent to South Carolina Federalist (and his colleague during the XYZ Affair) Charles Cotesworth Pinckney are particularly evocative of this perception. See Marshall to Pinckney, Mar. 4, 1801, & Nov. 21, 1802, *Papers of John Marshall* 6:89, 125–26.

20. As "Christopher Caustic," Thomas Greene Fessenden mocked "*genuine*-republican-slave-driving-nabobs of Virginia." See Christopher Caustic, *Democracy Unveiled; Or Tyranny Stripped of the Garb of Patriotism* (Boston, 1805), 3.

21. *Monthly Anthology and Boston Review*, Feb. 1810, and William R. Davie to John Steele, Sept. 25, 1803, both cited in Linda K. Kerber, *Federalists in Dissent: Imagery and Ideology in Jeffersonian America* (Ithaca, N.Y., 1970), 29, 31. Kerber points out, however, that the likes of John Quincy Adams persisted in seeking cross-sectional consensus toward achieving larger national purposes. Adams deplored expressions of anti-Virginia sentiments among his New England friends. See ibid., 32–33.

22. Caustic, *Democracy Unveiled*, 2–3.

23. *National Intelligencer*, Nov. 13, 1801.

24. *National Intelligencer*, Nov. 26, 1802.

25. *National Intelligencer*, Nov. 26, 1802.

26. Mercy Otis Warren, *History of the Rise, Progress and Termination of the American Revolution* (Boston, 1805), 3:303–6; James Warren cited in Rosemarie Zagarri, *A Woman's Dilemma: Mercy Otis Warren and the American Revolution* (Wheeling, Ill., 1995), 139.

27. David Simpson, *The Politics of American English, 1776–1850* (New York, 1986), 22–23.

28. Ibid., 42–49, 111.

29. *National Intelligencer*, Apr. 20, May 23, & June 13, 1803.

30. *National Intelligencer*, May 23 & June 13, 1803.

31. *National Intelligencer*, Feb. 21, 1806.

32. *Boston Chronicle* column reprinted in *National Intelligencer*, Aug. 3, 1803.

33. Smith, *The Loving Kindness of God Displayed in the Triumph of Republicanism in America*, cited in Wood, *Radicalism of the American Revolution*, 232.

34. *New-York Evening Post*, Nov. 22, 1803.

35. *United States Gazette* satire reprinted in *New-York Evening Post*, Jan. 24, 1815.

36. Jefferson to Attorney General Levi Lincoln, Oct. 25, 1802, and to Count de Volney, Feb. 8, 1805, *Writings of Thomas Jefferson*, ed. Lipscomb and Bergh, 10:339, 11:68.

37. O[rsamus] C[ook] Merrill, *The Happiness of America: An Oration Delivered at Shaftsbury on the Fourth of July, 1804* (Bennington, Vt., 1804), 3.

38. Ibid., 6, 15, 17. Using old imagery, Merrill cast independence as a "beam" of light which "sublimely rose above the dark mountains of Chaos, and shone with cheering radiance." As that light "diffused far and wide, its salutary and vivifying influence . . . attracted the attention of all classes of people, and engaged the meditations of a world."

39. Joel Barlow, *Prospectus of a National Institution, To Be Established in the United States* (Washington City, 1806), 16.

40. Adams to Rush, Mar. 26, 1806, Apr. 18, June 20, Sept. 27, 1808; Rush to Adams, June 13, 1808, in John A. Schutz and Douglass Adair, *The Spur of Fame: Dialogues of John Adams and Benjamin Rush, 1805–1813* (San Marino, Calif., 1966), 52, 107–20.

41. Jefferson to Andrew Ellicott, Nov. 1, 1806; to Wilson Cary Nicholas, Mar. 26, 1805; to Albert Gallatin, Oct. 12, 1806, in *Works of Thomas Jefferson*, ed. Ford, 10:299–300, 137–38, 294–95.

42. Earlier in Philadelphia, Burr had indicated to British ambassador Anthony Merry that he would be willing to serve London's interest by severing the eastern and western regions of the continent and perhaps to annex Mexico. Whether Burr literally intended to sever the union is not certain; he may have been interested in gaining attention and extracting money from this notoriously anti-American British representative. See Dumas Malone, *Jefferson the President: Second Term, 1805–1809* (Boston, 1974), 234–41. For a succinct narrative of Burr's activities, see Nathan Schachner, *Aaron Burr: A Biography* (New York, 1937).

43. Special Message to the Senate and House of Representatives, Jan. 22, 1807, and Jefferson to Leiper, Dec. 20, 1806, in *Works of Thomas Jefferson*, ed. Ford, 10:346–57, 329–30.

44. Entries of Nov. 8, 1804, Mar. 3, 1805, & Jan. 14, 1807, in *William Plumer's Memorandum of Proceedings in the United States Senate, 1803–1807* (New York, 1969), 186, 316, 574. At this time the word *crooked* generally meant unpredictable, perhaps opportunistic, but not dishonest.

45. Entry of Jan. 12, 1807, ibid., 570.

46. Plumer, *Memorandum of Proceedings in the United States Senate*, 547, 608; Merrill D. Peterson, *The Great Triumvirate: Webster, Clay, and Calhoun* (New York, 1987), 6–11.

47. First Inaugural Address, in Peterson, *The Portable Jefferson*, 290. The sense of America's distinct situation, both physical and moral, was almost a truism; Jefferson's meaning was reiterated as a statement of fact by Mercy Warren in the preface to her *History*, "An Address to the Inhabitants of the United States of America": "The world is now viewing America, as experimenting a new system of government, a FEDERAL REPUBLIC, including a territory to which the Kingdom of Great Britain and Ireland bear little proportion." (vii–viii.)

48. Whitman, *An Oration Commemorative of the Declaration of Independence . . .* , 19–20. See also Drew R. McCoy, *The Elusive Republic: Political Economy in Jeffersonian America* (New York, 1980), chaps. 1, 2, 8 & 9. Jeffersonians, responsive to Adam Smith's 1776 *The Wealth of Nations*, believed that commerce could easily get out of hand and upset the "natural order," especially if it ceased to encourage the expansion of agriculture. Jeffersonians, McCoy asserts, wanted an expansive economy without admitting that this was what they wanted. (Ibid., 187–88.)

49. Address of Dec. 20, 1805, published in *National Intelligencer*, Jan. 6, 1806.

50. Charlotte M. Porter, *The Eagle's Nest: Natural History and American Ideas, 1812–1842* (University, Ala., 1986), 5–7, 159–60.

51. *Notes on the State of Virginia*, ed. Peden, 24–25; Burstein, *The Inner Jefferson*, 35–41; Miller, *Jefferson and Nature*, 102–3.

52. McKinsey, *Niagara Falls*, 42, 89.

53. Albert Furtwangler, *Acts of Discovery: Visions of America in the Lewis and Clark Journals* (Urbana, Ill., 1993), 7–8.

54. Barbara McEwan, *Thomas Jefferson: Farmer* (Jefferson, N.C., 1991).

55. Williams to "a member of Congress," Feb. 12, 1804, in *National Intelligencer*, Jan. 3, 1806; "A CITIZEN," in *National Intelligencer*, Jan. 8, 1806. During Senate debate on the ramifications of Ohio statehood, another speculated: "Politicians have generally agreed that rivers unite the interests and promote the friendship of those who inhabit their banks; while mountains on the contrary, tend to the disunion and estrangement of those who are separated by their intervention." It was thus to the advantage of union to "make the crooked ways straight and the rough ways smooth." Senate debate of Dec. 19, 1805, reported in *National Intelligencer*, Dec. 27, 1805.

56. June 13 & 14, 1805, *The Journals of the Lewis & Clark Expedition*, ed. Gary E. Moulton (Lincoln, Neb., 1986–   ), 4:283–85, 289–90.

57. Ibid., 290–94.

58. See Furtwangler, *Acts of Discovery*, 23–24, 27–33.

59. Ibid., chap. 5. The vision, however, did not imply learning from the successes of the Indians in order to build a new culture alongside them; it was rather a narrow nationalist vision as John Quincy Adams described it in 1811, a continent "destined by Providence to be peopled by one *nation*, speaking one language, professing one general system of religious and political principles, and accustomed to one general tenor of social usages and customs."

60. Merrill, *The Happiness of America*, 7. In building his sentiment, the orator used dramatic contrasts between America and the Old World experience. America's natural "diversity of blessings," when tapped by a productive people, cemented union. Each state had its own "gifts" to be shared with the other states. Nature was conducive to republican union, "variety, and fullness, which would knit the whole together." The union of states was a strong fabric, immune from "those continual jealousies, and bloody dissentions, which distract the old world." Through its independence America had gained a "fertile source" of "sentiment, good will, conformity of habits and manners, and consequent intellectual extension" favorable to practical growth and "congenial with the spirit of Liberty." There were still "amazing prospects" in view, so that Americans could not look ahead with "indifference." The most evident portent in 1804 was the recent "*peaceful* acquisition of Louisiana," a "new and luminous

example" of open diplomacy, "eclipsing the boasted triumphs of conquerors and giving an important lecture to the world, upon the easiest method of being happy and prosperous . . . , extending the limits of a country, without being embroiled in the dire conflicts of ignoble ambition." (Ibid., 8–10.)

61. Second Inaugural Address, in Peterson, *Portable Jefferson*, 318.

62. Francis Jennings, *The Invasion of America: Indians, Colonialism, and the Cant of Conquest* (Chapel Hill, N.C., 1975); Robert F. Berkhofer, Jr., *The White Man's Indian: Images of the American Indian from Columbus to the Present* (New York, 1978); idem, *Salvation and the Savage: An Analysis of Protestant Missions and the American Indian Response, 1787–1862* (Lexington, Ky., 1965); Sheehan, *Seeds of Extinction*. In line with the self-serving ideology of "philanthropy" toward Indians, Jefferson instructed Meriwether Lewis to treat the natives he encountered "in the most friendly & conciliatory manner which their own conduct will admit." To Seneca chief Handsome Lake the President wrote of his "affectionate concern" for Indians' happiness and of his own "sincerity and zeal" to find humane solutions in white-Indian relations: "You are our brethren of the same land: we wish to see your prosperity as brethren should do." But the ultimate solution was, of course, conformity rather than diversity. Jefferson to Lewis, June 20, 1803; to Handsome Lake, Nov. 3, 1802, in Peterson, ed., *The Portable Thomas Jefferson*, 312, 306–7.

63. Hugh Williamson, *Observations on the Climate in Different Parts of America* (1811) and *An Attempt to Account for the Change in Climate . . .* (1789), cited in Sheehan, *Seeds of Extinction*, 37, 39.

64. Jefferson to William Duane, July 20, 1807, *Writings of Thomas Jefferson*, ed. Lipscomb and Bergh, 11:291.

65. *National Intelligencer*, May 28 & June 13, 1806.

66. Peterson, *The Great Triumvirate*, 17; Calhoun to Dr. James McBride, Feb. 16, 1812, *The Papers of John C. Calhoun*, ed. Robert L. Meriwether (Columbia, S.C., 1959), 1:90–91.

67. *Annals of Congress*, 9th Congress, 1st Session, Feb. 1806, 555–60.

68. Speeches of Dec. 12, 1811, & Oct. 25, 1814, in *Papers of John C. Calhoun*, 1:76–77, 254, 258–59.

69. Clay to Rodney, Dec. 29, 1812, *The Papers of Henry Clay*, ed. James F. Hopkins (Lexington, Ky., 1959–  ), 1:750–51; Peterson, *The Great Triumvirate*, 45. For a discussion of the post-Revolutionary generation's ascendance in Congress, see Ronald L. Hatzenbuehler and Robert L. Ivie, *Congress Declares War: Rhetoric, Leadership, and Partisanship in the Early Republic* (Kent, Ohio, 1983).

70. J. C. A. Stagg, *Mr. Madison's War: Politics, Diplomacy, and Welfare in the Early American Republic* (Princeton, N.J., 1983); Harry L. Coles, *The War of 1812* (Chicago, 1965); Steven Watts, *The Republic Reborn: War and the Making of Liberal America, 1790–1820* (Baltimore, 1987), 276–81, 305–11; Ketcham, *James Madison*, 593–97.

71. "Song," by John M'Creery of Petersburg, Virginia, composed and sung on July 4, 1815, printed in *Niles' Weekly Register*, Supplement to Volume 9, Feb. 24, 1816.

72. *New-York Evening Post*, Feb. 7 & Mar. 22, 1815.

73. Watts, *The Republic Reborn*, 285–89.

74. *Niles' Weekly Register*, Dec. 2, 1815, 230–32.

75. *Niles' Weekly Register*, Dec. 2, 1815, 238–40. Steven Watts has called Hezekiah Niles at this time "a self-conscious ideologue of productive, socially ambitious individualism." (See Watts, *The Republic Reborn*, 293.) Like Franklin's 1751 "Observations Concerning the Increase of Mankind," or Mercy Otis Warren's comments in her 1805 *History of the . . . American Revolution* concerning the "multitudes" attracted to "a land of such fair promise" (3:302–3), Niles, with census figures available, saw a doubling of the population every twenty-two years and saw impending greatness in the nation's status as a refuge for distressed Europeans.

76. This process is traced in the classic work of David Brion Davis, *The Problem of Slavery in Western Culture*.

77. Brown, *The Power of Sympathy*, 1:79–80, 82–84.

78. Richard S. Newman, "Prelude to the Gag Rule: Southern Reaction to Antislavery Petitions in the First Federal Congress," *Journal of the Early Republic* 16 (Winter 1996), 571–99.

79. *Notes on Virginia*, Query XIV; [William Loughton Smith], *The Pretensions of Thomas Jefferson to the Presidency Examined* (Philadelphia, 1796); Jefferson to Banneker, Aug. 30, 1791, and to Coles, Aug. 25, 1814, in Peterson, ed., *The Portable Thomas Jefferson*, 454–55, 544–47; Finkleman, *Slavery and the Founders*, 134–35.

80. Love of liberty was white America's credo, and the enslavement of African Americans could only be justified if they were understood to be happier as the property of the Southern gentleman than they might otherwise be. While liberal-minded Southerners of the early national period expressed an interest in eliminating slavery from the land—James Madison in the 1790s echoed William Hill Brown when he wrote that slavery rendered his section more aristocratic and less republican—others focused on the widely held belief that blacks were intellectually inferior, unfaithful, and lazy, and needed guidance and paternalistic care in order to sustain life. Revolutionaries of Madison's persuasion, though they reflected positively on the decency of some masters, were gravitating toward a new solution, either recolonization in Africa or diffusion through unsettled parts of the American West, in any case removal of blacks from white society. Madison's pragmatism on slavery is ably developed in McCoy, *The Last of the Fathers: James Madison and the Republican Legacy* (Cambridge, 1989); for commentary relating to the early 1790s, see ibid., 234–35; on slaves' habits see especially Eugene D. Genovese, *Roll, Jordan, Roll: The World the Slaves Made* (New York, 1974); see also Jan Lewis, "The Problem of Slavery in Southern Political Discourse," in Konig, ed., *Devising Liberty*, 265–97; Rollin G. Osterweis, *Romanticism and Nationalism in the Old South* (New Haven, Conn., 1949), chap. 2; Jordan, *White Over Black*.

81. Plumer, entries of Jan. 24–26, 1804, *Memorandum of Proceedings in the United States Senate*, 111–19.

82. Isabella Oliver quoted in Baym, *American Women Writers and the Work of History*, 76.

83. Tise, *Proslavery*, 42–50.

84. Ibid. And yet, to highlight the confusion over these unresolved, emotionally charged issues, Smith suggested at the same time that race prejudice would be reduced if emancipated slaves were settled on western lands and allowed to intermarry with whites there. Smith's was an unusual proposition for this time, given the widespread revulsion against miscegenation. See Jordan, *White Over Black*, chap. 15, quote at 544. Defensive Hezekiah Niles added critically of the British: "It appears to me quite as absurd for a person to clamor for the emancipation of the negroes and advocate the 'legitimacy of kings,' as it is for a planter, with a whip in his hand, to contend for the abject submission of his blacks, while he speaks of 'liberty and equality.' In both cases there is a *master*; but the latter is a less extensive evil than the former. . . . The Louisiana negro has just as much to say in the choice of a *master* as the natural born *Englishman*. . . . Your king is the greatest dealer in *human flesh* in the world—for many years past it has been his custom to buy any body that could and would hold a musket." (*Niles' Weekly Register*, Dec. 2, 1815, 239–40.)

85. Tise, *Proslavery*, 51, 191–93. Winthrop Jordan has noted that the genteel wife of magazine publisher Mathew Carey was "horrified" in 1806 by the emotions she witnessed among African-American worshippers at a camp meeting in Pennsylvania. (Jordan, *White Over Black*, 419.)

86. Joel Barlow, *Oration Delivered at Washington July 4, 1809, at the Request of the Democratic Citizens of the District of Columbia* (Washington, D.C., 1809), 1–5.

87. Ibid., 6–9, 14.

88. Joel Barlow, *The Columbiad* (Washington City, 1825), 232, 239–42, 249, 257.

89. *Niles' Weekly Register*, Supplement to Volume 9, Feb. 24, 1816, 83 ("Defence of Fort M'Henry" reprinted from the *Port Folio*, no longer a strictly Federalist newspaper); Jean V. Matthews, *Toward a New Society: American Thought and Culture, 1800–1830* (Boston, 1991), 16–18.

## 8. WITH PINIONS HIGH POINTED: 1816–28

1. From the *Saratoga* (N.Y.) *Journal*, reprinted in *Niles' Weekly Register*, Supplement to Volume 9, Feb. 24, 1816, 91–92.

2. Howard B. Rock, *Artisans of the New Republic: The Tradesmen of New York City in the Age of Jefferson* (New York, 1979), 90–91.

3. Robert H. Wiebe, *Self-Rule: A Cultural History of American Democracy* (Chicago, 1995), 39.

4. On the social and political ramifications of women's benevolence activities in this period, see Anne M. Boylan, "Women and Politics in the Era Before Seneca Falls," *Journal of the Early Republic* 10 (Fall 1990): 363–82.

5. Tise, *Proslavery*; George Dangerfield, *The Awakening of American Nationalism, 1815–1828* (New York, 1965), 97–101; John M. Grammer, *Pastoral and Politics in the Old South* (Baton Rouge, La., 1996), chap. 1. In 1831, Virginian John Hartwell Cocke, a Christian reformer and self-styled Man of Feeling, distinguished among his slaves "common cornfield hands" and those with "sensibilities." See Lewis, *The Pursuit of Happiness*, 141. The Southern argument would eventually crystallize in an essay by William Gilmore Sims titled "The Morals of Slavery."

6. Friedman, *Inventors of the Promised Land*, 181ff; Alison Goodyear Freehling, *Drift Toward Dissolution: The Virginia Slavery Debate of 1831–1832* (Baton Rouge, La., 1982).

7. "Address to the Auxiliary Colonization Societies and the People of the United States," *The African Intelligencer*, July 1820, 12, 29; *The African Repository, and Colonial Journal*, inaugural issue, Mar. 1825. Colonization was not without black adherents. Paul Cuffee, of mixed African and Native American heritage, was a free Quaker merchant and philanthropist who used his own money to finance the resettlement of thirty-eight freed slaves to Liberia in 1815. Cuffee died in 1817. His biography was first presented in *Memoir of Paul Cuffee a Man of Color . . .* (London, 1811).

8. "The Slaves," in *New-York Mirror, and Ladies' Literary Gazette*, Feb. 19, 1825, 297–98.

9. *New-York Advertiser*, Oct. 5, 1822.

10. Sheehan, *Seeds of Extinction*, esp. chap. 9, quote at 9–10.

11. This interpretation is borne out in Thomas R. Hietala, *Manifest Design: Anxious Aggrandizement in Late Jacksonian America* (Ithaca, N.Y., 1985).

12. Baron, *Grammar and Good Taste*, 26–30; Richard Bridgman, *The Colloquial Style in America* (New York, 1966), 41; Cmiel, " 'A Broad Fluid Language of Democracy' "; idem, *Democratic Eloquence: The Fight over Popular Speech in Nineteenth-Century America* (Berkeley, Calif., 1990), chaps. 3 & 4.

13. Rollins, *The Long Journey of Noah Webster*, chap. 8; Cmiel, *Democratic Eloquence*, 82–89. Jacksonian America did not make Webster's dictionary popular—that would wait for two enterprising brothers named Merriam and a later generation.

14. Mathew Carey, *Essays on Political Economy; Or the Most Certain Means of Promoting the Wealth, Power, Resources, and Happiness of Nations* (Philadelphia, 1822), 62–66. Carey, born in Dublin, Ireland, had been the moving force behind the patriotic *Columbian Magazine* in 1786 and the *American Museum* after that.

15. Herbert E. Sloan, *Principle and Interest: Thomas Jefferson and the Problem of Debt* (New York, 1995); McCoy, *The Elusive Republic*, esp. chap. 10.

16. Like Thomson, Hugh Henry Brackenridge arrived in America (from Scotland) with little fortune but read voraciously as a youth. He used his savings to matriculate at Princeton, then went on to edit *The United States Magazine* during the Revolution, before migrating to

Pittsburgh, where he practiced law and served in the state legislature. In Brackenridge's case, the design to win respectability was psychologically complex; he saw elements of his two fictional characters, scrappy Teague O'Regan and dignified Captain John Farrago, in himself. He was uncomfortable with his own search for financial security and social status. See also Boyd Stanley Schlenther, *Charles Thomson: A Patriot's Pursuit* (Newark, Del., 1990).

17. Paul A. Gilje and Howard B. Rock, eds., *Keepers of the Revolution: New Yorkers at Work in the Early Republic* (Ithaca, N.Y., 1992), 33–44, 51–53, and various illustrations.

18. Watts, *The Republic Reborn*, 43–58, 294–96; Dangerfield, *Awakening of American Nationalism*, 270.

19. Benjamin L. Oliver, *Hints for an Essay on the Pursuit of Happiness* (Cambridge, Mass., 1818), 39, 47, 88–95, 161–65, 200–2.

20. Harry Ammon, *James Monroe: The Quest for National Identity* (Charlottesville, Va., 1971), chap. 20; William Crafts, *An Oration on the Influence of Moral Causes on National Character* (Cambridge, Mass., 1817), 13.

21. *Niles' Weekly Register*, Mar. 6, 1819; David S. Heidler, "The Politics of National Aggression: Congress and the First Seminole War," *Journal of the Early Republic* 13 (Winter 1993), 501–30.

22. *Niles' Weekly Register*, Mar. 13, 1819, 41.

23. Dangerfield, *Awakening of American Nationalism*, chap. 4.

24. Debate in the House of Representatives, Feb. 15, 1819, reprinted in *Niles' Weekly Register*, Supplement to Volume 16, after Aug. 28, 1819, 161ff; *Annals of Congress*, Mar. 2, 1819, 15th Congress, 2nd Session, 1437.

25. *Liberty Hall & Cincinnati Gazette*, Jan. 25, 1820.

26. Glover Moore, *The Missouri Controversy* (Lexington, Ky., 1953), 171ff; Dangerfield, *Awakening of American Nationalism*, 126–29; Peterson, *The Great Triumvirate*, 59–68.

27. *Liberty Hall & Cincinnati Gazette*, Feb. 23, 1822.

28. *Liberty Hall & Cincinnati Gazette*, Mar. 2, 1822.

29. *Liberty Hall & Cincinnati Gazette*, Mar. 9, 1822.

30. *Liberty Hall & Cincinnati Gazette*, Mar. 23, 1822.

31. *Liberty Hall & Cincinnati Gazette*, Apr. 6, 13 & 20, 1822. A number of his contemporaries wrote of Calhoun's virtue and "manly independence." See Peterson, *The Great Triumvirate*, 86–87. At this point in his long career, Calhoun was indeed a nationalist; but as Andrew Jackson's Vice President he would become the symbol of states' rights in the nullification controversy of 1830–31, in which prominent South Carolinians asserted the state legislature's authority to nullify federal law.

32. Clay won the electoral votes of Ohio, Kentucky, and Missouri. Adams was dominant in New England. Jackson took Pennsylvania and New Jersey in the North, Indiana in the West, and most of the South. Jackson won approximately 43 percent of the popular vote and 99 of 261 electoral votes (to Adams's 84 and Clay's 37). The fourth candidate, William Crawford of Georgia, won the states of Georgia and Virginia.

33. Adams to Jefferson, Dec. 21, 1819, Feb. 21, 1820, Feb. 3, 1821; Jefferson to Adams, Jan. 22, 1821, *The Adams-Jefferson Letters: The Complete Correspondence Between Thomas Jefferson and Abigail and John Adams*, ed. Lester J. Cappon (Chapel Hill, N.C., 1959), 551, 561, 570.

34. Jefferson to Adams, Sept. 12, 1821, June 1, 1822, ibid., 575, 577–79. For a valuable discussion of the Adams-Jefferson correspondence in terms of national character and regional temperament, see William R. Taylor, *Cavalier and Yankee: The Old South and American National Character* (New York, 1961), 25–33.

35. Richard D. Brown, *The Strength of a People: The Idea of an Informed Citizenry in America, 1650–1870* (Chapel Hill, N.C., 1996), 109–10, 114–17; Peterson, *The Great Triumvirate*, 105–9.

36. Robertson, *The Language of Democracy*, chaps. 2 & 4; Hatch, *The Democratization of Christianity*, esp. chap. 5. Hatch notes the use of folk tales as a tool of persuasion by "communication entrepreneurs," who offered "true-to-life passion, simplicity of structure, and dramatic creativity" in a more colorful and less doctrinaire style of reaching and influencing the public. (Ibid., 138.) Kenneth Cmiel observes, with different emphasis, that in this period "distinct forms of high and low culture lived icily side by side," suggesting that a Webster did not necessarily reach into as many hearts as might be imagined. But that does not make him irrelevant by any means. He merely adapted, and stepped up his efforts to reach out. The erudite orator would insist by 1840 on his humble log cabin-like roots, in order to make certain he was connecting with more "middling" people. Cmiel's point is that it was only gradually that the class character of words was lost. He explains, "The contradictory push toward democratic rawness and pull to universal education created a kind of cultural vertigo. Even the traditional language of civil authority became unsteady." From the 1820s on, as informal speech became increasingly practical, the nationalist idiom extended beyond stately commemorations; more, not fewer, Americans were contributing to a nationalist voice. See Cmiel, *Democratic Eloquence*, 56–59.

37. "Adams and Jefferson," Aug. 2, 1826, in *The Papers of Daniel Webster: Speeches and Formal Writings*, ed. Charles M. Wiltse (Hanover, N.H., 1986), 1:238–39.

38. Ibid., 240; Burstein, *Inner Jefferson*, 266.

39. *Papers of Daniel Webster*, 1:240–41.

40. Ibid., 269–71.

41. *New-York Advertiser*, July 7, 11, & 14, 1826.

42. Henry Laurens Pinckney, *An Oration Delivered in St. Michael's Church, Before an Assemblage of the Inhabitants of Charleston, South-Carolina; on the Fourth of July, 1818* (Charleston, S.C., 1818), 11; Maier, *American Scripture*, 171,176; Merrill D. Peterson, *The Jefferson Image in the American Mind* (New York, 1960), 69–70, 100.

43. Pauline Maier writes with reference to the corresponding deaths of Adams and Jefferson: "Never before was interest in the American past greater than in the decade before 1826, and never was the sense of impending loss more widespread." See Maier, *American Scripture*, 178.

44. Poem in the *New-York American*, reprinted in the *New-York Advertiser*, May 25, 1827.

45. Dann, ed., *The Revolution Remembered*, xvi–xvii; Seymour, *Documentary Life of Nathan Hale*, 311–14, 355–56, 364–65; *New-York Mirror, and Ladies' Literary Gazette*, Apr. 15, 1826.

46. *New-York Advertiser*, May 31, 1826.

47. James Fenimore Cooper, *The Pioneers* (New York, 1985), 13.

48. Ibid.; Geoffrey Rans, *Cooper's Leather-Stocking Novels: A Secular Reading* (Chapel Hill, N.C., 1991), 56.

49. See especially Blake Nevius, *Cooper's Landscapes: An Essay on the Picturesque Vision* (Berkeley, Calif., 1976), 6–16, quote at 16. Examples of Cooper's language come from the texts of *The Pioneers* and *The Last of the Mohicans*. Additionally, in his *Notions of the Americans*, published in London in 1828 but composed in America sometime earlier, Cooper wrote with a similar opulence about the Hudson Highlands: "Rocks, broken, ragged, and fantastic; forests, through which disjointed precipices are seen forming dusky backgrounds; promontories; dark, deep bays; low sylvan points; elevated plains; gloomy, retiring vallies; pinnacles; cones; ramparts that overhang and frown upon the water . . ." Cooper called this variety "romantic beauty" for the imagination, "romantic" because it allowed one to conjure the setting of a romance. America lacked the ruined castles of Europe that the author's recent travels abroad had shown him, but America could boast superiority in the unrivaled dignity and grandeur of its natural scenery. See Nevius, *Cooper's Landscapes*, 20.

50. McWilliams, *The American Epic*; Josephine Miles, "The Romantic Mode," in Harold Bloom, ed., *Romanticism and Consciousness: Essays in Criticism* (New York, 1970), 173–80. Romanticism was not mere emotionalism. As Alfred Cobban has put it: "The Nature of most

of the romanticists is simply an emotionalized version of the Reason of the philosophes, its political effect being to place their views of society in a democratic setting." In that sense, then, there was no "replacement" of neoclassicism with romanticism, only a change in emphasis. Romantic tendencies most assuredly existed in the writings and sentimental assumptions of the age of Enlightenment, just as they were present in Shakespeare's world before that. Sentimentalism in the eighteenth century, though constricted by its obvious conventions, was in fact a stage in the development of nineteenth-century romanticism; with romanticism the imagination merely enlarged. Also, in spite of its less spontaneous approach to knowledge, the neoclassical embrace of reason did not cease to be satisfying to romantic minds. Classical and romantic have been described as "the systolic and diastolic of the human heart in history"; one pulse is stronger as the other becomes faint. See Cobban, "The Revolt Against the Eighteenth Century," in ibid., 136, and H. J. C. Grierson, "Classical and Romantic: A Point of View," in Robert F. Gleckner and Gerald E. Enscoe, eds., *Romanticism: Points of View* (Detroit, 1962), 52.

51. Smith, *Virgin Land*, chap. 6; Kay Seymour House, *Cooper's Americans* (Columbus, Ohio, 1965).

52. Faragher, *Daniel Boone*, 326–30.

53. See Roderick Nash, *Wilderness and the American Mind* (New Haven, Conn., 1967), chap. 3. Ascribing value to uncultivated parts of a country did not originate in the American imagination; an earlier European fascination with the wild brought together innocence and an innate nobility. From the 1820's, though, a romantic vocabulary developed, one that highlighted the influence on the imagination of excursions along rural pathways, through parks and peaceful cemeteries. The gradual industrialization of towns caused people to seek an accessible counterpoint to their increasingly compressed lives, experiencing nature without having to endure the loneliness of farm isolation. See Thomas Bender, *Toward an Urban Vision: Ideas and Institutions in Nineteenth Century America* (Lexington, Ky., 1975), chap. 4.

54. Perry Miller, "The Romantic Dilemma in American Nationalism and the Concept of Nature," *Harvard Theological Review* 48 (1955): 239–53. Karol Ann Peard Lawson significantly writes that "by the 1810s, the painter's eye firmly controlled the presentation and interpretation of native landscape views in American magazines, . . . explicitly proposed . . . as an inspiration for fine art that could dispel myths of cultural inadequacy." See Lawson, "An Inexhaustible Abundance: The National Landscape Depicted in American Magazines, 1780–1820," *Journal of the Early Republic* 12 (Fall 1992): 303–30, quote at 324.

55. Marx, *The Machine in the Garden*, 75–84.

56. Pinckney, *An Oration Delivered in St. Michael's Church* . . . , 4, 19.

57. Jefferson to Marquis de Barbé-Marbois, June 14, 1817, *Writings of Thomas Jefferson*, ed. Lipscomb and Bergh, 15:130; Randall, *Life of Thomas Jefferson*, 3:435–46; Merrill D. Peterson, ed., *Visitors to Monticello* (Charlottesville, Va., 1989), 74–79.

58. Benjamin F. Allen, *An Oration, Pronounced Before the Students of Brown University in the College Chapel, July 4, 1817* (Providence, R.I., 1817), 8–9.

59. Ibid.

60. Pinckney, *An Oration Delivered in St. Michael's Church* . . . , 6, 22–24.

61. "Address to the Patrons of the Liberty Hall and Cincinnati Gazette By the Carrier; on the Commencement of the Year 1820," Jan. 4, 1820, insert in *Liberty Hall & Cincinnati Gazette*.

62. Patrick V. McGreevy, *Imagining Niagara: The Meaning and Making of Niagara Falls* (Amherst, Mass., 1994), 5–7, 43; Webster to Mrs. George Blake (wife of a fellow Boston attorney), July 15, 1825, in *The Papers of Daniel Webster: Correspondence*, ed. Charles M. Wiltse (Hanover, N.H., 1974–86), 2:57–63; Carol Sheriff, *The Artificial River: The Erie Canal and the Paradox of Progress, 1817–1862* (New York, 1996).

63. Harry N. Scheiber, *Ohio Canal Era: A Case Study of Government and the Economy, 1820–1861* (Athens, Ohio, 1968), chaps. 1–4; Cayton, *Frontier Republic*, 110ff; Hurt, *The Ohio Frontier*, 370–71, 387–89.

64. James Hall, *Letters from the West* (London, 1828), 236, 251, 385.

65. Ibid., 236–37, 244–45.

66. Ibid., 313–16.

67. Thomas Hart Benton, *Thirty Years View* (New York, 1854), 13–14.

68. Ibid. History, Benton later wrote, would find the words to "do justice to the national, and to individual character," just as "felicity at home, and respect abroad" was making America "the envy and admiration of the civilized world." (Ibid., 111–13.) Everett cited in Fred Somkin, *Unquiet Eagle: Memory and Desire in the Idea of American Freedom, 1815–1860* (Ithaca, N.Y., 1967), 97–98.

69. "Speech at Faneuil Hall on the Election of 1825," Apr. 3, 1825, *Papers of Daniel Webster: Speeches and Formal Writings*, 1:172–73.

70. Ibid., 174.

71. Monroe's Eighth Annual Message, Dec. 7, 1824, in Podell and Anzovin, eds., *Speeches of the American Presidents*, 71–72. For a discussion of prosperity in the years after the War of 1812 as the apparent reward for a morally secure ideology, see Somkin, *Unquiet Eagle*, chap. 1. On foreign policy during the Monroe presidency, see Noble E. Cunningham, Jr., *The Presidency of James Monroe* (Lawrence, Kans., 1996), Ammon, *James Monroe*, chaps. 27 & 29, and Ernest R. May, *The Making of the Monroe Doctrine* (Cambridge, Mass., 1975).

## 9. Sentiment and Sympathy: Transitions

1. Gordon Wood provides a comprehensive picture of the civic consciousness and genteel behavior that self-cultivating gentlemen strove for during this period—without which masculine sensibility would not have acquired its public dimension. See Wood, *The Radicalism of the American Revolution*, 192–98; see also Bushman, *The Refinement of America*.

2. Jefferson perhaps best expressed the triumph of heart in his 1786 letter to Maria Cosway: "If our country, when pressed with wrongs at the point of a bayonet, had been governed by it's heads instead of it's hearts, where should we have been now?" Britain's "wealth and numbers" fell before American "enthusiasm" and "a few pulsations of our warmest blood." Jefferson to Cosway, Oct. 12, 1786, *Papers of Thomas Jefferson*, 10:451.

3. Royall Tyler, *The Contrast, A Comedy* (Philadelphia, 1790), Act I. The critical male tone with regard to female sensibility is typified in a diary entry of Virginia planter Landon Carter: "Passion is a dangerous thing in woman especially, for they have a vast fund of tears to make a gust and then for every connection to Pity poor Mama." After describing a misunderstanding with his wife over a payment, Carter added. "I could laugh at these things, was there not such abundance of smoak and fire and then a flood of tears." Entry of Apr. 10, 1777, in Jack P. Greene, ed., *The Diary of Colonel Landon Carter of Sabine Hall, 1752–1778* (Richmond, Va., 1987), 1089–90.

4. Tyler, *The Contrast*, Act IV. It should be pointed out at the same time, though, that there is intentional exaggeration of the characters by Tyler, and thus Colonel Manly's staunch regard for sensibility is mildly satirized. I thank Gordon Wood for contributing this important clarification. As the text below will show, even Henry Mackenzie was able to temper his moralism in prose with a recognition that sensibility was not always practical.

5. *General Advertiser (Aurora)*, May 3, 1792.

6. Crèvecoeur, *Letters from an American Farmer*, 41; Jefferson to Maria Cosway, Oct. 12, 1786, *Papers of Thomas Jefferson*, 10:447–48.

7. Adams, "Letters from a Distinguished American XII," written for *Parker's General Advertiser and Morning Intelligencer*, in Hutson, ed., *Letters from a Distinguished American*, 47–48; Henry Laurens to Thomas Fletchall, July 14, 1775, *Papers of Henry Laurens*, 10:214–18.

8. Paine, *Collected Writings*, 548.

9. *The Works of Joel Barlow*, 2 vols. (Gainesville, Fla., 1970), 1:12. Barlow's revised epic, the *Columbiad* (1807), would intensify his earlier conviction. From America's "genial soil," the "union'd banners" would wave, and carry across the seas to "an accordant world." In his prescription, "patriot views" and "moral views" were one and the same. See ibid., 241–42, 248–49.

10. From Shaftesbury's *Characteristics of Men, Manners, Opinions, Times*, cited in Barker-Benfield, *Culture of Sensibility*, 113; see also Gustafson, *Representative Words*, 260–62.

11. Cited in Robertson, *The Language of Democracy*, 36.

12. Washington to Benjamin Harrison, June 12, 1783, as published in the *Virginia Gazette*, July 5, 1783.

13. "The Trifler, No. V," in *Columbian Magazine*, September 1787; *The United States Magazine*, Jan, 1779.

14. Ramsay, *History of the American Revolution*, 1:173–74; Jefferson to the Marquis de Chastellux, Sept. 2, 1785, *Papers of Thomas Jefferson*, 8:468; Crèvecoeur, *Letters from an American Farmer*, 44–46. When calmly pursuing his affairs after the murder of Hamilton, Aaron Burr gently chastised his daughter Theodosia for her impulsive response to recent events: "Your anxieties about me evince a sort of sickly sensibility," he wrote. "I fear that you are suffering a debility, arising from climate or other cause, which affects both mind and body." See Aaron Burr to Theodosia Burr Alston, Mar. 10, 1805, in *Correspondence of Aaron Burr and His Daughter Theodosia*, ed. Mark Van Doren (New York, 1929), 203.

15. Ramsay, *History of the American Revolution*, 1:173.

16. *Pennsylvania Gazette*, Nov. 14, 1781.

17. Warren, *History of the Rise, Progress and Termination of the American Revolution*, iii–vi, 1–5.

18. Ibid., 1:237, 2:146, 3:247.

19. Ibid., 1:303–4.

20. Mackenzie, *The Man of Feeling*, 112.

21. Rush to Julia Rush, Dec. 9, 1775, *My Dearest Julia: The Love Letters of Dr. Benjamin Rush to Julia Stockton* (New York, 1979), 26–27; Sterne, *A Sentimental Journey*, 142–44.

22. Rush to Madison, Feb. 27, 1790, *Letters of Benjamin Rush*, ed. L. H. Butterfield (Princeton, N.J., 1951), 540–41. A similar prescriptive tone is found in Rush's *A Plan for the Establishment of Public Schools and the Diffusion of Knowledge in Pennsylvania* (1786) and *Thoughts Upon Female Education, Accommodated to the Present State of Society, Manners, and Government in the United States of America* (1787). These are reprinted in Frederick Rudolph, ed., *Essays on Education in the Early Republic* (Cambridge, Mass., 1965), 3–40.

23. Rush to Nicholson, Aug. 12, 1793, *Letters of Benjamin Rush*, 636.

24. Rush to Jefferson, Oct. 6, 1800, & Mar. 12, 1801, *Letters of Benjamin Rush*, 825–26, 831–32.

25. Zagarri, "Morals, Manners, and the Republican Mother," 206, citing and evaluating Rush's 1806 essay, "Of the Mode of Education Proper in a Republic."

26. Anya Jabour, " 'It Will Never Do for Me to Be Married': The Life of Laura Wirt Randall, 1803–1833," *Journal of the Early Republic* (Summer 1997): 193–236, quote at 203. For all his unpredictability, Aaron Burr, like Wirt, was remarkably determined to educate his daughter Theodosia to equal or exceed male competence. Impressed with Mary Wollstonecraft's *Vindication of the Rights of Women*, he proceeded to mold his daughter, while at the same time encouraging his wife's intellectual development.

27. Merrill, *The Happiness of America*, 4.

28. Ibid., 12, 17. Hume posed as a moral question the individual's determination of how far to "yield" to the "illusions" of an imagination that, without being reined in, tended to

drift "like a galley put in motion by the oars, carries on its course without any new impulse." "Our sensible perceptions," he noted, "have, therefore, a continu'd and uninterrupted existence." Imagination, of course, could not be cut off. Sympathy demanded it, "where the mind passes easily from the idea of ourselves to that of any other object related to us." See Hume, *A Treatise of Human Nature*, 198, 213–14, 266–67, 339–41.

29. Hall, *Letters from the West*, 315–16.

30. See Rodgers, "Sensibility, Sympathy, Benevolence . . . ," 124–26; also Roy Porter, "Against the Spleen," in Valerie Grosvenor Myer, ed., *Laurence Sterne: Riddles and Mysteries* (London, 1984), 84–98.

31. Hamilton to Edward Carrington, May 26, 1792, *Papers of Alexander Hamilton*, 11:440.

32. See McCoy, *The Elusive Republic*.

33. "Reynolds Pamphlet," Aug. 25, 1797, in *Papers of Alexander Hamilton*, 21:239–53; Rowson, *Charlotte Temple*, ed. Davidson.

34. "Reynolds Pamphlet"; disputing Hamilton during the buildup to publication of the pamphlet, Jefferson ally James Monroe charged that the New Yorker was "indelicate." (Monroe to Hamilton, July 21, 1797, *Papers of Alexander Hamilton*, 21:178.) In the wake of publication, James Madison characterized Hamilton as one guilty of deception: "Simplicity and candor are the only dress which prudence would put on innocence." Instead, Hamilton employed "rhetorical artifice." (Madison to Jefferson, Oct. 20, 1797, cited in ibid., 139.) See also a recent probing of Americans' assessment of the relationship between public and private conduct in Jacob Katz Cogan, "The Reynolds Affair and the Politics of Character," *Journal of the Early Republic* 16 (Fall 1996), 389–417. Cogan notes that Maria Reynolds, significantly retaining Aaron Burr as her divorce attorney in 1793, faded from the public view, eventually turned to evangelical religion, and lived out her sixty-six years according to the standard of feminine virtue expected of one embroiled as she was in a real-life tale of the politics of respectability.

35. "Reynolds Pamphlet."

36. Rowson, *Charlotte Temple*, 17. Literary critic Julia Stern notes of the narrative tone in *Charlotte Temple*: "A link to the figure of a mother, whether biological or symbolic, enjoyed with a woman or with a nurturing man of feeling, is figured as the object relation of ultimate value." (Stern, *The Plight of Feeling*, chap. 2, quote at 61.) It may be that female guardianship and female benevolence (surrogate motherhood) are better developed in the novel than the role of biological motherhood, but the statement still stands. In this way, the Jeffersonian persuasion is meant to sentimentalize the role of the nurturing political parent (surrogate of the biological) while idealizing the democratization of social relations more generally.

37. Henry Adams, *History of the United States of America During the Administrations of Thomas Jefferson* (New York, 1986 [1889]), 99–100. Curiously, when the Federalist press wanted to embarrass President Jefferson in 1803 after allegations of moral laxity were leveled at him, it, too, challenged: "If he has one remaining spark of sensibility," he would be "gnashing his teeth" and "finding himself truly a miserable being" at the revelations about his private and public character. See *Boston Gazette*, Jan. 6, 1803, citing James Thomson Callender in the *Richmond Recorder*.

38. Jefferson to Washington, Sept. 9, 1792, *Papers of Thomas Jefferson*, 24:351–59.

39. See Joanne B. Freeman, "Dueling as Politics: Reinterpreting the Burr-Hamilton Duel," *The William and Mary Quarterly* (Apr. 1996): 289–318. Freeman describes dueling as "public-minded personal disputes" and a means of adapting to a political culture that frowned on factionalism or "party spirit." That Hamilton stood his ground but did not fire his weapon at his adversary was meant to establish that his motives were sincere (as well as an expression of religious scruples). He had spoken against Burr in "severe" tones, but this was purportedly to espouse his consistent political principles, which Burr's political rise appeared to threaten. Jefferson's opinion was that dueling was "an imaginary honour." In the language of sensibility he asserted that the duel "bursts asunder all the ligaments of duty and affection and assigns to misery and ruin innocent and helpless families." See Dumas Malone, *Jefferson the President: Second Term, 1805–1809* (Boston, 1974), 130–32.

40. Abigail to John Adams, Mar. 2, 1776; John to Abigail Adams, Mar. 19, 1776, in *Adams Family Correspondence*, 1:352, 363; Gustafson, *Representative Words*, 251. On the dangers of sentiment, see Fliegelman, *Prodigals and Pilgrims*, 230ff.

41. Mason Weems, *A History of the Life and Death Virtues & Exploits of General George Washington* (New York, 1927), 25.

42. See John Ferling's portrayal of Washington's wartime character in "George Washington and the American Victory," in Ferling, ed., *The World Turned Upside Down: The American Victory in the War for Independence* (New York, 1988), 53–70.

43. See the extensive discussion of Hamilton's nationalist thinking in Elkins and McKitrick, *The Age of Federalism*, 92–114.

44. *New-York Evening Post*, July 21, 1804.

45. *Fragment of a Journal of a Sentimental Philosopher, During His Residence in the City of New-York, To Which Is Added, A Discourse Upon the Nature and Properties of Eloquence As a Science* (New York, 1809), 13–16.

46. Ibid., 20, 29–32.

47. Washington Irving, "Rip Van Winkle," in Haskell Springer, ed., *The Sketch Book of Geoffrey Crayon, Gent.* (Boston, 1978), 46–52. (Part of Richard Dilworth Rust, general ed., *The Complete Works of Washington Irving*.)

48. William Godwin, *Fleetwood: Or, the New Man of Feeling* (Alexandria, Va., 1805), quotes at 15–16, 20, 22; review reprinted in the *Port Folio*, Sept. 14 & 21, 1805, quote at 294. A separate 1805 printing of *Fleetwood* was brought out in New York.

49. This period witnessed, in Stuart M. Blumin's words, the "redrawing of society's most critical boundary." The transportation revolution, with new turnpikes, river traffic, and the railroad, caused larger merchants to give up the retail trade and permit people of more modest means to rise to respectability. See Blumin, *The Emergence of the Middle Class: Social Experience in the American City, 1760–1900* (Cambridge, 1989), quote at 107; Coontz, *The Social Origins of Private Life*, chap. 5; Joseph F. Kett, *Rites of Passage: Adolescence in America, 1790 to the Present* (New York, 1977); Mary P. Ryan, *Cradle of the Middle Class: The Family in Oneida County, New York, 1790–1865* (Cambridge, 1981), 165–79; Jean H. Baker, *Affairs of Party: The Political Culture of the Northern Democrats in the Mid-Nineteenth Century* (Ithaca, N.Y., 1983), chaps. 1 & 2.

50. *The Juvenile Port-Folio and Literary Miscellany*, Aug. 27 & Sept. 17, 1814, Jan. 14, Mar. 11, & May 6, 1815. The August 27, 1814, issue notably reprinted Harley's encounter with Old Edwards from *The Man of Feeling*. It should be noted that warning against the excess of sensibility dated back to Mackenzie's prime, when it was felt that a woman's overrefinement could sink her into a permanent state of melancholy. There is a subtle but important difference between the earlier emphasis on emotional depression and the nineteenth-century extension of the criticism to encompass the public embarrassment associated with a life wasted by such novels as led one to breathe a crippling air of unreality (to be discussed below). Sensibility was understood to be healthy as a gentle melancholy aroused in times of recognized sorrow, as the mourning of a lost relative, friend, or beloved public figure.

51. *New-York Mirror, and Ladies' Literary Gazette*, Jan. 1, Feb. 5, & Feb. 19, 1825, 179, 219, 236.

52. Sir Walter Scott, *Waverley* (Boston, 1912), 32; Ina Ferris, *The Achievement of Literary Authority: Gender, History, and the Waverley Novels* (Ithaca, N.Y., 1991), chap. 3; David Daiches, "Scott's Achievement as a Novelist," and Walter Bagehot, "The Waverley Novels," in A. Norman Jeffares, ed., *Scott's Mind and Art* (London, 1969), 21–52, 132–66. "Their emphatic masculinity," writes Nina Baym of Scott and James Fenimore Cooper, "helped make the novel an acceptable genre for men to write and boys to read." See Baym, *American Women Writers and the Work of History*, 153.

53. *American Minerva*, Mar. 24, 1795. The article called even "harmless" novels "trivial and dangerous" for "diverting the attention from some useful employment."

54. Beyond writing sentimental fiction, in which eighteenth-century female writers con-

fined themselves to expressing a view consistent with women's assigned role as guardians of public morality, certain female nonfiction writers were able to acquire an air of professionalism that permitted a larger, more general display of prudence and good sense (though history still remained a vehicle for moral instruction). See Cheryl Turner, *Living by the Pen: Women Writers in the Eighteenth Century* (London, 1992). For stylistic comparisons between Warren and Macaulay, as well as the nature of their correspondence, see Zagarri, *A Woman's Dilemma*, 54–55.

55. Herbert Ross Brown, *The Sentimental Novel in America, 1789–1860* (New York, 1959), 281–322, quote at 283–84.

56. For a discussion of the gendered meaning of legal and political representation and changes resulting from nineteenth-century democracy, see Nancy Isenberg, *Sex and Citizenship in Antebellum America* (Chapel Hill, N.C., 1998). For the distinctly Southern characteristics of women's relation to male authority, see Bertram Wyatt-Brown, *Southern Honor: Ethics and Behavior in the Old South* (New York, 1982), esp. chap. 9.

57. *A Voice from the Interior. Who Shall Be President? The Hero of New-Orleans, Or John the Second of the House of Braintree* (Boston, 1828), 3–12. This is not to suggest, however, that the entire eighteenth-century political-emotional vocabulary was unacceptable to supporters of Jackson. A particularly forceful 1828 pamphlet hailing Jackson's patriotism at New Orleans remarked on his ability to appeal to people's emotions, to "awe disaffection"; his example "cheered the desponding." Such language mirrored patriotic tracts of the eighteenth century. If a greater emphasis on Jackson's "energetic" presence distinguished him from past statesmen, his "spirit," like Washington's, "was infused into others." Another orator at this time placed him squarely within the Revolutionary tradition of virtue and sensibility, contrasting Jackson with Benedict Arnold: "Every fibre which can vibrate in the heart of an American is chilled at the name of an Arnold." Jackson's masculinity did not mean that he could not move people's hearts as the sensible Jefferson had done. The same writer linked the two charismatic leaders sentimentally: "The spirit of our ancestors still survives in the bosoms of their descendants, and the same voice which called upon a JEFFERSON to correct the errors of the first Adams now calls upon JACKSON to correct the errors of the second." See Isaac Hill's lead address and "Address by J. B. Thornton" in Isaac Hill, *An Address at Concord, N.H., January 8, 1828, the Thirteenth Anniversary of Jackson's Victory at New-Orleans* (Concord, N.H., 1828), 3–5, 33, 35.

58. *A Voice from the Interior*, 12–16. On Jackson's decidedly masculine sense of his private and public obligations, and with particular emphasis on vindication through the code duello, see Bertram Wyatt-Brown, "Andrew Jackson's Honor," *Journal of the Early Republic* 17 (Spring 1997), 1–36. On the Clay-Randolph duel, see Peterson, *The Great Triumvirate*, 140–42. As to the robustness of women in the Jacksonian perspective, frontier conditions had and would increasingly cause wives and mothers to undertake duties critical to family survival. Their nobility and heroism heightened as men's did; in literature they courted danger and underwent trials, adapting to an unrefined world. The domestic framework remained, women were seen as civilizers, but their ability to take on "masculine" qualities where necessary added a new dimension to their experience. See Julie Roy Jeffrey, *Frontier Women: The Trans-Mississippi West, 1840–1880* (New York, 1979), esp. 16–22.

59. *A Voice from the Interior*, 16–18.

60. Robert Remini, *The Election of Andrew Jackson* (Philadelphia, 1963), 151–54.

61. [Charles Hammond], *View of General Jackson's Domestic Relations, in Reference to His Fitness for the Presidency* (Washington, D.C., 1828), 7–12; Norma Basch, "Marriage, Morals, and Politics in the Election of 1828," *The Journal of American History* 80 (Dec. 1993): 890–918. On a wife's presumed passivity as her husband's "property," see Isenberg, *Sex and Citizenship in Antebellum America*, chap. 6.

62. Basch, "Marriage, Morals, and Politics in the Election of 1828"; *A Letter from the Jackson Committee of Nashville . . .* (Nashville, Tenn., 1827).

63. For details and commentary on political aspects of the so-called Hemings and Walker affairs, see Dumas Malone, *Jefferson the Virginian* (Boston, 1948), 447–51, and Malone, *Jefferson the President, First Term, 1801–1805* (Boston, 1970), 212–23. Debate over the truth or

falsehood of Jefferson's alleged sexual behavior has generated numerous popular as well as scholarly treatments, the most recent of which is Annette Gordon-Reed, *Thomas Jefferson and Sally Hemings: An American Controversy* (Charlottesville, Va., 1997).

64. For example, a piece of Jackson campaign theater established the Democrat's integrity as a military and political leader, followed by a dramatic scene in which Jackson encounters patriotic young women strewing flowers before the hero's path. He assures a "fair nymph" that he will join the victory festival "where will be mingled feelings of the liveliest character." See [James Frisby Brice,] *Andrew Jackson, An Interlude in Three Acts* (Annapolis, Md., Apr. 1828).

65. Elements of the moral and political drama surrounding the election of 1828 were replayed shortly thereafter in the so-called Peggy Eaton affair. Cabinet secretary and Jackson intimate John Eaton, on New Year's Day 1829, married Margaret O'Neil Timberlake—a reputedly promiscuous woman whom the Washington social elite shunned and whose reputation Jackson, still incensed over the attacks on his wife, staunchly defended. The men involved—in essence Jackson's cabinet and Vice President—took principled stands, all claiming to exhibit the appropriate kind of masculine honor. Acting on a supposed slight, John Eaton challenged one of his detractors to a duel: fellow cabinet member Samuel Ingham, whom he insulted in the press for being "incapable of acting as became a man." The same newspaper likened Ingham to a hysterical old woman, "unmanned by his fears." Alleged effeminacy, then, countered by condemning the Jacksonian image as, in one scholar's words, "hypermasculine pugnacity," "overaggressive masculinity." Once again, passion, if unrestrained, loomed as a national sin; yet in this instance Jackson's "manly" stand prevailed in public opinion, as well as the dictate that publicly dominant males acting boldly to defend a sense of honor expressed the American character. See Kirsten E. Wood, " 'One Woman So Dangerous to Public Morals': Gender and Power in the Eaton Affair," *Journal of the Early Republic* (Summer 1997): 237–75.

66. Robert Walsh, Jr., *The Jackson Wreath, Or National Souvenir* (Philadelphia, 1829), 82–85.

67. Smith, *First Forty Years of Washington Society*, 259–60. Predictably, Smith adopted the anti-Jackson view in the Eaton affair.

68. John G. Miller, *The Great Convention* (Columbus, Ohio, 1840), 3–4. I thank Nancy Isenberg for bringing this valuable source to my attention.

69. Ibid., 4–8.

70. Noah Webster, *An American Dictionary of the English Language* (New York, 1828), n.p. Note that Webster's definitions of *sensible* were ranked much as Johnson's had been, privileging the physiological, then indicating "moral perception." The modern meaning "intelligent, discerning; as a *sensible* man" was listed eighth in order.

71. Mackenzie, *The Man of Feeling*, 200–2.

72. Jack Greene has observed that the success of the Revolution brought European agreement with the idea of American exceptionalism as it related both to America the place and to the American people. A cluttered Old World, burdened by its population and propped up by stricter social distinctions, was giving way (in imagination if not in global political reality) to the active and industrious American experiment. See Jack P. Greene, *The Intellectual Construction of America: Exceptionalism and Identity from 1492 to 1800* (Chapel Hill, N.C., 1993), 167; similarly, Gay, *The Enlightenment*, 2:556–58.

73. The happiness of its society, Paine wrote, was owing to the "uniting" of "affections," just as the contest with Great Britain was about distinct "tempers," "passions and feelings," "feelings and affections." See Paine, *Collected Writings*, 5, 6, 26–29.

74. Benjamin F. Allen, *An Oration, Pronounced Before the Students of Brown University . . .*, 4–5.

## 10. LEGACIES OF NATIONAL CHARACTER

1. *National Intelligencer*, Feb. 18, 1806, during a debate over neutral rights.

2. "Address by Nathan B. Felton," in Hill, *An Address, Delivered at Concord, N.H., January 8, 1828 . . .* , 37.

3. "Essays on American Language and Literature," *North American Review* (Sept. 1815), cited in Cmiel, " 'A Broad Fluid Language of Democracy.' "

4. William Cullen Bryant, "Early American Verse," from *North American Review* (July 1818), in Parke Godwin, ed., *Prose Writings of William Cullen Bryant* (New York, 1884), 45–49; Albert F. McLean, *William Cullen Bryant* (Boston, 1989); see also Gustafson, *Representative Words*, chap. 9, "The Unsettled Language." Bryant used more rapturous language to project his nation's power in an 1821 Harvard commencement poem, comparing America, where the "free spirit of mankind, at length, / Throws its fetters off," to a comet swiftly racing "Into the depths of ages." See Somkin, *Unquiet Eagle*, 53–54.

5. "English Writers on America," in Springer, ed., *The Sketch Book of Geoffrey Crayon, Gent.*, 43–44.

6. Ibid., 44–49.

7. William L. Hedges, *Washington Irving: An American Study, 1802–1832* (Baltimore, 1965), esp. 1–33 and chap. 3.

8. Ibid., 114; see also Stanley Brodwin, ed., *The Old and New World Romanticism of Washington Irving* (New York, 1986).

9. Hedges, *Washington Irving*, 116–31; Smith, *Virgin Land*. See Rupert Wilkinson, *The Pursuit of American Character* (New York, 1988), for a sense of the problem in defining social character, of making visible the differences in outlook among classes and with respect to gender and other primary distinctions. Wilkinson also relates the observed romantic landscape, the concomitant rise of a culture of individualism and progress, and the need Americans have had to separate their culture from that of parent civilizations and declare uniqueness. It was as Henry Laurens Pinckney boasted in 1818: "America, separated from the world, wove the web of greatness from herself." See Pinckney, *An Oration Delivered in St. Michael's Church . . .* , 4.

10. "The Voyage," in *The Sketch Book of Geoffrey Crayon, Gent.*, 11–15.

11. Bryan Jay Wolff, *Romantic Re-Vision: Culture and Consciousness in Nineteenth-Century American Painting and Literature* (Chicago, 1982); Earl A. Powell, *Thomas Cole* (New York, 1990).

12. "An American Farmer," in *Niles' Weekly Register*, Oct. 22, 1836, 118.

13. Ibid.

14. See James C. Thompson, Jr., et al., *Sentimental Imperialists: The American Experience in East Asia* (New York, 1981) for an overview of this missionary impulse in foreign policy.

15. Cited in Smith, *Virgin Land*, 37.

16. *Leaves of Grass by Walt Whitman*, ed. Justin Kaplan (New York, 1983), 185–88.

17. Henry Adams, *The Education of Henry Adams: An Autobiography* (Boston, 1961), 249.

18. Cecilia Elizabeth O'Leary, " 'Blood Brotherhood': The Racialization of Patriotism, 1865–1918," in Bodnar, ed., *Bonds of Affection*, 53–81, citing Horace Potter, "Grant's Last Campaign," in *The Century* 35 (Nov. 1887).

19. Adams, *The Education of Henry Adams*, 180–81, 239.

20. Benedict Anderson, *Imagined Communities: Reflections on the Origin and Spread of Nationalism* (London, 1983), esp. 4–13, 30–36, quote at 6.

21. Ibid., 9.

22. Ernest Gellner, *Nations and Nationalism* (Ithaca, N.Y., 1983), 57.

23. Michael Lind's *The Next American Nation: The New Nationalism and the Fourth American Revolution* (New York, 1995) explores the political potential of a transracial "Trans-American majority"; Franz Schurmann's *American Soul* (San Francisco, 1995) advocates the spiritual engineering of a once soulful, of late static or directionless polity; David A. Hollinger's *Postethnic America* (New York, 1995) imagines the cross-cultural potential of a freshly enlightened moral community based on less arbitrary "affiliations" than multiculturalism provides. These and other similarly inspired works of the mid-1990s promote a "sensible" (in the modern understanding of the word) American worldview—differing perspectives, true, but all in large measure sympathetic to past enthusiasm and all actively advocating a more promising, updated sense of identity to allow America and the world to be remade jointly.

24. On the late nineteenth century, see especially Walter LaFeber, *The New Empire: An Interpretation of American Expansion, 1860–1898* (Ithaca, N.Y., 1963); also Thompson et al., *Sentimental Imperialists*, and Akira Iriye, *Across the Pacific: An Inner History of American-East Asian Relations* (New York, 1967); Melvyn P. Leffler, *A Preponderance of Power: National Security, the Truman Administration, and the Cold War* (Stanford, Calif., 1992), quote at 19.

25. *Time*, Feb. 23, 1981.

26. Hollinger, *Postethnic America*, 64–65.

27. Peter Biskind, *Seeing Is Believing: How Hollywood Taught Us to Stop Worrying and Love the Fifties* (New York, 1983), 3.

28. Wilkinson, *The Pursuit of American Character*, 73–75.

29. *The New York Times*, Feb. 2, 1996, A7.

# BIBLIOGRAPHY

## NEWSPAPERS AND MAGAZINES

*The African Intelligencer*
*The African Repository, and Colonial Journal*
*The American Magazine*
*American Minerva*
*Boston Gazette*
*Columbian Magazine*
*General Advertiser (Aurora)*
*The Juvenile Port Folio and Literary Miscellany*
*Liberty Hall & Cincinnati Gazette*
*National Intelligencer*
*The New American Magazine*
*The New England Magazine of Knowledge and Pleasure*
*The New-Hampshire Magazine*
*New-York Advertiser*
*New-York Evening Post*
*New-York Mirror, and Ladies' Literary Gazette*
*Niles' Weekly Register*
*Pennsylvania Gazette*
*The Pennsylvania Magazine*
*Port Folio*
*South-Carolina Gazette*
*The Time Piece; and Literary Companion*
*The United States Magazine* (Newark, N.J.)
*The United States Magazine* (Philadelphia)
*The Universal Asylum, and Columbian Magazine*
*Virginia Gazette*

## AUTOBIOGRAPHY, CORRESPONDENCE, ORATIONS, AND OTHER EIGHTEENTH- AND NINETEENTH-CENTURY PRIMARY SOURCES

Adams, Henry. *The Education of Henry Adams: An Autobiography*. Boston: Houghton Mifflin, 1961.

*Adams Family Correspondence*, ed. L. H. Butterfield. Cambridge, Mass.: Harvard University Press, 1963.

*The Adams-Jefferson Letters: The Complete Correspondence Between Thomas Jefferson and Abigail and John Adams*, ed. Lester J. Cappon. Chapel Hill: University of North Carolina Press, 1959.

Allen, Benjamin F. *An Oration, Pronounced Before the Students of Brown University in the College Chapel, July 4, 1817*. Providence, R.I.: Jones & Wheeler, 1817.

*Annals of Congress*. Washington, D.C.: Gales and Seaton, 1851–53.

[Anonymous.] *Fragment of a Journal of a Sentimental Philosopher, During His Residence in the City of New-York, To Which Is Added, A Discourse Upon the Nature and Properties of Eloquence As a Science*. New York: E. Sargeant, 1809.

*The Autobiography of Benjamin Rush: His "Travels Through Life" Together with His Commonplace Book for 1789–1813*, ed. George W. Corner. Princeton, N.J.: Princeton University Press, 1948.

Bartram, William. *Travels in Georgia and Florida, 1773–1774*. Annotated by Francis Harper. Philadelphia: The American Philosophical Society, 1943 [first published 1791].

Belknap, Jeremy. *The History of New-Hampshire*. Dover, N.H.: S. C. Stevens and Ela & Wadleigh, 1831 [copy of 1784 first edition].

*Belknap Papers*, 5th & 6th Series. Boston: Massachusetts Historical Society, 1877 & 1891.

Bingham, Caleb. *The Columbian Orator*. Boston: Caleb Bingham and Co., 1817.

Blair, Hugh. *Lectures on Rhetoric and Belles Lettres*. Philadelphia: Troutman & Hayes, 1833.

Brown, William Hill. *The Power of Sympathy*. New York: Columbia University Press, 1937 [facsimile reprint].

Brackenridge, Hugh Henry. *Modern Chivalry*, ed. Claude M. Newlin. New York: American Book Company, 1937.

Burke, Edmund. *A Philosophical Enquiry into the Origin of Our Ideas of the Sublime and Beautiful*, ed. James T. Boulton. London: Routledge & Kegan Paul, 1958.

Caustic, Christopher [Thomas Greene Fessenden]. *Democracy Unveiled: Or Tyranny Stripped of the Garb of Patriotism*. Boston: David Carlisle, 1805.

Crafts, William. *An Oration on the Influence of Moral Causes on National Character*. Cambridge, Mass.: Hilliard and Metcalf, 1817.

Crèvecoeur, Hector St. Jean de. *Letters from an American Farmer*. Garden City, N.Y.: Doubleday, 1964.

Davies, Samuel. *Religion and Patriotism the Constituents of a Good Soldier*. Philadelphia: James Chattin, 1755.

*Diary and Autobiography of John Adams*, ed. L. H. Butterfield. Cambridge, Mass.: Harvard University Press, 1961.

*Documents of the American Revolution, 1770–1783*, ed. K. G. Davies. Shannon, Ireland: Irish University Press, 1972.

Dwight, Timothy. *The Means of Establishing Public Happiness*. New Haven, Conn.: T. & S. Green, 1795.

*The Federal Songster: Being a Collection of the Most CELEBRATED Patriotic SONGS, Hitherto Published*. New London, Conn.: James Springer, 1800.

*The Federalist Papers*, ed. Clinton Rossiter. New York: Penguin Books, 1961.

Filson, John. *The Discovery of Kentucke and the Adventures of Daniel Boon*. New York: Garland Publishing, 1978 [facsimile of 1784 edition].

Fletcher, Ebenezer. *The Narrative of Ebenezer Fletcher, A Soldier of the Revolution*. Freeport, N.Y.: Books for Libraries Press, 1970 [1866].

Foner, Philip S., ed. *The Democratic-Republican Societies, 1790–1800: A Documentary Sourcebook of Constitutions, Declarations, Addresses, Resolutions, and Toasts*. Westport, Conn.: Greenwood Press, 1976.

Goodrich, Elizur. *The Principles of CIVIL UNION and HAPPINESS considered and recommended*. Hartford, Conn.: Hudson and Goodwin, 1787.

Hall, James. *Letters from the West*. Gainesville, Fla.: Scholars' Facsimiles & Reprints, 1967 [London, 1828].

[Hammond, Charles.] *View of General Jackson's Domestic Relations, in Reference to His Fitness for the Presidency*. Washington, D.C.: no publisher listed, 1828.

Henry, William Wirt. *Patrick Henry: Life, Correspondence and Speeches*. New York: Charles Scribner's Sons, 1891.

Hill, Isaac. *An Address at Concord, N.H., January 8, 1828, the Thirteenth Anniversary of Jackson's Victory at New-Orleans*. Concord, N.H.: Manahan, Hoag & Co., 1828.

Hume, David. *A Treatise of Human Nature*, ed. L. A. Selby-Bigge. Oxford: Oxford University Press, 1978.

*The John Gray Blount Papers*, ed. Alice Barnwell Keith. Raleigh, N.C.: State Department of Archives and History, 1952.

*The Journals of the Lewis & Clark Expedition, 1804–1806*, ed. Gary E. Moulton. Lincoln: University of Nebraska Press, 1986–.

*Letters from a Distinguished American: Twelve Essays by John Adams on American Foreign Policy, 1780*, ed. James H. Hutson. Washington, D.C.: Library of Congress, 1978.

*Letters of Benjamin Rush*, ed. L. H. Butterfield. Princeton, N.J.: Princeton University Press, 1951.

*Letters of Delegates to the Continental Congress*, ed. Paul Smith. Washington, D.C.: Library of Congress, 1976–.

Mackenzie, Henry. *The Man of Feeling*. New York: William Borradaile, 1821 [first published London, 1770].

———. *The Man of the World*. Philadelphia: David Hogan, 1799.

———. *The Pursuits of Happiness*. New York: G. F. Hopkins, 1801.

Martin, Wendy, ed. *Colonial American Travel Narratives*. New York: Viking Penguin, 1994.

May, Arthur. *An Inaugural Dissertation on Sympathy*. Philadelphia: Way & Groff, 1799.

Mayhew, Jonathan. *The Snare Broken*. Boston: Benjamin Edes, 1766.

Merrill, O. C. *The Happiness of America: An Oration Delivered at Shaftsbury on the Fourth of July, 1804*. Bennington, Vt.: Anthony, Naswell, 1804.

Miller, John G. *The Great Convention*. Columbus, Ohio: Cutler & Wright, 1840.

Montesquieu. *The Spirit of the Laws*, trans. and ed. Anne M. Cohler et al. Cambridge: Cambridge University Press, 1989.

Morse, Jedidiah. *The American Gazetteer*. Boston: S. Hall, and Thomas & Andrews, 1797 [facsimile reprint: New York: Arno Press, 1971].

Oliver, Benjamin L. *Hints for an Essay on the Pursuit of Happiness*. Cambridge, Mass.: Hilliard and Metcalf, 1818.

*Orations Delivered at the Request of the Inhabitants of the Town of Boston to Commemorate the Evening of the Fifth of March, 1770*. Boston: Peter Edes, 1785.

Paine, Thomas. *Collected Writings*. New York: Library of America, 1995.

*The Papers of Alexander Hamilton*, ed. Harold C. Syrett. New York: Columbia University Press, 1961–87.

*The Papers of Benjamin Franklin*, ed. Leonard Labaree et al. New Haven, Conn.: Yale University Press, 1959–.

*The Papers of Daniel Webster: Correspondence*, ed. Charles M. Wiltse. Hanover, N.H.: University Press of New England, 1974–86.

*The Papers of Daniel Webster: Speeches and Formal Writings*, ed. Charles M. Wiltse. Hanover, N.H.: University Press of New England, 1986.

*Papers of George Gilmer of Pen Park, 1775–1778, Miscellaneous Papers, 1762–1865, of the Virginia Historical Society*. Richmond: Virginia Historical Society, 1887.

*The Papers of George Mason*, ed. Robert A. Rutland. Chapel Hill: University of North Carolina Press, 1970.

*The Papers of George Washington*, Colonial Series, ed. W. W. Abbot and Dorothy Twohig. Charlottesville: University Press of Virginia, 1983–.

*The Papers of Henry Clay*, ed. James F. Hopkins. Lexington: University of Kentucky Press, 1959–.

*The Papers of Henry Laurens*, ed. Philip M. Hamer et al. Columbia: University of South Carolina Press, 1968–.

*The Papers of John C. Calhoun*, ed. Robert L. Meriwether. Columbia: University of South Carolina Press, 1959–.

*Papers of John Marshall*, ed. Herbert A. Johnson et al. Chapel Hill: University of North Carolina Press, 1979–.

*The Papers of Josiah Bartlett*, ed. Frank C. Mevers. Hanover, N.H.: New Hampshire Historical Society, 1979.

*The Papers of Thomas Jefferson*, ed. Julian P. Boyd et al. Princeton, N.J.: Princeton University Press, 1950–.

*The Papers of William Livingston*, ed. Carl E. Prince. Trenton: New Jersey Historical Commission, 1979–88.

Pinckney, Henry Laurens. *An Oration Delivered in St. Michael's Church, Before an Assemblage of the Inhabitants of Charleston, South-Carolina; on the Fourth of July, 1818*. Charleston: W. P. Young, 1818.

Plumer, William. *William Plumer's Memorandum of Proceedings in the United States Senate, 1803–1807*, ed. Everett S. Brown. New York: Da Capo Press, 1969.

Potter, John. *The Words of the Wise*. Philadelphia: Joseph Crukshank, 1790.

Ramsay, David. *The History of the American Revolution*, ed. Lester H. Cohen. Indianapolis: Liberty Fund, 1990 [1789].

*The Satiric Poems of John Trumbull*, ed. Edwin T. Bowden. Austin: University of Texas Press, 1962.

Schutz, John A., and Douglass Adair. *The Spur of Fame: Dialogues of John Adams and Benjamin Rush, 1805–1813*. San Marino, Calif.: The Huntington Library, 1966.

*The Selected Papers of Charles Willson Peale and His Family*, ed. Lillian B. Miller. New Haven, Conn.: Yale University Press, 1983–91.

Smith, Margaret Bayard. *The First Forty Years of Washington Society*. New York: Charles Scribner's Sons, 1906.

Smith, William. *Eulogium on Benjamin Franklin*. Philadelphia: Benjamin Franklin Bache, 1792.

Sterne, Laurence. *A Sentimental Journey Through France and Italy*, ed. Graham Petrie. New York: Penguin Books, 1967 [1768].

Stiles, Ezra. *The UNITED STATES Elevated to GLORY and HONOUR*. Worcester, Mass.: Isaiah Thomas, 1785.

Thacher, Peter. *The Nature and Effects of Christian Sympathy*. Boston: Benjamin Edes & Son, 1794.

Tyler, Royall. *The Contrast, A Comedy*. Philadelphia: Prichard & Hall, 1790.

*A Voice from the Interior. Who Shall Be President? The Hero of New-Orleans, Or John the Second of the House of Braintree*. Boston: True and Greene, 1828.

Warren, Mercy Otis. *History of the Rise, Progress and Termination of the American Revolution*. New York: AMS Press, 1970 [Boston, 1805].

Webster, Noah. *An American Dictionary of the English Language*. New York: S. Converse, 1828.

Whitman, Ezekiel. *An Oration Commemorative of the Declaration of Independence of the United States of America*. Portland, Me.: E. A. Jenks, 1801.

*The Works of Joel Barlow*. Gainesville, Fla.: Scholars' Facsimiles & Reprints, 1970.

*Works of Thomas Jefferson*, ed. Andrew A. Lipscomb and Albert Ellery Bergh. Washington, D.C., 1905.

*Writings of Washington*, ed. John C. Fitzpatrick. Washington, D.C.: U.S. Government Printing Office, 1931–44.

## SELECTED SECONDARY SOURCES

Anderson, Douglas. *The Radical Enlightenments of Benjamin Franklin*. Baltimore: Johns Hopkins University Press, 1997.

Bailyn, Bernard. *The Ideological Origins of the American Revolution*. Cambridge, Mass.: Belknap Press, 1967.

———, ed. *Pamphlets of the American Revolution, 1750–1776*. Cambridge, Mass.: Belknap Press, 1965.

Ball, Terence, and J. G. A. Pocock, eds. *Conceptual Change and the Constitution*. Lawrence: University Press of Kansas, 1988.

Banning, Lance. *The Jeffersonian Persuasion: Evolution of a Party Ideology*. Ithaca, N.Y.: Cornell University Press, 1978.

Barker-Benfield, G. J. *The Culture of Sensibility: Sex and Society in Eighteenth-Century Britain*. Chicago: University of Chicago Press, 1992.

Baym, Nina. *American Women Writers and the Work of History, 1790–1860*. New Brunswick, N.J.: Rutgers University Press, 1995.

Bellesiles, Michael A. *Revolutionary Outlaws: Ethan Allen and the Struggle for Independence on the Early American Frontier*. Charlottesville: University Press of Virginia, 1993.

Bercovitch, Sacvan. *The American Jeremiad*. Madison: University of Wisconsin Press, 1978.

———. *The Rites of Assent: Transformation in the Symbolic Construction of America*. New York: Routledge, 1993.

Berens, John F. *Providence and Patriotism in Early America, 1640–1815*. Charlottesville: University Press of Virginia, 1978.

Berkhofer, Robert F., Jr. *Salvation and the Savage: An Analysis of Protestant Missions and the American Indian Response, 1787–1862*. Lexington: University Press of Kentucky, 1965.

———. *The White Man's Indian: Images of the American Indian from Columbus to the Present*. New York: Alfred A. Knopf, 1978.

Bloch, Ruth H. *Visionary Republic: Millennial Themes in American Thought, 1756–1800*. Cambridge: Cambridge University Press, 1985.

Bloom, Harold, ed. *Romanticism and Consciousness: Essays in Criticism*. New York: W. W. Norton, 1970.

Bodnar, John, ed. *Bonds of Affection: Americans Define Their Patriotism*. Princeton, N.J.: Princeton University Press, 1996.

Boyd, Stephen R., ed. *The Whiskey Rebellion: Past and Present Perspectives*. Westport, Conn.: Greenwood Press, 1985.

Brissenden, R. F. *Virtue in Distress: Studies in the Novel of Sentiment from Richardson to Sade*. New York: Barnes & Noble, 1974.

Brown, Dennis E. *Grammar and Good Taste: Reforming the American Language*. New Haven, Conn.: Yale University Press, 1983.

Brown, Richard D. *Knowledge Is Power: The Diffusion of Information in Early America, 1700–1865*. New York: Oxford University Press, 1989.

———. *Revolutionary Politics in Massachusetts: The Boston Committee of Correspondence and the Towns, 1772–1774*. Cambridge, Mass.: Harvard University Press, 1970.

———. *The Strength of a People: The Idea of an Informed Citizenry in America, 1650–1870*. Chapel Hill: University of North Carolina Press, 1996.

Buel, Joy Day, and Richard Buel, Jr. *The Way of Duty: A Woman and Her Family in Revolutionary America*. New York: W. W. Norton, 1984.

Bullock, Steven C. *Revolutionary Brotherhood: Freemasonry and the Transformation of the American Social Order, 1730–1840*. Chapel Hill: University of North Carolina Press, 1996.

Burstein, Andrew. *The Inner Jefferson: Portrait of a Grieving Optimist*. Charlottesville: University Press of Virginia, 1995.

Bushman, Richard. *From Puritan to Yankee: Character and the Social Order in Connecticut, 1690–1765*. Cambridge, Mass.: Harvard University Press, 1967.

———. *The Refinement of America*. New York: Alfred A. Knopf, 1992.

Cayton, Andrew R. L. *The Frontier Republic: Ideology and Politics in the Ohio Country, 1780–1825*. Kent, Ohio: Kent State University Press, 1986.

Chaplin, Joyce E. *An Anxious Pursuit: Agricultural Innovation and Modernity in the Lower South, 1730–1815*. Chapel Hill: University of North Carolina Press, 1993.

Clark, Gregory, and S. Michael Halloran, eds. *Oratorical Culture in Nineteenth-Century America: Transformations in the Theory and Practice of Rhetoric*. Carbondale: Southern Illinois University Press, 1993.

Cmiel, Kenneth. *Democratic Eloquence: The Fight over Popular Speech in Nineteenth-Century America*. Berkeley: University of California Press, 1990.

Colley, Linda. *Britons: Forging the Nation, 1707–1837*. New Haven, Conn.: Yale University Press, 1992.

Commager, Henry Steele. *Jefferson, Nationalism, and the Enlightenment*. New York: George Braziller, 1975.

Cornell, Saul. *The Other Founders: Anti-Federalism and the Dissenting Tradition in America, 1788–1828*. Chapel Hill: University of North Carolina Press, 1999.

Dangerfield, George. *The Awakening of American Nationalism, 1815–1828*. New York: Harper & Row, 1965.

Dann, John C., ed. *The Revolution Remembered: Eyewitness Accounts of the War for Independence*. Chicago: University of Chicago Press, 1980.

Davidson, Cathy. *Revolution and the Word: The Rise of the Novel in America*. New York: Oxford University Press, 1986.

Davidson, Philip. *Propaganda and the American Revolution, 1763–1783*. New York: W. W. Norton, 1973.

Davis, David Brion. *The Problem of Slavery in Western Culture*. Ithaca, N.Y.: Cornell University Press, 1966.

DeMaria, Robert, Jr. *Johnson's Dictionary and the Language of Learning*. Chapel Hill: University of North Carolina Press, 1986.

Elkins, Stanley, and Eric McKitrick. *The Age of Federalism: The Early American Republic, 1788–1800*. New York: Oxford University Press, 1993.

Ellis, Joseph J. *After the Revolution: Profiles of Early American Culture*. New York: W. W. Norton, 1979.

———. *Passionate Sage: The Character and Legacy of John Adams*. New York: W. W. Norton, 1993.

Faragher, John Mack. *Daniel Boone: The Life and Legend of an American Pioneer*. New York: Henry Holt and Company, 1992.

Fehlen, Myra. *American Incarnation: The Individual, the Nation, and the Continent*. Cambridge, Mass.: Harvard University Press, 1986.

Ferling, John, ed. *The World Turned Upside Down: The American Victory in the War for Independence*. Westport, Conn.: Greenwood Press, 1988.

Ferris, Ina. *The Achievement of Literary Authority: Gender, History, and the Waverley Novels*. Ithaca, N.Y.: Cornell University Press, 1991.

Fischer, David Hackett. *Paul Revere's Ride*. New York: Oxford University Press, 1994.

Fliegelman, Jay. *Declaring Independence: Jefferson, Natural Language, and the Culture of Performance*. Stanford, Calif.: Stanford University Press, 1993.

———. *Prodigals and Pilgrims: The American Revolution Against Patriarchal Authority, 1750–1800*. Cambridge: Cambridge University Press, 1982.

Friedman, Lawrence J. *Inventors of the Promised Land*. New York: Alfred A. Knopf, 1975.

Furtwangler, Albert. *Acts of Discovery: Visions of America in the Lewis and Clark Journals*. Urbana: University of Illinois Press, 1993.

Gay, Peter. *The Enlightenment: An Interpretation*. 2 vols. New York: Alfred A. Knopf, 1966 & 1969.

Gilje, Paul A., and Howard B. Rock, eds. *Keepers of the Revolution: New Yorkers at Work in the Early Republic*. Ithaca, N.Y.: Cornell University Press, 1992.

Godbold, E. Stanly, Jr., and Robert H. Woody. *Christopher Gadsden and the American Revolution*. Knoxville: University of Tennessee Press, 1982.

Greene, Jack P., ed. *The American Revolution: Its Character and Limits*. New York: New York University Press, 1987.

Greene, Jack P. *Imperatives, Behaviors, and Identities: Essays in Early American Cultural History*. Charlottesville: University Press of Virginia, 1992.

———. *The Intellectual Construction of America: Exceptionalism and Identity from 1492 to 1800*. Chapel Hill: University of North Carolina Press, 1993.

———. *Pursuits of Happiness: The Social Development of Early Modern British Colonies and the Formation of American Culture*. Chapel Hill: University of North Carolina Press, 1988.

Gustafson, Thomas. *Representative Words: Politics, Literature, and the American Language, 1776–1865*. Cambridge: Cambridge University Press, 1992.

Hastings, George Everett. *The Life and Works of Francis Hopkinson*. Chicago: University of Chicago Press, 1926.

Hatch, Nathan O. *The Democratization of American Christianity*. New Haven, Conn.: Yale University Press, 1989.

———. *The Sacred Cause of Liberty: Republican Thought and the Millennium in Revolutionary New England*. New Haven, Conn.: Yale University Press, 1977.

Hoffer, Peter Charles. *Revolution and Regeneration: Life Cycle and the Historical Vision of the Generation of 1776*. Athens: University of Georgia Press, 1983.

House, Kay Seymour. *Cooper's Americans*. Columbus: Ohio State University Press, 1965.

Hurt, R. Douglas. *The Ohio Frontier: Crucible of the Old Northwest, 1720–1830*. Bloomington: Indiana University Press, 1996.

Isaac, Rhys. *The Transformation of Virginia*. Chapel Hill: University of North Carolina Press, 1982.

Isenberg, Nancy. *Sex and Citizenship in Antebellum America*. Chapel Hill: University of North Carolina Press, 1998.

John, Richard R. *Spreading the News: The American Postal System from Franklin to Morse*. Cambridge, Mass.: Harvard University Press, 1995.

Johnston, Henry P. *The Battle of Harlem Heights*. New York, 1897; rept. AMS Press, 1970.

Jones, Howard Mumford. *The Pursuit of Happiness*. Cambridge, Mass.: Harvard University Press, 1953.

Jordan, Winthrop D. *White Over Black: American Attitudes Toward the Negro, 1550–1812*. Chapel Hill: University of North Carolina Press, 1968.

Kerber, Linda K. *Federalists in Dissent: Imagery and Ideology in Jeffersonian America*. Ithaca, N.Y.: Cornell University Press, 1970.

——. *Women of the Republic: Intellect and Ideology in Revolutionary America*. Chapel Hill: University of North Carolina Press, 1980.

Klein, Rachel N. *Unification of a Slave State: The Rise of the Planter Class in the South Carolina Backcountry, 1760–1808*. Chapel Hill: University of North Carolina Press, 1990.

Koch, Adrienne. *Power, Morals, and the Founding Fathers: Essays in the Interpretation of the American Enlightenment*. Ithaca, N.Y.: Cornell University Press, 1961.

Kolodny, Annette. *The Land Before Her: Fantasy and Experience of the American Frontiers, 1630–1860*. Chapel Hill: University of North Carolina Press, 1984.

——. *The Lay of the Land: Metaphor as Experience and History in American Life and Letters*. Chapel Hill: University of North Carolina Press, 1975.

Konig, David Thomas, ed. *Devising Liberty: Preserving and Creating Freedom in the New American Republic*. Stanford, Calif.: Stanford University Press, 1995.

Kramer, Michael P. *Imagining Language in America: From the Revolution to the Civil War*. Princeton, N.J.: Princeton University Press, 1992.

Labaree, Benjamin Woods. *The Boston Tea Party*. New York: Oxford University Press, 1964.

Lewis, Jan. *The Pursuit of Happiness: Family and Values in Jeffersonian Virginia*. Cambridge: Cambridge University Press, 1983.

Looby Christopher. *Voicing America: Language, Literary Form, and the Origins of the United States*. Chicago: University of Chicago Press, 1996.

Maier, Pauline. *American Scripture: Making the Declaration of Independence*. New York: Alfred A. Knopf, 1997.

——. *From Resistance to Revolution: Colonial Radicals and the Development of American Opposition to Britain, 1765–1776*. New York: Alfred A. Knopf, 1972.

Malone, Dumas. *Jefferson and His Time*. 6 vols. Boston: Little, Brown, 1948–81.

Martin, Terence. *Parables of Possibility: The American Need for Beginnings*. New York: Columbia University Press, 1995.

Marx, Leo. *The Machine in the Garden: Technology and the Pastoral Ideal in America*. New York: Oxford University Press, 1964.

Matthews, Jean V. *Toward a New Society: American Thought and Culture, 1800–1830*. Boston: Twayne Publishers, 1991.

May, Henry F. *The Enlightenment in America*. New York: Oxford University Press, 1976.

McGill, V. J. *The Idea of Happiness*. New York: Frederick A. Praeger, 1967.

McGreevy, Patrick V. *Imagining Niagara: The Meaning and Making of Niagara Falls*. Amherst: University of Massachusetts Press, 1994.

McKinsey, Elizabeth. *Niagara Falls: Icon of the American Sublime*. Cambridge: Cambridge University Press, 1985.

McWilliams, John P., Jr. *The American Epic: Transforming a Genre, 1770–1860*. Cambridge: Cambridge University Press, 1989.

Miller, Charles A. *Jefferson and Nature: An Interpretation*. Baltimore: Johns Hopkins University Press, 1988.

Miller, Lillian B., and David C. Ward, eds. *New Perspectives on Charles Willson Peale*. Pittsburgh: University of Pittsburgh Press, 1991.

Moore, Arthur K. *The Frontier Mind: A Cultural Analysis of the Kentucky Frontiersman*. Lexington: University of Kentucky Press, 1957.

Morgan, Edmund S. *The Challenge of the American Revolution*. New York: W. W. Norton, 1976.

———— and Helen M. Morgan. *The Stamp Act Crisis: Prologue to Revolution*. Chapel Hill: University of North Carolina Press, 1953.

Mullan, John. *Sentiment and Sociability: The Language of Feeling in the Eighteenth Century*. Oxford: Oxford University Press, 1988.

Nash, Roderick. *Wilderness and the American Mind*. New Haven, Conn.: Yale University Press, 1967.

Nevius, Blake. *Cooper's Landscapes: An Essay on the Picturesque Vision*. Berkeley: University of California Press, 1976.

Onuf, Peter S. *The Origins of the Federal Republic*. Philadelphia: University of Pennsylvania Press, 1983.

————. *Statehood and Union: A History of the Northwest Ordinance*. Bloomington: Indiana University Press, 1987.

Peterson, Merrill D. *The Great Triumvirate: Webster, Clay, and Calhoun*. New York: Oxford University Press, 1987.

Porter, Charlotte M. *The Eagle's Nest: Natural History and American Ideas, 1812–1842*. University: University of Alabama Press, 1986.

Potter, Janice. *The Liberty We Seek: Loyalist Ideology in Colonial New York and Massachusetts*. Cambridge, Mass.: Harvard University Press, 1983.

Rans, Geoffrey. *Cooper's Leather-Stocking Novels: A Secular Reading*. Chapel Hill: University of North Carolina Press, 1991.

Robertson, Andrew W. *The Language of Democracy: Political Rhetoric in the United States and Britain, 1790–1900*. Ithaca, N.Y.: Cornell University Press, 1995.

Rock, Howard B. *Artisans of the New Republic: The Tradesmen of New York City in the Age of Jefferson*. New York: New York University Press, 1979.

Rock, Howard B., Paul A. Gilje, and Robert Asher, eds. *American Artisans: Crafting Social Identity, 1750–1850*. Baltimore: Johns Hopkins University Press, 1995.

Rollins, Richard M. *The Long Journey of Noah Webster*. Philadelphia: University of Pennsylvania Press, 1980.

Royster, Charles. *A Revolutionary People at War: The Continental Army and American Character*. Chapel Hill: University of North Carolina Press, 1979.

Sellers, Charles Coleman. *Mr. Peale's Museum: Charles Willson Peale and the First Popular Museum of Natural Sciences and Art*. New York: W. W. Norton, 1980.

Shain, Barry Alan. *The Myth of American Individualism: The Protestant Origins of American Political Thought*. Princeton, N.J.: Princeton University Press, 1994.

Shaw, Peter. *American Patriots and the Rituals of Revolution*. Cambridge, Mass.: Harvard University Press, 1981.

————. *The Character of John Adams*. Chapel Hill: University of North Carolina Press, 1976.

Sheehan, Bernard W. *Seeds of Extinction: Jeffersonian Philanthropy and the American Indian*. Chapel Hill: University of North Carolina Press, 1973.

Shields, David S. *Civil Tongues & Polite Letters in British America*. Chapel Hill: University of North Carolina Press, 1997.

Silverman, Kenneth. *A Cultural History of the American Revolution*. New York: Thomas Y. Crowell, 1976.

Simpson, David. *The Politics of American English, 1776–1850*. New York: Oxford University Press, 1986.

Slaughter, Thomas P. *The Whiskey Rebellion: Frontier Epilogue to the American Revolution*. New York: Oxford University Press, 1986.

Slotkin, Richard. *Regeneration Through Violence: The Mythology of the American Frontier, 1600–1860*. Middletown, Conn.: Wesleyan University Press, 1973.

Smith, Henry Nash. *Virgin Land: The American West as Symbol and Myth*. Cambridge, Mass.: Harvard University Press, 1950.

Somkin, Fred. *Unquiet Eagle: Memory and Desire in the Idea of American Freedom, 1815–1860*. Ithaca, N.Y.: Cornell University Press, 1967.

Stephanson, Anders. *Manifest Destiny: American Expansion and the Empire of Right*. New York: Hill and Wang, 1995.

Stern, Julia A. *The Plight of Feeling: Sympathy and Dissent in the Early American Novel*. Chicago: University of Chicago Press, 1997.

Thompson, Harold William. *A Scottish Man of Feeling: Some Account of Henry Mackenzie, Esq., of Edinburgh and of the Golden Age of Burns and Scott*. London: Oxford University Press, 1931.

Tise, Larry E. *Proslavery: A History of the Defense of Slavery in America, 1701–1840*. Athens: University of Georgia Press, 1987.

Tuveson, Ernest Lee. *Redeemer Nation: The Idea of America's Millennial Role*. Chicago: University of Chicago Press, 1968.

Van Doren, Carl. *Benjamin Franklin*. New York: Viking Press, 1938.

Vila, Anne C. *Enlightenment and Pathology: Sensibility in the Literature and Medicine of Eighteenth-Century France*. Baltimore: Johns Hopkins University Press, 1998.

Waldstreicher, David. *In the Midst of Perpetual Fetes: The Making of American Nationalism, 1776–1820*. Chapel Hill: University of North Carolina Press, 1997.

Wiebe, Robert H. *Self-Rule: A Cultural History of American Democracy*. Chicago: University of Chicago Press, 1995.

Wilkinson, Rupert. *The Pursuit of American Character*. New York: Harper & Row, 1988.

Wolf, Bryan Jay. *Romantic Re-Vision: Culture and Consciousness in Nineteenth-Century American Painting and Literature*. Chicago: University of Chicago Press, 1982.

Wood, Gordon S. *The Creation of the American Republic, 1776–1789*. Chapel Hill: University of North Carolina Press, 1969.

———. *The Radicalism of the American Revolution*. New York: Alfred A. Knopf, 1992.

Yazawa, Melvin. *From Colonies to Commonwealth: Familial Ideology and the Beginnings of the American Republic*. Baltimore: Johns Hopkins University Press, 1985.

Zagarri, Rosemarie. *A Woman's Dilemma: Mercy Otis Warren and the American Revolution*. Wheeling, Ill.: Harlan Davidson, 1995.

Zobel, Hiller B. *The Boston Massacre*. New York: W. W. Norton, 1970.

# INDEX